"While many both in the
philosopher is an oxymo
Over the last fifty years there has been a dramatic resurgence of faithful
Christians in academic philosophy. Many of the best young Christian
minds continue to flock to this discipline. Finally there is a tool to help
them think deeply and critically about the benefits of bringing their commitments to the authority of Scripture and the person of Jesus into their
study of philosophy. *Doing Philosophy as a Christian* will set the beginner
on the right path, and it will challenge the more advanced philosopher to
continue to become a more faithful follower of Christ. Not only will those
who study this book be better philosophers, they will be better able to lead
others into a deeper encounter with Christ."
GREGORY E. GANSSLE, Yale University

"Sooner or later, reflective Christians will face the question of what to do
with the academic discipline of philosophy. Garrett DeWeese rightly con-
tends that Jesus as Lord has an important bearing on this question. This
book aims to spell out this bearing of Jesus. In doing so, it merits careful
attention from all reflective Christians."
PAUL K. MOSER, Loyola University Chicago

"Garrett DeWeese's book fills a serious gap. Students in philosophy, as
well as professional philosophers, will find much insight into the important question of how Christian faith shapes the practice of philosophy. Not
all Christian philosophers will agree with all the positions taken, but all
can benefit from this fine example of what it means to be integrally Christian while seeking to do philosophy in a rigorous manner."
C. STEPHEN EVANS, Baylor University

"In this unique and uniquely important book, Garrett DeWeese carefully
and winsomely develops a clear, deep and cogent approach to the practice
of philosophizing as a Christian. In so doing, he demonstrates a rich
knowledge of Scripture, analytic philosophy and the history of philoso-

phy—a rare combination of intellectual virtue. Both students and professors of philosophy will benefit greatly from this astute and timely work, for which I have the highest admiration."

"With graduate degrees in theology and philosophy, and years of deep reflection, Garry DeWeese is uniquely qualified to write on how to approach philosophy from a Christian perspective. And *Doing Philosophy as a Christian* does just that. In page after page, DeWeese offers fresh insight and deep reflection about how to honor Jesus as Lord in the task of doing philosophy. This is a must-read for all interested in worldview development and the integration of Scripture with the field of philosophy."

CHRISTIAN WORLDVIEW ✚ INTEGRATION SERIES

Doing PHILOSOPHY as a Christian

GARRETT J. DeWEESE

IVP Academic

An imprint of InterVarsity Press
Downers Grove, Illinois

InterVarsity Press
P.O. Box 1400, Downers Grove, IL 60515-1426
World Wide Web: www.ivpress.com
E-mail: email@ivpress.com

InterVarsity Press® is the book-publishing division of InterVarsity Christian Fellowship/USA®, a movement of
students and faculty active on campus at hundreds of universities, colleges and schools of nursing in the United States
of America, and a member movement of the International Fellowship of Evangelical Students. For information
about local and regional activities, write Public Relations Dept., InterVarsity Christian Fellowship/USA, 6400
Schroeder Rd., P.O. Box 7895, Madison, WI 53707-7895, or visit the IVCF website at <www.intervarsity.org>.

Design: Cindy Kiple

ISBN 978-0-8308-2811-1

Printed in the United States of America ∞

Library of Congress Cataloging-in-Publication Data

DeWeese, Garrett J., 1947-
  Doing philosophy as a Christian / Garrett J. DeWeese.
    p. cm.
  Includes bibliographical references and index.
  ISBN 978-0-8308-2811-1 (pbk.: alk. paper)
  1. Christian philosophy. I. Title.
  BR100.D457 2011
  261.5'1—dc22

                                                                        2011013667

| P | 20 | 19 | 18 | 17 | 16 | 15 | 14 | 13 | 12 | 11 | 10 | 9 | 8 | 7 | 6 | 5 | 4 | 3 | 2 | 1 |
| Y | 28 | 27 | 26 | 25 | 24 | 23 | 22 | 21 | 20 | 19 | 18 | 17 | 16 | 15 | 14 | 13 | 12 | 11 | | |

Dedicated, with respect and appreciation, to

Alvin Plantinga
Dallas Willard
William Lane Craig

Three giants who in our day set the standard
for doing philosophy as a Christian

CONTENTS

SERIES PREFACE

A CALL TO INTEGRATION AND THE
CHRISTIAN WORLDVIEW INTEGRATION SERIES

Life is short and we're all busy. If you're a college student, you're *really* busy. There's your part-time job (which seems full time), your social life (hopefully) and church. On top of that you're expected to go to class, do some reading, take tests and write papers. Now, while you are minding your own business, you hear about something called "integration," trying to relate your major with your Christianity. Several questions may come to mind: What is integration anyway? Is it just a fad? Why should I care about it? And even if I do care about it, I don't have a clue as to how to go about doing it. How do I do this? These are good questions, and in this introduction we're going to address them in order. We are passionate about helping you learn about and become good at integrating your Christian convictions with the issues and ideas in your college major or your career.

WHAT IS INTEGRATION?

The word *integrate* means "to form or blend into a whole," "to unite." We humans naturally seek to find the unity that is behind diversity, and in fact coherence is an important mark of rationality. There are two kinds of integration: conceptual and personal. In conceptual integration, *our theological beliefs, especially those derived from careful study of the Bible, are blended and unified with important, reasonable ideas from our profession or college major into a coherent, intellectually satisfying Christian worldview.* As Augustine wisely advised, "We must show our Scriptures not to be in conflict with whatever [our critics] can demonstrate about the nature of things from reliable sources."[1] In personal integration we seek to live a unified life, a life in which we are the same in public as we are in private, a life in which the various aspects of our personality are consistent with each other and conducive to a life of human flourishing as a disciple of Jesus.

The two kinds of integration are deeply intertwined. All things being equal, the more authentic we are, the more integrity we have, the more we should be able to do conceptual integration with fidelity to Jesus and Scripture, and with intellectual honesty. All things being equal, the more conceptual integration we accomplish, the more coherent will be our set of beliefs and the more confidence we will have in the truth of our Christian worldview. In fact, conceptual integration is so important that it is worth thinking some more about why it matters.

SEVEN REASONS WHY INTEGRATION MATTERS

1. The Bible's teachings are true. The first justification for integration is pretty obvious, but often overlooked. *Christians hold that, when properly interpreted, the teachings of Holy Scripture are true.* This means two things. If the Bible teaches something relevant to an issue in an academic field, the Bible's view on that topic is true and thus provides an incredibly rich resource for doing work in that academic field. It would be irresponsible to set aside an important source of relevant truth in thinking through issues in our field of study or vocation. Further, if it appears that a claim on our field tends to make a biblical claim false, this tension needs to be resolved. Maybe our interpretation of Scripture is mistaken; maybe the Bible is not even talking about the issue; maybe the claim in our field is false. Whatever the case, the Christian's commitment to the truth of Scripture makes integration inevitable.

Adolfo Lopez-Otero, a Stanford engineering professor and a self-described secular humanist, offers advice to thinking Christians who want to have an impact on the world: "When a Christian professor ap-

---

[1]Augustine *De genesi ad litteram* 1.21, cited in Ernan McMullin, "How Should Cosmology Relate to Theology?" in *The Sciences and Theology in the Twentieth Century*, ed. Arthur R. Peacocke (Notre Dame, Ind.: University of Notre Dame Press, 1981), p. 20.

proaches a non-believing faculty member . . . they can expect to face a polite but condescending person [with a belief that they possess] superior metaphysics who can't understand how such an intelligent person [as yourself] still believes in things which have been discredited eons ago."[2] He goes on to say that "[Christian professors] cannot afford to give excuses . . . if they are honest about wanting to open spiritual and truthful dialogue with their non-believing colleagues—that is the price they must pay for having declared themselves Christians."[3] While Lopez-Otero's remarks are directed to Christian professors, his point applies to all thinking Christians: If we claim that our Christian views are true, we need to back that up by interacting with the various ideas that come from different academic disciplines. In short, we must integrate Christianity and our major or vocation.

   2. Our vocation and the holistic character of discipleship demand integration. As disciples grow, they learn to see, feel, think, desire, believe and behave the way Jesus does in a manner fitting to the kingdom of God and their own station in life. With God's help we seek to live as Jesus would if he were a philosophy professor at Biola University married to Hope and father of Ashley and Allison, or as a political philosopher at Baylor University married to Frankie.

   Two important implications flow from the nature of discipleship. For one thing, the lordship of Christ is holistic. The religious life is not a special compartment in an otherwise secular life. Rather, the religious life is an entire way of life. To live Christianly is to allow Jesus Christ to be the Lord of every aspect of our life. There is no room for a secular-sacred separation in the life of Jesus' followers. Jesus Christ should be every bit as much at home in our thinking and behavior when we are developing our views in our area of study or work as he is when we are in a small group fellowship.

   Further, as disciples of Jesus we do not merely have a job. We have a vocation as a Christian teacher. A job is a means for supporting ourselves and those for whom we are responsible. For the Christian a vocation (from the Latin *vocare*, which means "to call") is an overall calling

---

[2]Adolfo Lopez-Otero, "Be Humble, but Daring," *The Real Issue* 16 (September-October 1997): 10.
[3]Ibid., p. 11.

from God. Harry Blamires correctly draws a distinction between a general and a special vocation:

> The general vocation of all Christians—indeed of all men and women—is the same. We are called to live as children of God, obeying his will in all things. But obedience to God's will must inevitably take many different forms. The wife's mode of obedience is not the same as the nun's; the farmer's is not the same as the priest's. By "special vocation," therefore, we designate God's call to a [person] to serve him in a particular sphere of activity.[4]

As Christians seek to discover and become excellent in their special vocation, they must ask, how would Jesus approach the task of being a history teacher, a chemist, an athletic director, a mathematician? It is not always easy to answer this question, but the vocational demands of discipleship require that we give it our best shot.

Whatever we do, however, it is important that we restore to our culture an image of Jesus Christ as an intelligent, competent person who spoke authoritatively on whatever subject he addressed. The disciples of Jesus agreed with Paul when he said that all the wisdom of the Greeks and Jews was ultimately wrapped up in Jesus himself (Col 2:2-3). For them, Jesus was not merely a Savior from sin; he was the wisest, most intelligent, most attractive person they had ever seen.

In the early centuries of Christianity, the church presented Jesus to unbelievers precisely because he was wiser, more virtuous, more intelligent and more attractive in his character than Aristotle, Plato, Moses or anyone else. It has been a part of the church's self-understanding to locate the spiritual life in a broader quest for the good life, that is, a life of wisdom, knowledge, beauty and goodness. So understood, the spiritual life and discipleship to Jesus were seen as the very best way to achieve a life of truth, beauty and goodness. Moreover, the life of discipleship was depicted as the wisest, most reasonable form of life available so that a life of unbelief was taken to be foolish and absurd. *Our schools need to recapture and propagate this broader understanding of following Christ if they are to be thoroughly Christian in their approach to education.*

---

[4]Harry Blamires, *A God Who Acts* (Ann Arbor, Mich.: Servant Books, 1957), p. 67.

3. Biblical teaching about the role of the mind in the Christian life and the value of extrabiblical knowledge requires integration. The Scriptures are clear that God wants us to be like him in every facet of our lives, and he desires commitment from our total being, including our intellectual life. We are told that we change spiritually by having the categories of our minds renewed (Rom 12:1-2), that we are to include an intellectual love for God in our devotion (Mt 22:37-38), and that we are to be prepared to give others a reasonable answer to questions others ask us about why we believe what we believe (1 Pet 3:15). As the great eighteenth-century Christian thinker and spiritual master William Law put it, "Unreasonable and absurd ways of life . . . are truly an offense to God."[5] Learning and developing convictions about the teachings of Scripture are absolutely central to these mandates. However, many of Jesus' followers have failed to see that an aggressive pursuit of knowledge in areas outside the Bible is also relevant to these directives.

God has revealed himself and various truths on a number of topics outside the Bible. As Christians have known throughout our history, common sense, logic and mathematics, along with the arts, humanities, sciences and other areas of study, contain important truths relevant to life in general and to the development of a careful, life-related Christian worldview.

In 1756 John Wesley delivered an address to a gathering of clergy on how to carry out the pastoral ministry with joy and skill. In it Wesley catalogued a number of things familiar to most contemporary believers—the cultivation of a disposition to glorify God and save souls, a knowledge of Scripture, and similar notions. However, at the front of his list Wesley focused on something seldom expressly valued by most pastoral search committees: "Ought not a Minister to have, First, a good understanding, a clear apprehension, a sound judgment, and a capacity of reasoning with some closeness?"[6]

Time and again throughout the address Wesley unpacked this re-

---

[5]William Law, *A Serious Call to a Devout and Holy Life* (1728; reprint, Grand Rapids: Eerdmans, 1966), p. 2.
[6]John Wesley, "An Address to the Clergy," in *The Works of John Wesley*, 3rd ed. (Grand Rapids: Baker, 1979), p. 481.

mark by admonishing ministers to know what would sound truly odd and almost pagan to the average congregant of today: logic, metaphysics, natural theology, geometry and the ideas of important figures in the history of philosophy. For Wesley, study in these areas (especially philosophy and geometry) helped train the mind to think precisely, a habit of incredible value, he asserted, when it comes to thinking as a Christian about theological themes or scriptural texts. According to Wesley, the study of extrabiblical information and the writings of unbelievers was of critical value for growth and maturity. As he put it elsewhere, "To imagine none can teach you but those who are themselves saved from sin is a very great and dangerous mistake. Give not place to it for a moment."[7]

Wesley's remarks were not unusual in his time. A century earlier the great Reformed pastor Richard Baxter was faced with lukewarmness in the church and unbelief outside the church. In 1667 he wrote a book to meet this need, and in it he used philosophy, logic and general items of knowledge outside Scripture to argue for the existence of the soul and the life to come. The fact that Baxter turned to philosophy and extrabiblical knowledge instead of small groups or praise hymns is worth pondering. In fact, it is safe to say that throughout much of church history, Scripture and right reason directed at extrabiblical truth were used by disciples of Jesus and prized as twin allies.

In valuing extrabiblical knowledge, our brothers and sisters in church history were merely following common sense and Scripture itself. Repeatedly, Scripture acknowledges the wisdom of cultures outside Israel; for example, Egypt (Acts 7:22; cf. Ex 7:11), the Edomites (Jer 49:7), the Phoenicians (Zech 9:2), and many others. The remarkable achievements produced by human wisdom are acknowledged in Job 28:1-11. The wisdom of Solomon is compared to the wisdom of the "people of the east" and Egypt in order to show that Solomon's wisdom surpassed that of people with a longstanding, well-deserved reputation for wisdom (1 Kings 4:29-34). Paul approvingly quotes pagan philosophers (Acts 17:28), and Jude does the same thing with the noncanonical book *The*

---

[7]John Wesley, *A Plain Account of Christian Perfection* (London: Epworth Press, 1952), p. 87.

Assumption of Moses (Jude 9). The book of Proverbs is filled with examples in which knowledge, even moral and spiritual knowledge, can be gained from studying things in the natural world (ants, for example). Jesus taught that we should know we are to love our enemies, not on the basis of an Old Testament text but from careful reflection on how the sun and rain behave (Mt 5:44-45).

In valuing extrabiblical knowledge, our brothers and sisters in church history were also living out scriptural teaching about the value of general revelation. We must never forget that God is the God of creation and general revelation just as he is the God of Scripture and special revelation.

Christians should do everything they can to gain and teach important and relevant knowledge in their areas of expertise. At the level appropriate to our station in life, Christians are called to be Christian intellectuals, at home in the world of ideas.

4. Neglect of integration results in a costly division between secular and sacred. While few would actually put it in these terms, faith is now understood as a blind act of will, a sort of decision to believe something that is either independent of reason or makes up for the paltry lack of evidence for what one is trying to believe. By contrast, the Bible presents faith as a power or skill to act in accordance with the nature of the kingdom of God, a trust in what we have reason to believe is true. Understood in this way, we see that faith is built on reason and knowledge. We should have good reasons for thinking that Christianity is true before we completely dedicate ourselves to it. We should have solid evidence that our understanding of a biblical passage is correct before we go on to apply it. We bring knowledge claims from Scripture and theology to the task of integration; we do not employ mere beliefs or faith postulates.

Unfortunately, our contemporary understanding of faith and reason treats them as polar opposites. A few years ago I (J. P.) went to New York to conduct a series of evangelistic messages for a church. The series was in a high school gym, and several believers and unbelievers came each night. The first evening I gave arguments for the existence of God from science and philosophy. Before closing in prayer, I entertained several questions from the audience. One woman (who was a Christian) complained about my talk, charging that if I "proved" the existence of God, I would leave no room for faith. I responded by saying that if she were right, then we should pray that currently available evidence for God would evaporate and be refuted so there would be even more room for faith! Obviously, her view of faith utterly detached it from reason.

If faith and reason are deeply connected, then students and teachers need to explore their entire intellectual life in light of the Word of God. But if faith and reason are polar opposites, then the subject matter of our study or teaching is largely irrelevant to growth in discipleship. Because of this view of faith and reason, there has emerged a secular-sacred separation in our understanding of the Christian life with the result that Christian teaching and practice are privatized. The withdrawal of the corporate body of Christ from the public sphere of ideas is mirrored by our understanding of what is required to produce an individual disciple. Religion is viewed as personal, private and a matter of how we feel about things. Often, Bible classes and paracurricular Christian activities are not taken as academically serious aspects of the Christian school, nor are they integrated into the content of "secular" areas of teaching.

There is no time like the present to recapture the integrative task. Given the abandonment of monotheism, the ground is weakened for believing in the unity of truth. This is one reason why our *uni*versities are turning in to *multi*versities.[8] The fragmentation of secular education at all levels and its inability to define its purpose or gather together a coherent curriculum are symptoms of what happens when monotheism, especially Christian monotheism, is set aside. At this critical hour the Christian educator has something increasingly rare and distinctive to offer, and integration is at the heart of who we are as Christian educators.

5. The nature of spiritual warfare necessitates integration. Today, spiritual warfare is widely misunderstood. Briefly, spiritual warfare is a conflict among persons—disembodied malevolent persons (demons and

---

[8]See Julie Reuben, *The Making of the Modern University* (Chicago: University of Chicago Press, 1996).

the devil), human beings, angels and God himself. So far, so good. But what is often overlooked is that this conflict among persons in two camps crucially involves a clash of ideas. Why? The conflict is about control, and persons control others by getting them to accept certain beliefs and emotions as correct, good and proper. This is precisely how the devil primarily works to destroy human beings and thwart God's work in history, namely, by influencing the idea structures in culture. That is why Paul makes the war of ideas central to spiritual conflict:

> For though we live in the world, we do not wage war as the world does. The weapons we fight with are not the weapons of the world. On the contrary, they have divine power to demolish strongholds. We demolish arguments and every pretension that sets itself up against the knowledge of God, and we take captive every thought to make it obedient to Christ. (2 Cor 10:3-5 NIV)

Spiritual warfare is largely, though not entirely, a war of ideas, and we fight bad, false ideas with better ones. That means that truth, reason, argumentation and so forth, from both Scripture and general revelation, are central weapons in the fight. Since the centers of education are the centers for dealing with ideas, they become the main location for spiritual warfare. Solid, intelligent integration, then, is part of our mandate to engage in spiritual conflict.

6. Spiritual formation calls for integration. It is crucial that we reflect a bit on the relationship between integration and spiritual/devotional life. To begin with, there is a widespread hunger throughout our culture for genuine, life-transforming spirituality. This is as it should be. People are weary of those who claim to believe certain things when they do not see those beliefs having an impact on the lives of the heralds. Among other things, integration is a spiritual activity—we may even call it a spiritual discipline—but not merely in the sense that often comes to mind in this context. Often, Christian teachers express the spiritual aspect of integration in terms of doxology: Christian integrators hold to and teach the same beliefs about their subject matter that non-Christians accept but go on to add praise to God for the subject matter. Thus, Christian biologists simply assert the views widely accepted in the discipline but make sure that class closes with a word of praise to God for the beauty and complexity of the living world.

The doxological approach is good as far as it goes; unfortunately, it doesn't go far enough in capturing the spiritual dimension of integration. We draw closer to the core of this dimension when we think about the role of beliefs in the process of spiritual transformation. Beliefs are the rails on which our lives run. We almost always act according to what we really believe. It doesn't matter much what we say we believe or what we want others to think we believe. When the rubber meets the road, we act out our actual beliefs most of the time. That is why behavior is such a good indicator of our beliefs. The centrality of beliefs for spiritual progress is a clear implication of Old Testament teaching on wisdom and New Testament teaching about the role of a renewed mind in transformation. Thus, *integration has as its spiritual aim the intellectual goal of structuring the mind so we can see things as they really are and strengthening the belief structure that ought to inform the individual and corporate life of discipleship to Jesus.*

Integration can also help unbelievers accept certain beliefs crucial to the Christian journey and aid believers in maintaining and developing convictions about those beliefs. This aspect of integration becomes clear when we reflect on the notion of a plausibility structure. Individuals will never be able to change their lives if they cannot even entertain the beliefs needed to bring about that change. By "entertain a belief" we mean to consider the *possibility* that the belief *might* be true. If someone is hateful and mean to a fellow employee, that person will have to change what he or she believes about that coworker before treating the coworker differently. But if a person cannot even entertain the thought that the coworker is a good person worthy of kindness, the hateful person will not change.

A person's plausibility structure is the set of ideas the person either is or is not willing to entertain as possibly true. For example, few people would come to a lecture defending a flat earth, because this idea is just not part of our common plausibility structure. Most people today simply cannot even entertain the idea. Moreover, a person's plausibility structure is largely (though not exclusively) a function of beliefs already held. Applied to accepting or maintaining Christian belief, J. Gresham Machen got it right when he said:

> God usually exerts that power in connection with certain prior conditions of the human mind, and it should be ours to create, so far as we can, with the help of God, those favorable conditions for the reception of the gospel. False ideas are the greatest obstacles to the reception of the gospel. We may preach with all the fervor of a reformer and yet succeed only in winning a straggler here and there, if we permit the whole collective thought of the nation or of the world to be controlled by ideas which, by the resistless force of logic, prevent Christianity from being regarded as anything more than a harmless delusion.[9]

If a culture reaches the point where Christian claims are not even part of its plausibility structure, fewer and fewer people will be able to entertain the possibility that they might be true. Whatever stragglers do come to faith in such a context would do so on the basis of felt needs alone, and the genuineness of such conversions would be questionable, to say the least. And believers will not make much progress in the spiritual life because they will not have the depth of conviction or the integrated noetic structure necessary for such progress. This is why integration is so crucial to spirituality. It can create a plausibility structure in a person's mind, "favorable conditions," as Machen put it, so Christian ideas can be entertained by that person. As Christians, our goal is *to make Christian ideas relevant to our subject matter appear to be true, beautiful, good and reasonable in order to increase the ranking of Christian ideas in the culture's plausibility structure.*

7. Integration is crucial to the current worldview struggle and the contemporary crisis of knowledge. Luther once said that if we defend Christ at all points except those at which he is currently being attacked, then we have not really defended Christ. The Christian must keep in mind the tensions between Christian claims and competing worldviews currently dominating the culture. Such vigilance yields an integrative mandate for contemporary Christians that the Christian Worldview Integration

---

[9]J. Gresham Machen, address delivered on September 20, 1912, at the opening of the 101st session of Princeton Theological Seminary, reprinted in *What Is Christianity?* (Grand Rapids: Eerdmans, 1951), p. 162.

Series (CWIS) will keep in mind. There is a very important cultural fact that each volume in the series must face: *There simply is no established, widely recognized body of ethical or religious knowledge now operative in the institutions of knowledge in our culture.* Indeed, ethical and religious claims are frequently placed into what Francis Schaeffer called the "upper story," and they are judged to have little or no epistemic authority, especially compared to the authority given to science to define the limits of knowledge and reality in those same institutions. This raises pressing questions: *Is Christianity a knowledge tradition or merely a faith tradition, a perspective which, while true, cannot be known to be true and must be embraced on the basis of some epistemic state weaker than knowledge? Is there nonempirical knowledge in my field? Is there evidence of nonphysical, immaterial reality (e.g., linguistic meanings are arguable, nonphysical, spiritual entities) in my field? Do the ideas of Christianity do any serious intellectual work in my field such that those who fail to take them into consideration simply will not be able to understand adequately the realities involved in my field?*

There are at least two reasons why these may well be the crucial questions for Christians to keep in mind as they do their work in their disciplines. For one thing, Christianity claims to be a knowledge tradition, and it places knowledge at the center of proclamation and discipleship. The Old and New Testaments, including the teachings of Jesus, claim not merely that Christianity is true but that a variety of its moral and religious assertions can be known to be true.

Second, knowledge is the basis of responsible action in society. Dentists, not lawyers, have the authority to place their hands in our mouths because they have the relevant knowledge—not merely true beliefs—on the basis of which they may act responsibly. If Christians do little to deflect the view that theological and ethical assertions are merely parts of a tradition, ways of seeing, a source for adding a "theological perspective" to an otherwise unperturbed secular topic and so forth that fall short of conveying knowledge, then they inadvertently contribute to the marginalization of Christianity precisely because they fail to rebut the contemporary tendency to rob it of the very thing that gives it the authority necessary to prevent that marginalization, namely, its legitimate claim to give us moral and religious knowledge. Both in and out of the church Jesus has been lost as an intellectual authority, and Christian intellectuals should carry out their academic vocation in light of this fact.

We agree with those who see a three-way worldview struggle in academic and popular culture among ethical monotheism (especially Christian theism), postmodernism and scientific naturalism. As Christian intellectuals seek to promote Christianity as a knowledge tradition in their academic disciplines, they should keep in mind the impact of their work on this triumvirate. Space considerations forbid us to say much about postmodernism here. We recognize it is a variegated tunic with many nuances. But to the degree that postmodernism denies the objectivity of reality, truth, value and reason (in its epistemic if not psychological sense)—to the degree that it rejects dichotomous thinking about real-unreal, true-false, rational-irrational and right-wrong, to the degree that it believes intentionality creates the objects of consciousness, to that degree it should be resisted by Christian intellectuals, and the CWIS will take this stance toward postmodernism.

Scientific naturalism also comes in many varieties, but very roughly, a major form of it is the view that the spatio-temporal cosmos containing physical objects studied by the hard sciences is all there is and that the hard sciences are either the only source of knowledge or else vastly superior in proffering epistemically justified beliefs compared to nonscientific fields. In connection with scientific naturalism some have argued that the rise of modern science has contributed to the loss of intellectual authority in those fields such as ethics and religion that supposedly are not subject to the types of testing and experimentation employed in science.

Extreme forms of postmodernism and scientific naturalism agree that there is no nonempirical knowledge, especially no knowledge of immaterial reality, no theological or ethical knowledge. *The authors of the CWIS seek to undermine this claim and the concomitant privatization and noncognitive treatment of religious/ethical faith and belief.* Thus, there will be three integrative tasks of central importance for each volume in the series.

How Do We Engage in Integration? Three Integrative Tasks

As noted earlier, the word *integration* means "to form or blend into a whole," "to unite." One of the goals of integration is to maintain or increase both the conceptual relevance of and epistemological justification for Christian theism. To repeat Augustine's advice, "We must show our Scriptures not to be in conflict with whatever [our critics] can demonstrate about the nature of things from reliable sources."[10] We may distinguish three different aspects of the justificatory side of integration: direct defense, polemics and Christian explanation.

1. Direct defense. In direct defense we engage in integration with the primary intent of enhancing or maintaining directly the rational justification of Christian theism or some proposition taken to be explicit within or entailed by it, especially those aspects of a Christian worldview relevant to our own discipline. Specific attention should be given to topics that are intrinsically important to mere Christianity or currently under fire in our field. Hereafter, we will simply refer to these issues as "Christian theism." We do so for brevity's sake. Christian theism should be taken to include specific views about a particular area of study that we believe to be relevant to the integrative task, for example, that cognitive behavioral therapy is an important tool for applying the biblical mandate to be "transformed by the renewing of your minds" (Rom 12:2).

There are two basic forms of direct defense, one negative and one positive.[11] The less controversial of the two is a negative direct defense where we attempt to remove defeaters to Christian theism. If we have a justified belief regarding some proposition P, a defeater is something that weakens or removes that justification. Defeaters come in two types.[12] A rebutting defeater gives justification for believing not-P, in this case, that Christian theism is false. For example, attempts to show that the biblical concept of the family is dysfunctional and false, or that homosexuality is causally necessitated by genes or brain states and that

---

[10]Augustine *De genesi ad litteram* 1.21.
[11]See Ronald Nash, *Faith and Reason* (Grand Rapids: Zondervan, 1988), pp. 14-18.
[12]For a useful discussion of various types of defeaters, see John Pollock, *Contemporary Theories of Knowledge* (Totowa, N.J.: Rowman & Littlefield, 1986), pp. 36-39; Ralph Baergen, *Contemporary Epistemology* (Fort Worth: Harcourt Brace, 1995), pp. 119-24.

therefore it is not a proper object for moral appraisal are cases of rebutting defeaters. An undercutting defeater does not give justification for believing not-P but rather seeks to remove or weaken justification for believing P in the first place. Critiques of the arguments for God's existence are examples of undercutting defeaters. When defeaters are raised against Christian theism, a negative defense seeks either to rebut or undercut those defeaters.

By contrast, a positive direct defense is an attempt to build a positive case for Christian theism. Arguments for the existence of God, objective morality, the existence of the soul, the value and nature of virtue ethics, and the possibility and knowability of miracles are examples. This task for integration is not accepted by all Christian intellectuals. For example, various species of what may be loosely called Reformed epistemology run the gamut from seeing a modest role for a positive direct defense to an outright rejection of this type of activity in certain areas, for example, justifying belief in God and the authority of Holy Scripture. *The CWIS will seek to engage in both negative and positive direct defense.*

2. Polemics. In polemics we seek to criticize views that rival Christian theism in one way or another. Critiques of scientific naturalism, physicalism, pantheism, behaviorist models of educational goals, authorless approaches to texts and Marxist theories of economics are all examples of polemics.

3. Theistic explanation. Suppose we have a set of items that stand in need of explanation and we offer some overall explanation as an adequate or even best explanation of those items. In such a case, our overall explanation explains each of the items in question, and this fact itself provides some degree of confirmation for our overall explanation. For example, if a certain intrinsic genre statement explains the various data of a biblical text, then this fact offers some confirmation for the belief that the statement is the correct interpretation of that text. Christian theists ought to be about the business of exploring the world in light of their worldview and, more specifically, of using their theistic beliefs as explanations of various desiderata in their disciplines. Put differently, we should seek to solve intellectual problems and shed light on areas of puzzlement by using the explanatory power of our worldview.

For example, for those who accept the existence of natural moral law, the irreducibly mental nature of consciousness, natural human rights or the fact that human flourishing follows from certain biblically mandated ethical and religious practices, the truth of Christian theism provides a good explanation of these phenomena. And this fact can provide some degree of confirmation for Christian theism. *The CWIS seeks to show the explanatory power of Christian ideas in various disciplines.*

WHAT MODELS ARE AVAILABLE FOR CLASSIFYING INTEGRATIVE PROBLEMS?

When problem areas surface, there is a need for Christians to think hard about the issue in light of the need for strengthening the rational authority of Christian theism and placing it squarely within the plausibility structure of contemporary culture. We will use the term *theology* to stand for any Christian idea that seems to be a part of a Christian worldview derived primarily from special revelation. When we address problems like these, there will emerge a number of different ways that theology can interact with an issue in a discipline outside theology. Here are some of the different ways that such interaction can take place. These represent different strategies for handling a particular difficulty in integration. These strategies will be employed where appropriate on a case-by-case basis by the authors in the series.

1. *The two-realms view.* Propositions, theories or methodologies in theology and another discipline may involve two distinct, nonoverlapping areas of investigation. For example, debates about angels or the extent of the atonement have little to do with organic chemistry. Similarly, it is of little interest to theology whether a methane molecule has three or four hydrogen atoms in it.

2. *The complementarity view.* Propositions, theories or methodologies in theology and another discipline may involve two different, complementary, noninteracting approaches to the same reality. Sociological aspects of church growth and certain psychological aspects of conversion may be sociological or psychological descriptions of certain phenomena that are complementary to a theological description of church growth or conversion.

3. The direct-interaction view. Propositions, theories or methodologies in theology and another discipline may directly interact in such a way that either one area of study offers rational support for the other or one area of study raises rational difficulties for the other. For example, certain theological teachings about the existence of the soul raise rational problems for philosophical or scientific claims that deny the existence of the soul. The general theory of evolution raises various difficulties for certain ways of understanding the book of Genesis. Some have argued that the big bang theory tends to support the theological proposition that the universe had a beginning.

4. The presuppositions view. Theology may support the presuppositions of another discipline and vice versa. Some have argued that many of the presuppositions of science (for example, the existence of truth; the rational, orderly nature of reality; the adequacy of our sensory and cognitive faculties as tools suited for knowing the external world) make sense and are easy to justify given Christian theism, but are odd and without ultimate justification in a naturalistic worldview. Similarly, some have argued that philosophical critiques of epistemological skepticism and defenses of the existence of a real, theory-independent world and a correspondence theory of truth offer justification for some of the presuppositions of theology.

5. The practical application view. Theology may fill out and add details to general principles in another discipline and vice versa, and theology may help us practically apply principles in another discipline and vice versa. For example, theology teaches that fathers should not provoke their children to anger, and psychology can add important details about what this means by offering information about family systems, the nature and causes of anger, and so forth. Psychology can devise various tests for assessing whether a person is or is not mature, and theology can offer a normative definition to psychology as to what a mature person is.

A WORD ABOUT THIS BOOK

In this volume, Garry DeWeese argues that a genuine integration of Christian faith and philosophy profoundly affects how one does philosophy. He presents a model for integration, beginning with the very concept of philosophy as the search for wisdom leading to a flourishing life. He then works through the traditional subjects of philosophy, arguing in each for the view he believes best represents a consistent integration of biblical and theological commitments with the major philosophical issues. He concludes by making the case that doing philosophy as a Christian can and should lead to transformative spiritual formation.

We hope you can see why we are excited about this book. Even though you're busy, and the many demands on your time tug at you from different directions, we don't think you can afford not to read this book. So wrestle, ponder, pray, compare ideas with Scripture, talk about the pages to follow with others and enjoy.

A FINAL CHALLENGE

In 2001 atheist philosopher Quentin Smith published a remarkably insightful article of crucial relevance to the task of integration. For over fifty years, Smith notes, the academic community has become increasingly secularized and atheistic even though there have been a fair number of Christian teachers involved in that community. How could this be? Smith's answer amounts to the claim that Christians compartmentalized their faith, kept it tucked away in a private compartment of their lives and did not integrate their Christian ideas with their work:

> This is not to say that none of the scholars in their various academic fields were realist theists [theists who took their religious beliefs to be true] in their "private lives"; but realist theists, for the most part excluded their theism from their publications and teaching, in large part because theism . . . was mainly considered to have such a low epistemic status that it did not meet the standards of an "academically respectable" position to hold.[13]

Smith goes on to claim that while Christians have recaptured considerable ground in the field of philosophy, "theists in other fields tend to compartmentalize their theistic beliefs from their scholarly

---

[13]Quentin Smith, "The Metaphysics of Naturalism," *Philo* 4, no. 2 (2001): 1.

work; they rarely assume and never argue for theism in their scholarly work."[14]

This has got to stop. We offer this book to you with the prayer that it will help you rise to the occasion and recapture lost territory in your field of study for the cause of Christ.

Francis J. Beckwith
J. P. Moreland
Series Editors

---

[14]Ibid., p. 3. The same observation about advances in philosophy has been noted by Mark A. Noll in *The Scandal of the Evangelical Mind* (Grand Rapids: Eerdmans, 1994), pp. 235-38.

ACKNOWLEDGMENTS

Isaac Newton famously remarked in a letter to his rival Robert Hooke (dated February 5, 1676), "If I have seen a little further it is by standing on the shoulders of Giants." And if I have learned anything about doing philosophy as a Christian, it is by learning from those who have loomed above the crowd as exemplary Christian philosophers. I've dedicated this book to three giants, men whose impact on Christian philosophy, and philosophy in general, has been great. The shapes of the three men's careers differ markedly.

Alvin Plantinga is truly a philosopher's philosopher, making original and deeply important contributions in metaphysics, epistemology and philosophy of religion, yet throughout maintaining a happy and consistent Christian witness, seeing himself first of all as a scholar in service to the Christian community.

Dallas Willard has impacted numerous students and made significant contributions in logic, philosophy of mind, and history of philosophy with his interpretation of Husserl, but is better known among Christians generally for his work through several decades in the area of spiritual formation.

William Lane Craig's scholarship has focused on defending the historicity of the resurrection of Jesus and on the *kalām* cosmological argument. His research and writing on the latter has sealed his reputation as a significant thinker on the philosophy of time, but he devotes a considerable portion of his time and effort to apologetics, skillfully debating both philosophical and theological opponents of orthodox Christianity.

None of the three would endorse everything I've written here, but I trust that all three would be gratified to see that their understanding of what it is to do philosophy as Christians has been impactful and appreciated.

There are other near-giants to whom I'm also indebted. To thank them all would be impossible, but I must mention the most salient ones.

Francis A. Schaeffer was an evangelist and pastor and only an amateur philosopher, but reading him just after I graduated from college awakened me to the truth—so obvious in retrospect—that ideas have consequences. Time spent at Schaeffer's L'Abri in Switzerland brought home to me, with the surging impact of a tsunami, the way that the transcendentals of truth, goodness and beauty are central to a Christian worldview and an authentic Christian spirituality.

I have the great privilege to teach at Biola University in Southern California, where God has brought together a community of nearly three dozen philosophers, all committed to a comprehensive Christian worldview and to doing philosophy in service to the kingdom of God. Among them I must specially thank my department colleagues in the Talbot School of Theology: Scott Rae, J. P. Moreland, Doug Geivett, Dave Horner, Tim Pickavance, Bill Craig, and our regular visiting professor, David Hunt. I especially want to thank J. P. for his years of friendship and for modeling what I've tried to express in this book about being a Christian philosopher. And I cannot overlook the many students in the department with whom I've continued to learn what it means to do philosophy as a Christian. I'm humbled to be among such thinkers.

Among professional philosophers, I can only name a few who have had great influence on me, whether through their work or by their personal friendship or both: Billy Abraham, Robert Adams, Marilyn Adams, Bill Alston, Robert Audi, Tom Crisp, Greg Ganssle, Robert Garcia, Gary Habermas, Rob Koons, Norman Kretzmann, Andrew Newman, Eleonore Stump, Gregg TenElshof, Nicholas Wolterstorff, Linda Zagzebski, Dean Zimmerman.

Gratitude is due—and hereby expressed—to the editors of the series of which this book is a part, J. P. Moreland and Frank Beckwith, and to Jim Hoover, editor at InterVarsity Press. I have greatly tried their patience, and appreciate their grace and their advice. Thanks is also due to Joe Gorra for his excellent work compiling the index.

Much of the work on this book was done during a study leave granted by Biola University. I'm grateful to Biola's president, Barry Corey, to the Dean of Talbot School of Theology, Dennis Dirks, and to the Dean of the Faculty, Mike Wilkins, for their friendship, support and encouragement.

Finally, nothing like this could have been accomplished without the love, patience and encouragement of my amazing wife, Barbara.

1

WHY SHOULD YOU READ
THIS BOOK?

I am a philosopher because I am a Christian.
To many intellectuals, this probably sounds like saying
that I am a dog because I am a cat.

BRIAN LEFTOW

This question of the bearing of one's Christianity on one's philosophy,
is extraordinarily difficult, and there isn't much by way of guidance
or precedent or (recent) tradition with respect to it.

ALVIN PLANTINGA

Since you've begun reading this book, I'm assuming that you're interested in philosophy. More particularly, I assume you're interested in the question implicit in the title: Is there anything *unique* or *distinctive* about how a Christian does, or should do, philosophy, as opposed to the way that, say, a Buddhist, a Muslim or an atheist would? So let me begin by telling you why you should continue reading this book.

WHAT THIS BOOK IS ABOUT

The thesis of this book is that there *is* something distinctive about how a Christian should do philosophy, and in what follows I aim to draw out what I take to be some of the implications of this thesis.

The class of readers with whom I wish to engage consists first of all of Christians majoring in philosophy, or those young scholars who recently entered the profession, who have questions and concerns about how their Christian faith does, or should, affect the study of and perhaps a career in philosophy. These questions and concerns are generally lumped together under the rubric of "integration," as in "the integration of faith and X," where X is some specific body of knowledge or some specific project or career path.[1]

Nevertheless, I do *not* assume that everyone reading this book is a Christian; after all, the implicit question may well be interesting in its own right to many non-Christians curious to learn how, in Oxford professor Brian Leftow's image, a cat can think it is a dog. I believe there are ideas here that might stimulate the thinking of any budding philosopher, whatever her spiritual commitment.

I'll begin, as any good philosopher would, with some definitions, which will be rather informal. First, what is philosophy? Of course we all know that philosophy, *philosophia,* is literally "the love of wisdom." The next chapter will look closely at the idea of wisdom. For now, let's go for a simpler characterization.

Philosophy is thinking critically about questions that matter.[2] In this sense, all of us are philosophers. All of us at some time ask what is real. All of us wonder what or how we know. And all of us ponder what is the right thing to do in a given situation, or more generally, how we should live our lives. These questions lie at the heart of philosophy. For most people, answers to such fundamental questions are largely unexamined and perhaps even mutually inconsistent, but in forming such beliefs and acting on them, everyone is doing philosophy. As someone nicely put it, "Philosophy is common sense in a dress suit."

At a more developed level, 'philosophy' refers to a body of knowl-

---

[1]The preface to the series of which this book is a part, by general editors J. P. Moreland and Francis Beckwith, deftly lays out the conception of integration to which I hold and from which I write. I need not repeat what they have written there, but intend to show, in a very practical way, some implications of that vision of integration of faith and learning as applied to the field of philosophy.

[2]I shamelessly stole the phrase from the title of the widely used textbook authored by Ed Miller, my *Doktorvater* at the University of Colorado: Ed. L. Miller and Jon Jensen, *Questions That Matter: An Invitation to Philosophy,* 6th ed. (New York: Macmillan, 2008).

edge, often the subject matter of college courses, that organizes and presents the thinking of major thinkers throughout the ages about such things as reality, knowledge and values. It is this study of philosophy that I have assumed has aroused your intellectual passion and drawn you deeper into study and thought.

At a still more refined level, 'philosophy' is the specialized activity engaged in by certain "professional thinkers" who build on the thought of those who have gone before, utilizing certain tools and methods, with the goal of developing, presenting and defending carefully examined conclusions about reality, knowledge and values. Since philosophy is above all concerned with discerning the truth about these things, it is natural that philosophy has influenced every corner of life—both inside and outside academia—and that philosophical terms, tools, arguments and conclusions can be found in almost any book pulled from the library shelf.

What do I mean by "doing" philosophy? If you are indeed a member of my imagined readership class, you might be considering (or just entering) a career in philosophy—which pretty much means an academic position teaching philosophy, and commits you to a number of years as a graduate student. As a graduate student you make the transition from *learning* philosophy to *doing* philosophy—and indeed, if you are an advanced undergrad philosophy major, you have already begun to make the transition.

The difference between *learning* philosophy and *doing* it is easier caught than taught, easier shown than explained. As St. Thomas Aquinas noted somewhere, "The purpose of the study of philosophy is not to learn what others have thought, but to learn how the truth of things stands." It is the difference between knowing how Plato develops his argument in the *Republic* and critically evaluating his claims about the nature of justice; it is the difference between learning first-order logic and applying that learning to pointing out the logical fallacies in an argument, whether in a philosophy article, a political speech or a letter to the editor.

I do not think there is any difference between the way in which a Christian or a non-Christian *learns* philosophy; the people and the facts, the books and the arguments are what they are. But I claimed above that there is a difference in the way Christians *do,* or *should do,* philosophy. Now, this claim does not mean Christians apply first-order logic differently. What I mean by the claim does mean—well, for that, you'll have to read the book.

And finally, what do I mean by 'Christian'? I *don't* mean simply an heir of Western civilization, or someone who would pick a church rather than a mosque or a synagogue for a wedding. A Christian, in the sense I'll use the term, is one who *believes* certain propositions (e.g., Jesus, who is God incarnate, died on a cross and was resurrected three days later), *trusts* certain promises for personal salvation (e.g., Jesus' death was substitutionary, making payment for my sins that I could not make myself, thus securing God's forgiveness), and as a result has committed intentionally to *live* a life exemplifying as consistently as possible the values Jesus taught (e.g., faith, love, mercy, patience, peace, self-control). I will strongly resist the temptation to introduce sectarian distinctives, and try to remain in the tradition of "canonical theism," the broad stream of orthodoxy traceable to the church fathers and the ecumenical councils and creeds.[3]

HOW CAN THIS BOOK HELP YOU?

Now, suppose you are a Christian student majoring in philosophy and contemplating graduate study with the goal of becoming a professional philosopher. How can this book help you?

First, I hope reading the book will be an enjoyable and relatively easy task. I have deliberately sought to write in a conversational style that is (I trust) accessible and clear. That does not mean, I hope, that discussions along the way are simplistic, but rather that they are not encumbered with very much in the way of technical formalisms.

Second, I believe that the discussions that follow will challenge and provoke you. It's all too easy to slip into a way of pursuing any discipline (not just philosophy) according to a currently popular set of rules: in a fashionable style, accepting certain assumptions, following particular

---

[3]See William J. Abraham, Jason F. Vickers and Natalie B. Van Kirk, eds., *Canonical Theism: A Proposal for Theology and the Church* (Grand Rapids: Eerdmans, 2008).

strictures, avoiding awkward questions and rejecting (usually without reflection) unpopular conclusions. Part of what it is to do philosophy as a Christian means breaking some of these rules. Or so I say. And I hope to show by example at least this one philosopher's understanding of how this works, and so to prod your intellectual journey into paths that you might otherwise have avoided or overlooked.

Third, I hope you disagree with at least parts of what I say. Naturally I believe that what I say is correct, but I could be wrong. In wrestling with the claims and suggestions that follow, you'll be doing philosophy yourself, developing your own ideas of what it is to integrate Christian faith and the practice of philosophy.

Finally, I believe that there is no such thing as "neutral" philosophizing. I reject the idea that the proper method of doing philosophy is "methodological naturalism," to use a term in vogue in philosophy of science. One's pretheoretical, prereflective worldview commitments[4] and control beliefs[5] will always influence one's theoretical thought. But this does not mean that we're trapped behind concepts inherited from our linguistic and cultural (or religious) community. Rather, it means we should be self-reflectively aware of the worldview commitments and control beliefs from which we start, as well as those of others with whom we converse and argue, and we should be open to the possibility that at least some of our pre-theoretical commitments should be open to revision. Reflecting on his philosophical training, Oxford professor Basil Mitchell wrote,

> [The study of philosophy] was, to all appearances, a straightforwardly intellectual task, but it was one that made exacting spiritual demands of a kind that is not always appreciated by those whose spiritual battlefields lie elsewhere. It was necessary to hold on to one's Christian belief

---

[4]"A worldview is a commitment, a fundamental orientation of the heart, that can be expressed as a story or in a set of presuppositions (assumptions which may be true, partially true, or entirely false) which we hold (consciously or subconsciously, consistently or inconsistently) about the basic constitution of reality, and that provides the foundation on which we live and move and have our being." James W. Sire, *Naming the Elephant: Worldview as a Concept* (Downers Grove, Ill.: InterVarsity Press, 2004), p. 122.

[5]See Nicholas Wolterstorff, *Reason Within the Bounds of Religion*, 2nd ed. (Grand Rapids: Eerdmans, 1984). Wolterstorff argues—correctly, I believe—that control beliefs play a significant role in *any* intellectual inquiry.

and practice, tentative and underdeveloped though they were, while en-
deavoring to ensure that the criticisms to which they were being subjected were fairly and honestly faced.[6]

I think it is entirely appropriate for a Christian philosopher to begin
from and be guided by certain control beliefs that are explicitly Christian, and I aim to prod you into thinking through some of the implications of those commitments for philosophy, as I see them.

Further, I will encourage you to think about the role your religious
community plays in your philosophizing. As Christians, surely, we must
pay careful attention to what the biblical scholars and the historical and
systematic theologians say constitutes the essential core of orthodox
Christianity. And if we find ourselves tempted to reject any of that core,
we must tread very, very carefully, lest we cease to be Christian in our
philosophizing. (Of course there is a reciprocal contribution here. Christian philosophers can help the biblical scholars and the theologians to
properly frame questions, analyze concepts, argue for positions and offer
other philosophical tools essential to the theological task. This is the
sense intended by the medievals when they claimed that "theology is the
queen of the sciences and philosophy is her handmaid." They were not
dismissing philosophy as useless or unnecessary.)

Alvin Plantinga puts it this way:

> The point I want to make is that Christian philosophers should *explicitly*
> and *self-consciously* think of themselves as belonging to the Christian com-
> munity (and the community of Christian intellectuals); perhaps they
> should think of themselves *primarily* or *first of all* as members of the Chris-
> tian community, and only secondarily as members of, say, the philosophi-
> cal community at large, or the contemporary academic community.[7]

As I argue for and illustrate this in what follows, I hope that you'll be
challenged to reflect on your own worldview commitments and control
beliefs, whether you're a Christian or not, and about the role those

---

[6]Basil Mitchell, "War and Friendship," in *Philosophers Who Believe*, ed. Kelly James Clark
(Downers Grove, Ill.: InterVarsity Press, 1993), p. 40.
[7]Alvin Plantinga, "A Christian Life Partly Lived," in *Philosophers Who Believe*, ed. Kelly James
Clark (Downers Grove, Ill.: InterVarsity Press, 1993), p. 78.

commitments and beliefs play in your philosophizing. At the end of the day you may not come out where I've come out on some issues, but at least you'll have done the hard and rewarding work of thinking seriously (and critically!) about your philosophy and your faith.

THE PLAN OF THE BOOK

Part one, "Introductory Matters," begins with chapter two with a consideration of the concept of wisdom, especially as the term is used in the Bible, for if philosophy is the love of wisdom, we need to get clear on the concept. I'll suggest that much of contemporary philosophy has lost the practical goal of wisdom—that of discerning what makes for a good person, a good society, a good life.

In chapter three I argue for the more specific claim that for a Christian philosopher, commitment to the Christian faith should guide how one does philosophy, and I offer some thoughts on the popular but false opposition of faith and reason.

Chapter four concludes the introductory matters by looking at Jesus and philosophy. Jesus was certainly not a systematic, analytic philosopher, but that does not mean his teaching and life have nothing to say to Christian philosophers. In fact, I claim there is a certain normativity to Jesus' teaching that philosophers who are Christians must not dismiss. And more—I claim there is a normativity to Jesus' mission that Christian philosophers *dare* not miss. So in chapter four I'll have to cash out and defend these claims.

Part two, "The Inescapable Questions," takes up just that—the very difficult, absolutely fundamental questions of existence, knowledge and values—especially moral values. In these chapters I'll consider certain crucial issues, explore the major options, and suggest implications of a Christian worldview for our investigation of and responses to these issues.

This is an intimidating task. While not denying the contribution of philosophers from Muslim (e.g., Al-Ghazali, Avicenna, Averroës) or Jewish (e.g., Maimonides, Spinoza) faiths, the majority of philosophers in the 1200 years from St. Augustine to the Enlightenment were Christians, and most of them were monks (after all, who else had the leisure to read, think and write?). They thought deeply about the topics of philosophy and their Christian faith, and in some respects thought more deeply about these things than we contemporary thinkers are wont to do. Nevertheless, I will refrain from more than passing reference to the great medieval philosophers—this book cannot become a history; but in the shadow of these giants, I claim no great originality.

Part three, "Second-Order Questions," takes up two more delimited subject areas of philosophy—philosophy of mind and of science—selected because they offer clear opportunities for doing philosophy as a Christian. Again, I will look at crucial issues, major options and implications of Christian belief.

Part four, "The End of the Matter," tackles the not-so-obvious question, what does all this philosophy have to do with spiritual formation—a Christian's growth "in the grace and knowledge of our Lord and Savior Jesus Christ" (2 Pet 3:18 NASB). The apostle Paul tells us, "do not be conformed to this world, but be transformed by the renewing of your mind, that you may prove what the will of God is, that which is good and acceptable and perfect" (Rom 12:2 NASB). My contention is that doing philosophy as a Christian is a most excellent means of achieving that mental transformation.

One thing I won't do is trace the contours of what is often called a Christian worldview. That's a large, book-length task in itself.[8] But as we proceed, you'll be able to discern certain contour lines that I see as crucial for a reflective, orthodox Christian worldview. Now, I can't claim ecclesiastical authority for my views, and I readily acknowledge that other Christian philosophers can disagree and still be fine philosophers, exemplary Christians and good people. Nevertheless, throughout I will take stands on issues, stands that I will generally argue for, and which I believe are congruent with a biblical worldview.

It's quite probable that some readers will want to skip right to one of the chapters where their interest lies—say, epistemology or philosophy of mind—and see what they might find there to argue with or learn from. That's fine; I do that too. But I urge you, if you're one of those,

---

[8]Again, I refer you to the series preface at the beginning of the book.

to first read the remaining chapters in part one, which lay the groundwork for what I have to say in succeeding chapters.

A WORD ABOUT PHILOSOPHICAL METHOD

To think about what philosophy is about, or the possibility, nature and modal status of philosophical knowledge, or the relationship of philosophy to empirical science and psychology, or even how philosophy should be done, is to engage in the work of *metaphilosophy*. In what follows, I won't directly address metaphilosophical questions, but my discussion presupposes certain positions on them, and it is only fair to state some of my presuppositions at the outset.

First, as I already said, philosophy is about questions that matter, and by that I mean questions that matter for our understanding of how we should live (I'll say more about this in the next chapter). And since I'm writing as a Christian for Christians (at least primarily), I take it as given that there is a clear notion of how we should live, and so philosophical knowledge is possible. Contra such neopragmatists as Richard Rorty, who sees philosophy as therapy to cure us of the desire for truth, I believe that philosophy, done rightly, is a great boon in the search for truth.

Second, I believe that in most cases, philosophy can arrive at answers to central philosophical questions without crucially relying on the empirical sciences, and since much philosophical thought can establish the logical or metaphysical necessity of its conclusions, those conclusions will have *greater* authority than the logically contingent conclusions of the natural sciences when those conclusions conflict. This is not to say that philosophers don't, or shouldn't, take seriously the deliverances of contemporary science, but it is to say that science is not the intellectual master of philosophy.[9]

Third, my approach lies in the broad tradition called Anglo-American analytical philosophy. My approach will not be primarily historical. Historical studies, as in a history of philosophy or, more broadly, a history of ideas approach, can be very helpful and quite interesting, espe-

---

[9]See George Bealer, "'A Priori' Knowledge and the Scope of Philosophy," *Philosophical Studies* 81 (1996): 122-42.

cially when the interrelationship between political and cultural trends and philosophical ideas is investigated. And we can learn much from the ancients, the medievals and the early moderns. But history, even if a guide to the future, is not necessarily a guide to the truth. Both Aristotle and Kant can be wrong.

Also, I don't intend to delve into the Continental tradition in philosophy, which is decidedly antimetaphysical in nature. While there is much that could be said about the Continental tradition, marked by the trajectory from Nietzsche through Husserl and Heidegger and the structuralists and poststructuralists to Derrida and Foucault, I shall leave it aside. It is not that phenomenology has no important insights into our experience or that deconstructionism has nothing interesting to say about our reading of the history of philosophy or reading texts in general. It is, rather, my judgment that the Anglo-American analytical tradition better equips us to get clear on our concepts and to converge on truth.

Finally, a word about two philosophical tools: logic and conceptual analysis.

Logic. I sometimes encounter the objection, usually from well-meaning Christians, "Why is logic so important? You make it sound like logic is even over God!" I believe the question reflects a common misunderstanding of logic. If God did not exist, then logic would not exist (nor would anything else, for that matter). But if God does exist, then a whole lot of other things also exist, including the laws of logic. Arguably, numbers, sets, universals, propositions, relations and so on also exist. Another way to say this is that if *anything* exists, then everything that is *logically necessary* must exist. But nothing can exist at all unless something that is *metaphysically necessary* exists. And God necessarily exists in this latter sense, so all logical necessities depend on his existence.[10]

For example, consider the law of identity: God is who he is; he is not another God or a hallucinogenic mushroom. Consider, too, the law of

---

[10]I must acknowledge that some of my good friends disagree with this analysis of God's relation to abstract objects such as the laws of logic. This leads them to adopt a "fictionalist" or "conceptualist" account of universals. For more, see the discussion in chapter 5.

noncontradiction: God cannot be both essentially good and not-good. These laws (and other things that exist timelessly) would not exist if God did not exist, so they depend for their existence on God. But they were not created by God in the sense that he could have made them otherwise. So to say that the laws of logic apply to God is not to make logic sovereign over God. It is simply to recognize that once anything at all exists, then many other things also exist that cannot be any other way.

Another objection is this: "Well, there are many different logics. How can we tell which one is the right one? Isn't that pretty arbitrary?" Again, I believe this objection rests on a misunderstanding. The short answer is yes, there are many different logics. But we should keep two points in mind. First, there are also many different algebras and many different geometries. (Mathematicians and logicians, contrary to popular stereotypes, are very creative people!) Some of these different systems were devised for dealing with specific problems and do not claim universal validity (e.g., "fuzzy" logic, versions of multivalent logic and many systems of abstract algebra). Second, none of these systems could have been "built" apart from certain fundamental laws of thought. (If the law of noncontradiction did not hold universally, we could not even claim that there were different systems!)

A final objection goes this way: "Your logic is a relic of the male-dominated West, and it ignores Eastern logic and feminist logic, for example." Again, I think this reflects a deep misunderstanding. With regards to "Eastern logic," there really is no such thing. It is true that certain strands of Hinduism and Buddhism teach that contradiction lies at the heart of reality, that on the path to enlightenment one must learn to embrace contradiction. But as Mortimer Adler argued, as long as Hindus and Buddhists accept the results of modern science and technology, they are tacitly affirming the law of noncontradiction, which lies at the very foundation of science.[11]

As for "feminist logic," this is almost certainly a matter of emphasis and values, not different logics. We may grant, for the sake of argument, that women are in general more relational and more emotionally

---

[11]Mortimer Adler, *Truth in Religion: The Plurality of Religions and the Unity of Truth* (New York: Macmillan, 1990), pp. 69-76.

connected, and men more objective and linear in their thought. But of course women can use objective logic when required, and men can learn to value relationships and emotional connections. Difference in emphasis is not difference in kind.

Conceptual analysis. Philosophers want to be clear and precise in their work, to say as unambiguously and understandably as possible just what it is that they are in fact saying. So generally we see a large part of our work to be that of conceptual analysis. When doing conceptual analysis, most philosophers are not so much interested in how a term is used or what its function is in a natural language (or by a particular linguistic community)—although such investigation can provide helpful starting points—as they are in discovering the essence of that to which the concept applies, or even if it refers to anything at all. We want to know what entities in the world "fall under" the concept, and how we can tell that they do. So, for example, if we ask the question "What is justice?" the answer will be found in an analysis of the concept of justice—seeking what justice consists in, what its essence is—and not simply in an analysis of the ways in which the word is used or in an examination of the things to which the term is applied (for some of them, it might turn out, are misapplications of the term). The process of conceptual analysis is often carried on through progressively refining the analysis, seeking out possible counterexamples and then re-refining. It may seem tedious, perhaps, but the goal is clarity and precision.

IS THIS BOOK REALLY NECESSARY?

About now you may be wondering if this book is really going to be all that different from many other works already out there. That's a good question, and it deserves a forthright answer. The Preacher of Ecclesiastes warned, "Of making many books there is no end, and much study wearies the body" (Eccles 12:12). Why would I risk adding to general weariness? Because by design this is not like those other books that swim in the same pond.

First, this is not a general introduction to philosophy written from a Christian perspective. I won't introduce the major topics in philosophy, but rather will consider how to think about them from within a Christian worldview. Second, this isn't a general challenge to Christian students to develop a "Christian mind," to engage their learning broadly and deeply as a way to "love their God with all their mind." Others have done that very well.

Third, it isn't a book of apologetics. I won't make arguments for Christian theism or offer defenses against objections to theism or Christianity. But this I hope: Philosophy done from within the commitments of a Christian worldview will be ampliative, offering a holistic, deeply integrated vision of philosophy that should prove satisfying and attractive. That in itself would be a powerful apologetic. My aim is to offer an outline of how that might be done.

So, there you have it. This is why I think you should read this book. Come, join me on the exploration!

PART ONE

INTRODUCTORY MATTERS

Perhaps, at some level, philosophy is always the theology of
some ultimate concern. For philosophy is written in the service of a
particular world view and set of values. Almost always, something in a
thinker's world picture or values calls forth a nearly religious awe or
attracts a supreme, quasi-religious loyalty.

BRIAN LEFTOW

By any standard, the growth in numbers of openly confessing Christians among professional philosophers in the past half-century has been remarkable. To some, it's been alarming. Quentin Smith, as editor of *Philo,* an academic journal encouraging naturalism (roughly, the view that no supernatural entities exist), sounded the alarm:

> Naturalists passively watched as realist versions of theism . . . began to sweep through the philosophical community, until today perhaps one-quarter or one-third of philosophy professors are theists, with most being orthodox Christians. . . . But in philosophy, it became, almost overnight, "academically respectable" to argue for theism, making philosophy a favored field of entry for the most intelligent and talented theists en-

tering academia today. . . . God is not "dead" in academia; he returned to life in the late 1960s and is now alive and well in his last academic stronghold, philosophy departments.[1]

Does this resurgence of Christians in academic philosophy have any significance? I think that it does. I believe that at least one reason for the growing numbers of Christian philosophers is that the implications of a Christian worldview for doing philosophy are profound. If a Christian worldview is indeed an accurate response to the God-created world in which we find ourselves, then it is no accident that a Christian worldview has profound explanatory power and coheres deeply with our experiences and intuitions.

In what follows, I hope to clarify that claim, argue for and illustrate it, and perhaps bring you to believe it too.

As Oxford professor Brian Leftow said, these are matters of ultimate concern.

---

[1]Quentin Smith, "The Metaphilosophy of Naturalism," *Philo* 4 (2001): 3.

2

PHILOSOPHERS AND SAGES

HOKHMAH AND SOPHIA

Of all human pursuits, the pursuit of wisdom is the more perfect,
the more sublime, the more useful, and the more agreeable.

ST. THOMAS AQUINAS

There is no such thing as religiously neutral intellectual endeavor—
or rather there is no such thing as serious, substantial and relatively
complete intellectual endeavor that is religiously neutral.

ALVIN PLANTINGA

Philosophy, literally, is the "love of wisdom." Which, of course, raises the question, what is wisdom? I think it's best to approach the answer in a somewhat roundabout way so as not to force the answer though our philosophical sieve.

We humans need a sense of order to quiet our mind, and we find ample evidence of order in nature. Day follows night, autumn yields to winter, generation replaces generation.

Yet in the interpersonal realm, where we must function daily, where we live and love and work and play, the sense of order rapidly fades to obscurity. The uncivil scowl of the checkout clerk shatters the social order just as surely, though not as indelibly, as a terrorist's bomb or a drunk driver's weaving.

To meet the heartfelt need for some predictability, some guidance in interpersonal matters, cultures worldwide have developed the phenomenon of wisdom. A father watches his son and remembers much; deep empathy arises in mutual experience. Each generation must learn for itself that the stove is hot, yet the desire to share experiential knowledge is universal. "Folk wisdom" results, giving rise to proverbs, maxims, aphorisms, country-store horse sense and "old saws." Stemming as it does from diverse environs and divergent outlooks, folk wisdom is sometimes profound, often contradictory ("Look before you leap," but "he who hesitates is lost"). Still, wisdom represents the attempt to distill from countless repeated experiences of life the pure nectar of truth. Wisdom reflects our desire to pass on to others what we have discovered about life and the living of it.

Wisdom seen in this light has a slightly different hue from the color that the average person sees in the word. To most, wisdom relates not so much to practical living as to amassed knowledge, often arcane, usually impractical. Indeed, Webster's defines wisdom first as "accumulated philosophic or scientific knowledge," and only later as "good sense . . . a wise attitude or course of action."[1]

Wisdom, according to this popular view, is to be found in dusty libraries and futuristic laboratories, not in common sense and mundane activities. In fact, the absent-minded professor who can't find his spectacles perched on his nose and has all the social graces of a buzz saw, can still be thought of as wise.

Such a conception of wisdom, however, is at odds with the traditional place of wisdom in hundreds of cultures over thousands of years. As the venerable *Encyclopedia of Philosophy* notes,

> Wisdom in its broadest and commonest sense denotes sound and serene judgment regarding the conduct of life. It may be accompanied by a broad range of knowledge, by intellectual acuteness, and by speculative depth, but it is not to be identified with any of these and may appear in their absence.[2]

---

[1]*Webster's Seventh New Collegiate Dictionary* (Springfield, Mass.: G. & C. Merriam Co., 1965), s.v. "wisdom."
[2]Donald M. Borchert, ed., *The Encyclopedia of Philosophy*, 2nd ed. (Farmington Hills, Mich.: Macmillan, 2006), 9:793.

More importantly for our purposes, perhaps, such a conception is also at odds with the picture of wisdom we find in the Bible—especially the Old Testament—and in the ancient Near East, which gives the Bible its cultural background.

BIBLICAL WISDOM

The first point that meets us in investigating biblical wisdom is that it is teleological. Wisdom for its own sake is unknown. Biblical wisdom is a harnessed force, a tool fittingly designed for a particular application.

Passages speaking of God's wisdom spotlight this point. Paul claims that what people often take for wisdom is in reality foolishness. God's wisdom—true wisdom—is directed toward the goal of salvation (1 Cor 1:18-30). God's wisdom is revealed to the inhabitants of the spiritual realm in the salvation of the church (Eph 3:10-12). James counsels that true wisdom is directed toward peaceful living (Jas 3:13-18). Thus, theologian J. I. Packer writes,

> In Scripture wisdom is a moral as well as an intellectual quality. . . . To be truly wise, in the Bible sense, one's intelligence and cleverness must be harnessed to a right end. Wisdom is the power to see, and the inclination to choose, the best and highest goal, together with the surest means of attaining it.[3]

Much can be learned from an exhaustive study of wisdom and related concepts in the Bible. But in the Old Testament—in the Proverbs of Solomon and the other sages, in the anguished dialogues of Job and his friends, and in the bemused reportings of the Preacher of Ecclesiastes—we encounter the essence of wisdom in its most commonplace applications.

The unique nature of Old Testament wisdom does not lie in its religious character; pagan wisdom too is religious. It is rather the God of the Old Testament who, as source, revealer and sustainer of wisdom, floods it with a unique light.[4]

---

[3]J. I. Packer, *Knowing God* (Downers Grove, Ill.: InterVarsity Press, 1973), p. 80.
[4]Bruce K. Waltke, "The Book of Proverbs and Ancient Wisdom Literature," *Bibliotheca Sacra* 136 (July-September 1979): 236.

The Hebrew sages moved always within the overriding belief in the person of Yahweh, the God of the Covenant. He was the unalterable presupposition and prerequisite of wisdom ("The fear of the LORD is the beginning of wisdom," Prov 9:10). "The thesis that all human knowledge comes back to the question about commitment to God is a statement of penetrating perspicacity. . . . One becomes competent and expert as far as the orders of life are concerned only if one begins from knowledge about God."[5] His revelation through the Law and the Prophets was assumed, and wisdom was built on such revelation ("Where there is no revelation the people cast off restraint; but blessed is he who keeps the law," Prov 29:18; see also Jer 18:18).

The sages had a high view of God's sovereignty. From the Law, especially Deuteronomy, came a mentality that saw social events as direct encounters with Yahweh who controlled the social order. Therefore reality was not merely "there" in a neutral sense, impassively waiting passionless examination. Rather, reality had an effect on all people because Yahweh was active in reality.

The Hebrew sages were at all times far from pantheism, however. Yahweh moves in reality, but he was not identical to reality. Quite the contrary: freedom, rooted in faith in Yahweh, resulted from the very fact that he *transcended* physical reality. Consequently the practical doctrine of divine sovereignty never became deterministic or fatalistic for the sages, as did the wisdom of some of their neighbors.

The purpose of wisdom for the Hebrews, then, was not to examine the attributes of the pantheon of gods that determined their lives. The nature of Yahweh was already revealed in the moral principles and the legal code of the Torah, and was being expounded in the exhortations of the prophets. For the Hebrews, the purpose of wisdom was to search out the order in reality created by Yahweh (see Prov 8:22-31) and to experience a happy life by walking in that created order.[6] "Wisdom thus consisted in knowing that at the bottom of things an order is at work, silently and often in a scarcely noticeable way, making for a balance of events."[7]

---

[5]Gerhard von Rad, *Wisdom in Israel* (Nashville: Abingdon, 1972), p. 67.
[6]Waltke, "Book of Proverbs," p. 233.
[7]Gerhard von Rad, *Old Testament Theology* (New York: Harper & Row, 1962), 1:428.

This brings us to the Hebrew word for wisdom, *hokhmah*. Basic to the meaning of the word is a root indicating something that is firm, well grounded. Early in the development of the Hebrew language the word was applied to technical expertise. Bezalel was filled by God with *hokhmah*, translated "skill," to make artistic designs for the furnishings of the tabernacle (Ex 31:3-5). Others are recognized as being skilled at idol-making (Jer 10:9), bronze work (1 Kings 7:14), and seafaring (Ezek 27:8-9). Thus the concept conveyed to us by the word *hokhmah* is that of a person who is well grounded and skilled in one's particular field of endeavor. For the wise person, that field of endeavor is life itself. "Basically wisdom is the intensely practical art of being skilled and successful in life."[8]

Or, more succinctly still, wisdom in the Old Testament—*hokhmah*—is *the skill of living*.

THE CYCLE OF BIBLICAL WISDOM

Wisdom seeks to encompass life. An impossible task, perhaps, given the multiplicity of twists and turns any single life might take, and infinitely more complicated when wisdom seeks to transcend cultures and times. Yet that is the aim—and, to anticipate our destination, the achievement—of biblical wisdom.

To encompass a thing, one must return to the starting point. A circle is traced. In a way that startles us with its extent and symmetry, the Old Testament wisdom books trace a circle. No matter where the reader begins, she can find a unity. Regardless of the individual life situation of the student of wisdom, she will be led along an inclusive path which, after tracking wisdom through all possible worlds, returns her to her own life and her own situation, now well prepared to face that situation and its consequences wisely.

Circles, of course, have no defined beginning or ending. Just so, there is no prescribed beginning when the student prepares to open the three Old Testament wisdom books, Proverbs, Job or Ecclesiastes. But circles go 'round, and cycles are meant to be completed. Just so, elimi-

---

[8]William Dyrness, *Themes in Old Testament Theology* (Downers Grove, Ill.: InterVarsity Press, 1979), p. 189.

nating one or two of the three wisdom books gives an incomplete and ultimately unsatisfying picture of wisdom, and will leave the student deficient in a portion of the skill of living.

So we might begin with any of the three books. If we were deep in personal crisis, or had recently been walking with a friend through his tragedy, we might begin with Job. If we were dealing with a predominately young group, their thinking deeply informed by the ironic zeitgeist of postmodernism, we might begin in Ecclesiastes. And for a more systematic entry into the world of *hokhmah*, we should begin with Proverbs.

Proverbs: The paradigm. Entering the wisdom cycle in Proverbs has several advantages. First, we will be beginning with wisdom presented in its traditional guise: the proverbs and parables that seek to make the particular lessons of wisdom generally applicable. The Proverbs are, after all, much more familiar to most than the wisdom teachings of either Job or Ecclesiastes, despite our familiarity with the story of Job and with the "vanity" refrain of Ecclesiastes.

Proverbs presents us with general principles that cover normal cases. To use an analogy from language learning, the individuals and experiences we meet in the Proverbs are, so to speak, regular verbs. We can master a paradigm, learn a few rather simple rules, and move ahead confidently.

Job: The exception. However, as any student of language knows, not all verbs are regular. Sooner or later an exception is encountered that follows the paradigm not at all. In life, the exception to wisdom is the righteous sufferer. Rare indeed is the man or woman who lives even a score of years without experiencing or observing firsthand some significant undeserved suffering. Such an experience challenges the paradigm. "Hold on a minute. You didn't tell us there were irregular verbs that had to be learned individually!" Wait a second. You didn't say that there might be people who live consistently by the proverbial rules of wisdom and still have problems and pain.

Job speaks to those who have observed or lived the exception. When the traditional categories that explain the normal cases fail, Job shows that the question is not *why?* but *who?* and suggests that the way to a deeper knowledge of Who is through wisdom. When the righteous *do* suffer, it is to Job that we turn. When the night is dark and the storm raging, it is the book of Job that provides comfort and encouragement. Nietzsche said, "The thought of suicide is a great consolation; with the help of it one has got through many a bad night." But to the student of wisdom, to men and women of faith, it is Job's experience and Job's God who are the consolation.

Ecclesiastes: The existentialist challenge. But for those who live long enough, or observe cynically enough, or who, in the words of the French existentialist Albert Camus, have the courage to "eschew all fuzzy abstractions and plant themselves squarely in front of the bloody face of history,"[9] the question will arise as to whether the normal cases really are normal. There seem to be more irregular verbs than regular, so of what use is the paradigm? When exceptions outnumber regularities, what is normal? Of what use is wisdom?

Ecclesiastes answers this objection with its healthy dose of sanctified existentialism and proposes that life is not a puzzle to be mastered but a gift to be responsibly enjoyed. The way to enjoy life to the fullest, says Ecclesiastes, is to live it according to *hokhmah*—wisdom grounded in faith.

So we come full circle to Proverbs. Whether we see life as a seamless weaving, or a tapestry with noticeable flaws, or simply, looking from the underside, as a meaningless pattern of randomly oriented threads, the counsel is the same. Life is lived best when lived wisely. The meaning of *hokhmah* shades together with the six or seven other closely related Hebrew words,[10] but all have an intensely practical orientation. What wisdom meant to the Hebrew was not analytical philosophy but a practical skill that would lead to success in daily life.

With the sages, then, we plunge into a thought realm where wisdom is functional, where the order created by God can and must be known,

---

[9]Camus used the phrase in speaking of what the world expects of Christians.

[10]In the first chapter of Proverbs (Prov 1:1-5), Solomon places a prism in front of wisdom, breaking its clear white light into a spectrum of meanings. These shades of wisdom are not hard and fixed categories. They blur together at the edges, and any one can stand for wisdom as a whole. Yet their proximity here reveals the fine shades of meaning subsumed under the general category of wisdom: *musar* (discipline, instruction), *binah* (insight, understanding), *sekel* (prudence), *mezimmah* (discretion), *da'at* (knowledge) and *leqakh* (learning).

where choices can be objectively labeled good or bad, and where the skill of living can be learned.

WISDOM AND PHILOSOPHY

The conception of wisdom as the skill of living is, as I said, basic to the wisdom traditions of many cultures around the world. The Greek philosophical tradition, wellspring of Western philosophy, was just as practically directed as the wisdom traditions of other cultures, and at the same time more reflective and theoretical. Thales, the first philosopher in the Greek tradition, was, according to Diogenes Laertius, the first of the Seven Sages created in the archonship of Damasius at Athens about 582 B.C., or just after the fall of Jerusalem to the Babylonians (see 2 Kings 25; Jer 39–41). Thales was interested in knowledge in pursuit of happiness: according to him, the happy man is "one who has a healthy body, a resourceful mind, and a docile [that is, teachable—the Greek is *eupaideutos*] nature."[11] From Thales on, the central tradition in Greek philosophy was intensely practical, aimed at discerning the elementary principles of the world in order to determine what constituted the good life, and how to live it.[12] Of course we know that even among the pre-Socratics there were charlatans such as the Sophists, and the Academy after Plato began to focus less and less on the good life and more and more on arcane matters. The wisdom, *sophia*, that Thales, Socrates, Plato and Aristotle sought became over time a parody of itself, what Qoheleth,[13] that most philosophical of the Hebrew sages, would call "a chasing after the wind" (Eccles 1:14). Cicero (106-43 B.C.) observed sarcastically, "Somehow or other no statement is too absurd for some philosopher to make."[14]

In the history of philosophy one may easily trace the tension between critical thought aimed at discovering the nature of the good—

---

[11]As recorded by Diogenes Laertius, *Lives of the Eminent Philosophers*, trans. R. D. Hicks, Loeb Classical Library (Cambridge, Mass.: Harvard University Press, 1925), p. 39.

[12]See, e.g., Martha C. Nussbaum, *The Therapy of Desire: Theory and Practice in Hellenistic Ethics* (Princeton, N.J.: Princeton University Press, 1994).

[13]*Qoheleth* is the Hebrew title of the author of Ecclesiastes (traditionally, King Solomon). It has been translated "teacher," "preacher" or left untranslated.

[14]Cicero, *De Divinatione*, trans. W. A. Falconer, Loeb Classical Library (Cambridge, Mass.: Harvard University Press, 1923), p. 505.

good people, good societies, the good life—and critical thought aimed at increasingly more arcane theoretical distinctions. Well, perhaps the tension is traced *too* easily. For one has to look very hard to find a significant philosopher in the medieval or early modern period who focused on abstractions to the exclusion of practical ethics. While it is easy to point to and, perhaps naively, to ridicule some of the obscure metaphysical speculations of the scholastics, a solid case could be made that metaphysical theory was nearly always employed in the service of true wisdom as understood by the sages. As St. Thomas Aquinas said, "Of all human pursuits, the pursuit of wisdom is the more perfect, the more sublime, the more useful, and the more agreeable."[15]

Even in the modern period, that most metaphysical of philosophers, Gottfried Wilhelm Leibniz (1646-1716), wrote extensively on politics, law and ethics, as well as theology. And no less than Immanuel Kant noted, "It is the zeal of a sophist to inquire into any idle proposition and to set to the craving after knowledge no other limits than impossibility. But to select from among the innumerable tasks before us the one which humanity must solve, is the merit of the wise."[16] In short, through the development of the Western philosophical tradition, *sophia* and *hokhmah* were not adversaries. The historian Will Durant saw this; he once observed, "Knowledge is power, but only wisdom is liberty."[17] Nevertheless, though *sophia* and *hokhmah* had come a long way together, by the twentieth century their paths had begun to diverge. *Sophia* as the goal of the philosophers was beginning to lose its *telos* in the good life.

So what of the present? Philosophers of today are certainly a diverse lot, yet—to be honest—we are often much closer to the pseudo-*sophia* of the Sophists than to the true *hokhmah* of the sages. The *sophia* of the philosophers has frequently veered far from practical wisdom. I don't have in mind the distinction of whether we do metaphysics of material objects versus applied ethics, but rather our propensity to think small,

---

[15]Thomas Aquinas *Summa contra gentiles* 1.1.2.

[16]Immanuel Kant, *Dreams of a Spirit-Seer*, trans. Emanuel F. Goerwitz (New York: Macmillan, 1900), p. 115.

[17]Will Durant, "What Is Philosophy?" <www.willdurant.com/philosophy.htm>.

to focus tightly, to analyze unendingly, to love cleverness, and to regard argument as a game to be won.

Perhaps it's safer, this thinking small. While no philosopher today would face Socrates' death sentence for corrupting youth (or, at least, not in Western democracies), Baruch Spinoza stated what many of us have found from experience to be true: "I do not know how to teach philosophy without becoming a disturber of the peace."[18] But if we stick to the most abstract and abstruse, no complaints about us from parents of students will land on the dean's desk, and we can present papers at professional meetings without ridicule or riot. But I doubt if this figures large in the motivation of most philosophers. Most of us resonate with the words of an address by William James:

> I know that you, ladies and gentlemen, have a philosophy, each and all of you, and that the most interesting and important thing about you is the way in which it determines the perspective in your several worlds. You know the same of me. And yet I confess to a certain tremor at the audacity of the enterprise which I am about to begin. For the philosophy which is so important in each of us is not a technical matter; it is our more or less dumb [i.e., silent] sense of what life honestly and deeply means. It is only partly got from books; it is our individual way of just seeing and feeling the total push and pressure of the cosmos. . . .
>
> Philosophy is at once the most sublime and the most trivial of human pursuits. It works in the minutest crannies and it opens out the widest vistas. It "bakes no bread," as has been said, but it can inspire our souls with courage; and repugnant as its manners, its doubting and challenging, its quibbling and dialectics, often are to common people, no one of us can get along without the far-flashing beams of light it sends over the world's perspectives. These illuminations at least, and the contrast-effects of darkness and mystery that accompany them, give to what it says an interest that is much more than professional.[19]

---

[18]While widely attributed to Spinoza, this is a loose paraphrase of a statement Spinoza made in a letter to the Elector Palatine, declining the offer of a professorship of philosophy at the University of Heidelbert. Benedict de Spinoza, *On the Improvement of Understanding, Ethics, Correspondence*, trans. R. H. M. Elwes (New York: Dover Publications, 1955), Letter 54, p. 374.

[19]William James, "The Present Dilemma in Philosophy," in *Pragmatism* (New York: Longmans, Green, 1907) pp. 3, 6.

And yet, while we resonate with these words, if we're honest, many of us in the profession do not often regard ourselves as disturbers of the peace, or as assisting any but our best students in grasping the "far-flashing beams of light" that philosophy sends to illuminate the many different perspectives in the world.

Perhaps our tight focus is the inevitable result of increasing specialization: it's not that metaphysicians and epistemologists don't care or think about the good life, nor is it that ethicists have no interest in the justification of moral claims or in the objects of moral evaluation.

More likely, it's just that few have the time or interest (or intellect?) to master vast bodies of learning in several diverse fields. Perhaps also it is the result of the rejection of metaphysics by positivism and (to some extent) empiricism, and the postmodern turn away from essentialist metaphysics to social constructivism.

Yet it remains true that in many university philosophy departments, a state of suspicion, sometimes open hostility, persists between the M&E (metaphysics and epistemology) side of the house and the normative and applied ethics side. Consequently, many philosophy students in the Anglo-American analytical tradition pursue metaphysics and epistemology without the slightest thought of the implications of their study for the nature of the good life, and many others do ethical theory and applied ethics without considering the metaphysics of the objects of ethical evaluation, or the epistemology of ethical judgments.

In the world of philosophy today, then, rather than being close companions, *hokhmah* and *sophia* are often rivals.

I wonder and worry about those of us who claim to be Christian philosophers. Has *sophia* smothered *hokhmah*? T. S. Eliot was not speaking explicitly of contemporary philosophy in "Choruses from 'The Rock,'" but he might have been:

> O world of spring and autumn, birth and dying!
> The endless cycle of idea and action,
> Endless invention, endless experiment,
> Brings knowledge of motion, but not of stillness;
> Knowledge of speech, but not of silence;
> Knowledge of words, and ignorance of the Word.

All our knowledge brings us nearer to death,
But nearness to death no nearer to God.
Where is the Life we have lost in living?
Where is the wisdom we have lost in knowledge?
Where is the knowledge we have lost in information?
The cycles of Heaven in twenty centuries
Brings us farther from God and nearer to the Dust.[20]

TRADITION AND COMMUNITY

There is among us these days a cynical disregard for tradition, a chauvinism of the present. We hear Tevye in *Fiddler on the Roof* sing lovingly of "Tradition," and many of us smirk. But the sages thought differently. For if wisdom is distilled from experience, if patterns may be discerned in history, then the fathers may indeed have something worth attending to. "Tradition," said G. K. Chesterton, "means giving votes to the most obscure of all classes, our ancestors. It is the democracy of the dead. . . . Democracy tells us not to neglect a good man's opinion, even if he is our groom; tradition asks us not to neglect a good man's opinion, even if he is our father."[21]

The sages' regard for tradition is reflected throughout the wisdom literature in the frequent exhortations to sons to listen to their father's and mother's instructions (e.g., Prov 1:8). It is reflected as well in the exhortations to pay attention to the sayings of the wise (e.g., Prov 22:17). As I'm using the term, tradition may be considered to be the collected wisdom transmitted through a culture, and since true wisdom when employed generally results in successful living, tradition serves as guardrails or lane markers, keeping the wise on the road that has the greatest likelihood of leading to success.

Still, the sages understood that tradition can be misused. "Like a lame man's legs that hang limp . . . like a thornbush in a drunkard's hand is a proverb in the mouth of a fool" (Prov 26:7, 9). Some progress toward wisdom serves as prerequisite for properly handling tradition.

---

[20]T. S. Eliot, *The Complete Poems and Plays, 1909-1950* (New York: Harcourt, Brace & World, 1971), p. 96.

[21]G. K. Chesterton, *Orthodoxy* (1908; reprint, Chicago: Moody Publishers, 2009), p. 85.

Otherwise, the wisdom embodied in tradition might easily become grist for ridicule or be taken as guaranteed promises rather than general principles.

The link to doing philosophy as a Christian follows directly. The Christian philosopher, first and foremost, stands in the Christian Tradition, and so must understand it. (I use the capital T to indicate what I called in the previous chapter "canonical Christianity"; of course, each Christian, philosopher or not, also stands in a subtradition: Protestant, Roman Catholic, Eastern Orthodox; Calvinist/Reformed, Arminian/Wesleyan; and so forth.) The capital-T Christian Tradition sets the guardrails that must constrain the theological and philosophical theorizing of those who would claim to be Christian philosophers. As those who engage in critical thinking about the most important questions, with the end of understanding what constitutes a flourishing life, Christian philosophers must have a deeper understanding of Christian theology to do their work properly than, say, a Christian plumber. Theology is important to both, but is important to the professional life of the philosopher in a way that it is not to the plumber.

And there is also the philosophical tradition. Again there are subtraditions: Platonism, Aristotelianism, Thomism, Kantianism, nominalism and so forth. But to do philosophy of any kind, one must understand the tradition. For centuries, most of the significant work in Western philosophy was done by those working explicitly in the Christian Tradition, and if today's Christian philosophers ignore this work, it is their great loss.

Tradition enters the picture democratically, as Chesterton saw; it cannot be a dictator. For a dozen years I lived in Boulder, Colorado, where people seem to enjoy communicating with bumper stickers. For a time, a popular one read "Question Authority." Then another appeared: "Question Authority, But Raise Your Hand." The spirit of the second strikes me as correct. Respect for tradition or authority, not blind obedience or scornful rejection, characterizes wisdom.

Community too plays a role in the acquisition of wisdom. "He who walks with the wise grows wise," we are told (Prov 13:20). "Plans fail for lack of counsel, but with many advisers they succeed" (Prov 15:22).

Of course, almost all Christians, even philosophers, know that they must meet together (Heb 10:25), following the pervasive New Testament pattern of the church gathering for worship, teaching, prayer and fellowship (e.g., Acts 2:42). The term "one another" is found more than forty times in the New Testament epistles describing attitudes and actions that presuppose active community. Many of these texts imply that growth in understanding the truths of the gospel and the practices of love that should characterize disciples of Jesus (Jn 13:34-35) occurs in a healthy community. The Old Testament sages also understood this: "As iron sharpens iron, so one man sharpens another" (Prov 27:17).

But can the idea of community be extended to doing philosophy? Isn't philosophy a distinctly solitary pursuit? Well, yes; as usually practiced, a philosopher (who is most often an academic, generally a teacher) does individual research on a topic that has intrigued him, writes a paper, presents the paper at one or two professional philosophy meetings, then submits it for publication in a refereed journal. Breaking out of that model of doing philosophy proves hard. But I'd suggest that Christian philosophers should try. I'd suggest that we should consciously seek to cultivate a community of Christian philosophers with whom we can interact frequently and informally. (The academic societies such as the Society of Christian Philosophers, the Evangelical Philosophical Society or the Catholic Philosophical Society serve a vital purpose in the guild, but are too scattered geographically and meet so infrequently that they cannot serve the purpose I'm exploring here.) Perhaps members of one's own academic department, or of nearby schools, could plan regular and frequent informal lunches. Perhaps as well, Christians in other departments, or local pastors with a philosophical bent, could be included. In my own experience, some of the most fun, stimulating and enlightening times have been those informal bull sessions when we took the time to just "hang out" together, and some of my most rewarding work has been collaborating with colleagues in study groups, teaching interdisciplinary courses, and coauthoring papers and books.

I think it would be helpful, on a somewhat regular basis, to discuss with Christian colleagues such questions as these: Does this question or problem merit the time and effort to pursue researching it? What is your particular ongoing research interest, and how does it contribute to the task of the Christian philosopher? How should we understand the task of the Christian philosopher in the first place? And when a paper has been drafted, what more congenial place for comments and criticisms could be found? But criticism in this context should look not only at the formal validity of the logic and point to overlooked but relevant papers; it should also ask if the draft lies comfortably within the Christian Tradition, or if it pushes against the guardrails, does it do so justifiably and respectfully. I'd suggest that out of such discussions, iron sharpening philosophical iron, coauthored papers or books would emerge, demonstrating the communal dimension of Christian philosophy.

CONCLUSION AND PROLOGUE

As Alvin Plantinga reminds us in the epigraph to this chapter, "There is no such thing as religiously neutral intellectual endeavor—or rather there is no such thing as serious, substantial and relatively complete intellectual endeavor that is religiously neutral."[22] So I want to single out two themes which will recur throughout this book, by way of reminder to those of us who see ourselves as Christian philosophers, not simply philosophers who happen to be Christians.

The first theme is this: As Christian philosophers, we must practice in our profession what we claim in our confession. The apostle Paul reminded the Corinthians that Christ is not only the power of God but also the wisdom of God (1 Cor 1:24). True wisdom is Christocentric in its origin and its application. Specifically, I think that as Christian philosophers we have a solemn duty to discover what Jesus believed and taught, and then believe, teach and defend that. This is a beginning, of course; there is much in contemporary philosophy that Jesus did not directly address, just as there is much in modern physics that he did not speak to. But where he spoke, and where his words have direct implications for our subjects, we must listen and learn. Christian philosophers

---

[22]Alvin Plantinga, "A Christian Life Partly Lived," in *Philosophers Who Believe,* ed. Kelly James Clark (Downers Grove, Ill.: InterVarsity Press, 1993), p. 56.

should not be so eager to surf the cultural swell that we cannot hear and heed our Lord's clear teaching. But more on this in coming chapters.

Now for the second theme that I want to point out here: True wisdom—skillful living—will be impacted by metaphysics and epistemology, to be sure. But it will still be practical in the end. Christian philosophers can serve the Lord by doing what we do well—analysis, clarification, justification. But Christian philosophers should not ever lose sight of the fact that serving the Lord entails as well serving his people. Does our research and our teaching ultimately contribute to clarifying, demonstrating and confirming the truth of the *credenda* of the faith? Do we, in the end, have anything to contribute to the project of helping our culture understand and pursue genuine human flourishing? Will the church and the world be better for what we do?

So I believe that Christian philosophers must be philosophers *and* sages, those who can discuss the fine points of metaphysics, epistemology and ethics, but who also learn how to live skillfully. And if we have to master only one of the pair, let it be life, not logic.

3

PHILOSOPHY WITHIN THE
LIMITS OF RELIGION ALONE?

FAITH AND REASON

*I do not seek to understand that I may believe,
but I believe in order to understand. For this also I believe,—
that unless I believed, I should not understand.*

ST. ANSELM

*Faith and reason are like two wings on which
the human spirit rises to the contemplation of truth.*

POPE JOHN PAUL II

*A successful Christian philosopher is not first of all one who has
won the approval and acclaim of the philosophical world generally,
not someone who is "distinguished": it is rather one who has
faithfully served the Lord in the ways put before her.*

ALVIN PLANTINGA

In the last chapter, I suggested that it is perhaps too easy for contemporary philosophers to lose sight of the original and abiding purpose of philosophy—seeking to understand in order to live skillfully. That claim might not be terribly controversial. I doubt you could find a professional philosopher who denies that at the end of the day, somehow, what she does will make her a better person. She could well agree that her research into the metaphysics of material objects or two-dimensional semantics is perhaps somewhat removed from applied ethics, but she would almost surely deny that there is no relation between the abstract and the practical.

In this chapter I want to argue for a more controversial thesis: that authentic Christian philosophy should be philosophy done within the limits of religion. The phrase intentionally echoes—and reverses—the title of Immanuel Kant's 1793 work, *Religion Within the Limits of Reason Alone*.[1] Let me explain before you throw the book across the room!

Division of Labor, or Autonomy of Disciplines?

There is a valid notion of division of intellectual labor—physicians don't do basic research in molecular biology, particle physicists decide whether to take a raincoat or not after listening to the meteorologists, and historians find help for depression from psychologists. But often, in the two disciplines closest to the heart of this book, the notion of division of labor is pushed to autonomy of labor. Philosophy is *the* second-order discipline, after all—it is philosophy that asks questions about the meanings and methods and metaphysics of other disciplines, and philosophy does the hard work of integrating various disciplines. So it is easy for philosophers almost unconsciously to regard other disciplines as subordinate or ancillary to philosophy: after all, every discipline in the academy is related to philosophy by descent with modification![2]

Theologians are subject to the same temptation. Knowledge of God and his ways is the highest knowledge to which humans can aspire, so

---

[1]Immanuel Kant, *Religion Within the Limits of Reason Alone*, trans. Theodore M. Greene and Hoyt H. Hudson (La Salle, Ill.: Open Court, 1934), pp. 9-10. My use of the phrase borrows from Nicholas Wolterstorff, *Reason Within the Bounds of Religion* (Grand Rapids: Eerdmans, 1984).

[2]To be sure, some philosophers seek to "naturalize" their field, for example, W. V. Quine's claim that epistemology is a branch of empirical psychology, and many working in philosophy of mind seek to reduce the mental to the neurophysiological. On the other hand, George Bealer has famously argued for both the autonomy and the authority of philosophy vis-à-vis the empirical sciences: George Bealer, "'A Priori' Knowledge and the Scope of Philosophy," *Philosophical Studies* 81 (1996): 122-42.

dichotomy = division into two parts, two mutually exclusive, opposed, contradictory groups.

clearly theology should have pride of place in the academy. And since "his [Christ's] divine power has given us everything we need for life and godliness through our knowledge of him" (2 Pet 1:3), everything else is at best useful only at the margins.

The challenge of the church father Tertullian—"What has Jerusalem to do with Athens"—still holds powerful sway in some circles, even though I suspect Tertullian is often misunderstood (see below). He does seem to support a strict dichotomy between theology and philosophy (and other disciplines) when he writes, "Let our 'seeking,' therefore be in that which is our own, and from those who are our own, and concerning that which is our own—that, and only that, which can become an object of inquiry without impairing the rule of faith."[3]

For some, the Protestant motto *sola scriptura* has come to mean "me and my Bible—I don't need anything else." The medievals taught that "theology is the queen of the sciences, and philosophy is her handmaid." But some believe that beautiful vision of the order of the disciplines has today been upset—the handmaid has become the dominatrix!

REASON WITHIN THE LIMITS OF RELIGION

As you might surmise, I believe both views are in error. In this chapter I'll explore what may broadly be called the problem of faith and reason. It might also be termed the problem of authority and autonomy. My thesis, I'll warn you, will be more controversial than that of the last chapter:

> Doing philosophy as a Christian means doing philosophy under the authority of the Lord Jesus and of the Bible, the Word of God. It means reasoning within the bounds of religion. It means, in the end, doing philosophy in a way that aims intentionally at the ultimate goal of personal transformation into the image of Christ, and of extending a meaningful invitation to others to enter into that transformation—that is, of extending the kingdom of God on earth.

As I explain and defend this thesis, I'll first attempt to show that the

---

[3]Tertullian, *Prescription Against Heretics* 12, in *Ante-Nicene Fathers*, ed. Alexander Roberts and James Donaldson (Peabody, Mass.: Hendrickson, 1994), 3:249.

dichotomy between philosophy and theology is a false one. Then I'll explore the famous statement of St. Anselm, "I believe in order to understand," and what that means for Christian philosophers today. I'll attempt to outline a model of the relationship of faith and reason, and consider what Thomas Nagel called his "cosmic authority problem." Finally, I'll sketch just how, in my opinion, Christian philosophers can do their philosophical work to the glory of God.

Dispatching a Dichotomy

Philosophy's avoidance of theology. Just as surely as other disciplines need philosophy, philosophy needs other disciplines. And so too with theology. It should be clear that philosophy rightly takes into account deliverances of natural or social sciences, just as frequently as the deliverances of philosophical reflection rightly impact meanings and methods of the sciences. For example, scientific accounts of the essences of natural kinds revealed to philosophers that there are a posteriori necessities,[4] while reflection on standard justificatory practice showed the incoherence of pure empiricism, the presumed "official" epistemology of science.[5]

What about theology? Should philosophy take into account theological conclusions? One reason why perhaps it should not stems from the plurality of religions and the plurality of theologies within any religion. But why should that present a problem? Divisions persist within philosophy as well; surely we would not want to foreclose thinking about material constitution simply because Platonists and Aristotelians don't agree, nor do we suspend ethical reflection until consequentialists, deontologists and virtue theorists come to agreement. So the plurality of theologies is no reason to exclude theological claims from consideration in doing philosophy.

---

[4]Saul Kripke, *Naming and Necessity* (Malden, Mass.: Blackwell, 1972); Hilary Putnam, "The Meaning of 'Meaning,'" in *Mind, Language and Reality*, vol. 2 of *Philosophical Papers* (New York: Cambridge University Press, 1975).
[5]George Bealer and P. F. Strawson, "The Incoherence of Empiricism," *The Aristotelian Society, Supplementary Volume* 66 (1992): 99-138. Alex Rosenberg calls empiricism the "official epistemology" of science: *Philosophy of Science: A Contemporary Introduction*, 2nd ed. (New York: Routledge, 2005), pp. 88-89.

Well, then, perhaps the reason for excluding theology might be a conviction that whereas philosophy yields knowledge, theology is nothing more than blind faith, and so is not any different from mere opinion or personal preference. *De gustibus non est disputandum,* "There's no accounting for taste." But Christianity has seen itself since its inception as a *knowledge tradition,* not opinion or unfounded belief.[6] Words for "know" and "knowledge" occur more than 2000 times in the Bible, and are prevalent as well in the writings of the church fathers, the apologists and later theologians. For some two thousand years Christians have taken themselves to have knowledge.

Of course, comes the rejoinder, they *thought* they were dealing in knowledge, but we can see now that their beliefs were not well founded and so, as we do with astrologers who think they have knowledge, we are free to ignore such unjustified claims as irrational.

The Christian philosopher can respond in at least two ways. First, she could argue case by case that particular theological deliverances constituted knowledge, seeking to defeat objections to each individual putative case of knowledge. However, in addition to being tedious, any progress to be made here would depend on the Christian philosopher and the objector agreeing on a number of contentious points in epistemology, and/or a global definition of epistemic rationality. The prospects for such agreement seem dim.

The second response would recognize that the real issue here is one of worldviews. What is rational to accept or even provisionally to consider is determined by standards that are, to a degree, relative to a worldview. (I'll resist a diversion here into the very knotty problems of categorizing, defining or characterizing various concepts of rationality.) The Christian philosopher, committed as she is to the existence of a morally perfect, loving and authoritative God, will certainly be open to thinking differently about many matters in philosophy than an atheist philosopher who regards theistic belief as an evolutionary adaptation that has outlived its usefulness. As Alvin Plantinga advised,

---

[6]See James R. Stoner Jr., "The 'Naked' University: What If Theology Is Knowledge, Not Belief?" *Theology Today* 62 (2006): 515-27.

So the Christian philosopher has his own topics and projects to think about; and when he thinks about the topics of current concern in the broader philosophical world, he will think about them in his own way, which may be a *different* way. He may have to reject certain currently fashionable assumptions about the philosophic enterprise—he may have to reject widely accepted assumptions as to what are the proper starting points and procedures for philosophical endeavor. And—and this is crucially important—the Christian philosopher has a perfect right to the point of view and prephilosophical assumptions he brings to philosophic work; the fact that these are not widely shared outside the Christian or theistic community is interesting but fundamentally irrelevant.[7]

So it seems to me that the Christian philosopher is perfectly within her rights to take account of theological deliverances in doing philosophy. Let me say that even more strongly: The Christian philosopher, if she is doing philosophy as a Christian, *must* take account of the deliverances of Christian theology when those deliverances bear on the topic of her philosophizing, regardless of whether or not the wider philosophical community does.

Finally, the exclusion of deliverances of theology from philosophical thought might be a vague, inchoate fear that once theology is let into the room, inquisitions will follow. Perhaps this fear lies behind the "terror" of "unscientific, religious alternatives" in philosophy of mind that John Searle speaks of:

> Acceptance of the current [i.e., physicalist] views is motivated not so much by an independent conviction of their truth as by a terror of what are apparently the only alternatives. That is, the choice we are tacitly presented with is between a "scientific" approach, as represented by one or another of the current versions of "materialism," and an "unscientific" approach, as represented by Cartesianism or some other traditional religious conception of the mind.[8]

Admittedly, the history of Christianity (and indeed most other religions) reveals periods of intolerance and outright persecution of hetero-

---

[7]Alvin Plantinga, "Advice to Christian Philosophers," *Faith and Philosophy* 1 (1984): 258 <http://faithandphilosophy.com/article_advice.php>.
[8]John Searle, *Rediscovering the Mind* (Cambridge, Mass.: MIT Press, 1992), pp. 3-4.

dox views.[9] But a return to inquisitions is most improbable in our day. And I dare say that the vast majority of Christians would agree that if God himself tolerates unbelievers and seeks to persuade them by means of the attractiveness of the loving sacrificial work of Jesus and the loving Christian community (see Jn 17:20-23; 2 Cor 5:14-20), then it follows that Christians should not embark on a mission to force belief contrary to conscience.

I suspect rather that the "terror" that Searle alludes to is more closely related to Nagel's "cosmic authority problem" than it is to a return to inquisitions; I'll return to the authority problem below.

So I see no reason why philosophy should not pay attention to theology, and indeed, for a Christian philosopher, I see many reasons to do so.

Theology's suspicion of philosophy. What then of theology's need for philosophy? Clearly, theology needs other disciplines such as history, archaeology and linguistics. Many works in systematic theology define the discipline in terms of using data from "any and every source."[10] Theological argumentation relies on logic. And the study of historical theology shows that systematic theology must always interact with the burning philosophical questions of the day.

In "An Address to the Clergy," in 1756, John Wesley asks two questions, "What manner of men ought we to be?" and "Are we such, or are we not?" He discusses the natural gifts and acquired abilities that he thought were necessary for effective ministers. In terms of acquired abilities, Wesley includes, understandably, a thorough knowledge of Scripture and of Greek and Hebrew. He adds an understanding of the church fathers, of history and psychology, and of how the world really is. And he adds philosophy. He challenges his audience to ask themselves,

> Am I a tolerable master of the sciences? Have I gone through the very gate of them, logic? If not, I am not likely to go much further, when I have stumbled at the threshold. . . . Do I understand metaphysics; if not the

---

[9]For a well-modulated treatment, see the historical-sociological analysis of inquisitions by Rodney Stark, *For the Glory of God: How Monotheism Led to Reformations, Science, Witch Hunts, and the End of Slavery* (Princeton, N.J.: Princeton University Press, 2003), pp. 201-89.

[10]Lewis Sperry Chafer, *Systematic Theology*, vol. 1 (Dallas: Dallas Seminary Press, 1947), p. 5.

depths of the Schoolmen, the subtleties of Scotus or Aquinas, yet the first rudiments, the general principles, of that useful science? Have I conquered so much of it, as to clear my apprehension and range my ideas under proper heads; so much as enables me to read with ease and pleasure, as well as profit, Dr. Henry Moore's Works, Malbranche's "Search after Truth," and Dr. Clarke's "Demonstration of the Being and Attributes of God?"[11]

Immanuel Kant, whose personal religious commitments remain somewhat enigmatic, advised,

> I will even venture to ask whether it would not be beneficial, upon completion of the academic instruction in Biblical Theology, always to add, by way of conclusion, as necessary to the complete equipment of the candidate, a special course of lectures on the purely *philosophical* theory of religion.[12]

In his work on the Trinity, the evangelical theologian Millard Erickson writes,

> At this point, it appears unlikely that a great deal more will be contributed to the doctrine of the Trinity from the biblical studies, where probably most of the relevant biblical passages have been well examined. What is more likely, however, is that more progress will be made in understanding the conceptual factors in the doctrine of triunity. . . . The growing number of philosophers giving serious attention to philosophical issues related to Christian theology provide a valuable resource for theology.[13]

Philosopher and theologian William Lane Craig notes,

> One of the most noteworthy developments on contemporary philosophy of religion has been the ingress of Christian philosophers into areas normally considered the province of systematic theologians. In particular, many Christian philosophers have taken up a share of the task of formulating and defending coherent statements of Christian doctrine.[14]

---

[11]John Wesley, "An Address to the Clergy," in *The Works of John Wesley* (Grand Rapids: Baker Book House, 1979; reprint of 1872 edition issued by Wesleyan Methodist Book Room, London), 10:491-92.

[12]Kant, *Religion Within the Limits of Reason Alone*, pp. 9-10.

[13]Millard F. Erickson, *God in Three Persons: A Contemporary Interpretation of the Trinity* (Grand Rapids: Baker, 1995), pp. 343-44.

[14]In J. P. Moreland and William Lane Craig, *Philosophical Foundations for a Christian Worldview* (Downers Grove, Ill.: InterVarsity Press, 2003), p. 575.

ontological argument = an argument for God's existence ~~based~~ through abstract reasoning

I won't belabor the point further. It should be clear that the dichotomy between philosophy and theology is a false one. They are indeed two distinct disciplines, but they are not mutually exclusive and do not operate in hermetically sealed compartments, in principle and in practice isolated from each other. The Christian philosopher must then develop an understanding of how the two disciplines relate to each other, and how the two interact with his own faith. For one model of this relationship, let me turn to the great medieval philosopher-theologian, St. Anselm of Canterbury (1033-1109).

BELIEVING TO UNDERSTAND

It's a great tragedy that virtually all anthologies that include St. Anselm's ontological argument print only chapters two and three of *Proslogion*. Chapter one lets us listen in as St. Anselm, in prayerful contemplation, begins the *Proslogion* by affirming his desire to know God, but confesses his sinful inability. "I was created to see thee, and not yet have I done that for which I was made. O wretched lot of man, when he hath lost that for which he was made!" With genuine humility he concludes his short introductory chapter with this affirmation:

> I do not endeavor, O Lord, to penetrate thy sublimity, for in no wise do I compare my understanding with that; but I long to understand in some degree thy truth, which my heart believes and loves. For I do not seek to understand that I may believe, but I believe in order to understand. For this also I believe—that unless I believed, I should not understand.[15]

The tragedy is that the ontological argument that follows is often seen as a paradigm case of pure autonomous a priori rationalism, when in fact it is the continuation of a prayerful meditation and the culmination of Anselm's considered vision of the relationship of faith and reason. The penultimate sentence contains Anselm's famous statement, *credo ut intelligam*, "I believe in order to understand."

Anselm's opening prayer for understanding God's truth refers, of course, not just to the ontological argument for God's existence (chapters 2 and 3 of *Proslogion*), but to the whole project of the work—his

---

[15]Anselm, *Proslogion*, trans. S. N. Deane, 2nd ed. (Chicago: Open Court, 1962), chap. 1.

derivation of God's nature, up to and including his trinitarian nature and the blessedness of salvation.

But what does this mean, really—believing *in order to* understand? Surely a well-educated atheist can understand as much as an equally well-educated Christian, can't he? How can belief (which in Anselm's aphorism I take to be equivalent to religious faith) be logically prior to understanding?

We need to know that Anselm is moving within a stream of thought going back to Augustine, and even to Aristotle. The Latin *intellectus* means understanding, not merely cognizing. *Intellectus* is grasping the nature of something, of first principles. *Scientia* (equivalent to Greek *episteme*) is usually translated "knowledge," but it also is more specific— it's the grasping of something as a kind of systematic knowledge, for example, the conclusion of a demonstrative syllogism. The ultimate premises, the principles, of systematic knowledge are grasped by *intellectus;* the conclusions, seen in light of their logical relations to those principles, are known by *scientia.*

So Anselm's maxim does not mean that you can't know anything, so you have to rely on blind faith. Rather, the way into understanding is by believing (say, an authority, a map, a teacher, or—a fortiori—God), but the goal is to come to understand it, to grasp its nature.

I suggest then that there are at least two dimensions to Anselm's maxim, one more narrow and the other more broad. First, I'll assume that 'understanding' is more than justified true belief, that it is the mental state that only results from grasping a true explanation cast in terms of the nature of things.[16] The distinction between knowledge and understanding is then clear. A student may know how to state the Pythagorean theorem and know how to apply it to solve problems, but not understand it (in the sense I'm using the term) because he fails to

---

[16]See Michael Strevens, *Depth* (Cambridge, Mass.: Harvard University Press, 2008), p. 3. Strevens's characterization refers to scientific understanding; I take it as a generalized characterization of 'understanding' in any field. Admittedly, not all explanations invoke first principles: the notion of pragmatics enters here—the purpose for which an explanation is requested may be more limited. But if it is indeed a true explanation, it will be grounded in the natures of things. See also Jonathan L. Kvanvig, *The Value of Knowledge and the Pursuit of Understanding* (New York: Cambridge University Press, 2003), chap. 8, for a slightly different account of understanding.

grasp the first principles of Euclidean geometry. Or, suppose that a youngster was taught the Pythagorean theorem by a devious older sibling who offered an "explanation" in terms of Nordic mythology and Thor's intentions. And suppose further that the Thor story was sufficiently coherent that it seemed to explain the theorem. Still, even though the youngster might successfully solve real-world problems, she would have no understanding since the "explanation" was not true.

Take another example. We may imagine a scientist (Einstein, say) who accepts the notion of quantum entanglement but holds to some form of local hidden variable as the explanation of apparent nonlocality. Now, a local hidden variable would indeed be an explanation, but in this case it seems to be disproved by various experimental confirmations of Bell's inequality. Does Einstein really understand entanglement? (Well, perhaps that's unfair: does *anyone* really understand it?) I trust that these examples bring out what is relevantly different about understanding: it is brought about by grasping a true explanation grounded in the nature of things.

If this is right, then Anselm's believing in order to understand would mean this: One must first believe certain things about God and his nature before one can truly understand—grasp the nature of or the true explanation of them. Anyone can, with a little study, grasp the meaning of such doctrinal formulations as the Nicene Creed, the Chalcedonian Formula or the Westminster Confession—or even Anselm's modal ontological argument. But to truly *understand* them demands grasping the true nature of God, his attributes and his relations with his creation. *Fides quaerens intellectum*—"Faith seeking understanding"—is reported to have been Anselm's suggested title for the *Proslogion*. This is, of course, in accord with the thinking of Augustine, who remarked, "Understanding is the reward of faith. Therefore seek not to understand that you may believe, but believe that you may understand."[17]

All well and good, you might be thinking, but I'm not doing philosophical theology. What is the relevance of my belief—my Christian faith—to my interest in modal logic or environmental ethics? Here's

---

[17]Augustine, *Tractates on the Gospel of John*, trans. John W. Rettig (Washington, D.C.: Catholic University of America Press, 1988), 29.6.2.

where a broader aspect of Anselm's *credo* applies. If God is who the Christian faith says he is, and if he is the creator and sustainer of all that exists, and if Christian theology is the attempt to systematically present God's nature and his relations to creation, then theology will have something to say about *any* search for understanding. Faith will precede understanding.

But this isn't quite right yet, for it seems to place faith and understanding in distinct categories of cognitive activity. For Anselm and other medieval philosophers, however, the two are but distinct *stages* of one integrated intellectual operation. Faith seamlessly shades into understanding. While that may be foreign to contemporary ways of thinking, which divorce faith from other intellectual activities, the connections between faith and any intellectual work was obvious in the thought world of Augustine and Anselm (and Aquinas and Duns Scotus, and Luther and Calvin—indeed, for anyone before the Enlightenment). And for the Christian philosopher, the connections should be obvious as well.

Or so I say. And the rest of this book will explore some of those connections. But before pressing on, two further topics need clarification.

FAITH AND REASON, OR FAITH AND SIGHT?

All this talk of faith and understanding surely has raised the venerable problem of "faith and reason."[18] There's a popular view, reinforced by the writings of the "new atheists,"[19] that 'faith' picks out a mental activity that is opposed to reason. If one has justification-conferring evidence for a belief, that belief is by definition not faith. The corollary, of course, is that beliefs for which one does not have reasons are literally unreasonable, so faith is by definition unreasonable, and unreasonable beliefs must be exposed, attacked and abandoned. Sadly, in my opinion,

---

[18]There is a rather vast literature of varying quality on the topic of the relation of faith and reason, so vast that I won't even begin to give bibliographic references. And so as not to add needlessly to the literature, I'll try to keep this section brief. I'm not sure I have anything original to add to the available discussions anyway.

[19]The view is a staple of the attacks on religion in Sam Harris, *The End of Faith* (New York: W. W. Norton, 2003); Richard Dawkins, *The God Delusion* (New York: Houghton Mifflin, 2006); Christopher Hitchens, *God Is Not Great* (New York: Hatchette, 2007); and others.

there is a stream of contemporary Christianity that agrees, also viewing faith and reason as opposites. In this fideistic form of Christianity, attempts to offer apologetic evidence in support of Christian belief are downright harmful, for if you can "prove" something like the resurrection, then you don't need faith—but "without faith it is impossible to please God" (Heb 11:6).

Perhaps Tertullian is partially responsible for this view among some Christians. He famously asked, "What then hath Athens in common with Jerusalem? What hath the Academy in common with the Church?"[20] However, scholars recognize that this quote, out of context, is misunderstood and misused. In context Tertullian is rejecting the need to seek justification for Christian doctrine in the Greek philosophical tradition, apart from Scripture. This is also his point in an equally famous quote where he says, in reference to the resurrection of Christ, *credo quia absurdum*, "I believe because it is absurd."[21] But again context is crucial. Here Tertullian is refuting the heretic Marcion and his followers, who excised from their scriptures reference to the death of Christ. Tertullian argues that the accounts of Christ's crucifixion and resurrection cannot be fraudulent inventions, since no one would believe them if they were fiction. But the accounts are attested to by the apostles and have been passed down in Scripture and in the faith of the church. So, because the accounts are "impossible," they could not be fictions, and must be the truth. (If he were living today, he might well have said, "Truth is stranger than fiction.") So to claim Tertullian as a proponent of a division between faith and reason is just bad interpretation of a couple of his more provocative statements.

There's no competition. Although this view of faith and reason is common, perhaps even dominant on university campuses, I believe it rests on serious misunderstandings. First, it's clear that *any* fairly inclusive worldview ultimately rests on improvable assumptions. There's some debate as to whether Gödel's incompleteness theorem is applicable here, but it's demonstrable that even simple beliefs such as my belief

---

[20]Tertullian, *Prescription Against Heretics.*
[21]*De Carne Christi* 5.4; trans. Ernest Evans (SPCK, 1956) available at <www.tertullian.org/articles/evans_carn/evans_carn_04eng.htm>.

that other people have minds very similar to mine, that the world did not begin eight nanoseconds ago, or that slavery is immoral and unjust, cannot be *proved* conclusively. Even the fundamental laws of logic are treated as axioms, propositions that cannot be proved or demonstrated but must be accepted as starting points. In other words, they are accepted on faith.

Second, the faith-reason dichotomy often rests on the assumption that the sort of evidence that confers justification, and thus reasonableness, on a belief, must be empirical evidence. The sciences, especially the "hard" sciences of physics and chemistry and perhaps biology, are paradigm cases. If moral beliefs are justified at all, it seems, they must have some explanation in terms of science—in this case, evolutionary psychology (its lack of empirical support is conveniently ignored). But beyond that, belief in any immaterial or supernatural entities is 'faith.' But distinguishing faith and reason in terms of empirical justification is doomed to failure if only because what counts as 'empirical' and 'justification' are philosophical questions not decidable by empirical means (see chapter 9 for more on this). And once you allow philosophical arguments to count as evidence, then you must accept philosophical arguments as evidence for the existence of immaterial entities and for God.

Third, the faith-reason dichotomy is itself not biblical, although many people probably believe it is, right up there with "cleanliness is next to godliness." But the biblical distinction is between faith and sight: "We walk by faith, not by sight" (2 Cor 5:7 NASB). Jesus' words to "Doubting" Thomas underscore the point: "Because you have seen Me, have you believed? Blessed are they who did not see, and yet believed" (Jn 20:29 NASB). As the author of the epistle to the Hebrews puts it, "Now faith is the substance of things hoped for, the evidence of things not seen" (Heb 11:1 NKJV).

Beyond these statements that contrast faith to sight (i.e., empirical observation), there is the fact that throughout the Bible arguments are made and evidence is offered—often in the form of *reliable testimony*— to support beliefs. The evangelistic ministry of the apostles is characterized by terms such as *apologeomai/apologia*, "to give reasons, make a (legal) defense"/"verbal defense" (e.g., Acts 26:2; 2 Tim 4:16; 1 Pet

3:15); *dialegomai,* "to reason, speak boldly" (e.g., Acts 17:2, 17; 18:4; 19:8); *peithō,* "to persuade, argue persuasively" (Acts 18:4; 19:8); and *bebaioō,* "to confirm, establish" (Phil 1:7; Heb 2:3). All of these terms link faith and reason, they don't oppose them. And at the end of the Gospel of John the author tells us explicitly, "Jesus did many other miraculous signs in the presence of his disciples, which are not recorded in this book. But these are written that you may believe that Jesus is the Christ, the Son of God, and that by believing you may have life in his name" (Jn 20:30-31). John believed the evidence of Jesus' miraculous signs justified faith in Jesus as the Son of God and source of eternal life. This is not belief apart from—or in spite of—reasons.

One last biblical passage should finally put to rest the faith-reason distinction. The apostle Paul writes, "For though we live in the world, we do not wage war as the world does. The weapons we fight with are not the weapons of the world. On the contrary, they have divine power to demolish strongholds. We demolish arguments and every pretension that sets itself up against the knowledge of God, and we take captive every thought to make it obedient to Christ" (2 Cor 10:3-5). Now, arguments are demolished by arguments, and pretentions that there is no knowledge are answered by arguments showing adequate justification. Thoughts are made "obedient to Christ" not by sheer willpower, but by transformed ways of thinking (see Rom 12:2). Reason is not the enemy of faith, only of blind faith, of false faith, of misplaced faith.

***And yet* . . .** And yet, I can't ignore a fact of history that complicates the simple account I've just offered. In the history of Christian theology, there is a tradition from the Greek fathers through most of the medieval scholastics that faith *is* distinct from knowledge. There are technical epistemological issues involved here; roughly, though, the view turns on an understanding of knowledge *(scientia)* as demonstrable, deductively inferred from first principles and thus certain, whereas faith is based solely on what God says (reveals) and thus is not inferred from anything else. We find expressions of this epistemology in Clement of Alexandria (ca. 150-215), Origen (ca. 185-254), Chrysostom (ca. 374-407) and others. But the most systematic expression is in the work of St. Thomas Aquinas. He says, for example,

The existence of God and other like truths about God, which can be
known by natural reason, are not articles of faith, but are preambles to
the articles; for faith presupposes natural knowledge, even as grace presupposes nature, and perfection supposes something that can be per-
fected. Nevertheless, there is nothing to prevent a man, who cannot
grasp a proof, accepting, as a matter of faith, something which in itself
is capable of being scientifically known and demonstrated.[22]

Thomas's view here resembles the view I referred to earlier as fideistic
Christianity, but Thomas's reasons for holding his view are rather more
nuanced and principled, resting on a well-developed epistemology.

Much could be said about these matters, but I won't.[23] Rather, I'll
summarize my views on the issues and commend them to you (such
being an author's privilege). First, contemporary epistemologists reject
certainty as a criterion of knowledge and admit that much of what we
know is in principle defeasible (meaning it is possible that the belief
could be defeated—shown possibly to be false). Justification generally
is truth-indicative, not truth-guaranteeing.

Second, the term 'faith' bears considerable freight for Christians,
given the many biblical links between faith and salvation. Saving faith
differs from "mere" belief in at least these five crucial respects: (1) By
most accounts, beliefs are beyond one's voluntary control, although one
can, by developing the intellectual virtues, put oneself in position to
acquire more true beliefs and reject more false ones. Faith, on the other
hand, seems (on the surface, at least—this is not the place for the Cal-
vinist-Arminian debates) to have a significant voluntaristic element. In
the Scriptures, people are invited, urged, even commanded, to put faith
in God.

(2) Still, faith is not a different species of mental activity altogether;
it includes "mere" belief. Biblical faith certainly presupposes an affirmative attitude toward certain propositions.

(3) As the apostle James teaches, genuine faith entails certain behav-

---

[22]Thomas Aquinas *Summa theologica* 1a.2.2, Reply to Objection 1.
[23]For an excellent discussion see John Lamont, "A Conception of Faith in the Greek Fathers,"
in *Analytic Theology*, ed. Oliver D. Crisp and Michael C. Rea (New York: Oxford University
Press 2009), pp. 87-116.

ioral dispositions, while it is not clear that (all) beliefs do. Of course, salvation depends on faith, not the activation of the behavioral dispositions, but the kind of faith that saves does cause such dispositions.

(4) Faith, in contrast to "mere" belief, seems to involve a personal, existential trusting commitment. This seems to be brought out in the locution "believe *in* the Lord Jesus." Now, surely believing *in* someone presupposes belief *that* the person is of a certain trustworthy character, but the belief *in* adds the additional element of personal trust.

(5) As one who has a biblical faith, I can give reasons (evidence) why the beliefs included in my faith are rational, and by my lights more likely to be true than their denials. Ultimately, though, my faith does not rest on these reasons, but on the internal testimony of the Holy Spirit. The apostle John wrote, "We accept man's testimony, but God's testimony is greater because it is the testimony of God, which he has given about his Son. Anyone who believes in the Son of God has this testimony in his heart" (1 Jn 5:9-10). And St. Paul wrote, "The Spirit himself testifies with our spirit that we are God's children" (Rom 8:16). William Lane Craig draws the contrast nicely in terms of "knowing" that one's faith is true, grounded in the internal testimony of the Holy Spirit, and "showing" that one's faith is reasonable, which involves giving the evidences of natural theology and apologetics.[24]

My conclusion is that the early Greek/medieval scholastic epistemology, together with a desire to mark off faith from belief (and so also from knowledge), was responsible for the Thomistic idea that faith is something quite different from reason. Rather, I want to say that faith is more than, but not wholly distinct from, reason-justified belief. Let me illustrate with a parable. (Acknowledgment: I first heard a version of this parable from Francis Schaeffer, but have modified it over the years.)

The parable of the mountain climbers. Suppose you set out with three friends to climb the Mountaineer's Route on the east side of Mt. Whitney, at 14,497 feet, the highest peak in the lower 48. You got an early start from Whitney Portal and made camp higher than you had planned, at Iceberg Lake, only some 1600 vertical feet below the summit. Your

---

[24]William Lane Craig, "Classical Apologetics," in *Five Views on Apologetics*, ed. Steven B. Cowan (Grand Rapids: Zondervan, 2000), pp. 25-55.

summit day plans change a bit in light of your progress, and you decide to leave early and travel light. In the grey pre-dawn light you fill your summit pack with some food and water bottles, wind pants and shirt, and a light fleece, and head up.

The lower stretch of the East Couloir is still snow-packed, a bit of a surprise in late July, and you wonder aloud if you should have brought ice axes and crampons. Halfway up the couloir the snow has hardened into ice and you can no longer kick steps. The four of you stop for a drink and an energy bar and worry about what conditions above at the Notch and in the North Chute will be like. You decide that your best hope of summiting is to move left onto the East Buttress and deal with the more difficult and exposed rock climbing. After about thirty minutes you glance up and notice that the magnificent blue sky, such a contrast to the light granite of the East Buttress, is being overtaken with dark clouds pouring over Whitney's summit from the west. This isn't good, but you had checked the weather report and the forecast had said zero chance of precip. So you climb on.

Just fifteen minutes later you are enveloped in a cold fog, and the wind picks up out of the northwest. It's one of the Sierra's notorious and unpredictable sudden storms. You put on all the extra clothes you have in your daypacks, and debate turning back. Suddenly, it seems, a very cold sleet is falling, freezing on the rock and on your jackets. Visibility is now only about five or six feet. You try to downclimb with urgency, but discover you've made a rookie mistake: not prepared for the East Buttress, you don't know the route, and on your ascent you had failed to take notice of significant features on the route. Soon, unsure of just where you are, the four of you huddle together, trying to conserve warmth, and admit that your situation is desperate: If the temperature continues dropping and the wind doesn't abate, you face a real risk of dying of hypothermia.

One friend breaks the glum mood. "If there is a ledge about ten feet down below this ridge we're on, it'd be out of the wind. We could drop onto it, spoon together for the night, and survive till rescue came in the morning."

"Sure, out of the wind we'd probably survive, but you can't see more than six feet below—why think there's a ledge there?"

"Well, what's our alternative? I feel we'll make it, but the only way is if we drop onto that ledge. C'mon."

And with that, before the rest of you can stop him, he swings his legs over the side of the ridge and lets go. There's a long pause, followed by a muffled thump. Then silence.

Your shock would be greater if your own situation weren't so precarious. To paraphrase Dr. Johnson, nothing focuses the mind like death on a mountainside. So you begin again downclimbing with great care on the ice-covered rock.

Suddenly the silence is broken by a voice out of the fog and sleet: "Hey you climbers on the East Buttress: You're in a real fix. But there's a ledge about ten feet below you on the leeward side. If you drop off the ridge onto the ledge, you can huddle together and survive the night. Mountain rescue will get you in the morning."

"Who is this—God?" you shout back, incredulous, not daring to hope.

"No, it's Royal Robbins. I'm camped near your tent by Iceberg Lake."

Royal Robbins?! He's a legend—a superman—in American climbing, with many famous first ascents to his credit. Still, you have doubts. Is this voice for real? Can you believe that he's really Royal Robbins?

"If you're really Robbins, tell us—who made the first class VI ascent in the U.S.?"

"C'mon—that was me, along with Sherrick and Galwas, in 1954, on the Northwest Face of Half Dome. Ask something hard."

"Who climbed the NA Wall on El Cap with you?"

"Frost, Chouinard and Pratt. Took us over nine days. Now get with it—you're in a life and death situation up there."

After a couple more questions, drawing on your knowledge of climbing history and lore, you three are satisfied that you have good reason to believe that it is indeed Royal Robbins down there. Still, the fog is so thick you can't see five feet in front of you, let alone six or seven hundred feet below.

"How do you know just where we are? How do you know there's a ledge below us?"

"Look—about three feet above you, to the right, there's a quartz outcropping in the shape of a monkey's head. And just below you on the windward side there's a tiny bristlecone sapling trying to take root—should be about six inches high now."

A quick check shows that the voice—Robbins—incredibly has pinpointed your location.

"Come on, guys—don't waste more time in the wind. You're wet and freezing, the sleet is ice on your parkas. I'm telling you there's a wide ledge there. It's your only hope. Drop onto it now!"

You glance at each other. You have good reason to believe that this voice is who he says he is, Royal Robbins. If so, he surely has detailed first-person knowledge of the East Buttress. And you have good reason to believe that he knows your exact location as well as your desperate condition.

So you drop.

Here's the difference between "blind faith" and reasonable faith. The first climber to drop based his belief that there was a ledge below on his "feeling," and perhaps his wish/hope/desire, with no other evidence, and took essentially a flying leap in the dark. Unfortunately, this is what many people seem to think is the essence of religious faith.

The second climber to drop based his belief about the ledge on evidence: the testimonial evidence offered by the voice in the fog. But he had good reason to believe that the voice was who he said he was, and thus was in a position to offer trustworthy testimony. And he had good reason to believe that the voice did in fact know precisely his location and condition, and so his advice was trustworthy.

But these beliefs, even though they were justified (and we may suppose, for the sake of the story, true) were not yet 'faith' in the sense relevant here. What more was needed was the element of personal trust. When the second climber dropped, he was exercising reasonable faith, putting his personal trust in the "revelation" from Robbins. He did not have sight, but had reasons to support his beliefs, and so his existential commitment of trust was reasonable.

The application should be obvious. Rather than a blind faith based on feelings, or a cultural artifact from less enlightened times, or some

Freudian projection, the Christian has good reason to believe that God is who he says he is, and that God knows the human condition, and so is trustworthy *in excelsis* to speak "words of life" to our condition.

THE LIMITS OF RELIGION ALONE?

I've argued so far that philosophy and theology are not mutually exclusive disciplines, but rather mutually necessary for moving toward comprehensive knowledge. I've attempted to cash out for Christian philosophers what Anselm's motto, "I believe in order to understand," might mean. And I've argued that faith and reason join in the reasonable faith of a Christian.

But all this has been groundwork, so to speak. In the preface to the first edition of *Religion Within the Limits of Reason Alone*, Kant allows that though the theologian who "cares for the soul's welfare alone" can "censor" certain books, the theologian who is a member of the university faculty, charged with the "care of the welfare of the sciences," must limit the censorship so it "creates no disturbance in the field of the sciences."[25] For Kant, it seems, a pastor may recommend to his parishioners that they not read certain books, but he has no business trying to ban those books. For Kant, however, religion seems to have been a rather abstract and intellectual exercise the purpose of which was merely to offer material content to the notion of the good life that is the formal goal of morality. Such religion has almost nothing to say to "the sciences," and what little it does say clearly is limited by reason, as reason, for Kant, is entirely capable of apprehending the nature and requirements of morality.

The contrast I want to draw, though, is not with religion *simpliciter* but with the Christian faith. Religion includes rites and rituals, traditions and communities, and is a social phenomenon. My concern is with a narrower concept, the theological content of "canonical Christianity."[26] It is thus the "faith that was once for all entrusted to the saints" (Jude 3) as represented in the Apostles', Niceno-Constantinopolitan and Chalcedonian Creeds.

---

[25]Kant, *Religion Within the Limits of Reason Alone*, pp. 7-8.
[26]For extended discussions of "canonical Christianity," see, e.g., William J. Abraham, Jason E. Vickers and Natalie B. Van Kirk, eds., *Canonical Theism* (Grand Rapids: Eerdmans, 2008).

In my view, then, in contrast to Kant's view, the Christian religion is all-encompassing, overarching and undergirding. As a unified and coherent worldview, a Christian's faith should saturate her thinking, deliberating and deciding. It should guide her relationships with other persons, her use of material possessions, her treatment of the natural world and of course her relationship with God. The Christian faith, like other religious faiths, essentially makes claims about reality, which are either true or false. Moreover, competing worldview truth claims often have very different consequences for life. As C. S. Lewis put it,

> We are now getting to the point at which different beliefs about the universe lead to different behavior. Religion involves a series of statements about facts, which must be either true of false. If they are true, one set of conclusions will follow about the right sailing of the human fleet; if they are false, quite a different set.[27]

So my view is that religion alone should set the limits on a philosopher's activities. Let me quickly say that I do not believe that a philosopher needs a cleric's permission before submitting a paper to a journal. Course syllabi don't need a church's approval, and books don't need an imprimatur (aside from the role of official sanction given to doctrinal teaching). The limits, rather, are personal, self-imposed and self-maintained. Clearly a Christian philosopher has the ability to ask all sorts of what-if questions, to entertain positions well outside the mainstream of Christian thought and even to think through the implications of views that might seem contrary to Christian behavior. But I believe that a Christian philosopher has a duty *as a Christian* not to advocate for heretical theological views, for conclusions that are clearly contrary to biblical teaching or for positions that if adopted would undermine Christian virtue.

Who decides what views those are, you ask? Well, as a Protestant, I can't simply point to the documents giving the church's magisterial teachings. And I surely don't want to endorse a naive literalist reading of the Bible. So the best I can do to answer this question here is to say that Christian philosophers, through their own study of the Bible, the-

---

[27]C. S. Lewis, *Mere Christianity* (New York: Macmillan, 1960), p. 58.

ology and the history of doctrine, in interaction with the Christian community and especially the trained exegetes, hermeneuticians, theologians and historians in the church, must answer the questions for themselves. Humility and honesty are inescapable here. (In succeeding chapters you'll see where I try to apply my own constraints to philosophical questions as I try to give at least one way of seeing what it is to do philosophy as a Christian.)

To sum up in different terms, *worldviews aren't neutral.* The pretheoretical commitments of a worldview constitute control beliefs about ultimate reality, about where we look for epistemic justification and what kind of evidence could constitute justification, and about what sorts of things in the world have moral properties, and what constitutes our moral obligations. I believe that anyone can be self-critical, subjecting his worldview to reflective evaluation, but it is difficult. Philosophy is a most excellent tool for this exercise. But to think that we can philosophize about such things in a *neutral* way is a mistake; our worldview gives us an interpretive grid—a plausibility structure—for what we will even consider legitimate and profitable to think about. The problem with "methodological *neutralism,*" if I can give an old term a new twist, is not methodological but metaphysical. As reflective Christians, we understand that our worldview commits us to certain metaphysical positions that bring with them epistemological and ethical commitments as well.

Doing philosophy as a Christian, in full recognition of the limits our Christian faith imposes on us, should be no more objectionable than doing philosophy as, say, a materialist.

COSMIC AUTHORITY PROBLEMS

Paul Moser claims, "We are morally responsible for the questions we willingly pursue, just as we are similarly responsible for everything else we intentionally do."[28] I believe this is true, and it highlights the present question of limits, of authority and autonomy in doing philosophy.

Thomas Nagel is refreshingly honest about such things:

---

[28]Paul K. Moser, *The Elusive God: Reorienting Religious Epistemology* (New York: Cambridge University Press, 2008), p. 5.

I want atheism to be true and am made uneasy by the fact that some of the most intelligent and well-informed people I know are religious believers. It isn't just that I don't believe in God and, naturally, hope that I'm right in my belief. It's that I hope there is no God! I don't want there to be a God; I don't want the universe to be like that.

My guess is that this cosmic authority problem is not a rare condition and that it is responsible for much of the scientism and reductionism of our time.[29]

Of course no Christian philosopher would say those words! However, it might not be far off to imagine some philosopher who is a Christian muttering, "I don't want some theologian or church council dictating my conclusions in advance. I have an ecclesiastical authority problem. I want to follow reason where it leads!"

An attitude like this, in a philosopher who is a Christian, baffles me. If the Christian faith commits us to belief in an all-powerful, perfectly good, tri-personal God who is the creator and sustainer of all, then to not begin our philosophical work in conscious submission to the authority of that God and his revelation is simply foolishness.

As C. S. Lewis said, "The one thing that Christianity cannot be is moderately important."

DO ALL TO THE GLORY OF GOD

Ideas have power—power to inspire and edify, to enlighten and empower, to shape and mold, but also power to inhibit and tear down and imprison, and ultimately to kill the spirit, and sometimes the body as well. That's why, as Moser said, we are morally responsible for the questions we willingly pursue. And, I'd add, we are morally responsible for the conclusions we willingly reach.

If an argument we are pursuing leads to conclusions that are morally repugnant (infanticide is permissible), or self-refuting (there is no objective truth), or strikingly counterintuitive (persons are perduring four-dimensional spacetime worms), or contrary to experience (Laplacian physical determinism rules out free will), then I think it's time to

---

[29]Thomas Nagel, *The Last Word* (New York: Oxford University Press, 1997), pp. 130-31.

reexamine the presuppositions with which we began the argument rather than cling (perhaps with a perverse pride) to a "radical" or "novel" or "irreverent" position. Genuine but proportional pride in one's work is not wrong, but a Christian worldview has something to say about what kind of work one can legitimately take pride in.

"So whether you eat or drink or whatever you do, do it all for the glory of God" (1 Cor 10:31). This is the motivation of the Christian philosopher doing philosophy within the limits of religion alone.

4

JESUS AND PHILOSOPHY

If you hold to my teaching, you are really my disciples.
Then you will know the truth, and the truth will set you free.

JESUS (JN 8:32)

"Jesus is Lord" can mean little in practice for anyone who has to hesitate
before saying "Jesus is smart." He is not just nice, he is brilliant.

DALLAS WILLARD

The Definition of Chalcedon, which all orthodox Christians affirm, declares:

> [O]ur Lord Jesus Christ, at once complete in Godhead and complete in manhood, truly God and truly man, consisting also of a reasonable soul and body; of one substance with the Father as regards his Godhead, and at the same time of one substance with us as regards his manhood; like us in all respects, apart from sin; as regards his Godhead, begotten of the Father before the ages, but yet as regards his manhood begotten, for us men and for our salvation.[1]

No doubt there is deep mystery here, a divine metaphysic incomprehensible in its fullness by the human mind. The Christian doctrine of the incarnation claims that the eternal Son of God, the second person of

---

[1]The Fourth Ecumenical Council of the Church convened in Chalcedon, a city in Asia Minor now part of Istanbul, in A.D. 451. The most important of its declarations was its "definition" of the hypostatic union, of which this quote is a part.

the Trinity, became fully a man, Jesus of Nazareth; that in doing so he did not for a moment cease to be fully God; and that he did this "for us and for our salvation." These are astonishing claims, and challenging ones, claims that force Christians to think hard about how they can be true. However, for purposes of this chapter, I'll simply take the claims at face value, assuming they can be adequately explicated and defended.[2]

Jesus was not a philosopher, at least not in any ordinary sense of the term.[3] He wrote no books (but neither did Socrates), developed no grand metaphysics (but neither have most philosophers through the ages). He did not make his living by lecturing or teaching philosophy (but neither did Hume). So what does Jesus have to do with philosophy?

Much in every way, as the apostle Paul might say (see Rom 3:2). In this chapter I'll argue for two claims. First, that Jesus is Lord, and that title is more than an honorific one: it has implications for how we do philosophy. Second, that Jesus is credible, and that credibility is pervasive: Jesus should be trusted in all matters, not just when he preaches the gospel of the kingdom of God.

WHO DO YOU SAY THAT I AM?

According to the Gospels,[4] Jesus claimed to be the Messiah, the coming prince promised in the Old Testament, who would bring the rule of

---

[2]Much detailed work on explicating the claims of Chalcedon has been done by theologians and philosophers. See, for example, Stephen T. Davis, Daniel Kendall and Gerald O'Collins, eds., *The Incarnation: An Interdisciplinary Symposium on the Incarnation of the Son of God* (New York: Oxford University Press, 2004); Fred Sanders and Klaus Issler, eds., *Jesus in Trinitarian Perspective* (Nashville: B & H Publishing, 2007).

[3]In spite of George W. Bush's claim during the 2000 presidential campaign that Jesus was his favorite political philosopher.

[4]I'm assuming the basic historical reliability of the Gospels. For a defense, see, e.g., Craig Blomberg, *The Historical Reliability of the Gospels* (Downers Grove, Ill.: InterVarsity Press, 1987); Gary R. Habermas, *The Historical Jesus: Ancient Evidence for the Life of Christ* (Joplin, Mo.: College Press, 1997); N. T. Wright, *The Challenge of Jesus: Rediscovering Who Jesus Was and Is* (Downers Grove, Ill.: InterVarsity Press, 1999).

In addition to his explicit teaching, both the miracles and the resurrection of Jesus validate his claim to divinity. This is not an apologetics book, so I can't argue for this here. For astute scholarly defenses, see R. Douglas Geivett and Gary R. Habermas, eds., *In Defense of Miracles: A Comprehensive Case for God's Actions in History* (Downers Grove, Ill.: InterVarsity Press, 1997); N. T. Wright, *The Resurrection of the Son of God* (Minneapolis: Augsburg, 2003); Gary R. Habermas and Michael R. Licona, *The Case for the Resurrection of Jesus* (Grand Rapids: Kregel, 2004).

God to Israel, and beyond. But as Craig Evans notes, "Jesus saw himself not only as the Messiah, or Anointed One of the Lord, who, as the figure described in the vision of Daniel 7 was invested with divine authority, but as the agent whose suffering would provide atonement and redemption for God's people."[5] His disciples only gradually came to understand this claim, and even up to his resurrection they did not understand the means by which he would bring about the redemption of humanity.

In a significant incident recorded in Matthew 16:13-20, Jesus asked his disciples what the popular opinion of him was. They replied that most people thought Jesus was a prophet. "Who do you say that I am?" Jesus asked. Peter's ringing reply apparently represented the view of (most of) the other disciples: "You are the Christ [*Christos*, the Greek translation of the Hebrew *mashiyakh*, Messiah, Anointed One], the Son of the living God."

Jesus accepts this ascription, indicating that he is indeed the coming Ruler. And if so, it follows that the God-anointed Ruler has a legitimate authority, a rightful claim to be obeyed.

In an equally telling incident, while washing the disciples' feet at the Last Supper, Jesus said to them, "You call me 'Teacher' and 'Lord,' and rightly so, for that is what I am. Now that I, your Lord and Teacher, have washed your feet, you also should wash one another's feet. I have set you an example that you should do as I have done for you" (Jn 13:13-15). (Jesus makes this point explicitly in an earlier discourse called the "Sermon on the Plain": "Why do you call me, 'Lord, Lord,' and do not do what I say?" [Lk 6:46].)

If it follows that (in general), students should follow the example of their teachers, a fortiori they should follow the example of their Lord and Teacher. But "following the example" of the Lord and Teacher means not only doing what he does, but believing what he teaches. And Jesus explicitly claims authority to teach truth and condemns those who don't believe his teaching (e.g., Jn 5:37-47; 8:24, 45; 18:37).

It follows, then, that to believe that Jesus is the promised Messiah

---

[5]Craig A. Evans, "Jesus: Sources and Self-Understanding," in *Jesus and Philosophy: New Essays*, ed. Paul K. Moser (New York: Cambridge University Press, 2009), pp. 38-39.

entails believing also that he is Lord, who must be obeyed, and Teacher, who must be believed.

Now, clearly, there are those who claim to be Christians but don't often obey the teachings of Christ, and no Christian could rightly claim always to obey. The ugly image of the vicious and merciless sheriff or landlord (or banker or politician or fill-in-the-blank) who shows up at church every Sunday morning, piously singing hymns and pompously greeting the pastor, has too much of the ring of truth about it to be denied. But serious Christians, and fair-minded people of any or no faith, can recognize that as an aberration. The exception does not disprove the rule; every belief system has its share of hypocrites. The vast majority of Christians, though, have committed to following Jesus in everyday life, not just on Sunday. They generally succeed at avoiding the "really big sins," and are genuinely good people. They may not be saints, but they know moral perfection awaits the future state called "glorification."

And yet I think that we need a more fine-grained approach. The stark contrast between outright hypocrisy and moral mediocrity is too coarse. For Jesus' demands are radical and their implications run deep, as any reading of the Sermon on the Mount will hammer home (Mt 5–7). To follow Jesus does not mean living a shade above the lowest common moral denominator. "If you love those who love you, what reward will you get? Are not even the tax collectors doing that? And if you greet only your brothers, what are you doing more than others? Do not even pagans do that? Be perfect, therefore, as your heavenly Father is perfect" (Mt 5:46-48).[6]

To be a Christian philosopher means more than not spreading false rumors about your department chair in order to get the job (although why anyone would aspire to chairing a department, with associated "administrivia," is beyond me); it means more than honest and complete citations in papers, thoroughness in lecture preparation, fairness in grading, and treating students, colleagues and assigned authors with the respect they deserve. Are not all good professors doing that? No,

---

[6]See Michael Wilkins, *In His Image: Reflecting Christ in Everyday Life* (Colorado Springs: Nav-Press, 1997).

the exemplary behavior that a Christian philosopher exhibits must extend to his service to the community or the university, to his family life, to his church involvement. A Christian professor must display integrity of life, demonstrate those practices that accord with Christian commitment—in short, holiness. (Of course the same standard—holiness—goes for a Christian in any profession if she genuinely claims to follow Jesus.)

Jesus is Lord. Our allegiance to him supersedes and brings into proper balance all other allegiances, whether to a profession, an organization, a group or a nation. Our lives should reflect that.

"That's all well and good," you might be thinking, "But it's nothing we haven't all heard in sermons or read in books or learned in Bible studies."

True enough, but it bears repeating to remind ourselves of how easy it is sometimes to slide, almost unawares, into comfortable mediocrity. But I've rung the changes on this theme for another reason as well. If Jesus is Lord, he is worthy to be obeyed—and to be believed. A Christian accountant must be thorough and accurate, refusing to fudge accounts, following the letter (and the spirit) of the law, leaving an audit trail so others can see his work. A Christian engineer must also be thorough and accurate, refusing to cut corners, following the letter (and the spirit) of the latest applicable standards, fulfilling the terms of the contract as well as insuring public safety. Doing their work as Christian professionals clearly involves understanding what Jesus commands and obeying him on the job. But a Christian philosopher trades in ideas, in concepts, in truth-claims. So not only must she behave as Jesus commands, she has an additional duty that is not as clear in most other professions (except, of course, teaching professions)—a duty to discover, declare and defend the truth of what Jesus taught.

I argued in the previous chapter that a Christian worldview rightly can and indeed ought to shape the contours of our philosophy. We Christian philosophers need to live in a dialectic, cycling between our philosophizing and Jesus' teaching, each serving as a provisional heuristic for interpreting the other, but at the end of the day recognizing where the authority truly rests. Now, I'm not here arguing for a naive literalism in biblical interpretation. Far from it. But if we are to answer as Peter did, then—and please hear this as charitably as I intend it—a Christian philosopher must have more than a Sunday school–level grasp of Jesus' teaching.

JESUS AND THE BIBLE

If Jesus is the supremely authoritative teacher, and if he points to an authoritative source in his teaching, it follows that that source also is authoritative. One cannot read the Gospels without being struck by the frequency with which Jesus cites the Hebrew Scriptures (our Old Testament) as authoritative. Further, he regards not only the explicit statements of the text as authoritative, but when disputing with the religious leaders about interpretations or applications of particular passages, he cites other passages as authoritative guides to interpretation. Even when being tempted by the devil, Jesus replies by quoting Scripture to rebut the tempter's enticements (cf. Mt 4:1-11).

In the Sermon on the Mount, Jesus offers explicit teaching concerning the authority of the Scripture:

> Do not think that I have come to abolish the Law or the Prophets; I have not come to abolish them but to fulfill them. I tell you the truth, until heaven and earth disappear, not the smallest letter, not the least stroke of a pen, will by any means disappear from the Law until everything is accomplished. Anyone who breaks one of the least of these commandments and teaches others to do the same will be called least in the kingdom of heaven, but whoever practices and teaches these commands will be called great in the kingdom of heaven. (Mt 5:17-19)

Demonstrating that he regarded the precise wording of the text as authoritative, Jesus even makes appeal to the tense of a verb. Matthew 22:23-33 records Jesus' encounter with a group of Sadducees, who did not believe in a resurrection. Although the Sadducees tried to trap Jesus with a trick question, Jesus undercut their trap by appealing to the use of the present tense in a verse of Scripture: "But about the resurrection of the dead—have you not read what God said to you, 'I am the God of Abraham, the God of Isaac, and the God of Jacob'? He is not the God of the dead but of the living" (Mt 22:31-32).

If then Jesus has authority to teach and to be believed, it seems that authority is extended by his teaching to the Old Testament as well. And many theologians understand his words after the Last Supper to imply antecedent endorsement of the writings of the New Testament also; Jesus said, "But when he, the Spirit of truth, comes, he will guide you into all truth" (Jn 16:13).

So it isn't difficult to argue that the authority of Jesus extends to the entire Bible: what it teaches is to be believed (when properly interpreted, of course). The Christian philosopher cannot then ignore or avoid the teaching of either Jesus or the Bible.[7]

IS JESUS CREDIBLE IN *ALL* MATTERS?

I've argued that Jesus' claims to be the Lord (with all that implies given the background of the Old Testament) qualify him as authoritative not only for how we behave but also for what we believe. And I've argued that Jesus' explicit statements and implicit attitudes toward the Scriptures extend his authority to the whole Bible (properly interpreted, of course).

It seems to me that many sincere Christians adopt a quite different approach to Scripture. Consciously or unconsciously they restrict the locus of biblical authority to matters of "faith and practice." The idea seems to be that the eternal Logos, the Second Person of the Trinity, was incarnate as a first-century Palestinian Jew, and would have shared his contemporaries' beliefs about the material world, about human psychology, about history and so forth, and we need not grant first-century beliefs about such matters any authority over our beliefs.

And even in matters of "practice," it seems, Jesus cannot be regarded as ultimately authoritative. Didn't Jesus himself demonstrate progress in moral understanding, as in the portion of the Sermon on the Mount where he repeatedly counters moral understanding grounded in the Old Testament: "You have heard that it was said . . . but I say to you . . ." (Mt 5:21-48). And Jesus explicitly revises Mosaic law on divorce: "Moses permitted you to divorce your wives because your hearts were hard. But it was not this way from the beginning. I tell you . . ." (Mt 19:8).

---

[7]For more on this, see John W. Wenham, "Christ's View of Scripture," in *Inerrancy*, ed. Norman L. Geisler (Grand Rapids: Zondervan, 1980).

Thus some Christians have maintained that moral understanding can grow, mature, become more refined, through years of thoughtful reflection on moral philosophy. So, presumably, we should realize that we may well be more enlightened with respect to many contemporary issues than were the New Testament authors.

The upshot of this approach is that the "authority" of Jesus (or Scripture) is subject to revision as contemporary culture "advances." Now, the authority of a constitutional government may be revisable as the constitution is amended. But this is not the ultimate authority of the one who is "Lord and Master." His rightful authority does not derive from the consent of the governed.

Not all who seek to avoid the explicit teaching of Jesus (or the Bible) consciously deflate Jesus' (or the Bible's) authority. Two strategies are on offer that allow an interpreter to reject what seems to be explicit teaching and still affirm Jesus' authority. The first says that Jesus knew that some of what he said was false, but he was accommodating his teaching to the common cultural beliefs of his day. The second appeals to cognitive limitations that Jesus voluntarily assumed during the incarnation to claim that Jesus necessarily held false beliefs, and one proper role of contemporary interpreters is to correct Jesus' teaching. The accommodation strategy is more often explicitly employed; the cognitive limitations strategy is generally employed tacitly. But if my argument that Jesus is authoritative in matters of belief is to go through, I need to respond to both strategies.

Accommodation? It might well be that Jesus (and indeed the Holy Spirit, inspiring the authors of the books of the Bible) accommodated his teaching to popular belief. Let's say that accommodation occurs when a teacher (or parent or some other authoritative presenter) employs beliefs[8] that he knows to be false but that his audience takes to be true; he accommodates the falsehoods rather than explicitly correcting them. Parents often accommodate beliefs of their children (whether about Santa Claus, or where babies come from, or Uncle Dave being as strong as a superhero), without thereby endorsing them as true. So too,

---

[8]Strictly, I should here speak of propositions that are believed, but to do that throughout would be too pedantic.

the claim goes, Jesus sometimes accommodated the false beliefs of his audience in his teaching. And the same would go for the inspired writers of Scripture.

We need to tread very carefully here; this is territory that should be marked, as some medieval maps were, with the warning, "Here be dragons!" First, I think it's clear that some accommodation is found in Scripture. One salient illustration is the use of expressions referring to the rising or the setting of the sun (for example, in the Sermon on the Mount, Matthew 5:45). Now we easily explain this away as "phenomenological language," and it certainly is that. But it's also virtually certain that all people in biblical times really did believe that the sun moved—that it literally rose and set. Nevertheless, the point Jesus was making is unaffected by whether his listeners believed in a geocentric cosmology.

We need to make a distinction (a quintessential philosophical activity). Say that a *benign accommodation* occurs when an author employs a false belief of his audience but does not affirm the false belief. He may employ the false belief as an illustration, in a metaphor or simile, or as some other figure of speech without affirming it. But if the proposition serves as a premise of an argument, or if it is employed in an assertoric speech act, then the author is affirming it. And if he knows it to be false, it's a deception. He is either asserting what he knows to be false (and thus a lie), or using an unsound argument (and thus sophistry). In that case I'll say that it is not a benign but a *malign accommodation.*[9]

It should be clear that whether a putative case of accommodation is benign or malign turns on proper exegesis. We need to be as sure as we can be that we understand what the author intended to communicate, and what the original audience would have understood by the communication. Thus the need for biblical scholarship to play a role in discussion of particular cases.

Here's the payoff of this brief discussion. If we have good reason to believe that Jesus as Lord must be believed as well as obeyed (and by ex-

---

[9]It is possible, I think, to construct scenarios where malign accommodation may not be morally blameworthy, but I doubt such scenarios are too common in real life. I leave it to you the reader to invent and explore such cases on your own.

tension the same goes for the biblical text, as I argued above), then we must reject the notion that Jesus (or the biblical authors) ever engaged in *malign* accommodation. So if the best exegesis indicates that Jesus affirms something, as Christian philosophers we must take the affirmation seriously and not dismiss it as accommodation. And we must remember that Jesus' teaching very often employed enthymemes (arguments in which a premise or a conclusion is not directly stated) rather than clear, explicit syllogisms; we must be careful that we take seriously both the explicit and the implicit premises and not dismiss them as accommodations.

Here I'll offer just one (admittedly controversial) example. In Matthew 10, Jesus is encouraging his disciples that though they will face persecution in their mission to preach the gospel of the kingdom, they should not fear the persecutors, as God is in control. In verse 28 Jesus says, "Do not be afraid of those who kill the body but cannot kill the soul. Rather, be afraid of the one who can destroy both soul and body in hell" (Mt 10:28). A number of biblical scholars and Christian philosophers these days reject the explicit dualism of sayings like this, dismissing Jesus' statement distinguishing the soul from the body as accommodation to folk psychology.[10] (And others tend to write off his statement about hell as accommodation to first-century Jewish eschatology.) Most who do so explicitly appeal to "advances in the neurosciences" that have "discredited a dualist interpretation of the human person."[11] But a careful reconstruction of Jesus' argument seems to turn on a literal affirmation of the soul-body distinction, and so if this were accommodation, it would involve using false premises in an argument, and so would be malign. Now, I could be wrong in my understanding of the text, but if I'm right, it has deep implications for Christian philosophers doing philosophy of mind (see chapter 8 for more on philosophy of mind).

---

[10]There are difficult theological and philosophical issues here; exegetes, theologians and philosophers are not immune from influencing and being influenced by one another, and by contemporary psychology and neuroscience. Nevertheless, and perhaps because of the controversial nature of the passage, this serves well to illustrate my point.

[11]Joel B. Green, *Body, Soul, and Human Life: The Nature of Humanity in the Bible* (Grand Rapids: Baker, 2008), p. 32. Interestingly, although Green's book cites numerous biblical texts, this is not one of them.

Incarnational limitations? As I noted at the beginning of the chapter, orthodox Christian doctrine holds that Jesus of Nazareth was at the same time fully God and fully human. But it also holds that during the incarnation Jesus voluntarily refrained from the exercise of certain divine attributes. He could not have divested himself of any attributes essential to divinity, or he would have ceased to be (fully) God. The voluntary restriction on the exercise of his attributes is called the "kenosis," after the Greek word used in the great christological hymn in Philippians 2:5-11:

> Your attitude should be the same as that of Christ Jesus:
>   Who, being in very nature God,
>   did not consider equality with God something to be grasped,
>   but made himself nothing,
>   taking the very nature of a servant,
>   being made in human likeness.
>   And being found in appearance as a man,
>   he humbled himself
>   and became obedient to death—even death on a cross!
>   Therefore God exalted him to the highest place
>   and gave him the name that is above every name,
>   that at the name of Jesus every knee should bow,
>   in heaven and on earth and under the earth,
>   and every tongue confess that Jesus Christ is Lord,
>   to the glory of God the Father.

The Greek word in question here translated "made himself nothing" is variously translated "emptied himself" or "made himself of no reputation."

Theologians have proposed a number of ways to understanding what was involved in the kenosis; many agree that in order to live the "fully human" life that we see portrayed in the Gospels, Jesus would have had to limit his use of such attributes as omniscience, omnipresence and omnipotence.[12] To be sure, some theologians, such as St. Thomas

---

[12]For in-depth discussion of some of these issues, see Garrett J. DeWeese, "One Person, Two Natures: Two Metaphysical Models of the Incarnation," and Klaus Issler, "Jesus' Example: Prototype of the Dependent, Spirit-Filled Life," in *Jesus in Trinitarian Perspective*, ed. Fred Sanders and Klaus Issler (Nashville: B & H Publishing, 2007).

Aquinas, have held a view according to which Jesus enjoyed the "beatific vision" from the moment of his birth, and so did not experience cognitive limitations. But such a view seems to be at odds with the Gospels. Certainly cognitive limitations are in view in passages such as Luke 2:52, "Jesus grew in wisdom and stature, and in favor with God and men," and Matthew 24:36, "No one knows about that day or hour, not even the angels in heaven, nor the Son, but only the Father."

But limiting omniscience raises certain problems. I have cited with approval Dallas Willard's claim that those who say that Jesus is Lord should also hold that Jesus was brilliant; let's grant that for sake of argument. Let's grant that Jesus, perhaps far beyond his contemporaries, reflected on his beliefs and accepted as true only well-justified beliefs. And let's grant that as a brilliant person he was able to see (or intuit) connections between beliefs that would support or defeat certain beliefs, connections opaque to the average person. We can even go so far as to grant that Jesus had the most accurate noetic structure of any human who had ever lived. But even brilliant people hold false beliefs, and many of those false beliefs are justified, based on the total evidence available and the prudential use of the intellectual virtues. It would seem that in Jesus' day, false but justified beliefs would have included such beliefs as a geocentric universe, a relatively small cosmos in which there were no more than a few thousand stars, the indivisibility of atoms, combustion as the source of the Sun's heat, and so on. In addition to such false scientific beliefs, other examples of false justified beliefs might well have included beliefs of historical, geographical and sociological natures.

The difficulty, then, is this. Did Jesus authoritatively teach false propositions that he was justified in believing?

Those who wish to deflate Jesus' teaching authority often tacitly assume an affirmative answer to the question. But here too we need to tread carefully. Let's proceed by dividing the question into its two parts. First, did Jesus hold false but justified beliefs? And second, if so, did he authoritatively teach false propositions?

To answer the first question we need to ask whether holding a justified false belief is a defect, or more precisely, the sort of defect that would count against Jesus' moral perfection or against Jesus' being fully man and fully God simultaneously. It seems, on one hand, that there are such things as justified false beliefs; one can nonculpably believe a falsehood if one has done one's best to arrive at what one takes as the truth. For example, there have been a number of cases in the past decade or so where inmates have had their convictions overturned based on analysis of DNA evidence that was not available (and in some cases not even possible) at the time of the trial. Assuming that the prosecution and the defense each did their job with integrity, the jury members cannot be held at fault for arriving at a verdict based on the evidence presented. Yet on the other hand, clearly a person's noetic structure is more perfect if it contains fewer false beliefs, no matter how well justified, and if Jesus was perfect, that seems to entail that he held no false beliefs.

One might think that this could be sidestepped by a correct analysis of the relation of Christ's human intellect to his divine person, but I don't think this offers a way out. Several models have been suggested: (1) One reading of the scholastic model, refined from the decrees of several of the ecumenical councils, understands the human nature that Jesus assumed at the incarnation as a subsistent entity, complete with its own mind. So Jesus had two minds: a fully human mind (as part of his human nature) and a fully divine mind (as a part of his divine nature).[13] (2) A modified scholastic view seeks greater unity between the two minds of Christ, viewing them as separate centers of consciousness in one "soul" or person.[14] Analogies offered to help elucidate this view include dual consciousnesses in brain commisurotomy patients, or multiple personality disorder (now called dissociative disorder).[15] (3) A more recent view understands the dual natures of the incarnate Christ

---

[13]For exposition of this view, see, for example, Alfred J. Freddoso, "Human Nature, Potency, and the Incarnation," *Faith and Philosophy* 3 (1986); Richard Cross, *The Metaphysics of the Incarnation* (Oxford: Oxford University Press, 2002).

[14]The "scare quotes" call attention to the difficulty of using a biblical term like "soul" without assuming a certain metaphysic of human persons.

[15]For exposition of this view, see Thomas V. Morris, *The Logic of God Incarnate* (Ithaca, N.Y.: Cornell University Press, 1986). Trenton Merricks invokes hemisphere commisurotomy as a model for the social Trinity in "Split Brains and the Godhead," in *Knowledge and Reality: Essays in Honor of Alvin Plantinga on His Seventieth Birthday*, ed. Thomas Crisp, Matthew Davidson and David Vander Laan (Dordrecht: Kluwer Academic, 2006).

as abstract entities, sets of properties, and thus a nature cannot have a mind. So this view locates the mind of the incarnate Christ in the person of the eternal Son of God, but argues that in the kenosis, Christ voluntarily restricted his conscious mental activity (at least most of the time) to that which was like all other human beings—mediated by a human brain, finite, able to learn and gain understanding. There would be some sort of "partition" or "firewall" that precluded Christ's human mental activity—that consistent with finite human nature and mediated by brain activity—from "accessing" his omniscient divine intellect, except, perhaps, in rare cases.[16]

A moment's reflection on the different models reveals that whether more proximal to the divine nature, as in (3), or more distal, as in (1), the false belief is still held by the one single individual who was both God and man. If a false belief is a defect, it is a defect in all three models—since, after all, they are models of the hypostatic *union*. Still, there might be more here to help us deal with the difficulty, even though there's nothing to help us avoid it.

So we need again to draw some distinctions. Surely some false beliefs are blameworthy.[17] I would claim that for any adult living in Germany before or during World War II, the belief that all Jews should be exterminated is not only false, but the person holding the belief is in some sense morally culpable for that belief. I believe that human reason is sufficient to the task of determining the morality of genocide, irrespective of the beliefs or propaganda of the surrounding culture. While it might be natural, easy or socially respectable to accept the moral beliefs of the prevailing culture, in the case of the Final Solution I claim that it is morally wrong to believe that genocide is moral. I recognize that in making this claim I'm assuming that cultural relativism is false as a viable moral theory,[18] and I'm also assuming that beliefs and not

---

[16]See William Lane Craig, "The Incarnation," in J. P. Moreland and William Lane Craig, *Philosophical Foundations for a Christian Worldview* (Downers Grove, Ill.: InterVarsity Press, 2003), pp. 597-613; DeWeese, "One Person, Two Natures," and Issler, "Jesus' Example."

[17]Or, rather, a believer is blameworthy (in a sense to be determined) for holding the belief. In what follows, for convenience, I'll sometimes speak of the belief and sometimes of the believer as blameworthy. Nothing crucial is lost here in sacrificing precision for readability.

[18]See chapter 7 for the argument.

merely actions are objects of moral evaluation, a view that comports well with an agent-centered (as opposed to an action-centered or a consequence-centered) ethic. Both of these assumptions are controversial, but seem to me to sit more comfortably in a Christian worldview than the alternatives.

If I'm right about this, then there are certain (false) beliefs that Jesus could *not* have held because were he to do so, he would be *morally* blameworthy. He could not, for example, have believed (with some of the more extreme Zealots) that all Romans should be killed simply because they were not Jews.

There is also, I think, a sense of *epistemic* blameworthiness that attaches to beliefs accepted on insufficient evidence,[19] or hastily, or out of laziness or prejudice or self-interest, or on the basis of a wish, a hope or a "gut feeling." A person accepting a belief in one of these ways is violating an epistemic norm for rational belief formation. Someone may believe, say, that the Detroit Lions will win the Superbowl in spite of their known weaknesses, but that belief would be based on hope or desire (or fanatical commitment). Such epistemically blameworthy beliefs may well be harmless—or not, depending on the subject of the belief and on what actions the belief moves one to take. But even apparently harmless, epistemically blameworthy false beliefs are not desirable and are not compatible with the prefect rationality we would require from someone who we regard as our divine Lord.

I think it would be a defect in Jesus if he were to have held a false belief that is blameworthy in either of the senses just discussed. So the cognitive limitations of the incarnation do not allow for such beliefs. But I don't think we can see a single example in the Gospels of Jesus holding such a belief, nor do we have any reason to attribute this sort of defective belief to Jesus.

So we might conclude, at least tentatively, that the two clear cases where a person might be blameworthy in some sense for holding a false belief are not cases into which any putative false beliefs of Jesus might fall.

---

[19]I'm not here intending to reject the view of Reformed epistemology that certain beliefs need not have empirical evidential support; again, see chapter 6.

Is there, though, a class (or classes) of belief that, although false, can be held in a nonblameworthy way, however 'blameworthiness' is understood? Perhaps so. Perhaps we all hold a number of false beliefs, which would qualify as well-founded beliefs on any theory of justification, and for which we are unaware of, or misjudge as insignificant, potential defeaters. It is hard to see how any sort of blame or culpability could attach to such beliefs. Unless one holds a theory of justification according to which justification is truth guaranteeing, such a scenario seems not only possible but probable.

I cannot see that even a high Christology can rule out the possibility that as a man, Jesus held nonblameworthy false beliefs. But it does not follow that he would have asserted or taught anything false. Recall the three models of the relation of Christ's human intellect to his divine person. Defenders of (1), according to which minds go with natures, have traditionally held that the divine mind totally engulfs the human, so that the human mind is hardly more than a theoretical entity, scarcely operative at all. For example, Gregory of Nazianzus wrote, "It is clear to every one that he [Christ] knows as God and knows not as man."[20] On this view, then, the divine mind could perhaps prevent the human mind from acquiring false beliefs (although the process of belief formation of the human mind on this view is not discussed by its proponents); but surely if Christ knows as God knows, then Christ—that is, the single hypostasis in which the human and divine are united—does not believe falsehoods and so cannot teach falsehoods.

On (2), the two centers of consciousness view, as well as on (3), the single mind view, the divine center of consciousness, or the divine portion of the single mind, can access the human (although presumably, except possibly in rare circumstances, the human cannot access the divine mind). Thus the divine mental activity of Jesus would know if he had formed justified false beliefs and would be able to prevent him from teaching falsehoods, perhaps via the ministry of the Holy Spirit to Jesus. (Recall that Jesus himself told his disciples that the Holy Spirit

[20]Gregory of Nazianzus, "Fourth Theological Oration," in *Christology of the Later Fathers*, ed. Edward R. Hardy (Philadelphia: Westminster Press, 1954), p. 188.

would guide them into all truth, John 16:13.)[21]

It seems, then, that there is no reason to think that the epistemic limitations of the incarnation would entail that Jesus would teach falsehoods. So we can safely conclude that neither the accommodation argument nor the incarnational limitations argument succeed in undermining the ultimate authority of Jesus in matters of belief. Said differently, there remains no good reason to question Jesus' complete credibility in *all* matters. This conviction, I believe, should serve as the guardrails that keep the Christian philosopher on the correct intellectual road.

JESUS AND PHILOSOPHY

I've already granted that Jesus was not a philosopher in the contemporary sense of the word. Nevertheless, there are significant ways in which we can understand Jesus as fitting comfortably in the company of philosophers. We can see this by looking at two dimensions of the Gospel portrayals of Jesus: the style and focus of (much of) his teaching, and his use of sound arguments.

Jesus as sage and model. In a very interesting article, Luke Timothy Johnson discusses "four ways in which the figure of Jesus as found in the canonical Gospels (Matthew, Mark, Luke and John) gives rise to the sort of thinking that can properly be called philosophical."[22] I'll focus on two of Johnson's four ways in this section.

Johnson's first approach is to consider Jesus as a historical figure whose teaching can be considered as that of an ancient Jewish sage. Here, the focus is on the sayings of Jesus that reveal a "love of wisdom" or an intent to teach the "skill of living," as did the Hebrew sages (see chapter 2) as well as other ancient sages as reported, for example, by Diogenes Laertius. So many of the sayings of Jesus that convey a truth

---

[21]For those who are biblical inerrantists (as I am), the parallel with the doctrine of the inspiration of Scripture, whereby the Holy Spirit prevented the biblical authors from recording error, makes this proposal all the more probable. And if Jesus is authoritative in his teachings about and his attitude toward Scripture, we have additional reason to accept inerrancy. But I can't pursue this argument here.

[22]Luke Timothy Johnson, "The Jesus of the Gospels and Philosophy," in *Jesus and Philosophy: New Essays*, ed. Paul K. Moser (New York: Cambridge University Press, 2009), pp. 63-83.

about human nature or commend a particular moral behavior or manner of life can be understood as giving rise to philosophical thought, not merely insight into Jesus' psychology. The aphoristic nature of some of Jesus' teaching "resemble the short snappy observations that also find parallel in Jewish proverbs and Greco-Roman *apophtheg mata.*"[23] *Apophthegmata* were collections of aphorisms, for example, the *Apophthegmata Laconica,* a portion of the *Moralia* of Plutarch (A.D. 46-120), roughly contemporaneous with the Gospels. Examples include "Be on your guard against all kinds of greed; a man's life does not consist in the abundance of his possessions" (Lk 12:15) and the so-called Beatitudes (Mt 5:2-11). Johnson notes that as statements about life, such aphorisms can be considered as philosophical in the same vein as the sayings of Colon or Confucius, and he quotes Origen as expounding the principle:

> If the doctrine be sound and the effect of it good, whether it was made known to the Greeks by Plato or any of the wise men of Greece, or whether it was delivered to the Jews by Moses or any of the prophets, or whether it was given to the Christians in the recorded teachings of Jesus Christ, or in the instructions of the apostles, that does not affect the value of the truth communicated.[24]

And finally are direct exhortations concerning a manner of life, which closely resemble (at least in style, if not always in content) the instructions found within Greco-Roman philosophical schools, for example, the *Sovereign Maxims* of Epicurus, or the writings of the Stoics Marcus Aurelius and Epictetus. Johnson concludes that the many parallels between Jesus' sayings and the Greco-Roman tradition "confirm that these statements fit within an understanding of philosophy as a way of life, in which the point of language is less to describe reality than to change character."[25]

Another approach to Jesus focuses on his overall moral teachings aimed not only at accurate analysis of right and wrong, but of shaping

---

[23]Ibid., p. 66.
[24]Origen *Against Celsus* 7.59; cited by Johnson, "Jesus of the Gospels," p. 67.
[25]Johnson, "Jesus of the Gospels," pp. 67-68.

the dispositions of character. In this, Aristotle's two books on ethics
serve as a parallel. Aristotle not only taught that students need to learn
the maxims of moral behavior, but need exemplars after whom they
could model their behavior. Other ancient writers frequently wrote bi-
ographies of virtuous wise individuals to serve as models: Plutarch's
Moralia, Diogenes Laertius's *Lives of Eminent Philosophers* (ca. A.D.
300), and others. In this vein, we can read the Gospels as presenting
Jesus not only as a sage, a teacher of wisdom, but also as a moral exemplar; the narratives show us the character of one after whom we should
model our lives, much as the early dialogues of Plato present us with
the example of Socrates. So the Gospels sit easily alongside the principle stated by Seneca (4 B.C.–A.D. 65): *Verba rebus proba*, "Prove the words
by deeds." "Insofar as philosophy has to do with thinking about the
proper way of being human, the character of Jesus in the narrative Gospels ought to give rise to the most serious sort of thinking."[26]

In the end, Johnson concludes that "the Jesus of the Gospels has or
might give rise to the serious and disciplined thought worthy of the
name philosophy." I believe he has made a compelling case for this conclusion, and so the Christian philosopher cannot afford to neglect study
of Jesus along with study of, say, Socrates or Scotus, Hume or Kant.

Jesus and logic. Two recent studies have highlighted Jesus' use of
logic in argument,[27] and this is the feature of Jesus' public ministry that
I want to focus on in this section. It's common these days for critics of
Christianity, or religion in general, to disparage religious belief as "mere
blind faith," as contrasted with "sound, evidence-backed reason." The
assumption is that religious leaders must disparage rationality in order
to entice people to accept religious beliefs. (Even the apostle Peter faced
similar detractors. In his second epistle, he wrote, "We did not follow
cleverly invented stories when we told you about the power and coming
of our Lord Jesus Christ, but we were eyewitnesses of his majesty"
[2 Pet 1:16], and refers to his personal experience on the Mount of

---

[26]Ibid., p. 74.
[27]Dallas Willard, "Jesus the Logician," *Christian Scholar's Review* 27 (1999): 605-14; and Douglas Groothuis, *On Jesus*, Wadsworth Philosophers Series (Florence, Ky.: Wadsworth, 2003).
   The latter looks at more than the narrow issue of Jesus' use of logic.

Transfiguration as evidence for the truth of his teaching.) So Michael
Martin, for example, claims that Jesus "does not exemplify the important intellectual virtues. Both his words and his actions seem to indicate that he does not value reason and learning."[28] Yet a careful reading
of the Gospel passages used by Martin to support his case shows that
he is cherry-picking verses out of context and divorced from the overall
tenor and thrust of Jesus' teaching.[29]

In the previous chapter I argued that there is no impassable gulf dividing faith and reason, and that the mature faith of an intelligent
Christian is eminently reasonable. And we can find evidence to support
this view in Jesus' teaching. Dallas Willard points out that Jesus did not
offer a developed theory of logic, but that was not the point of his mission on earth. Rather, it is in his *use* of logic that he reveals himself to
be supremely rational. Willard writes,

> Jesus' aim in utilizing logic is not to win battles, but to achieve under-
> standing or insight in his hearers. This understanding only comes from
> the inside, from the understandings one already has. It seems to "well
> up from within" one. Thus he does not follow the logical method one
> often sees in Plato's dialogues, or the method that characterizes most
> teaching and writing today. That is, he does not try to make everything
> so explicit that the conclusion is forced down the throat of the hearer.
> Rather, he presents matters in such a way that those who wish to know
> can find their way to, can come to, the appropriate conclusion as some-
> thing *they* have discovered—whether or not it is something they par-
> ticularly care for.[30]

In his dialectical strategy, then, we expect—and find—Jesus em-
ploying logic without explicitly stating his argument in terms of num-
bered premises, and often in ways that leave it to his listeners to draw
the right conclusions. "His use of logic is always enthymemic, as is
common to ordinary life and conversation. His points are, with respect
to logical explicitness, understated and underdeveloped. The signifi-

---

[28]Michael Martin, *The Case Against Christianity* (Philadelphia: Temple University Press, 1991),
    p. 167.
[29]See Groothuis, *On Jesus*, pp. 24-26, for a response to several specific claims made by Martin.
[30]Willard, "Jesus the Logician," p. 607.

cance of the enthymeme is that it enlists the mind of the hearer or hearers *from the inside,* in a way that full and explicit statement of argument cannot do."[31] With that caution in mind, though, we can observe Jesus' use of logic in his arguments. Here are just a few examples.

1. In one of several disputes with the religious leaders over the nature of the Sabbath, Jesus employs an a fortiori form of argumentation. In the encounter recorded in Luke 13:10-17, Jesus healed a physically disabled woman. Charged by the Pharisees with breaking the Sabbath law, Jesus responded, "Doesn't each of you on the Sabbath untie his ox or donkey from the stall and lead it out to give it water? Then should not this woman, a daughter of Abraham, whom Satan has kept bound for eighteen long years, be set free on the Sabbath day from what bound her?" That is, if it is lawful for an animal to be released from physical restraints on the Sabbath in order to be led to water, a fortiori it is lawful to release a woman from her physical restraints. Luke then gives us a glimpse of how Jesus' logic impacted his audience: "When he said this, all his opponents were humiliated, but the people were delighted with all the wonderful things he was doing" (Lk 13:15-16). (A similar use of a fortiori argument, again in a Sabbath dispute, is found in John 7:21-24.)

2. In yet another Sabbath dispute, Jesus relies on showing the logical implication of certain acts done on the Sabbath but not considered unlawful, and showing the logical inconsistency of the Pharisees in charging him with Sabbath breaking. As recorded in Matthew 12:1-8, Jesus cites two examples. In the case of King David eating the "consecrated bread" in the tabernacle, which was according to the law reserved for the priests, the implication is that human need may justify doing what was ritually prohibited. The second example is the work done by the priests in the temple, which would constitute breaking the Sabbath law, but the implication is that fulfilling the necessary duties to facilitate worship justifies a technical violation of the law. Since the Pharisees accepted that both these cases were justified, it follows that the ritual law is not inviolable. Then in verse 7, Jesus quotes the prophet Hosea

---

[31]Ibid.

(Hos 6:6), to show that the greater issue was the character of the God who gave the law. "If you had known what these words mean, 'I desire mercy, not sacrifice,' you would not have condemned the innocent." That is, there is an inconsistency between the compassion desired by God and the Pharisees' attempt to use the law to oppress and harm people—in the name of God. This inconsistency is the reason Jesus often calls these leaders hypocrites.

3. From time to time, Jesus cites evidence to support his conclusions (or the conclusions that right-thinking people would have to draw). This certainly is in contrast to the picture of Jesus presented by Martin, who claims that the only reasons Jesus gives for believing in him as Messiah are either that the kingdom of heaven is at hand, or that those who do not believe would go to hell. Martin asserts that "no rational justification was ever given for these claims."[32] Yet what we see in reading the Gospels is quite the opposite. For example, the disciples of imprisoned John the Baptist come to ask Jesus on John's behalf if he is really the Messiah. Jesus most certainly did not say that they would go to hell if they did not believe. Rather, he said, "Go back and report to John what you hear and see: The blind receive sight, the lame walk, those who have leprosy are cured, the deaf hear, the dead are raised, and the good news is preached to the poor" (Mt 11:4-5). Now, the evidence cited by Jesus is significant, as those were the sorts of acts that the prophets had predicted that the Messiah would do.[33] Similar use of evidence is seen in Jesus' response to the charge of blasphemy in John 5:17-47.

4. Jesus' enemies often put questions with the intent of trapping him into a statement they could use against him. On one occasion, recorded in Matthew 22:15-22, a group of Pharisees and Herodians attempted to trap Jesus in his own words. We should realize that the Pharisees were nationalists who strongly opposed Roman rule, while the Herodians were supporters of the Herod dynasty, half-Jews who governed on Rome's behalf. The coalition of these two opposing parties put a trick question to Jesus: "Is it right to pay taxes to Caesar, or not?" If Jesus

---

[32]Martin, *The Case Against Christianity,* p. 167.
[33]See, for example, Isaiah 35:4-6; 61:1-2.

answered that it was, then the Pharisees would accuse him of disloy-
alty to Israel, of selling out to Rome. But if he said no, then the
Herodians would denounce him as an insurrectionist, an enemy of
Rome. After asking for a coin, Jesus asked whose image was on it.
"Caesar's," was the reply. "Give to Caesar what is Caesar's, and to God
what is God's," Jesus said. Jesus displays a very sharp intellect here,
neatly passing between the horns of the dilemma. The dilemma is not
exhaustive: Jesus is implying that the material coin of the realm belongs to the one whose image is on it, but humans, as bearers of God's
image, belong to God. Caesar's rule is earthly and temporal, but God's
rule is spiritual and eternal. So temporal, material things such as taxes
might rightly be owed the state, but ultimate allegiance, one's entire
life, is owed to God.

Other examples could be given, but these are sufficient to demonstrate Jesus' intellectual prowess in logical argumentation.[34] I'll close
this chapter by again quoting Willard.

> Paying careful attention to how Jesus made use of logical thinking can
> strengthen our confidence in Jesus as master of the centers of intellect
> and creativity, and can encourage us to accept him as master in all of the
> areas of intellectual life in which we may participate. In those areas we
> can, then, be his disciples, not disciples of the current movements and
> glittering personalities who happen to dominate our field in human
> terms. Proper regard for him can also encourage us to follow his exam-
> ple as teachers in Christian contexts. We can learn from him to use
> logical reasoning at its best, as he works with us. When we teach what
> he taught in the manner he taught it, we will see his kind of result in the
> lives of those to whom we minister.[35]

---

[34]See also John Stott, *Christ the Controversialist* (Downers Grove, Ill.: InterVarsity Press, 1970);
and James W. Sire, *Habits of the Mind: Intellectual Life as a Christian Calling* (Downers Grove,
Ill.: InterVarsity Press, 2000).
[35]Willard, "Jesus the Logician," p. 614.

PART TWO

THE INESCAPABLE QUESTIONS

If most of us are ashamed of shabby clothes and shoddy furniture,
let us be more ashamed of shabby ideas and shoddy philosophy.

ALBERT EINSTEIN

I do not know how to teach philosophy
without becoming a disturber of the peace.

BENEDICT SPINOZA

Let's face it. Philosophers are known above all for asking disturbing questions.

- What is real?
- How do I know?
- How should I live?

These are the inescapable questions that occur to nearly everyone at some point in life. Of course, very many people put these questions in the same category as the monster under the bed: something fearful to avoid looking at too closely when they're young, and something to be regarded as childhood silliness when they're older.

Perhaps hard, critical thinking about these things *is* fearful, since the answers we arrive at could well overturn our world. No wonder Spinoza was a disturber of the peace; no surprise that Socrates was convicted of "corrupting" the youth of Athens. As old maps of the world ominously declared, "Here be dragons," so in philosophy, "Here be conceptual dragons."

And perhaps hard thinking *is* silliness, for as the saying goes, *philosophia non panem torrit,* "philosophy bakes no bread."[1] So let's get on with practical stuff like making a living.

Yet the questions are inescapable, since there is probably not a single thing that any one of us could think, say or do that does not presuppose the answer to at least one of the inescapable questions.

A few people (to paraphrase George Bernard Shaw's pithy comment in another context) think hard about such questions. Some people think they think hard about such questions. Most people would rather die than think hard about such questions.

Philosophers are simply those who make a living out of thinking hard about them.

---

[1]The origins of this saying are obscure. But the second half of the saying is often overlooked: "but without philosophy no bread is baked." Even bakers have values, reasons, beliefs.

5

What Is Real?

Metaphysics

The feeling of wonder is the touchstone of the philosopher,
and all philosophy has its origins in wonder.

Plato

It is owing to their wonder that men both now begin
and at first began to philosophize.

Aristotle

The two most enjoyable activities of mankind are gossip and metaphysics—
the sparkles on the shallows of conversation about people, and the
vast ocean of thought about reality, where the deeper you dive,
the greater the darkness and the pressure grows.

Joseph Bottum

Wonder. Humility. Amazement. Even darkness and pressure. Such emotions swell when a thoughtful person contemplates the universe in which we live, a world of quarks and quasars, Beethoven's symphonies and birds' songs, the pastel shades of alpine wildflowers and the saturated hues of tropical rainforests. The natural world astounds us with its variety and complexity, its scales of size and time. The French mathematician and philosopher Blaise Pascal pondered,

Finally, what is man in nature? A nothing with respect to the infinite, an all with respect to the nothing, a mean between nothing and everything. Infinitely far removed from comprehending the extremes, the end of things and their principle are hopelessly hidden from him in an impenetrable secret; [he is] equally incapable of seeing the nothing from which he is taken, and the infinite in which he is swallowed up.[1]

As "first philosophy," metaphysics takes up the challenge to think critically about the world. The metaphysician asks questions that everyone considers at some time, but she will not content herself with easy answers. And she also asks questions that almost no one else has considered, as her thinking about the world goes ever deeper. Reality, it seems, yields answers reluctantly; yet at the end of the day, the wonder of the metaphysician issues in a vision of reality, clear and precise even if profound.

Richard Taylor writes in his introduction to metaphysics:

> We cannot live as fully rational beings without it [metaphysics]. This does not mean that metaphysics promises the usual rewards that a scientific knowledge of the world so stingily withholds. It does not promise freedom, God, immortality, or anything of the sort. It offers neither a rational hope nor the knowledge of these. Metaphysics, in fact, promises no knowledge of anything. If knowledge itself is what you seek, be grateful for empirical science, for you will never find it in metaphysics.
>
> Then what is its reward? What does metaphysics offer that is in its power alone to give? What, that this boundless world cannot give even to the richest and most powerful—that it seems, in fact, to withhold from these more resolutely than from the poor and humble? Its reward is wisdom.[2]

While I'm not so pessimistic about the possibility of metaphysics to yield knowledge, I agree that genuine wisdom, as discussed in chapter two, must draw from roots deeply and firmly planted in metaphysics, for no one can be truly wise who does not have a firm grasp on reality, even if it is in the form of a time-honored, rough-and-ready

---

[1]Pascal, *Pensées* (Paris: Bordas, 1966), #72 (my translation).
[2]Richard Taylor, *Metaphysics*, 4th ed. (Englewood Cliffs, N.J.: Prentice-Hall, 1991), pp. 6-7.

folk metaphysics. This, I think, was John Wesley's point in his "Address to Clergy":

> Do I understand metaphysics; if not the depths of the Schoolmen, the subtleties of Scotus or Aquinas, yet the first rudiments, the general principles, of that useful science? Have I conquered so much of it, as to clear my apprehension and range my ideas under proper heads . . . ?[3]

CRUCIAL ISSUES

While a vast array of topics fall under metaphysics, here I'll only consider two. Yet they are two of the inescapable questions, perennial challenges to any thoughtful person. These questions, in somewhat varied formulations, lay at the heart of the metaphysics of the pre-Socratics: Thales, Anaximander, Anaximenes, Pythagoras, Xenophanes, Parmenides, Heraclitus, Empedocles, Anaxagoras, Leucippus and Democritus. Plato and Aristotle thought long and hard about them, as did most later thinkers. Here, then, are the two inescapable metaphysical questions.

Why is there something rather than nothing? Existence is the ultimate mystery. Everything we know of in the universe is contingent; it might not have existed at all. Why then does anything at all exist? Below, I'll call this simply the Existence Question, or EQ.

What kinds of things are there? Given that something exists, the next inescapable question asks about the nature of what exists. Does reality consist in one thing, or one kind of thing, or many kinds of things? What are these kinds of things? And why these things and not others? I'll refer to this as the Kinds Question, or KQ.

MAJOR OPTIONS

With respect to the first inescapable question, EQ, the answers fall rather neatly into two classes: naturalistic and nonnaturalistic. With respect to the second, KQ, the classification of options is not nearly so neat. In canvassing the options, we'll begin with the first.

---

[3]John Wesley, "An Address to the Clergy," in *The Works of John Wesley* (London: Wesleyan Methodist Book Room, 1872; reprint, Grand Rapids: Baker, 1979), 10:491.

Why is there something rather than nothing? Asked expressly by philosophers as diverse as Leibniz and Sartre, the inescapable question of
existence was long assumed to have only two answers: Either it is natural—the universe was eternal, uncaused and so needing no explanation. Or it is supernatural—God (or gods) brought it into existence.

Natural options. Contemporary theoretical cosmology offers a number of variations on the eternal universe theme. Most can be classified
as multiple universe or "multiverse" theories. They share a presupposition that if the number of universes is multiplied to infinity, then in
some sense there is no need for an explanation of existence of the multiverse. One way to categorize the multiple universes postulated by
these theories is to divide them into spatially multiple, temporally multiple and other-dimensionally multiple multiverses, each depending on
a different universe-generating mechanism.[4]

Spatially multiple proposals envision the multiverse as something
like an expanding "quantum foam" of inflationary Big Bang cosmology, giving birth to perhaps infinitely many "bubble universes."[5] In
more recent versions, the multiverse is conceived as "cosmic landscape,"
an unimaginably large multidimensional "space" of mountains and valleys representing unstable ("peaks"—maxima) and stable ("valleys"—
minima) combinations of the various cosmic constants and laws of nature. The minima represent causally isolated "pocket universes," with
the laws of nature quite different in different pockets. This cosmic
landscape scenario is one possible interpretation of the fact that the very
difficult equations of string theory seem to have as many as 10^{500} solutions, each solution representing a really existing pocket universe.[6] The
different regions of the landscape emerge from cosmic inflation and
quantum fluctuations, and our universe is but one lonely region in

---

[4]For an alternative taxonomy, see Max Tegmark, "Parallel Universes," *Scientific American* (May
2003).

[5]Proponents of this view include John Archibald Wheeler's oscillating universe and Lee Smo-
lin's "fecund universe." See Lee Smolin, *The Life of the Cosmos* (New York: Oxford University
Press, 1997); Alex Vilenkin, *Many Worlds in One: The Search for Other Universes* (New York:
Hill and Wang, 2006).

[6]The landscape proposal is defended by Andrei Linde, Leonard Susskind and Martin Rees,
among others. See Leonard Susskind, *The Cosmic Landscape: String Theory and the Illusion of
Intelligent Design* (New York: Little, Brown, 2006).

which the laws just happened to be such as to favor life. In some versions of the "landscape" scenario, there are perhaps an infinite number of pocket universes in the multiverse, so the fact that there should be a region in which the laws are life-friendly should not surprise us; indeed there is an infinity of such regions.

"Temporally multiple" multiverse proposals envision an eternally cyclical universe.[7] In these versions, each universe is a "brane" (from membrane) in string theory, and from time to time branes come into contact, releasing enormous amounts of energy, causing a new cycle of cosmic evolution to begin in the respective branes. Theorists suggest that energy would be conserved in such collisions, thus allowing for a temporally infinite multiverse.

"Other-dimensionally multiple" proposals build on Hugh Everett's many-worlds interpretation of quantum mechanics. In this view, every time the quantum wave function "collapses," the universe splits into distinct worlds that occupy a place in an infinite-dimensional Hilbert space.

In any of these infinite multiverse scenarios the inescapable question isn't at all inescapable; indeed, it doesn't arise at all. Or so proponents suggest. For if there is indeed infinite space or infinite time or an infinite number of dimensions, then (so it is suggested), there can be no raising of EQ. For if everything exists, then the *why?* question is meaningless. Indeed, as Robert Mann suggests, the question turns back on those who deny the infinite multiverse and becomes, *why is there something rather than everything?*[8] What is everything?

Another sort of naturalistic option claims that the universe is necessary, containing its own explanation. As articulated by Bertrand Russell in his famous debate with Fr. Frederick Copleston, "The universe is without explanation"; it's illegitimate to ask about the cause of the

Is this everything?

---

[7]Paul Steinhardt and Neil Turok have argued for a cyclic model of the universe in a series of papers, e.g., "A Cyclic Model of the Universe," *Science* 296 (2002): 1436-39; "Cosmic Evolution in a Cyclical Universe," *Physical Review* D 65 (2002): 126003/1-126003/20; see also Paul Steinhardt, *Endless Universe: Beyond the Big Bang—Rewriting Cosmic History* (New York: Doubleday, 2007).
[8]Robert B. Mann, "The Puzzle of Existence," *Perspectives on Science and the Christian Faith* 61 (2009): 139-50.

world.[9] Recently some physicists have given this a new twist. The proposal is that the universe itself is probabilistically favored, if not necessitated, by the laws of nature, so that the laws of nature somehow explain the universe. For example, according to physicist and self-proclaimed "new atheist" Victor Stenger,

> the universe and its laws could have arisen naturally from "nothing." Current cosmology suggests that no laws of physics were violated in bringing the universe into existence. The laws of physics themselves are shown to correspond to what one would expect if the universe appeared from nothing. There is something rather than nothing because something is more stable.[10] *How is Nothing unstable?*

Clearly the naturalistic options have come far from the pre-Socratic philosophical concept of an eternal universe, but the conclusion—and perhaps also the motivation—is the same: there is no need for a Creator.[11]

Now, one additional remark needs to be made here concerning the *meaning* of 'existence.' As the famous dictum of Willard Van Orman Quine has it, "To be is to be the value of a [bound] variable."[12] But surely this isn't what 'to exist' *means*. It tells us nothing about the nature of existence, but only about certain implications of quantification in first-order logic. I think that Quine's slogan should be considered a verification condition for existence claims, or, more accurately, a criterion of ontological commitment: if sentences or theories that we regard

[9]Audio and transcription of the debate are widely available, e.g., at <www.ditext.com/russell/debate.html>. "A Debate on the Argument from Contingency" broadcast in 1948 on the Third Programme of the British Broadcasting Corporation, published in *Humanitas* (Manchester) and reprinted in Bertrand Russell, *Why I Am Not a Christian* (London: George Allen & Unwin, 1957).

[10]Victor Stenger, preliminary summary for a forthcoming book, *Why Is There Something Rather Than Nothing? The Self-Contained Universe*, <www.positiveatheism.org/hist/quotes/stenger.htm>.

[11]This conclusion is not the only logically possible one. For example, physicist and theologian Robert John Russell argues that an eternal creation is compatible with the Christian belief that God created *ex nihilo*, if appropriate qualifications are made: "T=0: Is It Theologically Significant?" in *Religion and Science: History, Method, Dialogue*, ed. W. Mark Richardson and Wesley J. Wildman (New York: Routledge, 1996).

[12]W. V. Quine, "On What There Is," *Review of Metaphysics* 2 (1948): 21-38; reprinted in *From a Logical Point of View* (Cambridge, Mass.: Harvard University Press, 1953). The qualification 'bound' is often found in statements of Quine's slogan, and while Quine does use the term 'bound variable' in his essay, the original phrasing omits 'bound.'

as true quantify over certain variables, then those sentences or theories contain an ontological commitment to the existence of entities that can be the values of those variables. Other views, for example, that *to exist* means *to exemplify a property,* are similarly unhelpful in understanding the *meaning* of existence.

My view is that existence is the ultimate primitive, the "substratum of the world."[13] It cannot be analyzed in terms of anything else more basic, and paraphrases of the meaning of *to exist* (e.g., *to be real, to be actual,* etc.) simply trade on the brute fact of existence. Now, even though I'll want to say something about necessary versus contingent existence, and to claim that if God did not exist as a necessary being, nothing else would exist either, I don't think such claims shed light on the nature or meaning of existence. So I'll treat it as brute, and move on.

Supernatural options. Quite simply, supernatural options deny that the universe could be uncaused, or self-caused (if that is even a coherent notion), or its own explanation. Consequently there must be some cause beyond the natural. Almost by definition such a supernatural cause would be a deity. While it's not inconceivable that a group of gods to-gether or in competition were the creative origins of the universe—the picture of the cosmogonies of many ancient cultures from south Asia to Mesopotamia to Greece—such pictures were recognized as inadequate even by pre-Socratic philosophers. Xenophanes (ca. 570 B.C.–ca. 475 B.C.), for example, often regarded as one of the earliest monotheists among Greek philosophers, satirized the pantheon of Homer and He-siod as anthropomorphic projections.[14] I think it's safe to say that in our day, the supernatural answer to EQ is monotheistic.

What kinds of things are there? If answers to the first inescapable metaphysical question are few, answers to the second, about the kinds of things that exist, are legion. The earliest Milesian philosophers were philosophical monists; they answered KQ by arguing that everything

---

[13]Reinhardt Grossmann, *The Existence of the World: An Introduction to Ontology* (New York: Routledge, 1992), pp. 91-119.

[14]Jonathan Barnes, *The Presocratic Philosophers,* rev. ed. (New York: Routledge, 1982), pp. 63-77.

was composed of one thing. Thales thought everything came from water; Anaximander proposed some indefinite original stuff; Anaximenes said air. Do we see here a presaging of contemporary naturalists' reduction of everything to fundamental microphysical entities such as strings? Heraclitus, who argued that the only constant was change, also held that there was an eternal, immutable *logos* or rational principle that directed all else. Might we find here a foreshadowing of natural law? And Parmenides (on many interpretations) was the strictest monist of all, arguing that there was only one thing, eternal, undifferentiated, unchanging, and all change and individuality was illusory. A prefiguring of the timelessly existing four-dimensional block universe, perhaps? Although the answers of the pre-Socratics sound quaint to modern ears, the reductive search for a single principle, a single kind of stuff, is distinctly modern.

Plato and Aristotle famously argued for a plurality of things within a basic duality of immaterial forms and matter, differing—again, famously—over whether or not there could be uninstantiated forms (among other rather important details, of course). Aristotle organized all entities into a small number of basic categories, and for centuries ontology—the study of what categories of things there are and their properties and relations—operated with various permutations of Aristotle's categories, into which all things that exist were somehow fit.

For reasons that I won't pursue here, the development of grand, all-encompassing metaphysical systems ground slowly to a halt toward the end of the nineteenth century, and many philosophers would say that the later Wittgenstein (he of the *Philosophical Investigations* of 1953, not of the *Tractatus Logico-Philosophicus* of 1921) presided at its funeral. But metaphysics, and even the more specialized field of general ontology, have seen something of a resurgence in recent decades. Once again questions of categories, of properties and substances, of material constitution, and so on, are receiving quite sophisticated attention.

We can only dip our toes in this vast sea, so in what follows I'll discuss only what seem to me to be potential implications of a Christian worldview for thinking about substances and properties and identity.

CHRISTIAN WORLDVIEW IMPLICATIONS

One might be forgiven for assuming that other than the dogma of God as creator, a Christian worldview would have less to say about metaphysics than about other philosophical areas such as epistemology or ethics. But I believe that assumption would be wrong. I'll try to show why I believe that, beginning with the obvious.

The first question: Why is there something rather than nothing? "In the beginning, God created . . ." The affirmation of the first verse of the Bible is echoed in the Apostles' Creed: "I believe in God the Father Almighty, Maker of Heaven and Earth." Central to a Christian worldview is the belief that only God exists eternally and necessarily *a se*—of himself. Everything else in the universe depends upon him and was brought into existence by him.

Christian thinkers have accepted as dogma the doctrine of creation, but have also offered arguments against the notion that the universe is eternal or infinite or noncontingent. Different forms of the cosmological argument aim at this conclusion. In the history of the cosmological argument, three versions have emerged as prominent:[15] The first claims the impossibility of an essentially ordered infinite regress. This version takes as a premise a feature of the universe such as motion, contingency or causality, and concludes that some entity exists that exemplifies the property of being the prime mover, necessary being[16] or first cause. The arguments of Plato, Aristotle and Thomas Aquinas are examples of this version, as is the recent work of Timothy O'Connor.[17]

The second version takes as a premise the requirement an explanation or reason for the existence of a thing, and concludes that a being

---

[15]Garrett J. DeWeese and Joshua Rasmussen, "Hume and the *Kalām* Cosmological Argument," in *In Defense of Natural Theology: A Post-Humean Reassessment*, ed. Douglas Groothuis and James Sennett (Downers Grove, Ill.: InterVarsity Press, 2005).

[16]Species of this type of cosmological argument can be subdivided by the sort of necessary being involved. The necessary being may be broadly logically necessary (exists in all possible worlds), causally necessary (exists as the first eternal cause in every world in which it exists) or factually necessary (exists as the first eternal cause in the actual world).

[17]Plato *Laws* 10.884-899d. Aristotle gives his argument in several places, for example, *Physics* 8.1-6.250b5-260a15. Although Aquinas offers the argument in several places, the best known is found in the first three of Thomas' famous Five Ways; Thomas Aquinas *Summa theologica* 1a.2.3. Timothy O'Connor, *Theism and Ultimate Explanation: The Necessary Shape of Contingency* (Malden, Mass.: Blackwell, 2008).

ontology is the study of being,
or of what is

exists that is the self-explaining sufficient reason. This version is associated with Benedict Spinoza, Gottfried Wilhelm Leibniz and Samuel Clarke.[18] A contemporary version—or, better, a contemporary argument that makes use of a version of the principle of sufficient reason— is defended by Richard Gale and Alexander Pruss.[19]

The third version is the *kalām* cosmological argument (KCA), the key claim of which is that the universe must have a temporal beginning, and the conclusion of which is that a being exists that does not have a temporal beginning, in other words, that is eternal. The *kalām* version seems to have been discovered by medieval Islamic philosophers, and is found in the writings of Avicenna, al-Ghazali and Averroës, among others.[20] Contemporary defenders include William Lane Craig and J. P. Moreland.[21]

The different versions of the cosmological argument have been the subject of considerable discussion in the past two or three decades, and the literature—both supporting and opposing the soundness of the arguments—is vast. In my view, there are good (meaning sound and cogent) presentations of each version; that is, in spite of potential defeaters raised in opposition, I don't see the arguments being com-

---

[18]Benedict de Spinoza, *Ethic* I, P16 and P17, Scholium, in *Central Readings in the History of Modern Philosophy*, ed. Robert Cummins and David Owen (Belmont, Calif.: Wadsworth, 1992), pp. 46-48. G. W. Leibniz, *Theodicy: Essays on the Goodness of God, the Freedom of Man, and the Origin of Evil*, trans. E. M. Huggard (London: Routledge & Kegan Paul, 1951), p. 127. Leibniz further defends his argument in several key places in his correspondence with Clarke. Samuel Clarke, *A Demonstration of the Being and Attributes of God*, reprinted in "Sixteen Sermons on the Being and Attributes of God, the Obligations of Natural Religion, and the Truth and Certainty of the Christian Revelation," *The Works of Samuel Clarke*, vol. 2 (New York: Garland Publishing, 1978).

[19]Richard M. Gale and Alexander R. Pruss, "A New Cosmological Argument," *Religious Studies* 35 (1999): 461-76. See also Alexander R. Pruss, "The Leibnizian Cosmological Argument," in *Blackwell Companion to Natural Theology*, ed. William Lane Craig and J. P. Moreland (Malden, Mass.: Blackwell, 2009), pp. 24-100.

[20]For al-Ghazali's argument, see *The Incoherence of the Philosophers*, trans. Michael E. Marmura (Provo, Utah: Brigham Young University Press, 2000), first discussion, first proof, pp. 12-30.

[21]William Lane Craig, *The Cosmological Argument from Plato to Leibniz* (New York: Harper & Row, 1980; reprint, Eugene, Ore.: Wipf and Stock, 2001); and William Lane Craig and Quentin Smith, *Theism, Atheism and Big Bang Cosmology* (New York: Oxford University Press, 1995); J. P. Moreland, *Scaling the Secular City: A Defense of Christianity* (Grand Rapids: Baker, 1987), pp. 18-42. See also J. P. Moreland, "A Response to a Platonistic and a Set-Theoretic Objection to the *Kalām* Cosmological Argument," *Religious Studies* 39 (2003): 373-90.

pletely overthrown. Give and take, move and countermove continue and will continue, such being the nature of philosophy, where hardly anything of importance is settled finally, once and for all, to everyone's satisfaction.

What is striking, however, is that the proponents of multiverse theories seem to be either completely ignorant of, or at best disdainful of, the strong cosmological arguments that are on offer. Perhaps the reason is that discussion of these arguments generally occurs under the rubric of philosophy of religion, a subject far removed from the ethos within which theoretical cosmologists work. But perhaps there's more going on here. Several of the major players in cosmology openly reject belief in God and claim that even the theoretical possibility of a multiverse renders belief in God explanatorily otiose.[22] Since multiverse theories of any variety are not empirically testable, and so would seem to violate one of the cherished criteria for qualifying as a scientific hypothesis,[23] one might be forgiven for regarding the multiverse as a counsel of desperation by atheists seeking to avoid the force of the Existence Question.

[handwritten: → relating to space - existing in space]

Spatially multiple universe theories face a strong defeater in arguments that the existence of an actual infinite collection of spatiotemporal entities is impossible, and temporally multiple universe theories face an equally strong defeater in arguments that it is impossible to traverse an infinite temporal series. Both arguments are part of contemporary versions of the *kalām* argument. Both are a priori arguments from the nature of infinity, the premises of which are grounded in modal intuitions. As such, they have the force of logical necessity, especially strong when opposed to arguments that a given mathematical

[handwritten: ✱ existed in the mind prior to experience.]
[handwritten: Based on theory not experiment (a= w/o prior)]

[22]See, for example, Susskind, *Cosmic Landscape*, p. 380. *[handwritten: ✱ USELESS]*

[23]Some cosmologists see this as no small embarrassment; see, for example, Lee Smolin, *The Trouble with Physics: The Rise of String Theory, the Fall of Science, and What Comes Next* (New York: Houghton Mifflin, 2006); Peter Woit, *Not Even Wrong: The Failure of String Theory and the Search for Unity in Physical Law* (New York: Basic Books, 2006). Of course, proponents of these theories *do* regard them as genuine science and are devoting considerable energy to attempting to derive some testable empirical consequences from the theories. But all versions of multiverse theories of which I'm aware regard the distinct universes (whether spatial, temporal or other-dimensional) as causally isolated and so in principle incapable of being tested empirically.

formalism might be given a certain physical interpretation. Now, it sometimes happens that a mathematical formalism, borrowed by physicists from the pure mathematicians to solve a particularly hard problem, has turned out to apply to hitherto-unknown physical entities.[24] However, it surely is not the case that just because there is a mathematical solution to an equation, that solution must be a real physical possibility. And arguments against the existence of actual infinities surely are grounded in stronger intuitions than those that support realist interpretations of, for example, the equations of string theory.

A serious theological problem also arises that calls into question multiverse theories. Robert Mann asks us to assume the simplest kind of multiverse, one that is infinite in extent and in available energy and with laws like those obtaining in our observable universe. We can then ask about the probability of realizing all possible configurations of possible physical systems.

> One such physical system is the human body—your own, for example. Since human DNA has a finite number of configurations, your body will have a duplicate in this infinite universe. It is possible to estimate how far away this body-double is—about $10^{10^{29}}$ meters away from here. Of course, this is but the nearest of many duplicates—infinitely many, since we have allowed the universe to have unbounded matter and energy. Most of these will be only physically identical, with presumably different personalities. . . . However, some will be nearly the same because the local environments and circumstances will be nearly the same. . . . Taking this to its extreme, it means that any given physical system, individual, or society will experience everything it can experience. . . . This might seem like a quaint and benign inference, more science-fiction than fact. Quaint it may be, but benign it is not.[25]

Mann goes on to suggest that the theological problems posed by the "Duplication Dilemma" mostly have to do with the lack of uniqueness. There are many copies of me and of you—and presumably of Christ as well. But some of those duplicate Christs do not die on the cross (since

---

[24]See the convincing examples given by Mark Steiner, *The Applicability of Mathematics as a Philosophical Problem* (Cambridge, Mass.: Harvard University Press, 1998).
[25]Mann, "The Puzzle of Existence," p. 147.

all possible experiences are realized in some duplicate region of the multiverse). Mann concludes, "It is not at all clear that the multiverse paradigm is scientifically beneficial. It is even less clear that this paradigm can be reconciled with any reasonable form of Christian theology."[26] I agree.[27]

The other-dimensionally multiple universe theories pose a somewhat different problem. Perhaps there is a way to deploy the arguments against actual infinites to defeat theories of an infinity of other dimensions, but it's not clear to me how to do that. But here we must make a distinction between the multiple dimensions implied by string theory and the multiple dimensions or many worlds posited by Hugh Everett. The latter seems so highly implausible that it hardly needs comment: surely Ockham's razor is applicable to such ontological profligacy. The multiple dimensions entailed by string theory are not themselves the problem, since current versions of string theory call for "only" ten dimensions, not an infinite number. The explanation that our universe contains the six extra dimensions "curled up" so tightly that we can't detect them—compactified Calabi-Yao manifolds at every point of space—is not very helpful. But I'm hesitant to rule out such possibilities; God is infinitely more creative than my imagination! But as I said, these extra dimensions aren't the problem. The problem lies in the vast number of possible solutions to the still-poorly understood equations of string theory—somewhere in the neighborhood of 10^{500} possible solutions.[28] Each solution represents a different configuration of laws, particles and forces—very different universes from the one we inhabit. Many will be unstable, most probably would not sustain life. But if each possible solution is taken to represent a real universe in the multiverse, it is the sheer number of worlds that raises problems. As Don Page notes, "String theory further suggests that there may be many different kinds of space. This whole collection of googolplexes of galaxies within each of googolplexes of different spaces within each of googols of kinds

---

[26]Ibid., p. 149.

[27]But I could be wrong; not all Christians are skeptical. A notable example is Don N. Page, "Our Place in the Vast Universe," and "Does God So Love the Multiverse?" in *Science and Religion in Dialogue*, ed. Melville Y. Stewart (Malden, Mass.: Blackwell, 2010), 1:371-95.

[28]The number is widely repeated; see, for example, Smolin, *The Trouble with Physics*, p. xiv.

of space makes up an enormously vast universe or multiverse."[29] With such vast numbers, the duplication dilemma returns, so at this point the theological response is the conclusion of Mann above, that it is irreconcilable with reasonable Christian theology.

Conclusion. Although our universe may indeed contain additional dimensions that are not yet empirically detectable, admitting this as a possibility does not at all commit us to accepting any multiverse theory. Both philosophical and theological arguments against vast or infinite multiverse theories are strong.[30] The claim that God is the uncreated creator of all, central to a Christian worldview, is left untouched. The answer then to EQ is that all that exists apart from God does so by his will and for his own glory. "You are worthy, our Lord and God, to receive glory and honor and power, for you created all things, and by your will they were created and have their being" (Rev 4:11).

The second question: What kinds of things are there? As I said above, the answers to KQ are legion, so we must restrict our discussion to a selected range of subjects that seem (to me, at least) to have significant overlap with a Christian worldview. And while I'll readily admit that my claims here may be more controversial than some other claims in this book, and I could be wrong about them, I hope at least to stimulate serious thought about the claims themselves. I'm concerned, as I've noted several times above, to present at least one concrete example of doing philosophy as a Christian—one example of how a Christian worldview impacts philosophy. While I do not claim it is the *only* Christian position, naturally I believe it is the position that comports best with a Christian worldview. You may, of course, disagree—but then, it is up to you to argue that, at the end of the day, your position is

what? (handwritten margin note)

---

[29]Page, "Our Place in the Vast Universe," p. 371. "Googol" is the name of a very big number, 10^{100}, and "googolplex" is even bigger, 10^{googol}. The term was coined in 1938 by the nine-year-old nephew of an American mathematician.

[30]I remain very skeptical of spacetime theories in which time is treated as another dimension rather than a parameter. Four-dimensionalism, or string theory's ten-dimensionalism, entail static time and a block universe. I believe that there are good arguments in favor of dynamic time, and it seems to me that the resulting metaphysic of space and time comport much better with our notions of temporal becoming, free will and the nature of God. See Garrett J. DeWeese, *God and the Nature of Time* (Aldershot, U.K.: Ashgate, 2004) and William Lane Craig, *Time and the Metaphysics of Relativity,* Philosophical Studies Series 84 (Dordrecht: Kluwer Academic, 2001) for arguments.

a better reflection of Christian worldview thinking than is mine.

A helpful way to begin will be to ask, if the Bible is true—or, if the creeds and doctrines of Christianity are true, or if a Christian worldview is largely accurate in its depiction of reality—then what must the world be like? While not logically equivalent, I think that these questions are close enough to give us purchase on our subject.

Universals and particulars. It certainly *seems* that we live and move in a world filled with objects of varying size and solidity, and which possess qualities such as shape, color, location and relative motion. But seemings, or perceptions, have been challenged since the dawn of Western philosophy. Many challenges are epistemological: Pyrrhonian skepticism, for example, challenges the justification of beliefs based on perceptions (and will be considered in the next chapter). Other challenges are metaphysical, denying that the external world and the objects it seems to contain exists at all: Berkeley, Kant, and in some sense the later British idealists such as F. H. Bradley, all deny that there is an objectively existing world apart from the ideas in the minds of perceivers.

Although Berkeley was an Anglo-Irish bishop, and Kant was raised in German pietism, it's safe to say that almost all Christians through the ages have been realists about the external world. And it seems to me that some sort of realism fits best in a Christian worldview. Why? Nowhere in the Bible is there a hint that the external world is unreal, that something like Berkeley's subjective idealism, or Kant's transcendental idealism, is correct. The Bible describes a world in which material things actually exist as mind-independent entities, and in which there are also myriads of immaterial beings—angels and demons, principalities and powers—and the supreme immaterial being, God himself. God himself often refers to things in the world in a way that is most straightforwardly taken as realist. And certainly it is hard to resist the conclusion that the creation account of things—stars, the sun and moon, mountains, seas and rivers, plants, animals and people—is an account of the creation of actually existing entities in a mind-independent world. God ascribes qualities to these things—colors, shapes, locations, times, numbers—again in a realist way.

Now this is not to recommend a naive biblical literalism or a naive form of realism. We can recognize phenomenological and figurative language in Scripture just as we can in everyday life. But surely the simplest explanation of the pervasive realist language in Scripture is that realism is true. The burden rests on the idealists to show why we should abandon realism—and a mighty burden it is. Of course Berkeley and Kant and the British idealists offered arguments for their views, rather sophisticated ones at that. But with such philosophers as G. E. Moore, it seems to me that the premises of the idealists' arguments are far less certain than is the commonsense view that there is a real world out there.[31] So without further delay, I'll assume there is a world filled with things that have qualities, and ask what sorts of things and qualities those are.

To speak as I've been doing about *things* and *qualities* is common sense, but it is already to say that there are at least two kinds of things in the world, and that we can tell the difference. And so begins ontology—studying the categories. Aristotle offered a thorough discussion of the categories in, of course, *Categories*, "a singularly important work of philosophy. It not only presents the backbone of Aristotle's own philosophical theorizing, but has exerted an unparalleled influence on the systems of many of the greatest philosophers in the western tradition."[32] Of course, each ontologist gives the categorization of the world his or her own unique slant; there is no canonical, generally accepted way to do what Plato called "carving reality at the joints."[33] All ontologists begin with the most general category, entity (a thing that has being); debate begins already at level two. Is the broadest division of entity that of universals and particulars? Abstracta and concreta? Ontologists differ.[34] But it isn't necessary for our purposes to decide these difficult

---

[31]G. E. Moore, "A Defence of Common Sense," and "Proof of an External World," in *Philosophical Papers* (London: Allen & Unwin, 1959).

[32]Paul Studtmann, "Aristotle's Categories," *Stanford Encyclopedia of Philosophy* (Fall 2008 edition), ed. Edward N. Zalta, <http://plato.stanford.edu/archives/fall2008/entries/aristotle-categories/>.

[33]Plato *Phaedrus* 265d-266a. In this vein, see Eli Hirsch, *Dividing Reality* (New York: Oxford University Press, 1993).

[34]See, for example, E. J. Lowe, *The Possibility of Metaphysics: Substance, Identity, and Time* (New York: Oxford University Press, 1998), pp. 179-83; Joshua Hoffman and Gary S. Rosenkrantz,

questions; I'll consider both divisions without taking a stand on which has priority.

A Christian worldview underwrites our ability to divide the world into kinds of things. For we read in Genesis that God created things "according to their kinds," implying that there are indeed kinds in the world.[35] God made us in his image, apparently with the capacity to recognize the kinds, and with our own capacity to create our own kinds of artifacts.

How do we locate the joints—discern the kinds? "Aye, there's the rub." Clearly we do, but how? According to what scheme? We can get a handle on KQ first by noticing that the things in the world differ from each other in ways small and large, and we divide and classify things by the qualities they exhibit. We find it natural to speak of shoes and ships and cabbages and kings (sealing wax, not so much these days), and it seems to us that these are distinct kinds of things; we're not merely following some rules for acceptable use of language. The sortal terms in our language, then, reflect real joints in the world. (A sortal is a term that names a concept that supplies identity criteria for things to which it applies.) It's natural, then, to think of individuals or particulars, properties or universals, and sortals or kinds.

Further, it has seemed natural to many philosophers (until recent times) to see at least some sortals as picking out natural kinds that share a *nature* or *essence*. A nature is a set of properties that are jointly sufficient for membership in a kind, while an essence is a property (or set of properties) that is necessary to the existence of a particular, which that thing possesses in every possible world in which it exists, and which it could not lack and still be the same thing that it is.

The question of whether properties are universals or are themselves particulars has challenged philosophers since Plato's day. This is the age-old "problem of universals" (or its close cousin, the "problem of the one and the many"). Of course there are debates about definitions of what is meant by 'universal' and 'particular,' about the nature of puta-

---

Substance: Its Nature and Existence (New York: Routledge, 1997), pp. 46-50.

[35]I have no clear understanding of what taxonomic rank the living "kinds" of Genesis 1 correspond to. I believe it is higher than species and likely higher than genus, lower than domain or kingdom, but beyond that I have no idea. But Genesis is clear that God created "kinds."

tive universals and particulars, and about identity conditions for universals and particulars—answers to which give rise to different metaphysical camps. (One thing all philosophy students quickly learn is that every question is bigger on the inside than it appears from the outside.) Subject to nuance and qualification, those who believe there are universals are metaphysical realists (a different sense of 'realist' than above); those who deny that there are universals are some form of nominalists. Shortly, I'll suggest what I take to be a defensible position on these issues grounded in a Christian worldview, and then I'll consider three objections to my preferred position.

We need to begin, though, with trying to get clearer on what we mean by 'universal' and 'particular,' though as I indicated this is already a matter of debate. Let us say that the distinction between universals and particulars is such that everything is one or the other; the two categories are mutually exclusive and jointly exhaustive. I propose that the correct account of the distinction is given in terms of the notion of *instantiation*. The idea is this. Imagine a particular Lego brick; it has a color (blue, say) and a shape (rectangular prism, say), and other qualities (such as mass, location, and chemical composition, which we can safely ignore here). The brick clearly is a particular—there are others in the box that are distinct from this one. But its color is apparently the very same color as some of the others, as is its shape. The brick "has" blueness and rectangularity; it instantiates these universals.[36] Call this brick George and another blue one in the box Jean. Then the following make clear sense:

(1) George is blue.
(2) Jean is blue.
(3) George is rectangular.
(4) Jean is rectangular.

These sentences say that George and Jean both instantiate blueness and rectangularity, but it is logically possible that they could instantiate

---

[36]There are subtle distinctions to be drawn between the notions of instantiation and exemplification, which I will not make; nothing significant in this discussion hangs on these fine distinctions. See Lowe, *Possibility of Metaphysics*, pp. 78-79, 204-5.

redness and squareness. But it is not logically possible that George could instantiate Jean, or vice versa. So universals are things that can be instantiated—they have instances—while particulars cannot be instantiated—they do not have instances. The realist claims that such universals really exist and are not mere *façons de parler*—ways of speaking.

Why this matters. But is any of this really important? The issues seem arcane to all but those enchanted by the wonders of metaphysics.

Here's one example of the importance of the question. Several years ago the Christian theologian Bernard Ramm argued that one reason for the breakdown of the family was the rise of nominalism (the denial that there are universals.) Why think that one cause for the breakdown of the family was a rejection of universals? According to Ramm, a realist says that the class of all families literally has certain properties in common, certain universals—having a father and a mother (at least in normal conditions), which in turn have certain important properties in common (being nurturing)—such that a group is not a family just because we say it is but, rather, because it exemplifies the same properties at all times and in all places. Nominalists claim that there is no such universal attribute of a family and so feel free to define a family in many different ways. We see this in our day when advocates of gay "marriage" claim that being a "family" is whatever one believes that it is—any group of consenting persons living together in a loving relationship.

As a second example, consider love. The realist believes that there is a property *being loving* that people and their actions may or may not exemplify. It is a real property, not just a word, and it is a universal that is present in all and only individual acts of love or loving people. In fact, since *being loving* is a real universal, *being loving* itself has further properties that we could discover. What are these second-order properties that the first-order property *being loving* has? Paul describes some of them in 1 Corinthians 13: patience, kindness and so on. Since love and its properties are real universals, passages like 1 Corinthians 13, in describing love, are describing reality as it is in all cultures. These descriptions give us true knowledge of reality—in this case, of properties understood as universals.

We could offer further examples, ranging from justice to gender, where denial of universals—and hence also of natures and essences—leads to very practical differences in epistemology, ethics and aesthetics. (I'll return to questions of natures again in chapter 8 in a discussion of personhood.) So it isn't merely a matter of metaphysical esoterica; it makes a practical difference.

The arguments for realism. Realists offer several lines of argument for the conclusion that (most) properties are indeed universals; I'll consider three. They are the argument from predication, the argument that properties themselves can have properties, and the argument that universals are the best explanation of laws of nature.

The argument from predication is a semantic argument. Reprising our earlier example of Lego bricks, we say that (1) "George is blue." The predicate "is blue" supposedly represents the property of *being blue,* or *blueness.* But *blueness* is a noun, and it is natural to think that as a noun it refers to some existing thing. So (1) is logically equivalent to

(1') *Blueness* characterizes George,

which clearly implies the existence of blueness. And when we go on to say that (2) "Jean is blue," or (2') *"Blueness* characterizes Jean," it is natural to think that we are predicating the very same thing—*blueness*—of Jean. George and Jean are particulars existing at wholly distinct locations, yet George's *blueness* is identical to Jean's *blueness.* So

(5) George's *blueness* is identical to Jean's *blueness.*

The realist claims that taking *blueness* as a universal that can be "wholly present" at many spatial locations at the same time is the best explanation of what we are doing when we make such predications.

A nominalist might want to paraphrase (1) as

(1"). George is a blue thing,

which refers only to a particular. Now a problem arises for the nominalist. For she would also want to say that (2) is equivalent to

(2") Jean is a blue thing.

Imagine that Sam is a yellow Lego brick that is the same rectangular

What Is Real?   135

shape as George and Jean, and Sally is a yellow square brick. In virtue of what, then, are George and Jean members of the set of blue things, while Sam and Sally are not? And in virtue of what are George, Jean and Sam members of the set of rectangular things, and Sally is not? If there are not properties, then in virtue of what are these sets natural groupings?

A resemblance nominalist might want to say something like this: George and Jean are members of a class of things that resemble each other. But in virtue of what is resemblance determined? They both resemble Sam also in their shape; how is one to decide in advance that the relevant criterion for resemblance class membership is color and not shape? That is, the color property *blueness* is ontologically prior to the class of blue things. Similarly, to say that George, Jean and Sam are members of the resemblance class of rectangular things, but Sally is not, the property of rectangularity must be prior to the class. But if the property is prior to the class, then it cannot be reduced to membership in the class.

An additional argument against resemblance class analyses of properties is this: It makes perfect sense to say

(6) Blue is more like red than it is like yellow,

or, equivalently,

(7) *Blueness* is more like *redness* than it is like *yellowness.*

Even if (6) may be construed as referring to particulars in resemblance classes, clearly (7) cannot be so construed.

The argument that properties themselves can have properties goes like this.

(8) Blue is a color,

says that the first-order property, blue, instantiates a second-order property, being a color. A nominalist would reply that (8) is merely a statement about particulars:

(8') Blue things are colored things.

But this won't work. Why not? Take a sentence with the same structure as (8'):

(9) Blue things are spatially extended things.

Then, since the nominalist claims that (8') is equivalent to (8), by
parity of reasoning,

(9') Blue is spatial extension.

But of course it isn't, and I take this as a *reductio* of the nominalist's
claim to eliminate second-order properties.

The third argument from laws of nature goes something like this.
Take a statement of a law of nature, say, Newton's law of gravitation:

(10) $F = G \dfrac{m_1 m_2}{d^2}$

This says that the gravitational force exerted by one body on another is
proportional to the product of their masses and inversely proportional
to the square of the distance between them. Let's ignore the complica-
tions of the general theory of relativity and assume (10) is true.

It would be bizarre to claim that (10) is merely an abbreviation of an
(almost) infinite conjunction of statements about each and every body
in the universe, rather than stating a universal generalization in terms
of properties (mass), relations (the distance between objects) and numbers (G, the gravitational constant)—all of which are most plausibly
taken as universals. If it were merely a statement of facts, that would be
consistent with (10) being only contingently true. But if so, the (10)
could not be used to ground the truth of a claim, say, that were there to
be another planet in the solar system at a certain distance beyond the
orbit of Pluto, of such-and-such a mass, then it would exert a force on
Pluto of such-and-such a magnitude. In other words, if (10) represents
an (almost) infinite conjunction of statements about each actually existing body in the universe, then it cannot ground the truth of counterfactuals. But the nature of the scientific enterprise is to make such counterfactual hypotheses regularly. So if nominalism holds, it is difficult to
see what becomes of the theorizing practice of science.

Even such statements as "gold is that element with atomic number

79" or "all metals expand when heated" are best explained by taking numbers, properties (such as heat, even construed as mean molecular kinetic energy) and natural kinds as real entities.

The best explanation, then, of the laws of nature and other scientific statements is that the universals that figure in them really exist.

All three of these arguments for universals accord with the prephilosophical picture of the world we find in Scripture, and so support the realism about universals that naturally arises in a Christian worldview.

Against realism. Several arguments may be lodged against realism about universals; fairness demands that we consider them. I've already indicated how a realist would respond to a nominalist objection to universals, although I should acknowledge that there are several versions of nominalism and additional arguments in the literature.[37]

First, there is a Kantian-style argument that metaphysical analysis does not, after all, study being *qua* being (as Aristotle famously said in *Metaphysics*). Rather, metaphysics is, for Kant, the study of how our mental categories impose structure on the empirical world. As E. J. Lowe points out, the error is

> supposing that metaphysics concerns the structure of our *thought* about being rather than being itself. It is true, of course, that we can only discourse rationally about the nature of being inasmuch as we are capable of entertaining thoughts about what there is or could be in the world. But this does not mean that we must substitute a study of our thought about things for a study of things themselves. Our thoughts do not constitute a veil or curtain interposed between us and the things we are endeavouring to think of, somehow making them inaccessible or inscrutable to us. On the contrary, things are accessible to us precisely because we are able to think of them.[38]

I agree with Lowe: Metaphysics is not talk about thought; it is talk about the world—possible because God has made us in his image and so able to apprehend directly much of his world.[39]

---

[37]See, for example, J. P. Moreland, *Universals*, Central Problems in Philosophy (Chesham, U.K.: Acumen, 2001).

[38]E. J. Lowe, *A Survey of Metaphysics* (New York: Oxford University Press, 2002), p. 14.

[39]For an account of how this apprehension of the world may be worked out, see J. P. Moreland

This conclusion also defeats the postmodern rejection of metaphysics, and especially its rejection of essentialism. Because postmodernists reject universal properties, they also reject essentialism. According to essentialism, a thing's essential properties are those such that if the thing in question loses them, it ceases to exist. A thing's essential properties answer the most fundamental question, what sort of thing is this? For example, being prime is an essential property of the number 13, being human is essential to Socrates, being omnipotent is essential to God, being H_2O is essential to water. An accidental property is one such that a thing can lose it and still exist. For example, being married to Xantippe is accidental to Socrates.

According to postmodernists, there is no distinction in reality between essential and accidental properties. Rather, this division is relative to our interests, values and classificatory purposes and, as such, the division is itself a social construction that will not be uniform throughout social groups. For example, as competent speakers of English, we would not classify dolphins and whales as 'fish.' But suppose there was a group of scientifically uninformed, coastal-dwelling fishermen who had long ago adopted English as their language (for pragmatic purposes, say), and who (again, for pragmatic purposes) classified any animals living in the sea as 'fish.' According to postmodernism, there is no right or wrong here; what counts as a 'fish' is determined by a group's linguistic practices.

Now, the point here is not simply about the use of a particular word, but the broader question of whether there is in principle a distinction to be made between fish and marine mammals. Suppose there was an international treaty protecting marine mammals in the waters frequented by the fishermen. Are they exempt from the law simply because of their use of the word 'fish,' or should they be required to look beyond the linguistic constructs of their group to genuine essential differences between fish and marine mammals?

Now while this fictional group of fishermen won't have implica-

and Garrett J. DeWeese, "The Premature Report of Foundationalism's Demise," in *Reclaiming the Center*, ed. Millard J. Erickson, Paul Kjoss Helseth and Justin Taylor (Wheaton, Ill.: Crossway, 2004).

tions for our faith, I think that it's clear that postmodern nominalism, if widely accepted, would have a disastrous impact on the objective existence of important universals relating to truth, values and Christian teaching.

Another objection to realism, or at least realism that takes such properties as color and shape as universals, goes like this. Imagine you were a neutrino created in a supernova event hundreds of thousands of light years from earth. You would have traveled across space at nearly the speed of light, passing unaffected through near-vacua, interstellar dust, perhaps giant gas planets and small metallic asteroids, and finally through the earth's atmosphere, through trees, rocks, barns, water, cows, people, paintings, computers—in short, through many different kinds of things. Your journey would be described simply as moving through regions of greater or lesser energy density, of higher or lower molecular kinetic energy, of varying distributions of elements and molecules. But even that misstates things: it is unlikely that you would "notice" the "boundaries" of atoms and molecules. Your trip diary might, in fact, simply report traversing various quantum fields. In short, neutrino-you would not find any joints at which to carve the world.

So science, it is claimed, shows us that a scientifically accurate picture of the world does not contain the sorts of divisions that we find natural. The scientific picture does not contain as universals any so-called secondary qualities such as color, sound, smell and taste—at least the first two of which figure prominently in our classification of things into kinds. What we are left with are the properties of the fundamental entities known to physics (be they quarks, strings or whatever), together with the physical properties that emerge from various aggregations of the fundamental entities.

It's not at all clear that even scientists could operate in such an austere ontology. Science makes use of "secondary qualities"—for example, observations of spectral red shift used to determine intergalactic distances, and "red," "white" and "brown" as characterizations of certain star types, or the sound of various bird calls to identify species: can all such secondary qualities be eliminated in favor of some more fundamental set of properties? Further, talk of species, genera and so on in the life sciences seems to invoke universals, as does talk of such properties as ecosystemic homeostasis. So I believe the elimination of natural kinds and dismissal of the "joints of the world" by an austere microphysical description of it are surely inadequate.

A theological objection? Finally, we need to consider an objection arising *from within* a Christian worldview. Paul Copan and William Lane Craig raise a theological objection.[40] God is uncaused, existing, as the theologians say, *a se*, of or from himself; he has the attribute of *aseity*. Everything else that exists, then, exists *ab alio*, of or from another. This surely is one of the implications of the doctrine of *creatio ex nihilo*. The problem this raises concerns the existence of universals. Properties, propositions, numbers, sets and mathematical objects are plausibly construed as abstract objects. While the distinction between concrete and abstract objects is, like most such fundamental distinctions in philosophy, quite difficult to draw precisely, this much at least seems clear: Abstract objects cannot possibly enter into a causal relation, whole concrete objects possibly can. Construed as abstract objects, then, properties such as colors are causally inert. Assume for purposes of illustration that the bullfighter's red cape, not the motion of the cape, causes the bull to charge. It isn't the abstract universal *redness* that arouses the bull, but its instance or instantiation in the cape.

Now, abstract objects are thought to exist necessarily—of logical necessity. Properties, propositions and the like exist in all possible worlds. So these propositions exist in all possible worlds:

(11) Necessarily, 13 is prime.
(12) Necessarily, blue is a color.
(13) Necessarily, anything colored is extended.

But it follows from these that the number 13, and the properties *being prime, being blue, and being a color* also exist in all possible worlds. But if only God exists necessarily, then surely abstracta cannot. As an argument:

(14) Necessarily, necessary objects have no cause (they exist *a se*).

---

[40]For the argument, see Paul Copan and William Lane Craig, *Creation Out of Nothing: A Biblical, Philosophical, and Scientific Exploration* (Grand Rapids: Baker, 2004), pp. 167-73.

(15) Necessarily, if abstract objects exist, then they are necessary objects.

(16) Therefore, necessarily, if abstract objects exist, then they have no cause (they exist *a se*).

(17) But only God exists necessarily, *a se*.

(18) Therefore, necessarily, abstract objects are not necessary.

(19) Therefore, necessarily, abstract objects do not exist.

The claim that abstract objects *do* exist we may call Platonism. So the claim of the theological argument we are considering is quite strong: Platonism is *necessarily* false. That is, properties are not universals at all.

Copan and Craig canvass alternatives to Platonism: nominalism, modified absolute creationism, fictionalism and conceptualism, but "are not prepared to pronounce judgment" as to which alternative is preferable for the theist.[41] The details need not concern us here, for it seems to me that the argument they offered trades on a modal equivocation. There are, in fact, several varieties of necessity, logical and metaphysical being the salient varieties here. It strikes me that the necessity in premise (17) is metaphysical, whereas the necessity in the other premises is logical. The conceptual jungle becomes thick rather quickly here, but in brief, here is my response. Any entity that is logically necessary exists in all logically possible worlds. However, if nothing metaphysically necessary existed, then nothing at all would exist, not even logically possible worlds. Consequently, possible worlds, and the necessary entities they contain, radically depend upon the existence of a metaphysically necessary being, God. God does not depend on logically necessary entities. However, given that something metaphysically necessary exists—God, then a whole lot of logically necessary things also exist in dependence on God.

Pace my friends Paul Copan and Bill Craig, I cannot see how, for example, the identity relation, or the property of God's being identical to himself, could be a useful fiction, or a creation of God's, or an antecedent concept in God's mind. And there are a number of other properties that seem necessarily true of God and necessarily logically prior to God's conceptualization of them or creation of them.[42] I would claim

[41]Ibid., pp. 173-95.
[42]In his 1980 Aquinas lecture at Marquette University, Alvin Plantinga fleshed out the argu-

that these logical necessities are grounded in the nature of being itself: once some thing has being, very many logically necessary things also do. God could not have being without the logical necessity of such things as properties, relations and propositions. But again, the dependence is asymmetrical: the logical necessities depend upon the existence of a metaphysically necessary being. Does this threaten God's absolute sovereignty or independence? No, not by my lights, because being itself entails the logical necessities. One might as well ask if God's sovereignty or independence is threatened by the fact that he is not voluntarily a trinity.

Copan and Craig have one other argument, which to my mind is a straw man. Discussing only the existence of mathematical sets, they show the unimaginably large number of sets that would exist if Platonism about numbers were true. They say, "The physical universe, which has been created by God, is an infinitesimal triviality utterly dwarfed by the unspeakable quantity of uncreated beings."[43] But just where is the supposed difficulty? One should not simply count up everything like this; surely concrete entities—the physical universe, together, I'd add, with the spiritual realm of angels—represent a set of beings clearly distinct from the set of abstract entities. Specially created by God, and able to stand in causal relations, *concreta* cannot be meaningfully compared with *abstracta* as Copan and Craig do—it's worse than comparing apples and carburetors.

Substances, essences and natures. The philosophical analysis of substance has a long and somewhat spotty history, beginning with Aristotle's *Categories* and *Metaphysics.* Aristotle himself is a source of some of this confusion. Notoriously, he seems to have a different conception of substance in his *Categories* than in his later *Metaphysics.* Specifically, in *Categories,* substance belongs to a category composed, roughly, of those things that exist in ontological independence of other things of the same sort. This notion is generally called *primary substance* or *first sub-*

---

ment: *Does God Have a Nature?* (Milwaukee: Marquette University Press, 1980). Copan and Craig interact with Plantinga, but in my view their critique fails due to the modal confusion I suggest in the text.
[43]Copan and Craig, *Creation Out of Nothing,* p. 173.

stance and refers to individuals. The Aristotelian ontology sees first substances as hylomorphic compositions—composites of form and matter. A substance is made up of various sorts of constituents: for example, its nature (or essence), which constitutes the substance as a member of a particular natural kind; its accidental properties, which inhere in the substance but do not exist independently of it; and its stuff or matter. In *Metaphysics,* however, Aristotle introduces another concept of substance, namely, that which different individual members of a natural kind share in common. This notion is generally called *second substance* and refers to a universal, a nature. Aristotle uses the same word, *ousia,* for both.

In contemporary ontology there are those who deny that there are substances; rather, there are things that are bundles of properties with no essential principle of unity or individuation. But a significant number of ontologists believe that a complete assay of the world must include substances in addition to properties and relations.[44] Roughly, the *classical view* is that a substance is an individual or particular that bears properties, that itself is not "had" by anything else, that persists through time, may have inseparable parts but is not composed of separable parts, and has a nature (natural kind essence) that is the principle of unity of its properties.[45] (This concept of substance is akin to Aristotle's primary substance, while the nature or kind essence is his second substance.) Most of the substances, thus understood, that we encounter in day-to-day life are material things, to the point that the common view held by most people takes substance as "stuff," the material *out of which* something is made, rather than as a thing—especially an immaterial or spiritual thing. On the common view, chemical elements are the paradigm cases of substances. It is important to realize, however, that the classical view took living organisms—individual human beings, butterflies, dogs, oak trees—as the paradigm cases of substances. In fact,

---

[44]See, for example, Hoffman and Rosenkrantz, *Substance: Its Nature and Existence;* Lowe, *Possibility of Metaphysics;* J. P. Moreland and William Lane Craig, *Philosophical Foundations for a Christian Worldview* (Downers Grove, Ill.: InterVarsity Press, 2003), chap. 10.

[45]For a much fuller discussion and defense of definitions similar to what I give below, see J. P. Moreland, *The Recalcitrant* Imago Dei: *Human Persons and the Failure of Naturalism* (London: SCM Press, 2009), pp. 104-8.

for centuries, most theologians held that all persons—human, angelic and divine—were spiritual substances. As Boethius (ca. A.D. 480-524) said, "A person is an individual substance with a rational nature."[46]

In recent years, belief in substances in general and spiritual substances in particular has fallen on hard times, even among many Christian thinkers. The current rejection of the reality of substances, especially as applied to persons, is usually the result of a significant error about the nature of a substance. Often today a substance is mistakenly taken to be a static, inert entity, incapable of entering into significant relationships. But there is nothing in the classical conception of substance that prevents persons (whether human or divine) from being substances even while strongly emphasizing the importance of relationships in our understanding of persons. There's more to say on the nature of persons as substances, but I'll save it for chapter eight.

Here, I'll only describe certain features of the classical view. But since this view has been so important throughout the history of philosophy, getting clear on what it entails is a most worthwhile endeavor, especially since much confusion rests on a misunderstanding of the traditional position.

1. Property possession. Substances are more basic than properties, and "own" their properties. It makes sense to ask of a property, "What has that property?" but it does not make sense to ask of a substance, "What has that substance?" Properties are in substances, but substances are basic in that they are not in or had by things more basic than them.

2. Unity and wholeness at a time. A substance is a whole, and as such, is a unity of properties, parts and capacities. First, a substance is a unity of properties that come together in groups, not individually, and that exhibit a deeper unity of properties than, say, the properties of a heap of salt. Second, a substance is also a unity of parts (either separable or inseparable). The difference between a property and a part is this: a property is a universal that would still exist even if a substance having it were extinguished from being, whereas a part is a particular that would not survive if a substance having it were extinguished.

---

[46]Boethius *Contra Eutyches and Nestorius* 3.

Finally, a substance is a unity of capacities (potentialities, dispositions, tendencies).[47] *Counterfactual statements* are true of substances in virtue of their capacities, dispositions and powers. For example, if the salt in this salt shaker were to be put in a glass of water, then it would dissolve. Such counterfactuals are explained by saying that a substance has a set of capacities that are true of it even though they are not actualized. The salt has the capacity of solubility while in the saltshaker.

A substance's ultimate capacities are possessed by it solely in virtue of the substance belonging to its natural kind. We've already noticed that substances fall into natural kinds: for example, the class of dogs, humans and so forth. This can be explained by saying that each member of a natural kind has the very same *nature.* A substance's nature includes its ordered structural unity of ultimate capacities. A substance cannot change in its ultimate capacities; that is, it cannot lose its ultimate nature and continue to exist. For example, Tim's ultimate capacities are his because he has a specific nature—*humanness*—that explains why he is a member of the *natural kind* "human." Tim may change his skin color from exposure to the sun and still exist, but if he loses his *humanness,* his inner nature of ultimate capacities that constitutes being human, then he ceases to exist.

A nature is roughly equivalent to an *essence;* the exception, when 'essence' is picking out an *individual essence* that is unique to a certain particular, might lead us to speak more perspicuously of *natures* and *kind-essences.* A thing's kind-essence provides the deepest, most informative answer to the question "What kind of thing is this?"

That these points about first- and higher-order capacities and natures are of great practical importance can be seen, for example, in this claim by ethicist Robert Wennberg:

> When an individual becomes permanently unconscious, the *person* has passed out of existence, even if biological life continues. There cannot

---

[47]Increased philosophical attention is being paid to the concept of dispositional properties, capacities and powers. See Alexander Bird, *Nature's Metaphysics: Laws and Properties* (Oxford: Oxford University Press, 2007), for an account that regards dispositional properties as metaphysically necessary, and Walter Schultz, "Dispositions, Capacities and Powers," *Philosophia Christi* 11 (2009): 321-38, for an account that grounds such properties in God's actions in a version of *creatio continuans.*

be a person where there is neither the capacity for having mental states nor even the potentiality for developing that capacity.[48]

According to Wennberg, taking the life of a permanently unconscious individual with biological life may be permissible because there is no person made in the image of God that is present.

But Wennberg's claims rest on a confusion between first- and higher-order capacities. A fetus or a permanently unconscious individual may not have the first-order capacities of consciousness, but that does not mean they lack the second-order capacity to have this first-order capacity again if certain things happen (normal development for the fetus; medical or miraculous healing for the unconscious patient). Indeed, if one is a human person, then part of one's very essence is the possession of higher-order capacities for consciousness regardless of what may be the case with respect to one's first-order capacities.

3. Identity and absolute sameness through change. A substance is a *continuant* that remains the same through change. In fact, a *change* can be understood as the gaining or losing of a property by a substance at or throughout a period of time. A substance regularly loses old separable parts, properties and lower-order capacities and gains new ones. But the substance itself underlies this change and remains the same through it. Events are different. A long event like a baseball game has temporal parts and, in fact, is the sum of its temporal parts. A baseball game is a sum of nine innings, and each inning is a temporal part of the game. By contrast, substances do not have temporal parts; they are fully present at every moment of their existence.

4. Law and lawlike change. As a substance like an acorn grows, it changes through time. These changes are law-like. That is, each new stage of development and growth comes to be and replaces older stages in repeatable, nonrandom, law-like ways. These law-like changes are grounded in a substance's nature. The acorn changes in specific ways because of the dynamic inherent capacities latent within its nature as an oak. Each natural kind of thing will have its own type of law-like

---

[48]Robert Wennberg, *Terminal Choices: Euthanasia, Suicide, and the Right to Die* (Grand Rapids: Eerdmans, 1989), p. 159.

changes that are normal for members of that kind, and these changes are grounded in the nature of substances of that kind.

Moreover, this nature sets limits to change. If a substance were to violate these limits, the substance would no longer exist. For example, as a caterpillar changes into an adult butterfly, the organism's inner nature specifies the precise sequence of stages the organism can undergo in the process of growth. The butterfly is numerically identical to the organism that was the caterpillar. But if, *per impossibile,* if the caterpillar turned into a fish, we would not say that the caterpillar still existed as a fish; rather, we would say that the caterpillar ceased to be and a fish came to be. Thus, the lawlike changes that are grounded in a substance's nature (1) specify the ordered sequence of change that will occur in the process of maturation; and (2) set limits to the kind of change a substance can undergo and still be counted as a member of its kind.

5. Final causality. The traditional doctrine of substance contrasts *efficient, material, formal* and *final causes.* An efficient cause is that *by means of which* an effect takes place; for example, when one billiard ball hits and moves another, the first ball is the efficient cause of the motion. A material cause is that *out of which* something is made, the matter or "stuff" of which something is made; for example, the clay or bronze out of which the statue is made. A formal cause is that *in accordance with which* something is made; it is the blueprint, the archetype, the essence of a thing; for example, the blueprint of a house, or the humanness of Tim. A final cause is that *for the sake of which* an effect or change is produced; for example, the switch is pushed, closing the circuit, for the sake of turning on the light; the eye functions for the sake of aiding one to see. Many advocates of the traditional view hold that an individual substance has, within its nature (formal cause), an innate, immanent tendency (final cause) to realize fully the potentialities within its nature. An acorn changes "in order to" realize a mature oak nature; a fetus grows with the end in view of actualizing its potentialities grounded in human nature.

However, the doctrine of final causality is viewed by many these days to be outdated and unscientific. Instead, it is often thought that efficient and material causes are all that is needed to explain a substance's change; for example, explaining an acorn's growth only requires citing the chemical parts and processes in the acorn, together with whatever biological laws supervene on those parts and processes. We cannot evaluate this claim here, but it should be pointed out that the notions of formal and final causes are primarily philosophical, and arguments for and against them are beyond the scope of science.

SUMMARY AND CONCLUSIONS

Now, this somewhat lengthy journey through the classical view of substances, natures and essences, dispositions, capacities and powers, the four causes, and the like, has a point beyond its clear and distinct intrinsic historical interest! That is, in order to account for the world as depicted in Scripture and in the creeds, some ontology very similar to that described is required. For the world of a Christian worldview is one containing particulars that may be grouped into kinds according to the essential properties of the natures they share, which is best explained by taking properties as abstract universals. It is a world in which humans share a nature, *humanness;* they have certain (first- and second-order) capacities grounded in that nature, and it is that nature, not legal fiat or cultural consensus, in virtue of which they are human. Such a metaphysic, which is thoroughly biblical, makes a hugely important difference in many moral decisions facing us today.

Additionally, it is in virtue of shared human nature that certain actions, attitudes or lifestyles of individuals may be judged to be inimical to true flourishing, and others as contributory or essential to flourishing. The "laid-back pluralism of the post-modern, that heterogenous range of lifestyles and language games which has renounced the nostalgic urge to totalize and legitimate itself,"[49] is a house of mirrors. There is a truth of the matter about human nature.

It is also a world in which human capacities for apprehending the external world around us are grounded in our ability to abstract from particulars the properties and natures of things, and so to make representations in art and literature, to pursue science and technology, and

---

[49]Terry Eagleton, "Awakening from Modernity," *Times Literary Supplement,* February 20, 1987, p. 194.

to experience the awe and wonder of a magnificent, orderly, beautiful world, one which at the same time is complex beyond comprehension, yet not so much as to be totally random and chaotic.

We were made for such a world as this, at least until in our resurrected bodies we enter the new heavens and the new earth. Our metaphysics must do justice to such a vision of our place in the universe and in God's program.

6

What Do I Know?

Epistemology

My people are destroyed from lack of knowledge.

Yahweh (Hos 4:6)

All men by nature desire to know.

Aristotle

*Our wisdom, in so far as it ought to be deemed true
and solid wisdom, consists almost entirely of two parts:
the knowledge of God and of ourselves.*

John Calvin

It's intriguing to observe that both Aristotle and Calvin opened major works with aphorisms on knowledge. It's also intriguing to note that as I write this, *The New York Times Guide to Essential Knowledge: A Desk Reference for the Curious Mind,* Revised and Expanded Second Edition, is about number 5000 on Amazon.com's sales ranking. (Also intriguing is the implicit question: what essential knowledge was left out of the first edition?)

Certainly, we think knowledge is very important in daily life. We trust a dentist and not a mechanic to treat a toothache because of the dentist's knowledge—even though the mechanic has lots of cool tools.

Similarly for lawyers, doctors and accountants. Knowledge is valuable; it counts for a lot.

Yet today as perhaps never before in history the notion of knowledge is suspect. Of course skepticism has a long history, from Pyrrho of Elis (360-270 B.C.) and Carneades (241-129 B.C.) of the "New" Academy, through the revival of Pyrrhonism in early modern philosophy. But in our day it's undoubtedly the influence of philosophical postmodernism that calls knowledge claims into question. The situation is now such that in many corners of academia, as well as in many realms of discourse in contemporary culture, any claim to know something is regarded as worse than mistaken—it is downright arrogant and intolerant.

Epistemology takes these questions head-on, asking what knowledge is, whether or not we can know anything (or what sorts of things can be known), and how we know them.

ISSUES AND OPTIONS

As always in philosophy, we must begin by defining concepts, and we begin that task by thinking about the prephilosophical, ordinary-language use of a term. We use 'knowledge' (and related verbal forms) in ways that indicate that we know (or, at least, think that we know) a lot of things. We make knowledge claims about a lot of things:

- Our immediate surroundings ("It's getting warm in here.")

- Our sensations ("This Coke tastes flat.")

- Our own mental states ("I'm really glad I got tickets to that concert.")

- Mental states of others ("She thinks I'm a real geek.")

- Facts about the world ("Paris, France, is larger than Paris, Texas.")

- Scientific facts ("Everything is made up of atoms, which are too small to see.")

- The past ("In 1492 Columbus sailed the ocean blue.")

- The future ("Tomorrow will be even hotter than today.")

- Mathematics ("7 + 5 = 12")

- Conceptual truths ("Triangles have three sides.")

- Moral truths ("It is always wrong for anyone to torture babies for fun.")
- Religious truths ("Jesus Christ is fully God and fully man.")

Of course, some might dispute whether any of these statements actually constitute knowledge, and it is possible that in some cases we might be mistaken, but examples like these form a good part of what we commonly take ourselves as knowing. Examples of these sorts are called *propositional knowledge;* each example could be preceded by "I know *that* . . ." followed by the respective proposition.

But we use 'knowledge' and make knowledge claims in other senses as well:

- Persons ("I know Jane; she couldn't possibly have cheated on that test.")
- Places ("I know Paris well; I lived there for four years.")
- Bodies of work ("Prof. Green really knows Shakespeare.")

Such examples of knowing someone or something directly we call *knowledge by acquaintance.* Almost certainly, knowledge by acquaintance will involve some propositional knowledge, but it is doubtful that all acquaintance knowledge can be reduced to propositions. At least introspectively, *knowing Jane* has a different "feel" than *knowing that the new girl is named Jane.*

There's a further sense in which we claim knowledge:

- Skills ("She knows how to play the oboe.")
- Abilities ("Tom knows how to read Hebrew, but he can't speak it.")

Such know-how is called *skill knowledge,* and while it too involves some propositional knowledge, skill knowledge is not reducible to knowledge of propositions.

And there is at least one further sense in which 'knowledge' is commonly used:

- A theoretical body of knowledge ("Any theory of origins must comport well with the best scientific knowledge.")

It's pretty clear that this body of knowledge is propositional, but it's equally clear that no single person has such knowledge in her head. So we can use 'knowledge' to refer to the collective body of knowledge of a special community, but it's primarily knowledge claims of individuals that concern epistemologists.

Now, for various reasons, propositional knowledge has loomed large in epistemology. One might wonder whether propositional knowledge has been elevated beyond its importance; more on this below. Still, we can accept provisionally that our interest is in propositional knowledge as illustrated by the first set of examples. (Hereafter I'll simply refer to 'knowledge,' and distinguish skill-knowledge and knowledge by acquaintance when necessary.) How do we define such knowledge?

The so-called Traditional Analysis of Knowledge (TAK) defines knowledge as *justified true belief:* K = JTB.[1] Hints of TAK are found as far back as Plato's suggestion that knowledge consists in true belief for which one can give a *logos,* a rational account (*Theaetetus* 201c-210b). And while Plato himself finally rejects this in favor of a theory of one's intellectual apprehension of the Forms, the TAK was pretty much the standard view until Edmund Gettier's notorious paper published in 1963, "Is Justified True Belief Knowledge?"[2] The paper launched a cottage industry of creating "Gettier problems" where, intuitively, we would say the believer, although holding a justified true belief, only got to the truth "by luck," and so does not have knowledge.[3] In response, many philosophers have cited the need for a "fourth condition," K = JTB + something to rule out Gettier cases. But no agreement on the fourth condition has been reached.

Other characterizations, definitions or analyses of knowledge have been offered in recent years. *Virtue epistemology* focuses on cognitive acts motivated by intellectual virtue, where the intellectual virtues are dispositions such as attentiveness, discernment, intellectual honesty and so forth. Linda Zagzebski, a prominent virtue epistemologist, defines knowledge as "a state of cognitive contact with reality arising out of acts of intellectual virtue."[4]

---

[1]See, for example, Richard Feldman, *Epistemology* (Upper Saddle River, N.J.: Prentice-Hall, 2003), pp. 8-24.

[2]Edmund Gettier, "Is Justified True Belief Knowledge?" *Analysis* 23 (1963): 121-23.

[3]I won't belabor this by citing examples; they are amply and creatively illustrated in any introductory epistemology textbook.

[4]Linda Trinkaus Zagzebski, *Virtues of the Mind* (New York: Cambridge University Press, 1996), pp. 270-71.

Dallas Willard proposes an "initial description" of knowledge as "the capacity *to represent a respective subject matter as it is, on an appropriate basis of thought and/or experience.*"[5] Somewhat idiosyncratically, Willard does not think knowledge entails belief; you can know something without believing it.

Other recent characterizations incorporate a "sensitivity principle," which says that we only know a proposition if we wouldn't believe it if it were false, or a "safety principle," which says (roughly) that we can only know what wouldn't be false if we were to believe it. And then there are contextualist characterizations of knowledge. We cannot linger in the very interesting conceptual territory opened by these approaches; I mention them only to indicate that the field of epistemology (as well as meta-epistemology) is alive and robust.

What all these differing characterizations or analyses have in common, though, is the notion that for a cognitive state to count as knowledge, it must be *justified*. There must be something associated with the (production of the) cognitive state that ties it to or indicates its truth in an appropriate way. Lucky guesses, gamblers' hunches, horoscopes and the like just don't cut it as justifiers. While this rough idea of justification seems commonsensical, the debate in the last several decades in epistemology has swirled around two features of justification, which I'll call its *structure* and its *"location"* (the reason for the scare quotes will become apparent below). It is these two issues that I want to consider in most of the remainder this chapter, as it seems to me that a Christian worldview has major implications for these two.[6]

We can begin to explore these issues by framing them as two pairs of options. One pair, having to do with the structure of justification, explores how beliefs are related to other beliefs and (or if) beliefs are related to nonpropositional evidence. The two options here are *coherentism* and *foundationalism*. The other pair, having to do with the "location" of justification, focuses on the "access requirement"—whether or

[5]Dallas Willard, "Knowledge and Naturalism," in *Naturalism: A Critical Analysis*, ed. William Lane Craig and J. P. Moreland (New York: Routledge, 2000), p. 31; italics his.

[6]Of course, the other two ingredients of TAK are not unimportant. The nature of *belief* involves issues in philosophy of mind, and the nature of *truth* is at its core a metaphysical concern.

not, and to what extent, a person must have cognitive access to the reasons or evidence that confer justification on a belief in order to claim the belief constitutes knowledge. Here the options are *internalism* and *externalism*.

CHRISTIAN WORLDVIEW IMPLICATIONS

Most of the remainder of this chapter will explore implications of a Christian worldview for these two debates about justification. I'll start off, though, with some reflections on implications for the skeptical problem mentioned at the beginning of the chapter.

Skepticism. As I said earlier, skepticism has a long history in Western philosophy, and in our day has been sympathetically presented by such philosophers as Richard Popkin and Barry Stroud.[7] Skeptical conclusions are often motivated by considering "Descartes's Demon" or the "Brain in a Vat" scenario (BIV). (While in earlier and more innocent times I often had difficulty getting students to take BIV seriously, the film *The Matrix* changed all that. The disturbing images of human "coppertops," bodies suspended in a chemical bath, kept alive through nutrient infusions, while their conscious experiences were generated by a vast computer program—the Matrix—connected to their brains by electrodes, have made BIV a genuine problem for many students.) More subtle skeptical challenges come from considerations of our perceptions of secondary qualities such as color, and the doubt that such perceptual experiences throw on justification of perceptual beliefs in general.[8]

Roughly, skepticism can be construed either as skepticism about knowledge ("You can't know anything") or as skepticism about justification ("You can never have good enough reason to claim to know"). The former version, sometimes classified as Academic skepticism (after Carneades' teaching in the late Platonic Academy) can be shown to be

---

[7]See, among their other works, Richard H. Popkin, *The History of Scepticism from Savonarola to Bayle* (Oxford: Oxford University Press, 2003); and Barry Stroud, *The Significance of Philosophical Scepticism* (Oxford: Oxford University Press, 1984).

[8]Barry Stroud, *The Quest for Reality: Subjectivism & the Metaphysics of Colour* (Oxford: Oxford University Press, 1994), is one such example.

self-defeating: if true, then we couldn't know that we can't know.[9] The
second version is more akin to Pyrrho's skepticism and is much slip-
perier to deal with. Both forms offer intriguing challenges to traditional epistemology, dealing with which can be most enlightening.[10]
Here, though, I want to point in another direction.

Roderick Chisholm showed that we can approach the general epistemological problem either as methodists or as particularists.[11] Methodists (not the Protestant denominational kind) search for a method
that we can be sure will deliver knowledge, and then simply employ
that method in our theorizing. However, in order to know what method
works, we need first to have a criterion to know what constitutes knowledge, and so which methods deliver knowledge. But that means we
can't start with methods after all. Instead, said Chisholm, we must start
with particular cases where we all would agree that we do indeed have
knowledge, and then build up our epistemological method from those
particular cases—we must, that is, be particularists.

This just seems right to many epistemologists. I really do take myself
to know a great many things (as in the list above). And I have greater
confidence in my belief that I do know these things than I have in the
soundness of the skeptical arguments that I *don't* know them, or in attempts to deliver skepticism a once-for-all, knock-down blow. To say it
differently, if we begin epistemology by trying to defeat skepticism, we
may never get beyond that. But if we begin with clear cases where we
do seem to know, we can postpone dealing with skepticism until we
have constructed a satisfactory epistemology, at which point we'll have
the tools to deal more effectively with the skeptical challenge.

Here a Christian worldview should play a major role as the Christian
philosopher does epistemology. For Christianity, as we noted in an earlier chapter, is a knowledge tradition, not merely a belief (or opinion or
preference) tradition. Christians through the ages, and their Jewish an-

---

[9]This is the version that St. Augustine attacks in *Contra academicos*. See *Against the Academicians and The Teacher*, trans. Peter King (Indianapolis: Hackett, 1995).
[10]See John Greco, *Putting Skeptics in Their Place: The Nature of Skeptical Arguments and Their Role
in Philosophical Inquiry* (New York: Cambridge University Press, 2000).
[11]Roderick Chisholm, *The Problem of the Criterion* (Milwaukee: Marquette University Press,
1973).

cestors, claimed knowledge. This should come as no surprise, since the Old and New Testaments are filled with assertions about knowledge. The Hebrew words for 'know' and 'knowledge' occur over one thousand times (in the literal sense) in the Old Testament, and the Greek words about the same number in the much shorter New Testament. And those figures don't include synonymous expressions like "I see that . . ." Many of the occurrences are quite unremarkable, indicating propositional knowledge of empirical facts (Gen 12:11; Acts 2:22[12]). Other occurrences relate to knowledge of moral facts (Prov 10:23; Eph 5:5). Still others have to do with knowledge of God, God's will or other spiritual realities (Gen 15:8-9; Is 49:26; Mt 13:11; 1 Cor 8:4). Sometimes individuals—or the readers of the text—are told that the author is making an argument or citing evidence *for the express purpose of imparting knowledge* (1 Jn 5:13) or *grounding belief* (Jn 20:31). Clearly, the authors of Scripture believed knowledge was possible. And so did Jesus (for example, Mt 16:2-3; Jn 7:17).

So I take it that skepticism of either sort is not an option for the Christian who is doing epistemology from within a Christian worldview. But there are three warnings I want to sound at this point. First, this is not to say that Christian philosophers should ignore challenges put forward by skeptics, especially when those challenges have created serious grounds of doubt for someone and are not mere clever intellectual puzzles. Second, I want to stress that the fact that even though I think Christians should be particularists who can make legitimate knowledge claims even without a fully-developed bomb-proof epistemology, this does not warrant an intellectual arrogance, or an unwillingness to look seriously at the evidence offered for (almost) any contrary claim.

Third, Christian particularism should not blur the distinctions between certainty, confidence and belief. Here's what I have in mind. Certainty is the property you attach to a true proposition about which you could not possibly be mistaken. Some mathematical and logical

---

[12]I will only cite one or two examples in each category, although dozens could be listed. Note that occasionally various English translations will employ a word other than "know" or its cognates for the respective Hebrew and Greek words.

truths are certain; we can know them *certainly*. For example, I cannot be mistaken in my belief that 7 + 5 = 12, that nothing can violate the law of noncontradiction, or that there could not be a green chocolate middle-C.[13] I cannot rationally doubt such things. However, the stock of propositions about which I can have certainty is not all that large; most of the really interesting things that I believe in life are such that I recognize that I *could* possibly be wrong about them. I claim to know that Mt. Everest is 29,035 feet in elevation, and I have good reasons to support that (I've read several reports about how that figure was arrived at)—but I could be wrong (for example, if errors were made in calculating the value of the equipotential geoidal surface directly below the summit of Everest).

So certainty is not required for knowledge. Knowledge is compatible with a measure of doubt. And this accords with Scripture, where we find texts such as Ephesians 5:5 which speak of "knowing with certainty" (NASB). We may think of this in terms of degrees of confidence. I have full confidence in something of which I'm certain, and a complete lack of confidence in something I know to be false. But in between my confidence varies *in proportion to the kinds and amount of evidence*[14] I have to support the belief. Say I ask a friend, "What is twenty-seven times thirteen?" and he immediately answers, "Three hundred fifty-one." I happen to know that he's good at math, so my belief that the answer is correct has some evidence. But his answer came rather too quickly, so I have some real doubt. So I do the math: *27 x 10 is 270; 27 x 3 is, well, 25 x 3, 75, plus 2 x 3, 6; so the answer is 270 + 75 + 6, or 351.* Clearly, having worked it out myself, I have stronger evidence and more confidence in the answer. And if, in addition, I work out the product on a trustworthy calculator, my degree of confidence is even higher, and my doubts are fewer.

My degree of confidence, then, will be inversely proportional to my degree of doubt. But since I can't be certain about everything I believe,

---

[13]I'm speaking of the tone, not the piano key (which, however oddly, might be replaced by some sort of strange confection).

[14]Here I'm using 'evidence' in a very loose sense to include other beliefs, arguments, physical evidence, perception, testimony, memory, introspection, etc.

it follows that I may have doubts—some stronger, some weaker—about most of my beliefs. *Doubt then is neither the opposite of belief nor the absence of belief, but rather an accompaniment of all but certain beliefs.* That's why it makes sense for the father of the epileptic boy to say to Jesus, "I do believe, but help me not to doubt" (Mk 9:24 NLT).

So it seems, on reflection, that the Christian philosopher will do epistemology as a particularist believing that knowledge is possible. She will not let the presence of doubt or the lack of certainty lead to skepticism, nor her confidence that she does have some knowledge lead to arrogance about all her beliefs.

The structure of justification. This brings us to questions about justification. People believe things for reasons; indeed, a belief without a reason is, by definition, unreasonable. The justification condition requires that the reason must meet a certain standard if the belief is to count as knowledge, even if true. The intuition is that even true beliefs must be properly grounded.

The obvious question about the structure of justification is whether it is best represented by *coherentism* or *foundationalism*. (Each has, of course, a number of subspecies, which for my purposes I can largely ignore.)

Coherentism. Let the term *noetic structure* refer to the ensemble of all of a person's beliefs together with the relations that hold between those beliefs. Coherentism as a theory of justification amounts to the claim that a proper noetic structure is one in which all beliefs cohere with other beliefs in a proper, acceptable way.

It is clear that we hold a great many of our beliefs because we hold other beliefs; that is, the reason we believe p is that we believe q and r and $s,$ and we believe that q and r and s entail $p.$ For example, if we believe that Jim is either in his apartment or at the library, and we come to believe that he is not in his apartment, then we believe he is at the library. We believe that smoking causes lung cancer because we believe that the statistical correlation between smokers and lung cancer victims is far too high to be mere coincidence, or perhaps just because we believe that the surgeon general wouldn't lie about something like that. Or we believe that even though that person at the far table in the restaurant looks just like Jane, it isn't her, because we believe she left for

Paris on Saturday, and no one can be in two places at once. These are all examples of beliefs that cohere with other beliefs: they are based on or fit with other beliefs, and they do so in the right kind of way, a way that is logically correct, so that if the other beliefs are true, then so is the new belief.

While I think that coherence is an important feature in a noetic structure, I don't think that it is an adequate theory of justification. Exploring two questions will bring this out. First, is coherence sufficient to indicate the truth of the beliefs? Second, is coherence with other beliefs the only permissible relation between beliefs in a proper noetic structure?

Is coherence sufficient to indicate the truth of beliefs in a noetic structure? No. Any well-written novel will contain a coherent system of propositions (or else it just doesn't "hang together"). But surely someone who believes all the propositions contained in a good novel will hold many beliefs that don't match up with the real world, no matter how coherent the beliefs are. In fact, there are an infinite number of fully coherent belief systems, only one of which corresponds to—accurately represents—reality. So coherence alone is insufficient to indicate truth.

Second, is coherence the only permissible relation in a proper noetic structure? Again, the answer is no. But to explain the negative answer, we need to look more closely at the notion of coherence. All parties agree that coherence involves at least logical consistency. That is, a set of beliefs does not cohere if two (or more) of them are contrary or contradictory. Beyond that, there are a number of ways to understand the coherence requirement.

One way would be that if a belief coheres with a set of previously accepted beliefs, then that positive coherence confers justification. On the other hand, if a belief fails to cohere with an accepted set, then that dis-coherence results in the belief being unjustified. But these two notions are not equivalent, so which one is the right way to conceive of the coherence requirement?

One might take the view that coherence is linear; that is, all the beliefs in a coherent set could be lined up in a chain with each belief being supported by one (or perhaps a very few) other belief(s). Such a system will be circular, since every belief must be supported by another belief, but such circularity might not be too troubling, provided the circle is large enough. On the other hand, one might view coherence as holistic, where each belief is supported by all (or perhaps a very great number) of other beliefs, so that the result is not a circular chain but a crosshatched web of mutually supporting beliefs. There is something right about both linear and holistic coherentism; indeed, I think that both notions play a role in justification, and I'll return to these ideas below. For now, though, the question is whether coherentism is the correct overall view of the structure of justification.

Whether positive or negative, linear or holistic, coherentism requires beliefs to be justified by their relation(s) to other beliefs. But it certainly seems that we hold a number of beliefs—and regard them as justified— that do not depend on other beliefs. When you step outside and see a high-contrast pattern of light and shadow and feel warmth on one side of your face, you simply believe the sun is shining. It would be far-fetched in the extreme to say you infer that the sun is shining, but even if you did infer that conclusion, it seems you would infer it from your sensory experiences and not from other beliefs. In fact, if all beliefs had to be based solely on other beliefs, it is hard to see how we could ever believe the deliverances of sensory experiences, of memory, or of intro-spective awareness or of rational intuition, to mention just a few of the main sources of beliefs. A good number of the beliefs you now hold are not after all based on other beliefs, but are based on nondoxastic (i.e., nonbelief) evidence. So if coherentism is true, then none of those be-liefs can be justified. But clearly that is not the case, so coherentism must be false.

But arguably there is another sense in which a form of coherentism is the correct view of justification, and that's the sense found in various forms of postmodernism. In Jean-François Lyotard's famous phrase, postmodernism is "incredulity towards metanarrative."[15] Lyotard means, in effect, that there is no objective standard, no "supreme court,"

---

[15]Jean-François Lyotard, *The Postmodern Condition: A Report on Knowledge* (Minneapolis: University of Minnesota Press, 1984), p. xxiv.

to which all rational people can appeal to adjudicate disagreements about reality. So truth is not determined by its correspondence to reality, but by various social constructions devised for different purposes. Every culture has its own "language game" (and sometimes more than one), which describes reality very differently from other language games. But since we cannot get outside our cultural-linguistic conditioning, we cannot adjudicate between differing views of reality found in different language games. We've all heard Stanley Fish claim that various "interpretive communities" determine their own truth, and Richard Rorty says that truth is what his peers will let him get away with saying.

So the postmodern consensus is a sort of coherentism, where "justification" is coherence with the beliefs of a cultural-linguistic community, with saying things in ways that are not objectionable to one's own community.

In addition to the same doubts that I raised about philosophical coherentism, I have even graver doubts about whether postmodern coherentism is compatible with a Christian worldview. For example, if there is no objective truth, what becomes of a claim such as "Jesus is Lord"? According to postmodern theologian Philip Kenneson, it is meaningless to say that such a claim is objectively true:

> Truth becomes internal to a web of beliefs; there is no standard of truth independent of a set of beliefs and practices. . . . Under the new paradigm, this sentence translates into something like "'Jesus is Lord' is consistent with the convictions and actions of Christians, but not with those of others." . . . It simply does not make sense to think of reality as it is in itself, apart from human judgments.[16]

It would seem to follow straightforwardly that in those cultural-linguistic communities that reject a Christian worldview, and so judge "Jesus is Lord" to be false, it would be simply wrong for a missionary

---

[16]Philip D. Kenneson, "There's No Such Thing as Objective Truth, and It's a Good Thing, Too," in *Christian Apologetics in the Postmodern World*, ed. Timothy R. Phillips and Dennis L. Okholm (Downers Grove, Ill.: InterVarsity Press, 1995), pp. 163-64. Surely it *does* make sense to think of reality as it was in itself before the creation of Adam, for surely God himself knew that structure.

to claim that Jesus is the way, the truth and the life. So what, one wonders, becomes of the Lord's command to go into all the world and preach the good news? To his credit, as a Christian, of course Kenneson is committed to evangelism. "We will be passionately evangelistic, trying to persuade others to our beliefs because if they believe what we believe, they will see what we see; and the facts to which we point in order to support our interpretations will be as obvious to them as they are to us."[17] But to believe something just is to believe that it is *true*. Unless the truth of the matter enters in, it is hard to understand what we are trying to persuade someone *of*. Why we should want someone to believe what we believe if what we believe were merely how we see things?

Foundationalism. Rejecting the image of circles or webs of justification, foundationalism holds that a properly constructed noetic structure has a foundation. That is, while some beliefs can be based on other beliefs, ultimately the chain comes to rest in a belief that is not based on other beliefs, but is based on some nondoxastic grounds. Foundationalism is a family of theories about the grounds of justification, and all versions hold the following theses:

1. A proper noetic structure is foundational, composed of properly basic beliefs (the foundation) and nonbasic beliefs, where nonbasic beliefs are based in an epistemically correct way either directly or indirectly on properly basic beliefs, and properly basic beliefs are not based on other beliefs.

2. A properly basic belief is a belief that meets some condition C (where the choice of C marks different versions of foundationalism).

3. The basing relation is irreflexive and asymmetrical, so that the foundational noetic structure is not circular.

There are two main varieties of foundationalism. *Classical foundationalism* holds that condition C is indubitability: the ground of the belief must guarantee the truth of the belief. (Cartesianism is the paradigm example of classical foundationalism.) *Modest foundationalism*

[17]Ibid., p. 164.

holds that condition C is something weaker than indubitability: the ground of the belief must be truth-conducive. (Further restrictions on condition C will mark the difference between different versions of modest foundationalism.)

Nearly all epistemologists recognize that classical foundationalism is too ambitious: as I said above, even granted that there are some indubitable beliefs, there simply aren't enough of them to ground our entire noetic structure. Further, it certainly seems that some beliefs that are not indubitable—that can be doubted—are properly basic. Classical foundationalism is motivated largely by the belief that certainty is a necessary condition of knowledge. But that is wrong.

Recognition of the failure of classical foundationalism has led far too many thinkers to assume that no form of foundationalism can succeed. For some, the dismissal of modest foundationalism along with its classical cousin is motivated by a prior commitment to a different theory of justification (such as coherentism), to a postmodern view according to which all statements must be interpreted relative to a linguistic community and should not be regarded as objectively true or false, or to some other philosophical position. Interestingly though, it seems that recent decades have seen a growing number of philosophers gravitating to a foundationalist view; coherentism is in retreat. Indeed, among contemporary epistemologists, modest foundationalism of some form is the "dominant position."[18]

But for others, the dismissal is due more to a suspicion that a reasonable account of properly basic belief cannot be given, that is, that condition C cannot be successfully cashed out. However, I think it is quite possible to give a satisfactory account of condition C. To see the way this might work, we need to explore the notion of grounds in greater detail.

We can say that the ground of a belief is an indicator of the truth of a belief, that the right kind of ground provides justification for a belief.

---

[18]See, for example, Laurence Bonjour, *Epistemology: Classic Problems and Contemporary Responses* (Lanham, Md.: Rowman & Littlefield, 2002); Michael R. DePaul, "Preface," in *Resurrecting Old-Fashioned Foundationalism*, ed. Michael R. DePaul (Lanham, Md.: Rowman & Littlefield, 2001).

Thus, the ground should be understood as epistemic rather than causal or pragmatic: The ground of a belief confers justification if it makes it probable that the belief is true, not if it causes a belief or if it shows the belief is useful in some way.

In this discussion, let us stipulate our use of two familiar terms to differentiate two kinds of grounds. We'll use *evidence* to refer to non-doxastic grounds and *reasons* to refer to doxastic grounds. This seems a natural usage, since in ordinary language *evidence* generally connotes something physical or otherwise external to an investigator, which is indicative of something else, whereas *reason* connotes some kind of inferential notion that is internal to the investigator's cognition. So we'll say that properly basic beliefs have evidence as their grounds and nonbasic beliefs have reasons as theirs.

In the case of nonbasic beliefs, the relation of reasons to nonbasic beliefs is relatively straightforward. Inference from a (possibly) true belief provides reasons for another belief, and if the former belief is justified and the inference is valid, then the latter belief is also justified. In essence, this would resemble linear coherentism. But we could also regard a belief as justified because it "fits" well with a number of other justified beliefs, in the model of holistic coherentism, if at least one of those other beliefs is a basic belief. That is, coherence with other justified beliefs is *a criterion* of justification—that is what is right about coherentism. As I said above, modest foundationalists do not deny that coherence is an important aspect of justified beliefs. But it just isn't the whole story.

The nature of evidence, however, and its relation to properly basic beliefs, is more complicated. To get at this issue, let's begin by identifying particular cases that we would regard as cases of properly basic beliefs (and remember, a basic belief is one that is not grounded on other beliefs). We could begin with those beliefs that are indubitable—which cannot rationally be doubted. Such beliefs fall into three classes: (1) self-evident, (2) incorrigible or (3) evident to the senses. Self-evident beliefs are those which, on inspection, we just see cannot be false. This class would include simple propositions of mathematics (e.g., 3 + 4 = 7) and logic (e.g., *modus ponens:* "If *p*, then *q*; *p*; therefore *q*"). Merely to understand such propositions is to see that they could not be false.

Incorrigible beliefs (like incorrigible teenagers) cannot be corrected. Introspective awareness of one's own mental states is generally regarded as incorrigible. If you tell me you are in pain, I can't correct you about that. I can't say, "No, you're wrong. You're mistaking being tickled for being in pain." Only you can say if you are in pain. Of course, you might be mistaken about the cause or location of your pain—think of the amputee's phantom limb pain—but you cannot be mistaken about the fact that you are in pain. (3) Beliefs about perceptual experience are also, and a bit more controversially, regarded as indubitable. But we need to be careful here, for the claim is not that you are actually seeing (hearing, touching) something. The claim is that a belief about a perceptual experience itself cannot be wrong, not that a belief about what is being perceived is actually as it is perceived to be. So my belief that "I am having a visual experience of a red-rose-shaped blotch in my visual field" cannot be wrong, although the derivative belief that "I am seeing a red rose" might be. (Of course, we almost never form beliefs of the first type; we almost always directly form the second type of belief. But the point here is that the first type of belief is indubitable.)

The three classes of indubitable beliefs are basic in that they are grounded not on other beliefs but directly on nondoxastic evidence. To say that they are properly basic is to say they are justified beliefs, that they are grounded in the right way on the right kind of evidence. These three classes of indubitable beliefs are the same foundational beliefs accepted by classical foundationalism. But as we noted above, there are good reasons to accept modest foundationalism. That would mean broadening the foundation of the noetic structure, accepting into the foundation beliefs that are not indubitable, that is, which are defeasible (meaning it is possible that they could be defeated—shown possibly to be false). How can we characterize the nature of evidence and its relation to beliefs that are not indubitable, evidence that is truth-conducive in such a way as to confer justification on the beliefs?

Again, the way to approach the question is by looking at particular cases. Take memory, for example. Memories themselves, whatever they may be, are not beliefs; they ground memory beliefs. But memory beliefs are defeasible. In general, the more distant the event remembered, the more insignificant it was, and the less "normal" our mental state at the time (e.g., if we were tired, drunk, depressed), the less trustworthy our memory.

Nevertheless, we surely are justified in taking some memory beliefs as properly basic. I clearly remember eating cereal for breakfast. I don't infer this from beliefs about an empty cereal box on the kitchen counter or about a distinctive aftertaste (although, perhaps, I could form my belief that way). No, I just remember, quite clearly, having cereal for breakfast this morning. Similarly, I clearly remember marrying my wife in Boulder, Colorado, forty years ago. I don't infer this from the belief that the ring on my finger or the picture on the wall must mean I am married. My belief, based directly on memory and not inferred from something else, clearly is justified.

Again, I don't infer (most) perceptual beliefs from other beliefs. I don't, for example, infer the belief that there is a rose in the garden from the belief that I'm seeing a rose, which in turn I infer from beliefs about my perceptual experience (that I'm being appeared to red-rose-ly). I just believe there's a rose there because I see a rose (or, more precisely, because I'm having the perceptual experience of seeing a rose). Of course, some perceptual beliefs are false, so perceptual beliefs are not indefeasible. But with time and some skill developed from trial and error, we can weed out most of our false perceptual beliefs. We see what looks like water on the road, but know we're driving across the Mojave on I-15, so it's very probable that it's a mirage. We hear a voice that sounds like Jane's, but we don't form the belief that it's her because we know she's in Paris.

Since memory and perception are the right kinds of evidence to ground memory beliefs and perceptual beliefs, respectively, such beliefs are properly basic, according to modest foundationalism. We could offer similar arguments to show the truth-indicative nature of testimony, or rational intuitions, or other putative basic sources of evidence. To generalize, then, if it can be shown that there are kinds of evidence that (nondoxastically) ground certain kinds of beliefs in a way that assures the likelihood of the truth of those beliefs, then those beliefs will be properly basic beliefs for the modest foundationalist. That is, condition C is met in those cases where it can be shown that a certain kind of evidence is conducive to forming (mostly) true beliefs.[19]

I've spent time on what is still a sketch of modest foundationalism because it's my claim that a modest foundationalism fits best with a Christian worldview. I'll repeat that I could be wrong about that; sincere Christians do indeed hold different positions. But the most important thing here is that, as I showed above, both the Bible and the Christian theological tradition claim that persons can and do have knowledge of a wide range of truths. The confidence that we do have knowledge permeates a Christian worldview and seems to me to best fit with a modest foundationalist epistemology.

Throughout, the Bible seems clearly to endorse some sort of properly basic beliefs—beliefs, again, that are grounded in nondoxastic evidence. For example, when questioned by the disciples of John the Baptist as to whether he was the promised Messiah, Jesus "replied to the messengers, 'Go back and report to John what you have seen and heard: The blind receive sight, the lame walk, those who have leprosy are cured, the deaf hear, the dead are raised, and the good news is preached to the poor'" (Lk 7:22). The veridicality of the messengers' perceptual beliefs is assumed as properly basic, and from them inferences about Jesus' person and mission can be drawn.

John assumes that testimonial beliefs are properly basic when he writes near the end of his Gospel, "Jesus did many other miraculous signs in the presence of his disciples which are not recorded in this book. But these are written that you may believe that Jesus is the Christ, the Son of God, and that by believing you may have life in his name" (Jn 20:30-31). John assumes it is proper to believe on the basis of testimony that Jesus did certain miraculous things, which then form the inferential basis for beliefs about Jesus' person and mission of salvation. In his first epistle, John says much the same thing: "That which was

---

[19]To spell this out in detail would require more space than I can devote here. For one way to work this out for perceptual beliefs, see J. P. Moreland and Garrett DeWeese, "The Premature Report of Foundationalism's Demise," in *Reclaiming the Center*, ed. Millard J. Erickson, Paul Kjoss Helseth and Justin Taylor (Wheaton, Ill.: Crossway, 2004), pp. 81-107.

from the beginning, which we have heard, which we have seen with our eyes, which we have looked at and our hands have touched—this we proclaim concerning the Word of life. The life appeared; we have seen it and testify to it" (1 Jn 1:1-2). Again the appropriateness of testimony as properly basic is assumed.

Peter also endorses perceptual and testimonial evidence as properly basic when he refers to his experience on the Mount of Transfiguration: "We did not follow cleverly invented stories when we told you about the power and coming of our Lord Jesus Christ, but we were eyewitnesses of his majesty. For he received honor and glory from God the Father when the voice came to him from the Majestic Glory, saying, 'This is my Son, whom I love; with him I am well pleased.' We ourselves heard this voice that came from heaven when we were with him on the sacred mountain" (2 Pet 1:16-18).

Finally, our personal assurance of salvation, according to Scripture, is grounded in what is assumed to be a properly basic, nondoxastic, immediate experience of the Spirit of God within us: "We accept man's testimony, but God's testimony is greater because it is the testimony of God, which he has given about his Son. Anyone who believes in the Son of God has this testimony in his heart" (1 Jn 5:9). "The Spirit himself testifies with our spirit that we are God's children" (Rom 8:16).

Perhaps I'm belaboring this point. But in light of the rejection of foundationalism (both classical and modest) by some Christian philosophers and theologians influenced by those philosophers, I'll reiterate my belief that a modest foundationalism fits best in a Christian worldview. It's true that the Bible doesn't teach any particular epistemology, but the knowledge claims explicit and implicit within a Christian worldview seem to me to be very difficult to reconcile with a coherentist structure of justification, whether the philosophical or the postmodern kind. When doing epistemology as Christians, then, it seems to me that we have good reasons to work to clarify, refine and defend modest foundationalism.[20]

---

[20]In addition to the Moreland and DeWeese chapter mentioned in n. 17, two other chapters in the same volume explore these issues in exemplary manner: Douglas Groothuis, "Truth Defined and Defended," and R. Scott Smith, "Language, Theological Knowledge, and the

The "location" of justification: Internalism and externalism. The debate between internalists and externalists turns on whether or not, and
to what degree, Michelle (say) must be aware of the reasons that would
confer justification on her belief in order for the belief to be justified for
her. Some hold that as long as the chain from evidence to Michelle's
belief is reliable, her belief is justified; it doesn't matter whether or not
Michelle is aware of the reliability of the chain. Since the factors relevant to justifying her belief are external to Michelle, this position is
called *externalism.* Others hold that, at least to some extent, Michelle
must be aware of the factors that justify her belief, or, at least in principle, she must be able to become aware of them. Since in this case the
factors relevant to justification are or can be internal to Michelle's cognitive process, this position is *internalism.*

A technical discussion of the issues involved is beyond the scope of
this book. But I must make the following observation. Suppose Michelle is faced with an inescapable life-or-death decision. Suppose further that through some process unknown to us, a process that is in fact
reliable and that we would recognize as reliable if we knew of and understood it, Michelle forms a belief that a certain course of action is the
correct one in this situation. But suppose as well that Michelle understands that she cannot give any reasons that justify her belief and that
she is even aware of some reasons that would count against its truth.
Now, surely it is not rational to act (especially in a life-or-death situation) on a belief that you have no reason to think is true and even have
reasons to think is probably false. But if externalism is correct, then
either epistemic justification must be divorced from rational decision
making, or some completely novel account of rationality must be given
that would make Michelle's decision to act on her belief rational after
all. This seems to me to be a very tall order to fill and suggests that the
internalist account is most likely correct.

In recent years the respected Christian philosopher Alvin Plantinga
has popularized the distinction between *justification* and *warrant.* For
Plantinga, warrant is an externalist notion, while justification is an in-

Postmodern Paradigm," in *Reclaiming the Center,* ed. Millard J. Erickson, Paul Kjoss Helseth
and Justin Taylor (Wheaton, Ill.: Crossway, 2004), pp. 59-69 and 109-33, respectively.

ternalist notion. For the externalist (such as Plantinga), Michelle's belief will have warrant if (roughly) the entire belief-forming process is functioning properly, whether Michelle is aware of that process or not.[21] For the internalist, Michelle must be aware (or be able to become aware) that the belief is based on reasons or evidence that make it probable that it is true, if it is justified for her. Since Plantinga and a few colleagues who are active in formulating and defending the externalist conception of warrant are Calvinists, their position has become widely known as *Reformed epistemology.*

Reformed epistemology has brought an interesting position into contemporary epistemology. But it is often misunderstood, at least at a more popular level. The Reformed epistemologist is not, as sometimes characterized, advocating fideism (believing with no reasons or in spite of defeaters for the belief). Rather, the Reformed epistemologist believes it is not necessary for a person to have direct, first-person access (whether actual or in principle) to the reasons—the entire proper-function process—which confer warrant on her position.

I want to note an important point. The difference between internalism and externalism, justification and warrant, has led to a distinction in Christian apologetics between Reformed epistemology and evidential apologetics. As usually characterized, a Reformed apologist believes Christian belief is warranted even if the Christian cannot give any reasons for holding his belief. (Indeed, Reformed epistemologists argue that belief in God, produced by what Plantinga, following Calvin, calls the *sensus divinitatis,* is properly basic.)

By contrast, the evidentialist apologist believes a Christian can be aware of good reasons that justify his belief. It is not clear that these positions are so very different, and I think the distinction is often overstated. I would agree that a youngster, Michael (say), growing up in a Christian home, regularly attending Sunday school, church and maybe even Christian school, might simply find himself believing in Jesus as

---

[21]Plantinga's full specification is that a belief has warrant if it is produced by a belief-forming faculty functioning properly in a congenial epistemic environment according to a design plan successfully aimed at truth. See his *Warrant and Proper Function* (New York: Oxford University Press, 1993) for a full exposition and argument.

his Savior, based on the testimony of all the people in his life that he loves and respects. Or perhaps he comes to faith based on the *sensus divinitatis.* In either case, Michael might not be aware of why his belief is justified. But the internalist could well maintain that in principle, he could become aware, and that is all the internalist requires for justification. Similarly, the Reformed apologist would agree that when Michael enters college, encounters significant intellectual objections to the Christian faith, meets sincere practitioners of other religions, and studies arguments for and against the existence of God in his philosophy of religion class, he might have sufficient epistemic defeaters to seriously weaken his belief in God. Now he can study the objections and rebuttals to the objections by Christian philosophers, he can read Christian apologetics and learn of the many lines of evidence supporting Christian faith, and so—by becoming aware of the evidence that grounds his belief—acquire justification (in the internalist sense) for the belief. In other words, the Reformed apologist, as an externalist, does not deny that a person can, and perhaps in some cases should, be aware of the evidence grounding his belief.[22]

Virtue epistemology. In recent years a position has emerged in epistemology that actually reaches back to Aristotle and St. Thomas Aquinas for inspiration. Known as *virtue epistemology,* the view holds that having knowledge, or justification, depends on exercising the proper intellectual virtues.

The basic idea of virtue epistemology is that if a person faithfully employs certain intellectual virtues, the person's resultant noetic structure will be proper; that is, it will contain (mostly) true beliefs. The intellectual virtues are dispositions such as open-mindedness, honesty, curiosity, courage, humility, fairness, carefulness, sound judgment and so on. Aristotle believed that a person exercising such virtues would discover the truth. Aquinas added the insight that the intellectual and moral virtues form a seamless whole (can someone really be intellectually courageous without being morally courageous, intellectually fair

---

[22]I take it that Plantinga himself accepts this sort of scenario: see, for example, his response to potential arguments against Christian belief in Part IV, "Defeaters?" in Alvin Plantinga, *Warranted Christian Belief* (New York: Oxford University Press, 2000), pp. 355-499.

without being morally fair, etc.?), so that both intellectual and moral virtue is needed to arrive at truth.

It is not entirely clear to me whether virtue epistemology is best regarded as a theory of knowledge (i.e., a replacement for TAK, the K = JTB analysis of knowledge), or as a theory of justification (i.e., an explanation of what constitutes having the right kind of reasons for holding a belief), or as something else. As a Christian, I applaud the emphasis on virtue—especially Aquinas's emphasis on the unity of the virtues—and believe that teaching critical thinking apart from considerations of moral and intellectual virtues will be defective. This certainly fits well in a Christian worldview. But by my lights, virtue epistemology is best taken as describing certain dispositions, certain habits of thought and behavior, the possession of which puts a person in a good position to form true beliefs. That is, virtue epistemology seems to me to be a theory of how to best go about acquiring and sustaining (mostly) true beliefs. It describes constraints on the character and methodology of the person who is searching for truth, and not on an alternative theory of justification or knowledge.

Knowing God. One final topic forces itself on us in this chapter, the question of how a person can know God. It's as clear as anything in philosophy that many really smart philosophers not only don't know God (by acquaintance) but they even deny knowing (propositionally) that he exists, because (so they believed) that proposition is false. In recent years the "problem of divine hiddenness" has received a good bit of attention from philosophers, but I won't try to summarize that interesting discussion.[23] Rather, I want to consider a narrower topic, the epistemology of knowing God.

A Christian worldview commits us not only to the proposition that God exists, but also to the claim that he can be known. Jesus himself said it plainly: "Now this is eternal life: that they may know you, the only true God, and Jesus Christ, whom you have sent" (Jn 17:3). If then God *can* be known, how?[24]

---

[23]See, e.g., Daniel Howard-Snyder and Paul K. Moser, eds., *Divine Hiddenness* (New York: Cambridge University Press, 2002).
[24]This theme is explored at length in Dallas Willard, *Knowing Christ Today: Why We Can Trust*

Recalling the discussion at the beginning of the chapter, knowing a person (by acquaintance) is not equivalent to propositional knowledge about that person, but in part depends on and entails propositional knowledge. But we can make a further distinction, I think. Call one sort of knowledge by acquaintance "recognition-knowledge." The ability to recognize the face of another person, often someone we've met only casually once or twice, is an amazing thing. (Somewhere between 2.5 percent and 10 percent of the population are affected to various degrees with the disorder known as prospagnosia, the inability to recognize faces. Whether caused by brain damage or a congenital disorder, the condition is deeply frustrating for those suffering from it.) Facial recognition is apparently a function dependent on several regions of the brain operating in concert; the operation is unconscious, and still largely mysterious. But one thing is clear: recognition-knowledge is not reducible to propositional knowledge. Asked to spell out just how we were able to recognize that person we met last month at a party when we met her again in a totally different context, most of us could only give vague characteristics like tall, with dark hair. How we picked her out from the millions of other tall brunettes cannot be reduced to propositions. (Similar recognition-knowledge is evident in picking out landscapes or cityscapes, recognizing a taste or smell we encountered some time ago, or identifying a musical composition after hearing only a very few notes.)

Interesting as recognition knowledge is, though, in a relationship there's another sort of knowledge by acquaintance, knowledge of a person's character. Call this person-knowledge.[25] Interestingly, person-knowledge depends significantly on both the knower and the known. For example, you can sit next to someone in class for a whole semester, have recognition-knowledge so you know him when you see him in the cafeteria, have propositional knowledge of his name, and perhaps his major and how good a student he is, but never person-know him, because you do not intentionally, volitionally, engage him at all. Or, you

---

Spiritual Knowledge (New York: HarperCollins, 2009).
[25]Not to be confused with "personal knowledge," explored by Michael Polanyi in his book of that name.

may not person-know him because he intentionally, volitionally, withholds sharing anything about himself in spite of your efforts to become acquainted. Both your will and his must be cooperatively engaged for you to come to have person-knowledge necessary for a genuine relationship, one based on mutual respect and personal care. He must purpose to reveal himself honestly, and you must purpose to accept that revelation at face value.

In several articles and a recent book,[26] Paul Moser has argued that the evidence that leads to person-knowledge of God (my term, not his) will be evidence that "is available in a way, and *only* in a way, that accommodates the distinctive purposes of a perfectly loving God." Moser continues,

> The latter purposes . . . would aim noncoercively but authoritatively to transform human purposes to agree with divine purposes, despite human resistance of various and sundry sorts. In addition, those purposes would . . . be anchored in God's character, and would not be at all arbitrary or whimsical.[27]

Our receiving God's purposive evidence, and thus volitionally knowing God as Lord, Moser claims, depends on our being willing to submit to God as perfectly authoritative and to be transformed by his redemptive purposes. Humans cannot expect to find evidence for God if they come as casual spectators.

> *Volitionalism* about knowledge of God's reality, in contrast to pure rationalism and pure empiricism, implies that the human will is a central human "source" (or, perhaps better, "avenue") of conclusive evidence and knowledge of God's reality. More accurately, it implies that the yielding of the human will to a demand of perfectly authoritative evidence from God is a central source, or avenue, *within humans* of conclusive evidence of God's reality.[28]

Moser further refines the notion of volitional knowledge of God as

---

[26]Paul K. Moser, *The Elusive God: Reorienting Religious Epistemology* (New York: Cambridge University Press, 2008).
[27]Ibid., p. 3.
[28]Ibid., pp. 60-61.

"*filial* knowledge of God as one's perfectly authoritative and loving *Father* to whom one yields as God's child in response to a perfectly authoritative and loving call to repentance and fellowship."[29]

Now, I am in deep sympathy with Moser's development—reorientation, as he says—of religious epistemology. Jesus surely teaches this lesson. Some people of Jerusalem, debating just who Jesus was, argued, "'But we know where this man is from; when the Christ comes, no one will know where he is from.' Then Jesus, still teaching in the temple courts, cried out, 'Yes, you know me, and you know where I am from'" (Jn 7:27-28). They did have propositional knowledge about Jesus. But the very next day Jesus faced a more hostile group of Pharisees. "'You do not know me or my Father,' Jesus replied. 'If you knew me, you would know my Father also'" (Jn 8:19). Propositional knowledge did not result in person-knowledge, and certainly not in *filial* knowledge.

In spite of Bertrand Russell's famous complaint ("Not enough evidence, God!"), it seems right that person-knowledge or filial knowledge of God will be quite unlike casual, spectator knowledge; the purposes of a perfectly authoritative, perfectly loving God's revealing himself will surely not be to allow finite flawed creatures to treat him as some lab specimen. I suspect Russell (and many other atheists) have a deep unwillingness to submit to God as authoritative (recall the discussion of the "cosmic authority problem" in chapter 3). Since they do not volitionally desire to know God as he is, he has no requirement to offer evidence that he is what they want him to be.

But I do have some quibbles with Moser. Surely person-knowledge *presupposes* that the person in question exists! Or, at least, if I have no reason to think it's likely that the person exists, I won't be interested in pursuing person-knowledge.[30] I have no interest (aside from talking with my grandchildren) in knowing anything about SpongeBob SquarePants, and would never look for evidence for the pineapple under the sea where he reportedly lives. (That sums up the totality of all I know, or ever want to know, about the cartoon character.) Of course

---

[29]Ibid., p. 95.
[30]See Garrett J. DeWeese, "Toward a Robust Natural Theology: Reply to Paul Moser," *Philosophia Christi* 3, no. 1 (2001): 113-18.

the analogy is grossly inadequate, but I think the point is clear. Many people need at least some minimal assurance that such a person possibly exists before investing whatever is necessary to gain person-knowledge, whether of an intelligent sea-sponge or a perfectly loving, supremely authoritative God.[31]

Here is where I place a higher value on natural theology than Moser does. He calls the arguments of natural theology "at best incidental, even a dispensable sideshow."[32] Well, perhaps so, in comparison to the surpassing blessedness of knowing God. But perhaps not, as evidence that there is in reality a God who has spoken to us in his Word and in his Son, and calls us into a transforming relationship as we submit to his purposes for us.[33] Insofar as the arguments of natural theology give us reasons to believe that there is a necessarily existent, intelligent personal agent, the creator of all that exists apart from him, who is morally perfect and who can be known, I believe they serve a valuable purpose.

THIS I KNOW . . .

A Christian worldview commits the Christian philosopher to the claim that we do indeed have, or that it is possible to have, knowledge of various sorts of things, including knowledge about the natural world, about the past, about other persons, about supernatural beings and about God himself. Doing epistemology as a Christian means going about constructing and defending a theory of knowledge that makes sense of these knowledge claims.

---

[31]Even the "devotional experiment" urged by Pascal in connection with his famous "wager" is proposed for a person who has *some* evidence for God's existence which is roughly counterbalanced by contrary evidence.

[32]Moser, *The Elusive God*, p. 25.

[33]Recall the parable of the mountain climber in chapter 2.

7

WHAT SHOULD I VALUE?

ETHICS AND AESTHETICS

"Beauty is truth, truth beauty,"—
that is all ye know on earth, and all ye need to know.

JOHN KEATS

We shall set ourselves to show that in so far as statements of
value are significant, they are ordinary "scientific" statements;
and that in so far as they are not scientific, they are
not in the literal sense significant.

A. J. AYER

At the heart of liberty is the right to define one's own concept of existence,
of meaning, of the universe, and of the mystery of human life.

JUSTICE ANTHONY KENNEDY,
PLANNED PARENTHOOD V. CASEY

Wise living, the aim of philosophy, requires not only that we understand what is real, and what knowledge is, and how we can rightly claim to have knowledge. Wise living also requires that we understand what we should value—what we should spend time, money, effort and thought in pursuing, and what sort of value time, money, effort and thought have. *Axiology* is thinking critically—philosophically—about such questions. Very broadly, axiology is the study of value—what value is and what has it.

Immediately we face the question of definition. 'Value' sounds suspiciously vague and disturbingly person-relative: We hold on to many items that have only sentimental value, and when we're gone, likely no one else will value them. Some values are distinctly personal, matters of taste. I value Bach above Brubek, and both above Beyoncé; you may reverse the order of valuation. And we both may be mystified as to why someone values a "velvet Elvis" painting enough to purchase it and hang it in the living room. And no matter how much you want to get for an item in a garage sale or for the used car you put up on Craigslist, its 'value' is—at least in economic terms—only what the market will support.

Of course, there are different sorts of value, such as cultural value. In the culture of the United States, freedom of speech is highly valued, while in another culture, restraint and not speaking ill of one's elders might be more highly valued. And there are subcultural values as well. Older generations of Americans universally would dress up when going to church and remove their hats when entering the sanctuary, as signs of respect. Such symbolic actions seem to have no real value for a younger generation who apparently show their respect differently.

Some things have only instrumental value, for what further things they might be used to obtain. Money is (or should be) in this category. Other things have intrinsic value; they are worth possessing simply for their own sake. A classic example here is happiness. If someone asked you, "Why do you want to make money?" you'd surely have a ready answer or two in terms of ends which money could help you attain. But if someone asked you, "Why do you want to be happy?" you'd probably think the questioner wasn't being serious. Clearly happiness is valued for its own sake. Still other things—health, for instance—are mixed, both instrumental and intrinsic, valuable both in themselves and for what their possession enables you to attain.

I'm sure there are still other ways to slice the pie and label the slices. But I want to focus on only two categories of value in this chapter—aesthetic and ethical—as I believe a Christian worldview has the greatest impact on these axiological categories. For ease of exposition, and since (as will become apparent) I believe they are distinct kinds of values, I'll treat them separately in this chapter.

Issues and Options: Aesthetics

John Keats penned a poetic thesis of the Romantic movement in his "Ode on a Grecian Urn," but it's poetry, after all. Beauty is not truth, and neither beauty nor truth are goodness. And yet the three are related in some hard-to-define sense, and have been classed among the "transcendentals." The tradition from Plato and Aristotle though Aquinas and the Scholastics regarded the transcendentals as properties of Being, transcending time and place—transcending, that is, the limits of particulars. Consequently they also transcend personal tastes, cultural values and religious traditions. The transcendentals were proper objects of affection, proper aims of a well-ordered and fulfilled life.

The doctrine of the transcendentals is poorly understood today, but I have neither the expertise nor the space to pursue the topic here. I mention it simply to note this: In the long tradition of philosophy and medieval philosophical theology, truth, goodness and beauty were regarded as immutable and objective.

Not so today.

"Beauty is in the eye of the beholder" is such a common aphorism that questioning it is right up there with questioning motherhood and the infield fly rule. Yet it should be questioned, and (with proper qualifications) I believe it is false. Or so I'll argue.

Aesthetics is one of those roads less traveled in philosophy. I dare say most philosophy graduate students have never taken a formal course in aesthetics, and—full disclosure—neither have I. Yet through reading, supervising several students' independent studies in aesthetics, and reflections on implications of a Christian worldview, I believe I do have a bit to say here—even though it will be brief and sketchy. I leave it to you, if you're interested in the subject, to pursue the aesthetic quest more formally.

At the outset, I should distinguish between aesthetics, understood as critical philosophical investigation of beauty, and philosophy of art.

Not all art is or should be beautiful, but the nature of beauty itself is a question independent of art.[1] Here I want to focus narrowly on the question of beauty.

Subjectivism. Immanuel Kant's "third critique," the *Critique of Judgment*, is still widely influential. In it he speaks of "judgments of taste," arguing that two necessary (but not jointly sufficient) features of such judgments are subjectivity and universality.[2] By 'subjectivity,' Kant meant to call attention to the subjective feeling of pleasure or displeasure experienced when contemplating art. By 'universality,' however, Kant held that a person's judgment of beauty, based on her subjective experience of pleasure, was in addition universal or normative, such that when she judged something to be beautiful, she was "demanding the same delight from others."

In these more pluralistic, less naive days, though, the normative aspect of Kant's judgment of taste has been widely abandoned in favor of a purely subjective concept of beauty. The sense of pleasure Kant referred to has needed explication, and a plethora of explications have been given, so that in the literature it is difficult to see any consensus as to what makes a particular experience an aesthetic experience, or, more narrowly, how the subjective pleasure of the experience of beauty differs from other pleasurable experiences.

The result is a very liberal pluralism: if something (a painting, a piece of music, a landscape) gives you a certain sort of pleasure, then it's beautiful *to you*. I dare say this is by far the most popular "man on the street" view. But as I already indicated, I think this confuses personal taste or preference with genuine aesthetic judgment.

Objectivism. The objectivist will claim that while certainly there is a necessarily subjective component in aesthetic judgments, those judg-

---

[1]For more on the philosophy of art, I recommend Nicholas Wolterstorff, *Art in Action: Toward a Christian Aesthetic* (Grand Rapids: Eerdmans, 1998); especially noteworthy is his rich and fertile concept of art as world projection, which helps us understand how ugliness can legitimately be a part of art, and to distinguish exquisitely crafted decoration from skillful intentionality in art. More general in nature is Stephen Davies, *The Philosophy of Art* (Malden, Mass.: Blackwell, 2006). Prof. Laura Smit of Calvin College has compiled an incredibly thorough bibliography for theological aesthetics, <www.calvin.edu/admin/provost/faith/documents/aesthetics_biblio .pdf>.
[2]Immanuel Kant, *Critique of Judgment*, trans. Werner S. Pluhar (Indianapolis: Hackett, 1987).

ments can rightly be examined and can themselves be deemed correct or incorrect. That is, there is an objective standard such that the mere experience of aesthetic pleasure alone is insufficient to secure the truth or correctness of the judgment.

Objectivism attempts to explicate the concept of beauty in an objective way, that is, in a way that is independent of the judgments or experiences of any single individual or group of individuals. Differences among objectivists arise concerning such issues as whether beauty is a transcendental, simple property, or a complex property; whether or not beauty is a degreed property; whether 'beauty' refers to the same property when used of visual art or music or a landscape or a face; whether beauty must be tied to a perceptual experience (or whether, say, deaf Beethoven could experience the beauty of his Ninth Symphony); whether abstract structures such as mathematical equations can rightly be said to be beautiful; and whether beauty is a 'self-presenting' property, or is such that observers need (some degree of) training to apprehend it. And that's just for starters.

CHRISTIAN WORLDVIEW IMPLICATIONS: AESTHETICS

Clearly, philosophical aesthetics investigates a wide range of issues. And by my lights, a Christian worldview has implications for the philosopher thinking about such matters. I'll try briefly to draw out what to me seem to be some of the more salient implications in what follows.

Objective beauty. If the supremely authoritative God declares something beautiful, that would seem to be the strongest possible grounds, within a Christian worldview, for maintaining that beauty is objective (that is, independent of human judgments). And there are a number of biblical texts where God, or his authorized spokesmen, do in fact ascribe beauty to things.

Beautiful things, beautiful people. Among those things called beautiful in the Bible are the starry sky (Job 38:31), a singing voice (Ezek 33:32), a city in its setting (Ps 48:2), the land of Israel (Jer 3:19), jewelry (Ezek 7:20), clothing (Ezek 27:24), trees (Ezek 31:3; Dan 4:12) and, of course, people, especially women (see the many uses of "beauty" in the book of Esther; the word is used sixteen times in the Song of Solomon), in both their physical appearance and their "inner beauty" of character (1 Pet 3:3-4).[3]

The rich diversity of the things called beautiful leads me to reject the idea that beauty is a simple property.[4] Extrapolating from the biblical examples, I believe that a talented performance of a Puccini aria, a Monet water lily painting, and the view of Mount Rainier from amidst the dwarf spruce and plethora of wildflowers above Paradise ranger station are all beautiful. But the Puccini is a human creation and a human performance and must be experienced serially. The Monet canvas is also a human creation but can be experienced as a whole, or attended to in segments in no particular order, while the Rainier vista is (so I believe) a divine production using natural geological and botanical processes and is dramatically affected by time of day, season and weather. In order to account for the ascription of beauty to such diverse objects, I conclude that 'beauty' is a complex property that supervenes on an appropriate interplay (sorry—I can't be more precise) of such properties as melody and harmony (or color and tone), salience and balance, rhythm and voicing (or texture). Performance arts and plastic arts, persons and personalities and landscapes, if beautiful, all share in some degree these properties.

Clearly, different cultures will produce works that exemplify these properties in quite different styles, but with a bit of work one can rather easily distinguish a cultural style from the properties constitutive of beauty. And culture, experience and education contribute to personal taste, so that while a particular work may be judged beautiful, one may still not like it. (I for one regard Mozart's music generally as exemplifying the properties constitutive of beauty, but knowing something about Mozart's life, and that most of his compositions were produced to en-

---

[3]A critic might claim that these biblical texts are instances of accommodation—God using, for the sake of communication, certain culturally-relative beliefs about beauty without thereby implying anything about beauty as a universal property. I'd simply reply that it's quite difficult to articulate a consistent hermeneutic that allows a principled distinction to be drawn between accommodation and assertion when it comes to property ascription as opposed to physical object or event description (e.g., "the sun rose," or the ancient cosmology reflected in Genesis 1).
[4]I admit to being attracted to the manner in which ancient and medieval philosophers explicated beauty as a transcendental. Perhaps there is a way to bring this idea together with my understanding of beauty as a complex property, but I don't see that way clearly enough.

tertain or titillate his aristocratic patrons, I simply don't care for most Mozart compositions. On the other hand, being a guy who loves the Colorado mountains, I admit to loving John Denver, although in my view his songs exhibit beauty to a much lower degree than Mozart's sonatas. One can recognize beauty and not prefer it, and prefer mediocrity and not call it beautiful.)

I have only a couple additional points to raise about beauty. First, if God calls certain things beautiful, then clearly they are beautiful, regardless of human judgments about them. And this holds for things in our experience as well as things we can't experience, such as the beauty of angelic beings (Ezek 28:12-17, which many commentators take to be a description of the angel Lucifer). If so, then *pace* Kant, (human) subjective experience is not a necessary condition of beauty. When stepping onto the surface of the moon, Buzz Aldrin exclaimed, "Beautiful, beautiful. Magnificent desolation." I believe that there was beauty there the day before Apollo 11 landed, even though no human judgments of the beauty had been made.

Beautiful God. Finally, in addition to such immaterial entities as personality and angels that may legitimately be called beautiful, we need to face the ultimate: God himself is beautiful! The psalmist proclaims, "One thing I ask of the LORD, this is what I seek: that I may dwell in the house of the LORD all the days of my life, to gaze upon the beauty of the LORD and to seek him in his temple" (Ps 27:4). And he exhorts, "Ascribe to the LORD the glory due his name; worship the LORD in the beauty of his holiness (Ps 29:2 NKJV). If God is beautiful, then surely he is so regardless of human judgment, and was so in the eternity before humans appeared on earth. There is much more to say here, but I must refrain.[5]

Parenthetical application. Since God declares things good or beautiful, then it is true that there are objective values of goodness and beauty (and the like). And since God made humanity in his image, it is reason-

---

[5]See, for example, F. Duane Lindsey, "Essays Toward a Theology of Beauty," *Bibliotheca Sacra* 131 (1974): 120-36, 209-18, 311-19. See also the sweeping and challenging work of David Bently Hart, *The Beauty of the Infinite: The Aesthetics of Christian Truth* (Grand Rapids: Eerdmans, 2004).

able to believe both that we are able to recognize truth, goodness and beauty, and to rejoice in the true, the good and the beautiful.

But, as philosophers through the millennia have recognized, it might well take education to develop our innate capacity to apprehend these values. In our day, when courses such as art appreciation or music appreciation, not to mention art and music themselves, are being cut from school curricula, when the value of a good liberal arts education is being questioned, when exposure to great prose and poetry is rare in public schools, perhaps the church should take upon itself the task of educating in aesthetic values. This begins, of course, with demonstrating those values. Those responsible for church architecture, decoration and landscaping should at least raise the issue of beauty. Church musicians should think about the beauty of music and lyrics—and this is not a criticism of contemporary styles in worship music, for as I said above, beauty can be exemplified in vary many different styles. And what if a Sunday school class devoted a number of weeks to looking at photographs or reproductions of great religious art of past centuries and asking what—in addition to the subject matter—makes this work great?

If it's true that God made us to enjoy beauty (among other things), then shouldn't the church be a place of beauty?

ISSUES AND OPTIONS: ETHICS

Every day we are confronted with opinions and choices that have important consequences. We need to know how to judge whose opinion is correct; we need to know how to make the right choices. And intuitively we know that the "right" choice, the "correct" opinion, is in many cases not merely a matter of what works best or what will be approved of by the company we keep. Some choices and opinions are clearly moral in character.[6]

Just what makes one judgment a moral judgment and another judgment merely good advice? What makes certain behavior ethical (or unethical) and other behavior simply a matter of preference? It is difficult to specify a precise set of necessary and sufficient conditions that are

---

[6]While a few philosophers distinguish *morals* and *ethics,* most do not, and I'll use the two terms interchangeably.

met by all and only moral judgments. Still, we can point to a set of characteristics common to all or most ethical claims, characteristics that serve to set off the ethical from the nonethical.

The basic characteristic of a moral judgment, I think, is its *obligatory nature*. A certain sense of *oughtness* that attaches to moral judgments differs from the sort of oughtness attached to pieces of advice or norms of etiquette. Moral claims are imperatives, not recommendations. A friend may ask, "Why should I take your advice?" and you'd hear it as an invitation to a good argument. A child may ask, "Why should I be polite?" and you can engage in a discussion about behaviors that ease social settings and facilitate relationships. But if someone asked, "Why should I be moral?" you probably would think there was something seriously amiss in the questioner's worldview. For moral judgments seem to carry their own reasons, their own obligation. So while someone may wonder whether a particular ethical judgment is true or correct, it doesn't seem that one can really understand what an ethical judgment is and not agree that if it is correct, then it is obligatory (even if, at the end of the day, that person refuses the obligation).

Further, as obligatory, moral judgments are *authoritative*, overriding preferences, customs, etiquette and even (at times) law. Explaining the obligatory and authoritative nature of moral judgments is one crucial task of moral philosophy, and as I'll show below, one of the most difficult outside of a Christian worldview.

A second characteristic of a moral judgment is that it is *universalizable*—it applies to all morally responsible creatures in relevantly similar circumstances. Admittedly, there are some philosophers (and many more in other disciplines) who would relativize moral judgments either to individuals or to cultures at a particular time, but this is the minority view among philosophers; I'll return to this issue as well below. However, if moral truths are universal truths, then they apply to all possible moral agents in all possible worlds, that is, they are *necessary truths*.[7]

So being obligatory, authoritative, universalizable and necessary seem to be necessary properties of moral truths. The set may not be

---

[7]See, for example, Gregory E. Ganssle, "Necessary Moral Truths and the Need for Explanation," *Philosophia Christi* 2 (2000): 105-12.

jointly sufficient to precisely define moral truths; nevertheless, I believe these characteristics do suffice in a very large number of cases to enable us to pick out moral from other sorts of judgments.

METAETHICS

There are several distinct ways to approach the study of ethics. *Descriptive ethics* seeks to describe and clarify the ethical standards and behaviors of a group or a culture without making judgments as to the correctness of the standards and behaviors, and it is more properly part of anthropology or sociology than of philosophy. *Metaethics* seeks to answer questions about the meaning of ethical terms, about the structure of ethical theories, and about the source and nature of moral values and obligations. *Normative ethics* attempts to explain how to make judgments about which actions or attitudes are obligatory, permitted or prohibited under different ethical theories and, in consequence, to explain ascriptions of moral praise or blame. And *applied ethics* explores the ethical requirements of normative theory in a particular area, such as environmental, business or biomedical ethics.

Metaethics helps us slice the pie of different ethical theories so we can see comparisons and contrasts more easily. Let me put it a bit differently. Recognizing the obligatoriness of moral claims, almost all philosophers would agree that the *formal principle* of morality is "You ought to do what is good." Disagreement comes in explicating the *material principle,* "The good consists in ____." Metaethics tracks different ways of cashing out the material principle.

After mapping the territory of ethical theories, I'll return to three of the most important and widely held views about what makes actions right or wrong and how we should live.

Noncognitivism. The first division is between *noncognitive* and *cognitive* theories. The difference is this: noncognitive theories do not take ethical judgments as having truth value—they deny that the material principle can be meaningfully filled out—while cognitive theories hold that ethical judgments are either true or false. But if ethical judgments have no truth value, what do they express? Noncognitive theories fall into two general categories: *emotivism* and *prescriptivism.* These theo-

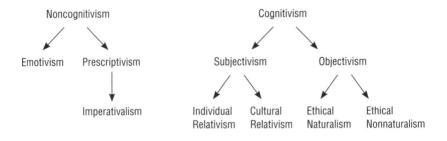

Figure 7.1. Metaethical "map" of ethical theories

ries say, respectively, that moral statements are really either statements of emotions or prescriptions for action. And since statements of emotion ("Yuck!" or "Yippee!") or prescriptions ("Take two aspirin and call me in the morning") are neither true nor false, moral judgments are neither true nor false either, even though on the surface they often look like simple declarative sentences.

Emotivist theories claim that when someone expresses a moral judgment, he is only expressing how he feels about an action. So "Abortion is wrong" means "I really feel awful about abortion," while "Promise keeping is good" means "I like people to keep their promises." Sometimes, emotivism is characterized as the "hooray/boo theory" of morality. ("Hooray for promise keeping! Boo for abortion!")

Emotivists are correct to note the emotion that often accompanies a moral judgment, but they are wrong to reduce moral judgments to mere statements of emotion. In fact, most of us intend our moral judgments to be understood as statements about moral praiseworthiness or blameworthiness of actions or agents. ("That murder was heinous." "This politician should be held accountable for his lie.") We do not believe for a minute that such statements are really nothing more than expressions of how we feel about some action or agent, and it seems to be rather arrogant for the emotivist to tell us we don't really mean what we think we are saying.

Prescriptivist theories of morality say that a moral statement is something like a doctor's prescription. If you go to your doctor and she gives you a prescription for your ailment, you might be foolish not to take the prescription as directed. If she's a good doctor, then it's good advice.

Similarly, moral statements should be regarded as advice—which could be either good or bad advice, depending on the qualification of the person making the statement and other relevant circumstances. A stronger version of prescriptivism is imperativalism, according to which moral statements are imperatives that command us to do or to refrain from doing something. Of course, we are confronted all the time with imperatives ("Merge left," "Sign on the line," "Don't miss this sale," "Don't torture"), and whether or not we obey them, or even regard them as binding on us, depends a lot on who issues the command, what the relevant circumstances are at the time, what the penalty for disobeying might be and whether or not we regard the command as a moral imperative.

In other words, we can tell the difference between a moral imperative and some other kind of imperative, which should show that moral statements cannot simply be reduced to imperatives. The person who misses the sale might wind up spending more money, perhaps even be fiscally foolish, but the person who participates in ritual torture is morally blameworthy.

In short, noncognitivist theories of morality completely fail to account for the strong intuitive sense we have of the difference between expressions of emotion, advice or commands, on the one hand, and genuinely moral judgments on the other hand, which carry obligation. They cannot account for the different sort of disapproval society gives to those who are simply foolish or impolite and to those who are regarded as genuinely immoral.

Cognitivism. So if moral statements have truth value—if a moral judgment is either true or false—what determines the truth value? If the material principle can be meaningfully cashed out, how do we characterize different versions? Different cognitive theories give different answers to this question. The broad division within cognitivist ethics is between subjective and objective theories. Now something is *subjective* if it depends on what is in a person's mind (thoughts, beliefs, fears, hopes, etc.), while something is *objective* if it is completely independent of anyone's thoughts, beliefs and so on. Subjectivist ethical theories take ethical statements to be either true or false, but they locate the truth maker for the statement in the thoughts, beliefs or other internal states of the moral subject or community. Ethical subjectivism can be further subdivided into *cultural relativism* and *individual relativism*.

Objectivist ethical theories claim that ethical judgments are true or false because of the way the world is, irrespective of what beliefs anyone might hold about the world. Moral objectivists deny that beliefs or thoughts are relevant to the truth of a moral judgment. Ethical objectivism can be subdivided into *ethical naturalism* and *ethical nonnaturalism*, depending on the nature of the grounds of the moral truth.

There's another important way of looking at the territory. This involves asking whether the moral theory is action-centered, or outcome-centered, or agent-centered. Deontological theories ground moral obligation in a duty to perform certain actions, and so are action-centered. Divine command theories generally fit this category. Consequentialist theories focus on the results of an action, and so are outcome-centered. Utilitarianism, hedonism and ethical egoism are examples. Virtue theory focuses on the character of the moral subject, and so is agent-centered. The virtue ethics of Aristotle or Thomas Aquinas are agent-centered examples. While there is some overlap, this way of distinguishing moral theories is at times quite helpful.

It's easy to see how different normative theories can be located on the metaethical map. Take Kant's deontological (duty-based) theory, for example. Kant believed that it was true that all persons at all times have a duty to act according to the categorical imperative, which says, in one formulation, "Act only according to that maxim by which you can at the same time will that it should become a universal law."[8] This theory is a cognitivist, objectivist theory. Whether or not it is further classified as naturalist or nonnaturalist depends on one's views of how such a maxim should be grounded. (While it might at first sound like this is a noncognitive, imperativalist theory, it's clear that Kant thought that it was a cognitive, objective theory.)

Utilitarianism, to take another example, holds (roughly) that an action is moral if its consequences lead to the greatest good for the great-

---

[8]Immanuel Kant, *Foundations of the Metaphysics of Morals*, trans. Lewis Beck White, 2nd ed. (New York: Macmillan, 1990), p. 38.

est number. If the notion of "the good" in a particular version of utilitarianism is cashed out in terms of objective properties that hold regardless of personal or cultural opinions, then this version of utilitarianism is a cognitivist, objectivist, ethical naturalist theory. But if "the good" is cashed out in terms of the beliefs or subjective values of a person or a culture, then this version of utilitarianism would be a cognitivist, subjectivist, individual or cultural relativist theory.

One final example: In Plato, the Form of the Good is the ground for moral judgment. An action is good to the degree that the action participates in the Form of the Good. But clearly, the forms are nonnatural entities, so Platonic ethics is cognitivist, objectivist, ethical nonnaturalist.

With this sketch of the territory, I'll now draw out what I see as the major implications of a Christian worldview for doing moral philosophy.

CHRISTIAN WORLDVIEW IMPLICATIONS: ETHICS

Consideration of the implications of a Christian worldview for doing ethics should need no justification: the connection is obvious. For many people, religion is just a code of ethics, and for others the primary function of religion is to impose some sort of public moral consensus. I won't reiterate why I think these are seriously deficient views of religion—especially Christianity. Rather, I'll simply agree that it's in the area of ethics that implications of a Christian worldview are more easily seen than in other areas of philosophy. And that's as it should be, if the end of philosophy is wise living. Christianity teaches the following principles:

1. God is a perfectly good being who created the universe with a "moral grain."

2. God made humanity in his image, including the capacity for rational decision-making and moral accountability.

3. Human flourishing is greatest when decisions are made in conformity to the moral character of God.

4. The ground of moral judgments about human motives and actions is the perfect moral character of God.

5. At least some human moral obligations and prohibitions are grounded in explicit divine commands.

It's clear as well from the Bible that certain things can be truly judged to be morally good or evil: actions (to cite but one example among many: Mt 5:16), agents (Mt 5:45), motives (Mt 12:33-36), character (1 Cor 15:33), and the good can be known (see the references to the "knowledge of good and evil" in Gen 2–3; see also Heb 5:14).

So for biblical and theological reasons, with which good philosophical arguments agree, ethical noncognitivism should not be an option when doing philosophy as a Christian. These theories cannot square with a theology that sees God as morally perfect and as commanding people to live morally good lives. In a Christian worldview, moral judgments are either true or false: we must be cognitivists.

Ethical cognitivism has two clear subdivisions, subjectivism and objectivism. What are Christian worldview implications here?

Subjectivism. Subjectivist theories of ethics agree that ethical statements have truth value, but they hold that whether a particular ethical statement is true or false depends on what people think. Cultural moral relativism is the view that the common moral beliefs of a culture are what make moral statements true or false; they determine that what is moral is relative to the beliefs of the culture. An act is moral within a particular culture if and only if it is judged to be moral by that culture.

Moral relativism. Because cultural moral relativism is so widely held, we should think closely about the issues involved. First, what sort of arguments can be advanced to support relativism? The usual defense of the position begins with the observation that moral codes differ considerably from one culture to another and from one era to another. Anthropologists have filled volumes detailing differing moral standards in various cultures. One culture buries its dead, another burns its dead, while a third eats its dead. One culture holds bribery to be immoral, while another regards such "gifts" as a normal way of doing business. Even within our own country, views on morality have changed. Divorce, extramarital sex and consumption of alcohol were all at one time regarded as immoral (at least by a large segment of the population), while racial segregation was not. This leads to a thesis of descriptive relativism (DR):

(DR) What is believed to be moral differs from culture to culture and from age to age.

While a case can be made that the moral codes of different times and cultures do not differ as much as is often claimed, nevertheless, for the sake of argument, I'll grant (DR). But what follows from the descriptive thesis? Most arguments for moral relativism draw a normative conclusion of cultural relativism (CR):

(CR) Therefore, what is moral differs from culture to culture and from age to age.

But it is clear, when formalized, that (CR) does not immediately follow from (DR). There is a missing or suppressed premise, a dependency thesis (DT):

(DT) What is moral depends on what is believed to be moral.

With (DT) included as a premise in the argument, (CR) does indeed follow. But why should we believe (DT)? No one who is not already willing to accept the conclusion (CR) would accept (DT), and if the argument depends on (DT), the argument clearly begs the question.

Tolerance. So the most obvious way to formulate an argument for moral relativism is a failure. Why else, then, might someone want to accept (CR)? Probably the most common reason today is a defective view of tolerance. Ask the average college undergraduate or the average progressive or liberal city-dweller (country people tend to be more conservative, both politically and ethically), and you'll be told that it is somehow wrong to judge another person or an action to be immoral. Why? Because we must be tolerant. The opposite of tolerant is bigoted, and it is morally wrong to be bigoted. Tolerance has become the supreme virtue in our culture, such that the only thing that can't be tolerated is intolerance (and never mind that this is self-refuting).

Of course, the refusal to make a judgment about the morality of an action is not genuine tolerance; it's moral cowardice, or intellectual laziness, or just plain confusion. True tolerance is the view that even if I believe that you are wrong, I will not use coercive force to enforce my belief. (Of course there are exceptions, notably for actions that harm others.) A truly tolerant person does not refrain from making judgments, but rather refrains from using power to coerce others to change their beliefs, relying instead on persuasion.

So tolerance as an argument for ethical relativism also fails, since it must rely on a defective notion of tolerance. If, then, both the argument from descriptive relativism and the argument from tolerance fail, and it is relatively easy to see that they do, why do so many—and sadly, in my view, many Christians as well—persist in holding to a relativist view of morality? Perhaps it is not too far off the mark to suggest that in our society, with its emphasis on individualism, rights and liberties, a new tacit social contract has emerged: I won't judge you if you don't judge me. This seems especially true in the case of so-called victimless crimes, notably those related to sex.

Against cultural relativism. Totally apart from the failure of arguments for ethical relativism, there are good arguments against it. I'll point out just three. First, cultural relativism makes criticism of other cultures impossible, because if that culture believes action A is moral, it is not relevant that our culture believes A is immoral. In any university, there will be students who refuse to judge Nazi Germany's Final Solution as immoral. "Well," they'll say, "of course it would be wrong for *us* to do that, but if *they* didn't think it was wrong, it wasn't wrong for them." And (appallingly) these students maintain that position no matter what the issue is: slavery, human sacrifice, female genital mutilation, torture, terrorism—no practice was wrong if the culture didn't think it was wrong. But surely we *can* make judgments about different cultures. We do not need to be a perfect society ourselves before we can criticize another on moral grounds. It seems clear to me that anyone thinking within a Christian worldview *must* judge that Nazi Germany was wrong, no matter what the culture believed; the slave trade was wrong, no matter cultural consensus; female genital mutilation is wrong, no matter how entrenched the tradition might be.

Second, cultural relativism makes the moral reformer immoral. For if what a culture believes is moral is in fact moral, then anyone who challenges that culture's beliefs is by definition immoral. Internal criticism is impossible. The abolitionist William Wilberforce was morally wrong, as were Mahatma Gandhi and Martin Luther King Jr. But that just can't be right. If a moral theory yields such counterintuitive results, so much the worse for the theory.

Finally, cultural relativism is an unstable position and will reduce ultimately to moral anarchy. The reason is that it is not possible to give a non-question-begging definition of culture in this context. What constitutes the relevant culture with respect to a moral judgment? Is it the particular local community? (The Supreme Court has ruled that local community standards are relevant when considering what constitutes pornography.) Or is it a single state? (Prostitution is legal in Nevada.) Or a region? (The South, prior to the Civil War, would have regarded slavery as moral.) Or the whole nation? the so-called Western world? Or something more narrow—evangelical Christians, Ivy League sororities, CEOs earning in excess of $10 million per year? Sooner or later, the definition of culture will invoke common beliefs as one identifying characteristic of a culture, with the result that a "culture" consists of "those who agree." But this is not at all helpful. It amounts to the claim that something is wrong only for those who believe it is wrong, which finally reduces to individual ethical relativism or moral anarchy.

Individual ethical relativism. Is it in fact the case that individual ethical relativism is moral anarchy? By my lights, yes. It is the condition described by the book of Judges: "All the people did what was right in their own eyes" (Judg 21:25 NRSV). It is the condition described by Thomas Hobbes (1588-1679) in *Leviathan:*

In such condition there is no place for industry, because the fruit thereof is uncertain: and consequently no culture of the earth; no navigation, nor use of the commodities that may be imported by sea; no commodious building; no instruments of moving and removing such things as require much force; no knowledge of the face of the earth; no account of time; no arts; no letters; no society; and which is worst of all, continual fear, and danger of violent death; and the life of man, solitary, poor, nasty, brutish, and short.[9]

John Calvin (1509-1564) said somewhere that no matter how bad a human government is, God grants that it is never so bad as anarchy. Individual relativism is unlivable. If a person believes it is not wrong for him to steal, rape or murder, what recourse does the victim have? Even if the individual relativist approves of legislation against such things in the interests of an orderly society, how can she not feel morally wronged (not merely legally wronged) if she's the victim? In short, while many may be moral relativists when "doing to," they soon become nonrelativists when "being done unto."

A Christian worldview understands that God, the all-knowing, perfectly good, supremely authoritative creator, has labeled certain things as good and others as evil. If there is any ground for an objective moral judgment, surely it is God's pronouncement. So subjectivism about morality does not sit at all well within a Christian worldview. And again, we've seen that philosophical argument supports a Christian worldview position.

Objectivism. We come now to the general class of objectivist ethical theories, those which hold that the truth or falsehood of moral statements does not depend on the thoughts or beliefs of any individuals or cultures. Objectivist theories fall into one of two categories, either *ethical naturalism* or *ethical nonnaturalism.* Both, though, are often labeled *moral realism,* since they agree that moral properties are real features of the world and not dependent on the mental life of any creatures.

Ethical naturalism. Ethical naturalists believe that moral properties are defined in terms of, or are reducible to, properties described by the natural (and perhaps the social) sciences. Some versions of natural law theory and some accounts of natural rights are naturalist theories in this sense. Aristotle believed (very roughly) that the necessary conditions of human flourishing could be "read off" the nature of human beings, and that to withhold anything necessary for flourishing was

---

[9]Thomas Hobbes, *Leviathan,* in *The English Philosophers from Bacon to Mill,* ed. Edwin A. Burtt (New York: Modern Library, 1939), p. 161.

immoral. For example, he said that humans need adequate food, shelter, clothing and (at least a modest amount of) leisure to be able to flourish, and so people had a moral right to these things. Jeremy Bentham, the father of utilitarianism (1748-1832) believed it was natural, and therefore moral, for humans to minimize pain and maximize pleasure. John Stuart Mill (1806-1873) further developed utilitarianism, claiming that what was moral was to seek the greatest good for the greatest number. Note that in both cases—pain and pleasure for Bentham and the greatest good for the greatest number for Mill—what counts as moral or immoral can be measured by the natural or social sciences. They are natural properties of the world. (I already noted briefly that there are versions of utilitarianism that take "the greatest good" as being that which commonly held cultural beliefs take to be the good. Such versions are subjectivist, not objectivist.)

It seems to many philosophers, and I concur, that ethical naturalism makes a mistake in reducing moral to natural properties. It is not at all clear that normative (moral) properties can be reduced to, or defined in terms of, natural (nonmoral) properties. For natural properties do not in themselves carry any normative notions; they just are. So something else must invest certain properties with moral qualities (e.g., causing gratuitous pain is morally wrong) while not so investing other properties (e.g., singing off-key is not morally wrong). In other words, there must be a meta-theory that determines which natural properties give rise to moral properties, and it cannot itself be naturalistic or an infinite regress results.

Ethical nonnaturalism. In contrast to naturalist theories, ethical nonnaturalism holds that ethical properties are irreducible features of the universe. Just as there are physical facts and properties, so too there are moral facts and properties. We already noted that Plato believed that goodness, justice and the like were eternal forms that existed just as surely as redness, squareness or the form of man. Some contemporary nonnaturalists want to avoid the language of Platonic forms but still posit the existence of irreducibly nonnatural moral properties in the universe. And religions like Christianity, which locate the source of morality in the nature of God, also yield nonnaturalist ethics.

CHRISTIAN NORMATIVE ETHICS

I'd like now to consider what I see as Christian worldview implications for three widely held normative ethical theories: outcome-centered *consequentialism,* action-centered *deontology* and agent-centered *virtue ethics.* But before we get to that, I need to address three preliminary matters. First, what do we expect an ethical theory to give us? Well, roughly, we want a way to tell what's the right thing to do. We want a guide to making moral decisions. Given that we accept the formal principle—Do what is morally good—we want to know how to flesh out the material principle: What *is* morally good? So we expect a moral theory to help us identify what makes for moral goodness (and moral wrongness). But notice that we don't expect a moral theory to tell us *why* we should do the right thing. That's really a metaethical question with significant worldview implications, and I'll return to it at the end of the chapter.

Second, it is important to note that as an evangelical Christian, I emphatically do not believe that anyone can be saved simply by being morally good. Discussions of moral theory are not discussions of soteriology (the theology of salvation). But, equally emphatically, I believe that all people *ought* to be moral, and that as Christian philosophers we should be able to make a persuasive argument that certain actions are moral or immoral, arguments that appeal to everyone whether or not they accept the authority of Scripture.

Third, I need to sound a caution against a practice I've seen adopted by some undergraduates in ethics classes. They often seem to assume that all that is needed in order to act morally is to find *some* rationale in *some* ethical theory for the action they're contemplating. They become eclectic ethicists, picking and choosing among theories to find the one theory that will "give them permission" to do what they want to do anyway. But ethical theory is not like that. Morality is not a cluttered toolbox of different theories, each ready to be employed for a different problem or to get a desired moral principle. The moral life should be a seamless, tightly woven fabric.

Consequentialism. Consequentialism refers to any moral theory that judges the moral value of an action based on its outcome or consequences. We should always seek to do that action which has good consequences and to avoid those actions which have bad consequences. Of course, spelling out just what constitutes "good consequences" is no small matter, and different answers give different forms of consequentialism.

The most popular form of consequentialism is utilitarianism. As it is usually stated, the principle of utilitarianism is always to seek "the greatest good for the greatest number." At first, the utilitarian principle may seem to be a fine ethical principle: it seems clear, comprehensive and easy to apply. But further consideration reveals that it is none of these. First, it is not clear, for it involves two superlatives; and it is impossible in almost every case to maximize both the good and numbers of people. And the two are not strictly commensurable. Suppose you had $100,000 to distribute as you saw fit, provided that you used it to secure "the greatest good for the greatest number." Would you give one dollar to 100,000 people? Or $100,000 to one person, or . . . ? Utilitarianism fails after all to give clear guidance in moral decision making.

Second, it is not comprehensive. To see this, ask, how do you define the "good"? We already encountered Bentham and Mill. Bentham takes "good" as maximization of sensual pleasure and minimization of pain, while Mill takes "good" as coming in degrees, where the intellectual pleasures are higher than sensual pleasures. Since Bentham and Mill, various analyses of "good" have been given by proponents of utilitarianism. But the point is that utilitarianism itself does not help at all in deciding what the good consists in, so as a moral theory it is incomplete, needing some additional theory to specify the nature of the good.

Third, it is not easy to apply. For often actions have unintended consequences, and what we think is likely to bring about good might turn out to do just the opposite. Further, how far must you look? The moral ripples of certain actions spread widely and last long, and who of us can know the comparative consequences of our actions with any reasonable degree of confidence?

In response to questions such as these, utilitarianism has undergone extensive refinement and today comes in a number of different varieties. I won't look at the details of any, for I claim that at the end of the day, utilitarianism of any variety will turn out to be an unsatisfactory theory for individual ethical decision making. Three thought experiments (which have been widely discussed in the relevant literature) will highlight the difficulties that plague any version of utilitarian theory.

First, utilitarianism can possibly lead to a perversion of justice. Say you are sheriff in a small town that has seen a recent murder that was clearly racially motivated. You have carefully investigated, but you have no leads, no idea who the murderer might be. Unrest grows, and rioting breaks out as the racial minority smells a cover-up. Word reaches you through an informant that the most militant sector of the minority will themselves kill one person of the racial majority at random each night until "justice is done." Now, as sheriff, you know you have just jailed a mentally incompetent vagrant whom you could frame for the murders. Suppose you reasonably believe this would end the rioting, prevent additional killing and restore calm. What would the utilitarian principle say is the right thing to do here? Plausibly, consequentialism would tell you to frame the vagrant. This is a very counterintuitive example of the end justifying the means, but that's just the point: consequentialism evaluates an action based on its outcome—its end. Yet, surely the nature of the action itself must have some bearing on its morality.

Second, utilitarianism might place a person in a situation that demands violating very deeply held moral principles. British philosopher Bernard Williams offers this example:

> Jim finds himself in the central square of a small South American town. Tied up against the wall are a row of twenty Indians, most terrified, a few defiant, in front of them several armed men in uniform. A heavy man in a sweat-stained khaki shirt turns out to be the captain in charge and, after a good deal of questioning of Jim which establishes that he got there by accident while on a botanical expedition, explains that the Indians are a random group of inhabitants who, after recent acts of protest against the government, are about to be killed to remind other possible protesters of the advantages of not protesting. However, since Jim is an honored visitor from another land, the captain is happy to offer him a guest's privilege of killing one of the Indians himself. If Jim accepts, then as a special mark of the occasion, the other Indians will be

let off. Of course, if Jim refuses, then there is no special occasion and Pedro here will do what he was about to do when Jim arrived, and kill them all. Jim, with some desperate recollection of schoolboy fiction, wonders whether if he got hold of a gun, he could hold the captain, Pedro and the rest of the soldiers to threat, but it is quite clear from the set-up that nothing of that kind is going to work: any attempt of that sort of thing will mean that all the Indians will be killed, and himself. The men against the wall, the other villagers, understand the situation, and are obviously begging him to accept. What should he do?[10]

Now suppose Jim has carefully constructed his moral character around a principle of nonviolence, believing that this is the teaching of the Lord Jesus in the Sermon on the Mount (Mt 5–7; cf. esp. Mt 5:39-46). Williams asks why it is that Jim should be constrained by the theory of utilitarianism to perform an action that so clearly violates his moral integrity, just because someone else has set up the situation in such a way that the utilitarian calculus comes out like this. How is it that Jim's character and the nature of the act don't enter into the ethical evaluation of the situation?

Third, utilitarianism often has the odd consequence that you should want everyone else to be a deontologist (doing their duty—see next section) while, secretly, you are a utilitarian. Imagine that you are in London during the Battle of Britain, and the prime minister has declared that, in order to conserve coal for the industries supporting His Majesty's military, everyone should keep the heat in their apartments at 62 degrees. Now you know that the British will certainly do their duty and keep their apartments cold. But, you reason, your overall happiness would be greatly increased if you could heat yours to 72 degrees. No one would know the difference, and the small additional amount of coal you burned would surely not make a difference to the war effort. Utilitarian calculus says that since cheating on the temperature of your apartment would increase overall happiness, provided everyone else does their duty, you should in fact cheat and keep it private. But how is it that a moral theory can have the implication that you should want

---

[10]Bernard Williams, "A Critique of Utilitarianism," in *Ethics: Discovering Right and Wrong*, ed. Louis Pojman, 2nd ed. (Belmont, Calif.: Wadsworth, 1995), p. 121.

everyone else to follow a different theory, that you should keep quiet about it and break the rules?

In fairness, utilitarians have offered responses to these and other problems that have been raised, but a great many ethicists have found the responses inadequate. It seems highly doubtful that the end can justify the means (in all but the most extreme and improbable circumstances, perhaps), that outcomes are the sole object of moral evaluation, and that the nature of the action and the character of the agent have no role to play.

Before leaving the discussion of consequentialism, however, let me say that in my opinion, asking about the greatest good for the greatest number is often a good place to start when considering matters of public policy. Suppose you're on a city council considering a project to widen a freeway. The project is predicted to result in greatly improved traffic flow and shorter commutes for thousands (thereby saving gas and reducing pollution), and in a 20 percent lower accident rate on the freeway, thereby reducing accident-related deaths by eight per year. But the project also will result in 190 families being displaced from their homes. And suppose that you and a majority of the council think that the project will indeed result in the greatest good for the greatest number, so under the doctrine of eminent domain, you condemn the homes. But in going ahead, you'll encounter the problem of distributive justice. The greatest good for the greatest number almost always entails greater harm for a few. So in using a utilitarian approach to public policy, government officials must always be ready to offer just compensation to those who have been harmed by a utilitarian decision.

Deontology. While consequentialism claims that the good outcomes of an act make the act morally good, deontological ethics (from the Greek *deon*, "that which is necessary or right") focuses on the nature of the act itself. Consequentialism says the end justifies the means; deontology says this is never the case. Consequentialism claims that nonmoral values (e.g., happiness, avoidance of pain) determine the moral rightness or wrongness of an act; deontology says (most) acts themselves have intrinsic moral qualities, and it is our duty to do that which is moral. Since keeping promises is moral and breaking promises is immoral, you should keep your promise even if the foreseeable consequences are highly negative. You are responsible only for doing your duty, not for altering your duty to achieve different outcomes.

Although some deontologists have focused on individual acts, most deontological theories have argued that ethical rules are the proper way to think about our moral duty. Rules such as "Tell the truth," "Keep your promises" and "Don't commit murder" are examples. What rules like this have in common is that they are universalizable; that is, if action A is morally right (or wrong), then for anyone in circumstances relevantly similar, A would also be right (or wrong).

Two further distinctions must be mentioned here. First, deontologists differ among themselves as to how moral duties can be known. Intuitionists believe that we know moral duties through our conscience, while rationalists hold that it is through use of our reason that we discover our moral duties. It seems likely that both aspects have a place in the moral life. For our conscience certainly does serve as a source of moral knowledge (cf. Rom 2:15). But there seem to be many situations where the issues are so complicated—think especially of the many difficult moral choices presented to us by advances in biotechnology—that we must apply reason carefully in analyzing the relevant moral factors before us.

The second distinction is that between absolutism and objectivism. Absolutists believe that an adequate moral theory will never produce conflicting duties, that moral principles are all of equal force and cannot be overridden. Objectivists (here used in a different sense than in metaethical theory) claim that while moral duties are universal, they are not necessarily without exception. Moral duties override all other kinds of considerations, but they come in a form such that there is a hierarchy among them. The objectivist often distinguishes prima facie duties—those which at first glance seem to hold—from actual duties. To illustrate the difference, consider the oft-discussed case of the Dutch woman who hides Jews from the Nazis. When the SS troops arrive at the door, the absolutist would say she has a duty to tell the truth, while the objectivist would say that the duty to save lives overrides the duty to tell the truth. The objectivist might even tell her that while truthful-

ness is a prima facie duty, the Nazis, because of their immoral intentions, have forfeited their moral claim to being told the truth. Note that
rather than being a lesser of two evils, this is the greater of two goods.

The Divine Command Theory of Morality. It's easy to see why Christians throughout the ages have found some sort of deontological ethics
very amenable to their worldview. And while some regard an ethical
system grounded in God's commands to be a separate category, I'll
treat it as a version of deontology. For if the "chief end of man is to
glorify God and enjoy Him forever," as the Westminster Shorter Catechism puts it, it surely follows that doing this includes obeying God's
commands. The Christian's duty is to obey.

More generally, the Divine Command Theory (DCT) holds to
three theses: First, morality depends on God. Second, any action is
required (prohibited, permitted) only if it is required (prohibited, permitted) by a command of God. And third, if God does not exist, then
there is no morality. (Recall the words spoken by Ivan Karamazov in
Fyodor Dostoyevsky's *The Brothers Karamazov:* "If there is no God,
then everything is permitted.") Under the DCT, "morally right"
means "commanded by God," while "morally wrong" means "prohibited by God."

The DCT is faced immediately with an objection called the "Euthyphro dilemma" (named for Plato's dialogue, the *Euthyphro,* in which
Socrates asks Euthyphro, "Do the gods love what is pious because it is
pious, or is it pious because the gods love it?"). As an objection to the
DCT, the dilemma goes like this: either (i) God commands action A
because A is moral, or (ii) A is moral because God commands A. Presumably the theist does not want to accept (i) and admit that the standard of morality is external to God. Nor apparently would the theist
want to accept (ii). If (ii), allegedly, then God could command anything
whatever—theft, rape, genocide—and it would be moral. Thus morality is arbitrary.

While some Christian thinkers have taken the second horn of the
dilemma (ii), most have held that the dilemma is a false one. If God is
essentially morally perfect, then God would not—indeed, could not—
command just any act whatsoever; and if God is thus understood, this

modified DCT avoids the force of the Euthyphro dilemma.[11]

But two other problems face a modified DCT. The first has to do with the specification of moral (or immoral) acts and the second with the nature of public morality. The first simply notes the great complexity of moral problems that we face in our world, problems such as stem cell research, genetic engineering, preemptive war against terrorism and producing genetically modified foods. It is dubious that any clear command of God can be applied unambiguously to these problems, so the DCT fails to deliver on its promise. (This is not to say that moral principles from divine revelation may not be applied to complex contemporary moral issues. But the DCT supposes divine commands, not moral principles, constitute the ground of morality. Applying principles is quite different from obeying direct commands.)

The second problem faced by the DCT has to do with the public square. How should a religiously based morality be applied in a religiously pluralistic society? It could be argued that biblical law should be the law of the land (roughly, a position called Reconstructionism), but most theologians do not believe that the laws of ancient Israel are applicable in any straightforward way outside their theocratic context. And even if they were, we would land again squarely in the specification problem. I believe that a better approach is hinted at in two relevant passages in Scripture.

In the first two chapters of Amos, the prophet reports the Lord's judgment on six nations surrounding Israel and then on Israel itself. The six nations, which were not recipients of Israel's divinely revealed Law, are judged for what today would be called crimes against humanity, while Israel is judged for violations of the Mosaic law. And in Romans 2:1-16, the Gentiles are held accountable not to the letter of the Law, but to the standard of their own conscience. The point is this: there is a standard of morality available to all people through their conscience and through their use of reason, apart from divine revelation

---

[11]Whether God is essentially morally perfect—whether or not he has genuine moral freedom—is an issue that has been much discussed of late. See, for example, Wes Morriston, "Omnipotence and Necessary Moral Perfection: Are They Compatible?" *Religious Studies* 37 (2001): 143-60; and T. J. Mawson, "Omnipotence and Necessary Moral Perfection Are Compatible: A Reply to Morriston," *Religious Studies* 38 (2002): 215-23.

(and that standard is sufficient to show their just condemnation before God and need of salvation). Thus I think that moral arguments in the public square can and should be made based on moral intuition and natural reason, even while moral arguments among God's people may invoke the surer standards of revelation. But this argument from natural morality is not available under the DCT.

Clearly a Christian worldview claims that God has revealed a number of moral commands which it is our duty to obey, and Scripture contains an array of moral principles which we can and should bring to bear on ethical decisions we face. I don't in any way wish to minimize the obligation that these direct commands and moral principles put on believers. But at the end of the day, I don't think that the DCT is an adequate *general* moral theory.

Virtue ethics. Virtue theory has a long and distinguished pedigree, going back to Aristotle and Plato, running through Thomas Aquinas and including many contemporary advocates. In contrast to both deontological and consequentialist theories, which focus on actions and outcomes, respectively, virtue ethics focuses on the character of a good person and the quality of the good life. It addresses the development of good character and emphasizes community and relationships.

Virtue theory is *teleological* in that its aim is to develop dispositions that enable a person to live well. A virtue is a disposition, a skill of sorts. Virtues thus are character traits that enable a person to achieve the goal of *eudaimonia*, "happiness," not in the sense of momentary pleasurable satisfaction, but in the sense of flourishing, well-being, an excellent life. Classic virtue ethics includes a commitment to essentialism, which roughly is the idea that human beings have an essence or nature (see the discussion of natures in chapter 5). On this view, the truth about human nature provides the grounds for understanding ideal human functioning. One who functions ideally and skillfully in life is one who functions properly in accordance with human nature. Human nature defines what is unique and proper for human flourishing, and a bad person is one who lives contrary to human nature. Thus, in Romans 1:26-27, Paul argues that homosexuality is wrong because it is "against nature"; that is, it is contrary to proper human functioning in accordance with the essence of being human.

Given a correct understanding of proper human functioning, virtue ethics spells out what constitutes a good character—the sum total of dispositions to think, feel, judge, desire and act in such a way as to flourish. Virtues go beyond the distinctly moral virtues and include "intellectual virtues" such as studiousness, intellectual curiosity and rationality, as well as "natural virtues" such as courage (one can be a courageous crook as well as a courageous Christian). Indeed, as Aquinas argued, there is a unity among the virtues, so that one who is lacking in one area cannot be wholly virtuous in other areas. A person who is intellectually lazy, prejudiced or complacent cannot be a truly virtuous agent any more than can the genius who is an inveterate liar. Traditionally, virtue ethics includes at least the "four cardinal virtues" of prudence, justice, courage and temperance. Christianity added the distinctively Christian virtues of faith, hope and love.

Aristotle, in the *Nichomachean Ethics,* investigates how virtue is developed and emphasizes the role of examples and instruction, of friends and laws. For Christian thinkers, the spiritual disciplines have been central to understanding character. A spiritual discipline, such as fasting, solitude or silence, is a repeated activity aimed at developing habits that train a person in a life of virtue. Practicing a spiritual discipline is very much like practicing the scales on a piano. One does not practice the scales to get good at playing the scales. Rather, one practices the scales to form the habits necessary for becoming an excellent piano player. Similarly, one does not perform spiritual disciplines to get good at them but, rather, to get good at life. A spiritual discipline is a means to forming dispositions relevant to the development of character and virtue.

One additional feature of virtue theory deserves comment. Virtue is at least partially person-relative. Let me hasten to state that this does not mean it is an individual relativistic theory. Here's why. As an example, take the (natural) virtue of courage. Aristotle taught that a virtue is in most cases the mean between two vices. Courage then is the mean between cowardice on the one hand, and foolhardiness on the other. Consider Sam and Sue, walking together in the dark to their cars

in a parking lot after a long work day. Sam is very unathletic and out of
shape, and rather timid. Sue, on the contrary, is very athletic, holding
four or five black belts in various martial arts, with a history of coura-
geously confronting threats. They are accosted by a group of five juve-
niles who demand their money and car keys. Sam, rather than melting
in a pool of cowardice, throws his wallet and keys in one direction and,
attempting to grab Sue's hand, sets off running in the opposite direction. Sue, though, in a scene reminiscent of the movies, throws a roundhouse kick, taking out three of the gang, and quickly subdues the other
two. Now, given Sam's personal situation, his act was courageous *for*
him, while given Sue's skills, her action was courageous *for her.* If Sue
had run away though, given her abilities, it would have been cowardice—the same action that was courageous for Sam. But suppose that
the same scenario unfolds a couple nights later to Sam, alone. Recalling
Sue's valor, he also attempts a roundhouse kick, pulls a groin muscle,
and falls to the ground where he is beaten and robbed. Again, given his
lack of skills, this action was foolhardy for him—the same action that
was courageous for Sue. The illustration might be a bit farfetched, but
I think the point is clear: while far from being infinitely flexible, many
virtues are person-relative in the sense that a virtuous action *for that*
person in those circumstances depends relevantly on the person's background, knowledge, abilities and certain features of the situation.

I think that this limited person-relativity is reflected in the Bible.
Truth-telling surely is a virtue commended throughout the Bible. However, in Exodus 1, as the slavery in Egypt is becoming unbearably op-
pressive, the Hebrew midwives are ordered to kill male babies. They do
not do so, and lie to Pharaoh. But rather than chastise the midwives for
lying, we read, "So God was kind to the midwives and the people increased and became even more numerous. And because the midwives
feared God, he gave them families of their own" (Ex 1:20-21). Similarly, in Joshua 2, the Canaanite prostitute Rahab hid the two Hebrew
spies on her roof, and lied, saying they had already left. Later, her life
was spared (Josh 6:17) because she saved the spies. In both these cases,
I maintain, and in others as well, we can see that virtuous behavior is
relative to the person and the situation. This is not to say that the indi-

viduals—indeed, all of us—should not grow in virtuous character and conduct, but rather to allow that under virtue theory, there is a measure of flexibility in applying the pure, exalted standards of virtue.

Virtue ethics has secured a wide following throughout the history of ethics and has enjoyed something of a revival in recent years. And it is easy to see why. Its core notions of the flourishing life, the good person, character and virtue capture much of what is central to the moral life.

Yet virtue ethics is not without its critics. Two objections are often raised against it. The first objection is the claim that given naturalistic evolutionary theory, several notions at the core of virtue theory, while not logically impossible, are nevertheless implausible. Such things as an overarching purpose to life, genuine essences or natures, and notions of proper and improper functioning, are hard to harmonize with a view that depicts humans as creatures that have evolved through a blind process of chance and necessity.

One response might be found in the work of some contemporary virtue ethicists, such as Alasdair MacIntyre, who seek to explicate virtue ethics without essentialism. Roughly, virtues are features judged to be skills relevant to the good life as that is understood relative to the narrative embodied in different traditions. A tradition is a community whose members are united by a core of shared beliefs and a commitment to them. Thus, virtues are not grounded in an objective human nature; rather, they are linguistic constructions relative to the valuations and commitments of different traditions. But I have doubts that this approach can prove successful. In addition to being subject to the criticisms of moral relativism noted above, I doubt that MacIntyre's notion of virtue can make sense of our deepest moral intuitions or the nature of moral obligation. I have a deep conviction that there is an objective difference between a good and a bad person, between a life lived well and a life lived poorly, and that the difference is more than a matter of cultural customs.

A second response that can be made would be simply to deny that there is a logical contradiction between naturalistic evolution and virtue theory. But we grant that the two do not sit easily with each other. So perhaps this conflict (together with other problems with Darwinism) is further evidence that evolution needs serious modification if not rejection.

The second objection is that virtue ethics simply fails to give guidance in resolving moral dilemmas and in knowing what to do in various moral situations. This is especially true when virtue ethics is compared with rule-based ethical theories such as rule-utilitarianism. Rule-based theories are far better suited for providing such guidance than is virtue ethics.

This objection is overstated if it means that virtue theory provides no guidance at all for the moral life. The role of example (asking questions such as "What would Jesus do in this situation?" or imitating the actions or the thinking of virtuous people) does provide guidance for leading a morally superior life. In its focus on character dispositions, virtue theory captures the truth that virtuous actions depend on virtuous character.

I believe that from the perspective of a Christian worldview, virtue ethics is the most viable theory of morality, even though some very able Christian philosophers defend other theories. First, virtue theory is not exclusive of consequentialist or deontological considerations; the virtuous person will use her intellect, emotion, judgment and desire together in weighing both relevant duties and possible outcomes in her deliberations about the right ethical decision. Second, virtue theory, because it is in part person-relative, surely fits well with a Christian worldview's emphasis on grace rather than strict application of law.

Third, virtue theory, in focusing on the development of character marked by dispositions to virtuous behavior, accords supremely with the Bible's emphasis on continued growth in holiness and responsibility for motives as well as actions and consequences.[12] And finally, in Aristotle's recommendations to study virtuous people to learn from them what virtuous character looks like, we see a parallel to the New Testament's teaching that we should be imitators of virtuous people (1 Cor 4:16; Heb 6:12), and supremely the example of Jesus (1 Cor 11:1; 1 Pet 2:21).

---

[12]See, for example, Benjamin W. Farley, *In Praise of Virtue: An Exploration of the Biblical Virtues in a Christian Context* (Grand Rapids: Eerdmans, 1995).

One final caution must be sounded. There are those who dislike talk of virtue (or perhaps morality in general), on the grounds that moral goodness is beyond human ability and only possible for a Christian who is empowered by the Holy Spirit. These critics quote passages such as Romans 3:9-18, where Paul, quoting from several Old Testament texts, says such things as "There is no one righteous, not even one. . . . There is no one who does good, not even one." But I think this reflects a deep confusion between morality as the grounds of salvation and morality as the grounds of human flourishing. True— in the end, a flourishing life depends upon a relationship with God; Jesus said that he came that we might "have life, and have it to the full" (Jn 10:10), and he taught that "eternal life" was constituted by knowing the only true God, and Jesus Christ, whom God had sent (Jn 17:3). Nevertheless, Jesus also acknowledged that even wicked people could do good things: "If you, then, though you are evil, know how to give good gifts to your children, how much more will your Father in heaven give good gifts to those who ask him?" (Mt 7:11). No one merits salvation by doing moral good, but it does not follow that moral good is impossible. Benjamin Farley puts it well:

> Throughout the Bible, one truth reigns supreme that provides the fundamental metaphysics of any biblical ethics of character: *no one is saved by exercising virtue; nor is anyone damned for the lack of it. God and God's grace come first.* Only then can everything else be seen in its proper perspective—from the human response of faith, hope and love, to the value of the classical virtues with their capacity to deepen personhood and mold character. As long as this order is preserved, human life ceases to be, contrary to Sartre's dictum, a "useless passion," and becomes a wonder, and we as creatures, "a little lower than God" (Ps 8:5).[13]

WHY BE MORAL?

In concluding the discussion of ethics, I want to return to the metaethical question mentioned above: Why should I be moral? Note that this is not a question that normative ethics can answer; the role

---

[13]Ibid., p. 3; emphasis in original.

of a normative theory is to spell out what moral or immoral actions consist in and how to go about moral decision making. But those projects assume the obligation to live a moral life. There really are two questions here. The first is, "Why should anyone at all be moral?" Perhaps the best answer to that question comes from such fictional portrayals as William Golding's *Lord of the Flies;* perhaps it is best summarized by Hobbes's depiction of "man in the state of nature" (that is, as we are left to ourselves), a "state of war of every man against every other man," where life is "solitary, poor, nasty, brutish and short." This, as Christians, we recognize as the reign of sin, resulting in moral anarchy. And (apart from regeneration), the corrosive effects of sin must be checked by individual and social acceptance of and attempts to live by a moral code.

Second, we can ask, "Why should *I* be moral?" This question asks, in effect, why I should adopt a moral point of view and seek to live a morally good life. We can understand this question as Glaucon put it to Socrates in Plato's *Republic.* He asks why we should prefer to be a virtuous person who is unsuccessful and is regarded by his peers as immoral, rather than an immoral person who is successful and appears to be highly moral. Answering the question "Why I should be moral?" will tell me why I should desire to be good even if I seem bad rather than to be bad but seem good.

Socrates' answer to Glaucon (to which the whole *Republic* is devoted) ultimately arrives at the claim that the harmony of one's soul is incompatible with an immoral life. To ask if you should desire to be moral is like asking if you should desire to be healthy. The immoral person will not, in the end, be able to enjoy his unjustly enriched life.

But it isn't at all clear that there aren't people with such amoral character that they could enjoy their ill-gotten gains anyway. These are people for whom the "harmony of the soul" is an empty notion. They seem quite content in their disharmonious soul, perhaps using their ill-gotten material goods or positions of power to anesthetize any last tremors of concern arising from their moral apathy. (Think only of the many moral failings of politicians in recent years.) And on the other side, don't we all know good people who are quite unhappy? I've found that even if Socrates' answer seems attractive to students, even if they do catch a fleeting dream of a harmonious soul, they have very little difficulty imagining someone for whom Socrates' answer has no appeal. So it seems that I need another sort of answer to the question, "Why should *I* be moral?"

Think again about the question. Is the *should* a moral or a practical *should*? If the answer is that it is a moral *should*, then it assumes that the moral point of view has already been adopted: it is moral to be moral. But that is trivial for the person who has already adopted the moral point of view and will not help at all for the one who hasn't. So we should (in the practical sense!) take the *should* in the question to be a practical or rational *should*. In this sense the question asks what practical or rational justification can be given for being moral.

Well, as rational people, we attempt to formulate a life plan, a reasonable manner of living our lives, a consistent guide to negotiating life and living it skillfully, "eudaimonistically," so that we flourish as persons. And we formulate our life plan in accordance with our worldview. So clearly, if our worldview incorporates features such as right and wrong, if, as it were, morality is built into the universe, then immoral actions will "go against the grain of the universe" and our lives cannot reasonably be expected to go as well as if we were to go "with the grain."

Rational people, according to a Christian worldview, have a moral conscience—the faculty by which we discern moral properties and discriminate moral from immoral actions and states of affairs. (Indeed, the inability to tell right from wrong is a legal basis for an insanity defense.) Further, the conscience seems to be the faculty that delivers to us the sense of obligation I spoke of earlier. So for a rational person, the deliverances of conscience must play a role in a worldview and in developing a life plan. A secularist can simply accept conscience as a brute fact about persons, or as an evolutionary adaptation conducive to survival, and leave it at that.

Once the nontheist grants that there are basic moral obligations in the universe to which conscience points, then envisioning a rational life plan must include a commitment to morality as best as it can be understood. And this will lead him to think about normative ethics. Even nontheists then have reason to be moral. And they *can* be good—even very good—people without believing in God. My claim is that, at the end of the day, they don't have a very compelling explanation of why they *should* be.

The problem is that whether conscience (and the morality to which it points) is a brute fact, or an evolutionary adaptation, there is no explanation of the obligatoriness—the oughtness—of moral judgments. Practical reasons for being moral just do not capture the sense of moral obligation we've noted: there's a real distinction between a practical *ought* ("You ought to follow your doctor's orders") and a moral *ought* ("You ought to treat people as ends, not as means").

In a naturalistic universe we can easily identify goods that are necessary for flourishing, and others that increase happiness, and we can say, with Aristotle, that pursuit of such goods in a way that allows others also to pursue them is virtuous. But as George Mavrodes has pointed out in a widely read essay, morality at times obligates us to forego some of these goods.[14] For example, we believe that a mother and a father are obligated to forego pursuit of certain personal goods in order to provide for the health and safety of their child. We deem a father who abandons his child in order to enjoy greater personal freedom and prosperity to be morally blameworthy, as is a mother who uses her limited resources to buy illegal drugs and lets her baby starve.

So here at last we come to what I believe is one of the most significant features of a Christian worldview. I claim that of all worldviews, the biblical worldview is the one that can best account for moral obligation. It does so, as I've noted, in terms of a morally perfect creator who imbued creation with a moral grain and created humans in his image with the responsibility to be moral and the capacity to discern moral truths. We *ought* to be moral because God, who made us, made us to be moral. As so often in philosophical discussions, rather than terminating in a natural brute fact, the Christian explanation terminates in a perfect personal being. But I want to be clear: I am not claiming that only Christians can be moral, or that only Christians recognize the

---

[14]George I. Mavrodes, "Religion and the Queerness of Morality," in *Moral Philosophy: A Reader*, ed. Louis P. Pojman (Indianapolis: Hackett, 1993), pp. 254-62.

obligatoriness of moral judgments. My claim is that a Christian world-view makes much better sense of that obligatoriness than any other.

THE MEANING OF LIFE

Finally, I will add a far-too-brief concluding thought to this chapter. The French existentialist Albert Camus wrote,

> Judging whether life is or is not worth living amounts to answering the fundamental question of philosophy. All the rest—whether or not the world has three dimensions, whether the mind has nine or twelve categories—come afterwards. These are games. . . . I have never seen anyone die for the ontological argument . . . the meaning of life is the most urgent of questions.[15]

And Camus was spot-on, in my opinion. But how does the question of the meaning of life fit in a chapter on value, primarily ethical value? Too often, in both popular and scholarly circles, discussions of ethics are divorced from questions of ultimate meaning. Ethics consist of norms agreed upon by society, and particular moral precepts may change as society changes. On the other hand, questions about the meaning of life are purely individualistic (see the quote by Justice Kennedy in the epigraph to this chapter).

But the division between ethics and ultimate meaning is rather recent. As many authors have shown, the ancient and medieval tradition—at least until William of Ockham and Duns Scotus—nearly unanimously accepted the direct connection between personal happiness as the aim of a well-lived life and a theory of morality that conduced to happiness.[16]

Perhaps the modern reluctance to see any necessary link between personal happiness and morality is due to the hijacking of the classical notion of *eudaimonia* in the utilitarian writings of Jeremy Bentham and John Stuart Mill, where it is cashed out in terms of pleasure, and in the ethical egoist philosophy of Ayn Rand's "objectivism." But recent years

---

[15]Albert Camus, *The Myth of Sisyphus and other Essays*, trans. Justin O'Brien (New York: Knopf, 1955), pp. 3-4.
[16]For the classic exposition of this theme, see Julia Annas, *The Morality of Happiness* (Oxford: Oxford University Press, 1993).

have seen a recovery of interest in the classical vision where morality
was tied to the ultimate purpose of life. As the Stoic Seneca wrote,

> As often as you wish to know what is to be avoided or what is to be
> sought, consider its relation to the Supreme Good, to the purpose of
> your whole life. For whatever we do ought to be in harmony with this;
> no man can set in order the details unless he has already set before him-
> self the chief purpose of his life.[17]

Christian ethicists too are articulating this vision, understanding
that the greatest good, the *summum bonum*, of life is found in knowing
God, and only in that relationship can true happiness be found. As St.
Augustine put it,

> [God] himself is the fountain of our happiness; he himself is the end of
> all of our longing. In choosing him, or rather, since we had lost him
> through neglect, in re-choosing him, . . . we strive toward him by love,
> so that by attaining him we might rest, happy because we are perfected
> by him who is our end. Thus, our good, the end which is extensively
> disputed among the philosophers, is nothing other than to cling to
> him.[18]

A well-developed Christian worldview will integrate the transcendentals—truth, goodness and beauty—into a vision of a flourishing
human life, in which morality plays *a* (not *the*) constitutive role,
grounded in an understanding of the nature of God, and humans as his
image bearers. As the Westminster Shorter Catechism succinctly puts
it in Question 1: "What is the chief end of man? Man's chief end is to
glorify God, and to enjoy Him forever."

Contributing to the articulation of that integrated vision should, I
submit, form the overarching framework within which the Christian
philosopher does not only ethical theory but all philosophy.

---

[17]Seneca, "On the Supreme Good," *Epistle LXXI, Ad Lucilium Epistulae Morales*, trans. Richard
M. Gummere (Cambridge, Mass.: Harvard University Press, 1962), p. 73.
[18]Augustine *City of God* 10.3, in *Political Writings*, ed. Michael W. Tkacz and Douglas Kries
(Indianapolis: Hackett, 1994), p. 73.

PART THREE

SECOND-ORDER QUESTIONS

Those who wish to succeed must ask
the right preliminary questions.

ARISTOTLE

Good philosophy must exist, if for no other reason,
because bad philosophy must be answered.

C. S. LEWIS

- Who or what am I?
- What is nature?
- Whom do I serve?

In addition to asking—and proposing to answer—the inescapable questions, philosophy also explores questions about specialized topics, such as philosophy of logic, philosophy of language, philosophy of time and philosophy of mind.

And philosophy asks a certain sort of questions about other disciplines as well, questions about the meaning of terms and concepts, the methods of investigation, and the kinds of questions and answers posed

in these other disciplines. Philosophy of science, philosophy of education and philosophy of religion are such enquiries.

We'll look at two examples in the following chapters. We might
have also looked at philosophy of law, or political philosophy, or philosophy of education, or others. But two will suffice: philosophy of
mind and philosophy of science.

In this endeavor, philosophy is a "second-order" discipline, assisting
in achieving clarity and precision in articulating the preliminary questions of other disciplines. Second-order questions are, for example,
"What is science, and how do you tell science from pseudo-science?" "Is
it coherent to speak of a being called God who has the attributes traditionally ascribed to him?"

These are questions that are philosophical, not scientific or religious.
And so, as we think about doing philosophy as a Christian, we need to
think about such second-order questions.

8

WHO AND WHAT AM I?

PHILOSOPHY OF MIND

I think we ought to hold not only that man has a soul,
but that it is important that he should know that he has a soul.

J. GRESHAM MACHEN

What a piece of work is a man, how noble in reason,
how infinite in faculties, in form and moving how express and admirable,
in action how like an angel, in apprehension how like a god!
the beauty of the world, the paragon of animals.

SHAKESPEARE

How can we square this self-conception of ourselves as mindful,
meaning-creating, free, rational, etc., agents with a universe that
consists entirely of mindless, meaningless, unfree,
nonrational, brute physical particles?

JOHN SEARLE

Any reflective thinker who ponders the nature of the world around her, the support for her beliefs, the morality of her actions, will inevitably find her critical gaze turning on herself. What is she, in the world—a substance, a bundle of properties, a biological machine, an embodied soul? It seems to her that at least some of her decisions and actions are freely taken; is that an illusion? And if free will is an illusion, then what of morality—is it simply a way to talk about helpful or harmful behavior, or a way to feel better as a society for locking up someone who looks strange or behaves differently? What comes after death, if anything? Is there a God? How can she know?

Second only to the question of whether or not God or a supernatural realm exists, the question of what a human person is, is central to a worldview. Whether one believes that a person with an individual identity is an illusion (as in Hinduism) or an evolved complex biological machine (as in naturalism) or an embodied soul made in the image of God (as in Judaism and Christianity), that belief will make all the difference in how one lives one's life, influencing one's beliefs about free will, knowledge, morality and much more.

ISSUES AND OPTIONS

Philosophical anthropology, somewhat broader than philosophy of mind, is the arena of philosophical thinking about such questions.[1] In order to keep this chapter to a manageable length, I'll assert the author's privilege to restrict the discussion to just three topics: First, how should we understand what a human person is—what, if anything, do we mean by the term 'soul'? This will involve discussions of the venerable mind-body problem, the origins of consciousness, qualia—the subjective "feel" of certain perceptual experiences—and the like. These are the sort of questions receiving an enormous amount of attention in philosophy of mind, and they will bring us to a discussion (and my defense) of substance dualism. Second, do human persons have anything like free will, and if so, how? While philosophy of mind discusses these questions, action theory also enters the picture. And finally, within the context of a Christian worldview, I'll consider the central

---

[1] In my own very subjective view, philosophy of mind is the most difficult subdivision of philosophy. I have benefited greatly from the work of George Bealer, John Cooper, Stewart Goetz, William Hasker, Richard Swinburne and J. P. Moreland, and freely acknowledge my debt to them for much of what I have written in this chapter. They certainly would not all agree with each other, nor with me, on all points, but together they offer strikingly strong arguments against physicalism and for some form of substance dualism.

Christian doctrine of the resurrection of the body, and suggest how in my view that doctrine should impact the thinking of the Christian philosopher on these topics.

Substance dualism. It's a truism that in the long history of philosophical thought, as well as in popular or folk psychology, most people have believed in a soul of some kind and would generally be classified as substance dualists. According to substance dualism, a person's various conscious states—feelings, sensations, thoughts, desires, intentional choices—are immaterial and not physical states, and the thing that "has" these states—the I, self, ego, soul—is not the brain but, rather, is an immaterial subject that somehow interacts with the brain, and through it, with the body. This "self" is often called the "soul,"[2] but we should recognize that the philosopher's use of the word is not perfectly congruent with either the biblical use of the word nor with the way most theologians use the term. To say that the soul is a substance is to say that it is a thing that has properties and is neither something that is "had" by another thing, nor is it constituted by a bundle of properties or mental states. (I'll offer a more precise characterization of substance dualism below.)

Many philosophers who deny dualism still will admit that it is the commonsense view. The history of theological anthropology reveals the same thing. Most Christians through the centuries have believed that men and beasts have souls; or, more accurately, they have believed that a human person *has* a body and a soul. The human soul, while not by nature immortal,[3] is capable of disembodied existence upon death and, eventually, of being reunited with a resurrected body. The Christian hope, according to the Bible, is not the immortality of the soul, but the resurrection of the body.

The early to middle decades of the twentieth century saw the rise of several forms of behaviorism, the attempt to reduce all mental talk to

---

[2]For example, Richard Swinburne, *The Evolution of the Soul,* rev. ed. (New York: Oxford University Press, 1997).

[3]There's a lot of talk in Christian circles about "the immortal soul." But in Christian theology, only God is essentially immortal. The continuing existence of everything else, including human souls, is contingent on God's sustaining power. Humans have, then, only conditional immortality.

talk of behaviors. However, recognition of the possibility of perfect
pretenders pretty much undermined behaviorism's claim to be able to
reduce the mental to the behavioral. And today, the landscape appears
decidedly different, much less friendly to dualism. The past fifty years
have seen increasing antipathy to acknowledging anything like a
spooky "ghost in the machine," reinforced by the remarkable successes
in brain research.

Physicalism. Since about the middle of the twentieth century, a prevailing current in philosophy has been toward "naturalizing" the analysis of concepts and issues, locating them within the best available (or
the future theoretically complete) natural sciences, especially physics,
chemistry and biology, and clarifying and systematizing the philosophical concepts in the language of the natural sciences. Now, the natural
sciences are committed to an objective, third-person description of the
natural world, so subjective descriptions such as qualia, the "felt experience" of perceptions, and even conscious experience itself, must be reduced to a third-person description given in terms of neurophysiological processes or else eliminated from a naturalistic ontology. The result
has been different versions of physicalism, the thesis that mental states
and properties just are brain states. Some form of physicalism is held by
the majority of philosophers of mind today, doubtless because of prior
commitment to a naturalist worldview.

Two physicalist strategies are deployed: reductionism and eliminativism (or the identity thesis).[4] According to physicalism, a human person is a physical thing—a body or a brain—and all of a human being's
features are either entirely physical or they emerge from and depend
entirely on one's physical states. Crispin Wright notes that this poses a
dilemma for naturalism:

> On one horn, if we embrace this naturalism, it seems we are committed
> either to reductionism: that is, to a construal of the reference of, for ex-
> ample, semantic, moral and psychological vocabulary as somehow being
> within the physical domain [i.e., reductionism]—or to disputing that

[4]See J. P. Moreland, "If You Can't Reduce, You Must Eliminate: Why Kim's Version of Physicalism Isn't Close Enough," *Philosophia Christi* 7 (2005): 463-73.

the discourse in question involves reference to what is real at all [i.e., eliminativism]. On the other horn, if we reject this naturalism, then we accept that there is more to the world than can be embraced within a physicalist ontology—and so take on a commitment, it can seem, to a kind of eerie supernaturalism.[5]

Reductionism attempts to retain mental properties while showing that mental phenomena are emergent, epiphenomenal properties, reducible to underlying brain states. On this view, brain states cause mental states, but mental states themselves have no causal power. Eliminativism simply eliminates the mental altogether, identifying mental properties, for example, being in pain, with first-order physical properties, for example, having C-fibers firing. David Papineau and Paul Churchland are representative of philosophers who simply deny the reality of the mental.[6]

Functionalism. Another current contributing to the dismissal of substance dualism has been the convergence of cognitive science and computer science. Research in artificial intelligence and advances in neural network simulations have given rise to functionalism, which has both "topic-neutral" and physicalist forms. The basic idea of functionalism is that mental states and properties are constituted wholly by their functional role. We can think of the "mind" as a black box with certain inputs and outputs. For example, physical stimuli, such as pain in one's hand, result in behavioral outputs, such as removing one's hand from the hot stove. Central to many (but not all) versions of functionalism is the concept of "multiple realizability," according to which the functional role labeled by some mental state or property is analyzed independently from consideration of the underlying physical system that realizes the functional role. Hence, not only human brains, but also (sufficiently advanced) computers, and possibly alien life forms with noncarbon-based chemistry, could instantiate mental states.

---

[5]Crispin Wright, "The Conceivability of Naturalism," in *Conceivability and Possibility*, ed. Tamar Szabo Gendler and John Hawthorne (New York: Oxford University Press, 2002), p. 401.
[6]David Papineau, *Philosophical Naturalism* (Oxford: Blackwell, 1993), pp. 114-26; Paul Churchland, *Matter and Consciousness* (Cambridge, Mass.: MIT Press, 1984), pp. 47-49.

Thought experiments such as John Searle's famous "Chinese Room,"[7] inverted spectrum possibilities[8] and "Twin Earth" scenarios[9] have lessened the appeal of topic-neutral forms of functionalism. So in what follows I'll ignore this form of functionalism. And it seems that much research into the structure of the brain assumes or concludes with a physicalist version of functionalism according to which the physical structure of the brain and its modular organization are directly analogous to a computer. Yale psychology professor Paul Bloom explains:

> The neurons are made up of parts like axons and dendrites, which are made up of smaller parts like terminal buttons and receptor sites, which are made up of molecules, and so on.
>   This hierarchical structure makes possible the research programs of psychology and neuroscience. The idea is that interesting properties of the whole (intelligence, decision-making, emotions, moral sensibility) can be understood in terms of the interaction of components that themselves lack these properties. This is how computers work; there is every reason to believe that this is how we work, too.[10]

If our minds were reducible to the functioning of our brains on the model of a computer, then they would necessarily operate on algorithmic patterns. However, physicist Roger Penrose has argued that while aspects of the functioning of the *brain* can be modeled on computers (part of the motivation behind research in artificial intelligence), there are several features of the human *mind* that *cannot* be algorithmic, such as creativity, certain forms of humor and mathematical insight, and Penrose has employed such notions as Gödel's incompleteness theorem and fractal geometry in his argument.[11] Further, physicalist forms of

---

[7] John Searle, "Minds, Brains and Programs," in *Behavioral and Brain Sciences* 3 (1980): 417-57.
[8] E.g., Ned Block, "Troubles with Functionalism," in *Readings in Philosophy of Psychology* (Cambridge, Mass.: Harvard University Press, 1980).
[9] Originally offered in support of an argument against semantic internalism by Hilary Putnam, "The Meaning of 'Meaning,'" reprinted in *Mind, Language and Reality* (New York: Cambridge University Press, 1975), the argument has often been extended to issues in philosophy of mind.
[10] Paul Bloom, "First Person Plural," *The Atlantic*, November 2008 <www.theatlantic.com/doc/200811/multiple-personalities>.
[11] Roger Penrose, *The Emperor's New Mind: Concerning Computers, Minds, and the Laws of Physics* (New York: Oxford University Press, 1989).

functionalism are susceptible to the same sort of critique that I'll offer below against physicalism in general, so with this brief nod, I'll close the discussion of functionalism.

Another pair of options. Arguments for reductivist or eliminativist physicalism exact a high price in terms of the denial of features of our own consciousness and mental life that we justifiably know that we have. Jaegwon Kim admits, "if a whole system of physical phenomena that are prima facie not among basic physical phenomena resists physical explanation, and especially if we don't even know where or how to begin, it would be time to reexamine one's physicalist commitments."[12] Two radically different approaches to dealing with this problem are represented by Colin McGinn and David Chalmers. McGinn wonders,

> How can mere matter originate consciousness? How did evolution convert the water of biological tissue into the wine of consciousness? Consciousness seems like a radical novelty in the universe, not prefigured by the after-effects of the Big Bang; so how did it contrive to spring into being from what preceded it?[13]

For McGinn, consciousness is such a novelty, so inexplicable in naturalist terms, that he concludes that there must be some unknown natural properties that link the physical and the mental, but he concludes that humans do not have the cognitive faculties to grasp these properties, and so we must forever be agnostic about their nature.

Chalmers also finds mental phenomena problematic, but his preference is for panpsychism, the view that every particle of matter in the universe has some sort of rudimentary or incipient consciousness.[14] According to Chalmers and other panpsychists, consciousness emerges from a suitably complex configuration of particles. But the unity of consciousness presents a difficult problem for panpsychism. The particles composing the brain stand in certain contingent spatial and causal relations, and panpsychism has no explanation of how *these* particles

---

[12]Jaegwon Kim, *Mind in a Physical World* (Cambridge, Mass.: MIT Press, 1998), p. 96.
[13]Colin McGinn, *The Mysterious Flame* (New York: Basic Books, 1999), pp. 13-14.
[14]David J. Chalmers, *The Conscious Mind: In Search of a Fundamental Theory* (New York: Oxford University Press, 1996).

and relations can give rise to a unified, single consciousness, while some other arbitrary arrangement will not.

Neither McGinn's agnosticism nor Chalmers's panpsychism seem satisfactory. One denies that an explanation of consciousness will ever be had by humans, the other distributes consciousness over all matter in the universe but cannot explain how consciousness emerges in a unified way just from the sort of aggregate of particles that are human brains.

The postmodern "soul." Postmodernism comes in various forms, of course; in fact, it probably has more forms than proponents! However, as a consciously held philosophical view, postmodernism denies such things as essences—natures of things. Rather, what things there are, and what those things are, are products of a sociolinguistic community. They are constructs, not givens. In the face of postmodernism's "incredulity towards metanarrative" (Lyotard), there can be no transcultural, multinational, historically continuous account of what it is to be a human person. "[A]ll ideas about human reality are social constructions."[15] The self, too, "is a social construction, a creation of language, a reification of the first person pronoun 'I.'"[16] It's important to realize that what's at stake here is more than a person's self-image, or her idea of what she'd like to be. Rather, according to postmodernism, there simply is no self. Psychology professor Kenneth Gergen writes, "postmoderns are populated with a plethora of selves. In place of an enduring core of deep and indelible character, there is a chorus of invitations. Each invitation 'to be' also casts doubt on the wisdom and authenticity of the other."[17] Similarly, Paul Bloom himself "gives up the idea that there is just one self per head. The idea is that instead, within each brain, different selves are continually popping in and out of existence. They have different desires, and they fight for control—bargaining with, deceiving, and plotting against one another."[18] Gergen and

---

[15]Walter Truett Anderson, *Reality Isn't What It Used to Be: Theatrical Politics, Ready-to-Wear Religion, Global Myths, Primitive Chic, and Other Wonders of the Postmodern World* (New York: HarperCollins, 1990), p. 3.

[16]J. P. Moreland, *The Recalcitrant* Imago Dei: *Human Persons and the Failure of Naturalism* (London: SCM Press, 2009), p. 13.

[17]Kenneth Gergen, *The Saturated Self: Dilemmas of Identity in Contemporary Life* (New York: Basic Books, 2000), p. 174.

[18]Bloom, "First Person Plural."

Bloom may not fully embrace the philosophical postmodern view of persons, but their work, dismissive of a single, unified, coherent self, feeds into the postmodern view.

While this might appeal to those who want constantly to "reinvent themselves," it faces serious defeaters in arguments that the human person or self persists through time and is not constituted simply by continuity of a biological organism (a human body). The postmodern view also is at odds with recent developments in psychological theory, notably cognitive behavioral therapy and the empirical evidence of neuroplasticity.[19] However, as anyone knows who has wrestled with postmodern dogma, it's like wrestling with a tar baby. Rational argument—an artifact of Western, male-dominated modernism—is replaced with assertion, story and sarcasm.[20] So rather than engage directly the postmodern view of persons, I'll let the positive arguments below stand for themselves. Flies may be irritating, but will not topple an elephant.

Christian physicalism. A final option to mention is "Christian physicalism." There seems to be an increasing trend among Christian philosophers toward a nonreductive version of physicalism, roughly, the view that holds that mental properties supervene on, but are not reducible to or identical with, a person's brain, together with his body and perhaps also his surrounding cultural or relational environment. And this trend can be spotted as well among certain biblical scholars and theologians.[21] The reasons that Christian physicalists give for rejecting an immaterial soul are varied, but two stand out. First, the success of neurophysiology has supposedly called into question the existence of a

---

[19]See, for example, Jeffrey M. Schwartz and Sharon Begley, *The Mind and the Brain: Neuroplasticity and the Power of Mental Force* (New York: HarperCollins, 2002).

[20]A superb example is Jacques Derrida's refusal to engage seriously with John Searle: Jacques Derrida, *Limited Inc* (Chicago: Northwestern University Press, 1988).

[21]Among biblical scholars and theologians who hold this view, see Ray S. Anderson, "On Being Human: The Spiritual Saga of a Creaturely Soul," and Joel B. Green, "'Bodies—That Is, Human Lives': A Re-Examination of Human Nature in the Bible," in *Whatever Happened to the Soul?* ed. Warren S. Brown, Nancey Murphy and H. Newton Malony (Minneapolis: Fortress, 1998). Representative of Christian philosophers accepting some form of physicalism, see Nancey Murphy, *Bodies and Souls, or Spirited Bodies?* (New York: Cambridge University Press, 2006); and Kevin Corcoran, *Rethinking Human Nature: A Christian Materialist Alternative to the Soul* (Grand Rapids: Baker, 2006).

substantial soul by demonstrating the radical dependence of the "mental" on the brain, if not the identity of the mind and brain.[22]

Second, some assert that biblical revelation depicts the human person as a holistic unity, whereas dualism is a Greek concept falsely read into the Bible. Christians, we are told, should be committed to a Hebraic monism, not to a Greek dualism. Biblical scholars have recognized that the strong versions of dualism that seem to permeate the church are not so much part of the biblical teaching on the nature of humans as they are part of the cultural/philosophical background, namely, Gnosticism in the first three centuries, Neoplatonism in the first five centuries, and a strong version of Cartesianism in modern times. The resultant Gnostic-Neoplatonic-Cartesian dualism may rightly be seen to be at odds with the biblical picture of physico-spiritual holism. But one could, of course, reject this strong form of dualism in favor of a more holistic Augustinian-Thomistic dualism without going so far as to deny the existence of the soul altogether.[23]

Now, I don't question the sincerity of these scholars' motives nor the seriousness with which they take their work. But by my lights, nonreductive physicalism does not sit comfortably in a Christian worldview. I think the biblical teaching, which I'll outline shortly, suffices to rebut the argument that dualism is a foreign import into the Bible. And I believe that arguments against "generic" physicalism can be brought against nonreductive physicalism, as I'll suggest below. Finally, I'll argue that the Christian doctrine of the resurrection of the body, together with a plausible account of personal identity, poses a serious defeater for Christian (nonreductive) physicalism.

CHRISTIAN WORLDVIEW IMPLICATIONS

Christian philosophers of all sorts acknowledge the indispensable role of

---

[22]Recent advances in neuroscience form the basis for Joel Green's rejection of dualism: Joel B. Green, *Body, Soul, and Human Life: The Nature of Humanity in the Bible* (Grand Rapids: Baker, 2008).

[23]For a defense of a holistic, Augustinian-Thomistic dualism as consonant with biblical teaching, see John W. Cooper, *Body, Soul, and Life Everlasting: Biblical Anthropology and the Monism-Dualism Debate* (Grand Rapids: Eerdmans, 1989); and J. P. Moreland and Scott B. Rae, *Body and Soul* (Downers Grove, Ill.: InterVarsity Press, 2000).

the Bible in forming a Christian worldview. Parts of Scripture shine a crystal clear and obvious divine light on our world. Other parts, however, seem quite distant, impenetrably foreign, dark and dimly lit. But even the most difficult passages can be grasped with the help of skilled exegetes and theologians. Moreover, of course, in Scripture we find the teachings of the Lord Jesus.[24] So I'll begin by outlining what I see as the most important biblical considerations for philosophical anthropology.

Biblical teaching. Despite some recent arguments to the contrary mentioned in the previous section, both the Old and the New Testament writers have traditionally been understood as affirming that a human person consists of both material and immaterial parts in functional unity.[25] I disagree with those who would claim that anthropological dualism can rightly be dismissed as the result of projecting Greek thought into the Bible.

The case for Old Testament anthropological dualism rests on two lines of evidence. First, in the *locus classicus* describing the creation of Adam (Gen 2:7), the Lord God formed Adam from the dust of the ground, breathed into him the breath of life, and he became a "living soul" (KJV) *(nefesh hayyah),* the implication being that a "living soul" consists of both a material part (the dust) and an immaterial part (the breath of life). In the Old Testament, two key anthropological terms are *nefesh* (soul) and *ruakh* (spirit). Although the Hebrew words have a wide semantic range,[26] both have occurrences where they seem clearly to mean an immaterial center of thought, desire and emotion; a continuing locus of personal identity that departs at death, reunites with a resurrection body, and is that which God adds to the body to make a living person (to pick out just four: Gen 35:18; 1 Kings 17:21-23; Ps 146:4; Ezek 37). In this sense, *nefesh* and *ruakh* are used of disembodied spirits (angels) and even of God himself.

---

[24]I am assuming that the extra-biblical "Gospels" are of little to no value in presenting us with the teachings of Jesus. See Darrell L. Bock, *The Missing Gospels: Unearthing the Truth Behind Alternative Christianities* (Nashville: Thomas Nelson, 2006).

[25]For a thorough defense of this claim, see Cooper, *Body, Soul, and Life Everlasting.*

[26]See, for example, Robert Saucy, "Theology of Human Nature," in *Christian Perspectives on Being Human,* ed. J. P. Moreland and David M. Ciocchi (Grand Rapids: Baker, 1993), pp. 38-41.

Second, *refaim* is the Old Testament term for the dead in Sheol, and frequently it refers to what can only be understood as disembodied persons there (Ps 88:10-12; Is 14:9-10). The Old Testament affirmation of a disembodied intermediate state explains Old Testament warnings about necromancy (communicating with the dead; cf. Deut 18:11; 1 Sam 28).

In the New Testament, the evidence for some form of substance dualism is equally powerful. Death is referred to as a giving up of the spirit *(pneuma)* in Matthew 27:50. The dead in the intermediate state are described as spirits or souls (Heb 12:23; Rev 6:9-11) prior to bodily resurrection. Jesus rested his argument against the Sadducees' denial of the resurrection on the fact that the patriarchs continued to be alive after their burial (Mt 22:23-33), and he promised the thief on the cross that he would be in paradise that very day—that is, that the thief would continue in uninterrupted existence after his death (Lk 23:42-43). Paul affirmed the disembodied intermediate state when he claimed that that to be absent from the body was to be with the Lord (2 Cor 5:1-10), and he believed that during a visionary experience he may well have been temporarily disembodied himself (2 Cor 12:1-4).

I argued in chapter four that those who are Christians owe an intellectual allegiance to Jesus as Lord. So what did Jesus believe about the soul? While none of Jesus' discourses expanded on questions of theological anthropology, we have a few hints. In the Gospels we find the word "soul," *psychē*, on the lips of Jesus about ten times, not counting parallels. In most of these contexts it could be translated "person" or "life." But in Matthew 10:28 Jesus warns, "Do not be afraid of those who kill the body but cannot kill the soul. Rather, be afraid of the one who can destroy both soul and body in hell." It is highly unlikely that "soul" here should be understood as "person" or "life." Jesus must think that it is possible for the body to be destroyed and the soul live on, or for both body and soul to be consigned to hell. This seems to be the clear interpretation of Jesus' words, and if correct, contradicts physicalism and supports dualism.

A second relevant passage is Jesus' teaching about the resurrection in John 5:26-29: "For just as the Father has life in Himself, even so

He gave to the Son also to have life in Himself; and He gave Him authority to execute judgment, because He is the Son of Man. Do not marvel at this; for an hour is coming, in which all who are in the tombs will hear His voice, and will come forth; those who did good to a resurrection of life, those who committed evil to a resurrection of judgment" (NASB). Two points: First, those who are in the tombs hear Christ's voice. And if the dead hear the Lord's voice, they must exist in some conscious intermediate state. Now, a physicalist might want to claim this is a reference to bodies, for it is bodies that go into tombs. But biblical scholars demonstrate that "in the tombs" is a first-century Jewish figure of speech for "dead." N. T. Wright,[27] John Cooper[28] and others have shown the widespread first-century Jewish belief in a disembodied intermediate state (certainly among Pharisees, though the Sadducees, clearly a minority, are ambiguous). This puts the burden of proof on anyone who claims that Jesus' teaching should be understood to refer to temporary bodies. Second point: Jesus makes it very clear that it is those who did good—those very persons, and not perfect replicas—who are resurrected to life, and those who committed evil—those very persons—who are resurrected to judgment.

Given these texts, I believe it is extremely likely that Jesus believed in the existence of an immaterial soul. And so too should Christian scholars, if Jesus is our intellectual Lord. Or so it seems to me.

The nature of God. A no less important point is this. Christian philosophers, operating within a Christian worldview, surely regard God (more precisely, the three divine Persons of the Trinity) as the paradigm case of personhood. And surely most Christians would also regard angels as clear cases of persons. John Calvin begins his masterful *Institutes of the Christian Religion* with these words:

> Our wisdom, in so far as it ought to be deemed true and solid Wisdom, consists almost entirely of two parts: the knowledge of God and of ourselves. But as these are connected together by many ties, it is not easy to

[27]N. T. Wright, *The Resurrection of the Son of God* (Minneapolis: Augsburg Fortress, 2003), especially pp. 129-205.
[28]Cooper, *Body, Soul, and Life Everlasting.*

determine which of the two precedes and gives birth to the other. For, in the first place, no man can survey himself without forthwith turning his thoughts towards the God in whom he lives and moves; because it is perfectly obvious, that the endowments which we possess cannot possibly be from ourselves.[29]

Similarly, Alvin Plantinga, in his celebrated essay "Advice to Christian Philosophers," says,

How should we think about human persons? What sorts of things, fundamentally, *are* they? . . . The first point to note is that on the Christian scheme of things, *God* is the premiere person, the first and chief exemplar of personhood . . . and the properties most important for an understanding of our personhood are properties we share with him.[30]

J. P. Moreland has formulated this into an argument,[31] which I'll rephrase somewhat:

1. God the Father, God the Son and God the Holy Spirit are paradigm cases of personhood.

2. If something is a person, then it resembles the paradigm cases in relevantly similar ways.

3. The relevantly similar way of resemblance is (i) being a spiritual substance, (ii) essentially characterized by actual and potential properties of consciousness.

4. A human person is a person.

5. Therefore, a human person is (i) a spiritual substance, (ii) essentially characterized by actual and potential properties of consciousness.

Now, while some of Moreland's premises are not uncontroversial, it seems to me that the burden of proof for someone claiming to be working within a Christian worldview will be on the one who denies the conclusion—that is, who denies that there is such a thing as a substantial soul.

---

[29]John Calvin, *Institutes of the Christian Religion* 1.1.1, trans. Henry Beveridge (Grand Rapids: Eerdmans, 1962).
[30]Alvin Plantinga, "Advice to Christian Philosophers," *Faith and Philosophy* 1 (1984): 264-65.
[31]Moreland, *Recalcitrant* Imago Dei, p. 128.

The image of God.

Then God said, "Let us make man in our image, in our likeness, and let them rule over the fish of the sea and the birds of the air, over the livestock, over all the earth, and over all the creatures that move along the ground." So God created man in his own image, in the image of God he created him; male and female he created them. (Gen 1:26-27)

The doctrine of the *imago Dei* is another important piece of a Christian worldview, but one that is difficult to penetrate. There are only four texts that use the term: Genesis 1:26-27; 9:6; 2 Corinthians 4:4; and Colossians 1:15. The latter two refer to Christ who, as the Second Adam, perfectly reflects the image of God. So it is far from easy to say just what the *imago Dei* consists in. Exegetes and theologians through the years have offered a wide variety of interpretations, but most at some point draw from the immediate context of Genesis 1, together with the role of Christ as King, and see in the term some reference to ruling over the earth as God's vice-regents.[32]

If humans were created for the purpose of ruling as stewards in God's place (among other purposes, most likely), what does that imply about human persons and their nature? I think it is fair to draw the following conclusions. Humans must have the capacities of consciousness and self-awareness, so as to grasp their role and responsibilities. They must be capable of relating spiritually to God, "the great King over all the earth" (Ps 47:2), whom they are to serve by ruling. They must be rational creatures, capable of discerning good and evil, right and wrong, beauty and ugliness, and of making decisions based on such values. They must be morally responsible for their actions. They must have the capacity of relating to other humans, communicating with them not just about present experiences and the immediate environment, but about the past, the future, and abstract ideas; they must have the capacity for language and creativity.

Doubtless these and other implications of the *imago Dei* could be

---

[32]See, for example, John H. Walton, *The Lost World of Genesis One* (Downers Grove, Ill.: InterVarsity Press, 2009), pp. 68-71, 138-19; Eugene H. Merrill, *Everlasting Dominion: A Theology of the Old Testament* (Nashville: B & H Academic, 2006), pp. 169-73.

(and have been) teased out and amplified in book-length studies, and I can't delay here to explore them further. But the Christian doing philosophical anthropology or philosophy of mind should keep the *imago Dei* in mind as the framework for his theoretical work. Insisting on the *imago Dei* as a key to understanding human persons may open the Christian philosopher to charges of "speciesism," and it may force him to swim upstream against the naturalizing current, but at the end of his work he should be moved to wonder and worship and sing with the psalmist, "What is man that you are mindful of him, the son of man that you care for him? You made him a little lower than the heavenly beings and crowned him with glory and honor" (Ps 8:4-5).

Other aspects of a Christian worldview bear on our discussion; the two most important are the frequent apparent appeals to free will in the Bible, and the doctrine (alluded to already) of the resurrection of the body. I'll say something about these matters in later sections.

SUBSTANCE DUALISM

As I've already clearly indicated, I believe a version of substance dualism is both defensible philosophically and the view that fits best within a Christian worldview. It's now time to explore what such a substance dualism involves.

The word *substance*, to most modern ears, connotes "stuff"—the chemistry—rather than "thing" or "individual" (recall the discussion in chapter 5). Many contemporary theologians, not conversant with the history or recent literature on substance, reject substance language simply because they understand *substance* to be an inert, static object. But that is a gross misunderstanding of the philosophical usage of *substance*. Similarly, in criticizing contemporary theologians who claim that the medieval notion of personhood has been superseded in modern thought, Alfred J. Freddoso concludes that "those who make assertions like this have a disappointingly superficial and unduly selective acquaintance with the voluminous recent philosophical literature on substance, personhood and personal identity."[33]

---

[33]Alfred J. Freddoso, "Human Nature, Potency, and the Incarnation," *Faith and Philosophy* 3 (1986): 29.

The claim of substance dualism is that there are two kinds of substances—material and spiritual. A *material substance* has spatial location and extension, is metaphysically (conceptually) divisible, and is essentially characterized by the properties (actual and potential) of an ideal physics and chemistry. A *spiritual substance*, by contrast, is not spatially extended (though on some accounts it may be located, for example, a human soul is normally located in a spatial region overlapping the body), is metaphysically indivisible, and is essentially characterized by the properties (actual and potential) of consciousness. This definition of a spiritual substance allows for the possibility of animal souls.

With this in mind, I'll define a *person* as an individual, essentially characterized by an appropriately complex and structured set of mental properties, faculties (a natural grouping of capacities) and higher-order capacities (of an appropriate complexity so as to rule out animals). As noted above, for the Christian, God serves as the paradigm case of properties of personhood. The structured set of mental properties or capacities essential to personhood includes (but is not necessarily limited to) these:

(a) Consciousness (including sensation, thought, belief, desire and volition)

(b) Self-consciousness (awareness of self as a unified subject and second-order awareness of one's first-order mental states)

(c) Agency, the capacity to initiate self-guided actions

(d) Moral responsibility

(e) Relationality, the capacity for relationships with other persons, including the immaterial person of God

(Note: As I understand it, these definitions capture what it is to be a spiritual substance and a person. They also allows for the orthodox Christian doctrine of the Trinity, according to which the Godhead is tri-personal without thereby being three substances, which in my view would come too close to tri-theism. So on this view, the Godhead is a single spiritual substance "within" which there are three divine Persons. But in every other case about which we know, individual persons are spiritual substances. But these are deep waters, flowing with much mystery, and I must resist the desire to attempt to navigate them here.)

If this (or something close to it) captures what it is to be a person, then we can see that 'person' is a genus concept admitting different species of persons: divine, angelic and demonic, human, and perhaps Martian or Klingon as well. To say it differently, 'person' is a determinable, and 'human person' is a determinate. So all that remains here is to characterize what it is to be a human person.

A *human person*, I would then say, is a spiritual substance essentially characterized by the properties and capacities (actual and potential) of personhood, which begins its life embodied in an organism of the species *Homo sapiens*, and the normal state of which is to be embodied.

Now it is not necessary to interpret substance dualism according to a Cartesian model, a mysterious "ghost in a machine." I believe that a more biblical version of dualism sees the human person as a functional unity of body and soul, for which being embodied is the normal condition, but that allows the human person to survive disembodied in "the intermediate state" between death and the resurrection of the body.[34]

All well and good, you might say, but why should we believe that there is any such thing as a spiritual substance? Merely defining a thing does not entail its existence. But let's assume for the moment that what people generally have believed about their "self" or "soul" is captured in the definition of a spiritual substance (or something close to this definition), can we offer any arguments to motivate such belief? In other words, can we offer arguments the conclusions of which lead to the denial of physicalism? I think the answer clearly is yes.

We should begin with a couple of methodological points. Clearly, neuroscience has made great advances in recent years and has uncovered an array of correlations between activity in specialized regions of the brain and certain thoughts, sensations, emotions and even intentional acts of the will. Such empirical successes are taken to provide strong support for physicalist accounts of mind. But as we all know, correlation is not causation.

---

[34]Cooper, *Body, Soul and Life Everlasting;* Moreland and Rae, *Body and Soul.*

Further, we need to ask about theory adjudication. When we are presented with competing theories that claim to explain some phenomenon, on what rational basis do we accept one and not the other? Well, traditionally such features as empirical adequacy and explanatory power are crucial; simplicity, elegance and fecundity (the ability to generate novel lines of research) are also important. But the latter group of qualities is notoriously subjective and difficult to evaluate; and it is well known, with respect to the former group, that data underdetermine theories, and incompatible theories can be empirically equivalent. Nevertheless, an important feature in evaluating explanatory power is the presence of phenomena that one theory can explain but the other cannot, or can only by invoking clearly ad hoc hypotheses. If one set of facts is recalcitrant, defying explanation under one theory, but perfectly explainable under another, then the second has greater explanatory power with respect to those facts.

I'll begin my argument for substance dualism by pointing out a number of recalcitrant facts for physicalism that should—aside from an antecedent commitment to naturalism—alert us to the possibility that there must be another concept of personhood.

Recalcitrant facts for physicalism. Serious scholars in psychology, neuroscience and philosophy of mind—nearly all committed naturalists—have noted a cluster of recalcitrant facts that, as things stand now, defy explanation in naturalistic terms. Serious physicalism must explain this cluster of mental phenomena in terms of a causally closed physical world, in which explanation begins with the smallest entities known to physics (particles, fields, strings or whatever the best theory turns out to be), together with their properties and dispositions. As macro-structures are formed from micro-structures, new structural properties might emerge, properties that are exemplified by larger structures but not by their micro-constituents. So, for example, the structure of a single molecule of water, H_2O, is explained in terms of the theory of bonding orbitals of oxygen and hydrogen; the liquidity of water (a suitably large collection of H_2O molecules), in terms of intermolecular interactions, and so on. Now mental phenomena, on this account, must follow a bottom-up explanatory story beginning with atoms (or their constituents) and ascending through increasingly complex structures of chemistry and biology, all told within an overarching Darwinian evolutionary story. Recalcitrant facts are just those that cannot be fit into such a story. Here are a few examples:

A salient type of phenomenon that is recalcitrant for physicalism is comprised of those mental states that are only describable in first-person and not third-person terms. Among these are qualia, the "raw feels" of conscious experience. Why something red "feels" different from something blue cannot be explained in third-person terms of wavelengths of light. The taste of pineapple, indescribable but unforgettable, cannot be reduced to the chemistry of pineapple juice. Emotions aroused by music cannot be predicted on the basis of sound frequencies. A third-person description of such phenomena in the language of natural science invariably omits something very important and very personal, something about the world that we know.[35] As such, the existence of qualia is a recalcitrant fact for physicalism. (A number of philosophers, committed to some form of physicalism but unwilling to eliminate qualia, claim the label "qualia freak."[36] Most of them, however, regard qualia as epiphenomenal—as emerging from physical properties but having no causal power. Often the term "property dualism" is used for this view; however, in what follows, when I use "dualism" I'll mean by the term substance dualism.)

Second, many mental states are intentional—that is, they have an "of-ness" or "about-ness"; they are directed at some object apart from themselves. But no natural arrangement of purely physical objects has intentionality. Natural arrangements are produced either by law-like necessity or random, stochastic processes. But neither chance nor necessity creates intentionality.[37] (That's one reason why neither the arrangement of planets nor of tea leaves can mean anything about something else. Astrology reduces to necessity, tea leaf arrangements to

[35]Although he now disavows parts of it, the classic source for this "knowledge argument" for qualia is Frank Jackson, "What Mary Didn't Know," *Journal of Philosophy* 83 (1986): 291-95.
[36]I believe the term entered the literature with Frank Jackson's paper "Epiphenomenal Qualia," *Philosophical Quarterly* 32 (1982): 127-36, but it is used widely.
[37]See George Bealer, "Materialism and the Logical Structure of Intentionality," in *Objections to Physicalism*, ed. Howard Robinson (Oxford: Oxford University Press, 1993), pp. 102-26.

chance—or at least to chaotic movements in the brewing tea.) So intentionality poses a recalcitrant fact for physicalism.

Third, mental states lack properties that physical objects and states necessarily possess, namely, location and spatial extension. If you imagine a green patch, say, no amount of searching in your brain matter will find an extended green patch. It's important here to understand that while study of your brain by fMRI (functional magnetic resonance imaging) might find a particular region of the brain more highly active when you think of a green patch, the researchers will have no way of knowing what you're imagining unless you tell them. The "green-patch experience" is not describable in third-person descriptions of brain activity. And even should it turn out that (almost) every human being shows the same heightened brain activity in the identical region of the brain when thinking of a green patch, nothing in that region of neurons is the extended green patch. And if that's not convincing, imagine hearing middle-C on a piano or tasting fresh pineapple: the sound and the taste are not located or extended in the brain. Consequently, since mental states lack properties that physical states necessarily possess, they cannot be identical. This is a further recalcitrant fact for physicalism.

Another problem for physicalism is human cognition—how we think. Harvard professor Marc Hauser identifies four traits that distinguish human from animal cognition and account for our "humaniqueness."[38] These are (1) generative computation, the ability to create virtually unlimited combinations of words, things and concepts, using recursive and combinatorial operations; (2) promiscuous combination of ideas from different domains of knowledge; (3) mental symbols that encode both real and imagined sensory experience, thus forming the basis for a rich system of communication; and (4) abstract thought, the contemplation of things beyond empirical experience. As an evolutionary biologist, Hauser has some vague suggestions as to how such traits might have evolved, but he admits that "the roots of our cognitive abilities remain largely unknown," and still expresses hope "that neurobiology will prove illuminating." Indeed, these distinctive

[38]Marc Hauser, "Origin of the Mind," *Scientific American* 301, September 2009, pp. 44-51.

traits are recalcitrant in a naturalistic evolutionary worldview.

Finally, there is the whole complex notion of "what it is like to be" you or me—or a bat, for that matter.[39] Consciousness has an irreducible subjective quality to it that cannot be captured in a third-person scientific description, and so it too is a recalcitrant fact for physicalism.

None of these facts is a problem for substance dualism, however. So in light of serious motivation for dualism apart from its historical and commonsense appeal, it seems that the Christian philosopher is on solid epistemic ground if he defends dualism as the view most consonant with his worldview.

Dualism defended. A number of arguments have been offered over the years in defense of substance dualism, but I only have room to sketch one, or rather, one family of arguments: the Modal Argument.

Versions of the Modal Argument (hereafter MA) have been defended by Richard Swinburne, George Bealer, Charles Taliaferro, E. J. Lowe, Stewart Goetz and Alvin Plantinga, among others.[40] In all its various forms, MA proceeds generally by arguing that, necessarily, I have different properties than my body, and concludes that I am not identical with my body or a proper part of my body. In support, the arguments rely on strong conceivability as indicative of metaphysical possibility. So various versions of MA claim that it is conceivable that "I" survive the destruction of my body (Swinburne), or that "I" have different persistence conditions than my body and so could survive partial or total replacement of the physical parts of my body (Plantinga), or that "I" am a simple entity while my body is a composite entity (Goetz). Different versions argue that since the mental properties or conscious states that constitute what "I" am are not those physical properties that

---

[39]See the well-known essay by Thomas Nagel, "What Is It Like to Be a Bat?" *Philosophical Review* 83 (1974): 435-50; widely reprinted.

[40]Swinburne, *Evolution of the Soul;* George Bealer, "Mental Properties," *Journal of Philosophy* 91 (1994): 185-208; Charles Taliaferro, *Consciousness and the Mind of God* (Cambridge: Cambridge University Press, 1994); E. J. Lowe, *An Introduction to the Philosophy of Mind* (Cambridge: Cambridge University Press, 2000); Stewart Goetz, "Modal Dualism: A Critique," in *Soul, Body, and Survival: Essays on the Metaphysics of Human Persons,* ed. Kevin Corcoran (Ithaca, N.Y.: Cornell University Press, 2001), pp. 89-105; Alvin Plantinga, "Materialism and Christian Belief," in *Persons: Human and Divine,* ed. Peter van Inwagen and Dean Zimmerman (New York: Oxford University Press, 2007), pp. 99-140.

characterize my body (or a proper part of it), necessarily I am not a physical entity (Lowe, Bealer). Indeed, it's possible, I believe, to construct a version of MA using just about any of the recalcitrant facts cited above.

Of course, the literature abounds with discussion, rebuttal and defense of these arguments, and likely the dialectical merry-go-round will continue well into the future. Nevertheless, MA has great intuitive appeal. In my view, the modal intuitions in the various forms of MA all stem from our most basic introspective awareness of ourselves, our awareness of those uniquely first-person aspects of conscious experience.

Objections. Objections to substance dualism, it seems to me, take three forms: ideological, scientific and conceptual. The ideological objection takes a commitment to naturalism as an axiom of thought in the "scientific age." In their critique of naturalism, Goetz and Taliaferro summarize:

> The unified incorporation of all phenomena in a natural scientific philosophy means that the difference between a fully conscious human being . . . and any inanimate matter and energy is chiefly a matter of complexity, configuration, and function, rather than of nature or substance.[41]

So for a person committed to naturalism as an ideology, dualistic theories are simply disallowed. Whatever human beings are, they are purely physical products of the random walk of evolution. This is not the place to take on a critique of naturalism;[42] suffice it to say that the recalcitrant facts cited above serve as evidence against naturalism, as does the coherence of the entire Christian worldview.

The scientific objection to dualism largely takes the form of a "gee whiz" argument: Look at the amazing advances neurobiology has made in recent decades. Just give the brain scientists a little more time, and they'll be able to explain consciousness, qualia and all the rest. But this isn't much of an argument, once we understand that correlation is not causation. In the view of Christian substance dualists, human beings

---

[41]Stewart Goetz and Charles Taliaferro, *Naturalism* (Grand Rapids: Eerdmans, 2008), p. 21.
[42]See Goetz and Taliaferro, *Naturalism;* William Lane Craig and J. P. Moreland, eds., *Naturalism: A Critical Analysis* (New York: Routledge, 2000).

begin their lives as embodied souls, and embodiment is the normal state for humans, although disembodied existence of the soul is also possible. It is a contingent fact that while embodied, human cognitive functions are mediated by the brain—we think, perceive, remember, deliberate and so forth. using our brain. But those mental operations are operations of the soul using the brain, not of the brain itself; contingent correlations are unsurprising. We would expect to find that psychoactive drugs, brain injury, tumors, strokes and dementia affect mental processes. And we would also expect to find that changing habituated patterns of thought would lead to observable changes in the brain's function. And we find both, of course. So the findings of neurobiology do not pose much of a problem for dualists.[43]

The primary conceptual objection to dualism is the difficulty—the objectors would say, the impossibility—of giving an account of mental causation. Even property dualists, who do not want to eliminate mental phenomena like qualia, do not regard the mental as having causal power. And prima facie, this *is* hard to understand. Jaegwon Kim writes,

> At the very interface between the mental and the physical, where direct and unmediated mind-body interaction takes place, the non-physical mind must somehow influence the state of some molecules, perhaps by electrically charging them or nudging them this way or that. Is this really conceivable? . . . Most physicalists . . . accept the causal closure of the physical not only as a fundamental metaphysical doctrine but as an indispensable methodological presupposition of the physical sciences.[44]

However, I will briefly offer three responses to the problem. First, for those operating within a Christian worldview, this cannot be a knock-down defeater. The argument for the causal closure of the physical is incompatible with orthodox Christianity. For God is an immaterial being who can exert power over the physical world, so immaterial-material causation cannot be a logical or metaphysical or nomological impossibility. Second, an account of mental causation need not involve

---

[43]This is not to say that some purported results of neurophysiological research pose no problem. Research sometimes outpaces interpretation.
[44]Jaegwon Kim, *Philosophy of Mind* (Boulder, Colo.: Westview Press, 1998), pp. 132, 147-48.

anything so crass as Descartes's posit of the pineal gland as the locus of the interaction. Bealer offers one account of both mental-to-mental and mental-to-physical causation.[45] But I'm inclined to think that our desire for an account or model of mental causation is fueled by our general familiarity with accounts of macro-level physical causation ("The window broke because the baseball hit it at a high speed"). I suspect that a full account of mental causation, when available, will look quite different from physical causal accounts, and for the moment perhaps we should be content to say that it is clear to me that I have the basic mental power to initiate actions, which include certain movements of my body, even though I do not now have a fully-developed theory of how that causal nexus works.

And that brings me to the third response to the problem of mental causation. I simply seem to be able to directly experience it. Countless times each day I decide (mental) to act (physical), and I do—directly. When I introspect my actions, they certainly seem to be brought about directly by a mental intention. Now, I could be operating under a pervasive and persistent illusion, of course, but since my direct awareness of mental causation fits well within my worldview and accords with a reasonable theory of substance dualism, I see no reason to assume it is illusory.

So in the absence of any decisive defeater to dualism, then, and given the known difficulties associated with physicalism, there seems little reason to abandon a view that has such a distinguished history and fits so well with a Christian worldview.

THE IDEA OF FREE WILL

It's doubtless true that the ubiquitous, natural, commonsense belief of almost all persons in almost every time and place has been that they are free to make (at least certain) decisions, and that praise or blame is rightly attached to the decisions, actions and consequences that follow. Yes, various cultures believed (and some still do) that various gods and demons, or the stars, or natural forces, or some "metaphysical" force

---

[45]George Bealer, "Mental Causation," *Philosophical Perspectives* 21 (2007): 23-54.

(the fates? karma?), or God Almighty, controlled or influenced many decisions. Sometimes that belief brought a comfortable escape from responsibility, sometimes anguish at being the prisoner of fate. But even in those cultures, I believe, all but the most ardent believers live their lives *as if* they had free will (and even they, I suspect, often find themselves apparently acting freely).

Yet the problem of free will is a notoriously difficult one, a problem argued about for as long as people have been doing philosophy. Freedom of the will may be distinct from freedom of action; maybe not. Freedom may be compatible with various kinds of determinism; maybe not. Free will must be robust if moral responsibility is to be assigned; maybe not.

Clearly we can't get into much of this discussion here, but equally clearly the question of whether humans do have free will, and if we do, how we should understand free will, is of crucial importance to our conception of who we are as persons. What I propose to do here is sketch an argument for the sort of robust view of free will that I think is correct, consider what notion of free will fits with physicalist accounts of mind, and conclude with a few theological observations from within a Christian worldview.

Alternatives. Determinism is the only view compatible with a physicalist construal of persons. As we have seen, physicalists hold to the causal closure of the physical. If every "mental" event is really just a physical event, it is brought about deterministically by an antecedent physical event. Every event is caused or necessitated by prior factors such that, given these prior factors, the event in question had to occur. We really have no more freedom as persons to decide between different courses of action than billiard balls have to decide between different trajectories when struck by the cue ball. We may have the illusion of acting freely, but it's just that—an illusion.

There are different forms of determinism with different stories about just what is the cause of the determined outcome. It might be the laws of physics and chemistry, as in physical causal determinism. Or it might be genetic, where our genes determine what we do (which might reduce to physics and chemistry), or psychological, where our character, formed in the past, determines what we do. Or it might be theological, where God "brings about whatsoever shall come to pass." Or it might be determinism or fatalism of some other sort.

Yet the illusion of freedom, if it is an illusion, is a powerful one. John Searle notes that the experience of making apparently free choices is so compelling that people cannot act as if the experience is an illusion. Even the strictest physicalist, he says, when offered a choice of entrees by the waiter, cannot say, "Look, I'm a determinist—che serà serà. I'll just wait and see what I order."[46] The clear alternative is a libertarian concept of freedom.

Libertarians embrace free will and hold that determinism is incompatible with it. Real freedom requires a type of control over one's action—and, more importantly, over one's will—such that, given a choice between doing A (eat that apple) or B (refrain from eating the apple, eat the donut instead), nothing determines that either choice is made. Rather, the agent herself must simply exercise her own causal powers and will to do one of the alternatives. When an agent chooses to do A, she also could have chosen to do B without anything else being different inside or outside of her. She is the absolute originator of her own actions. When an agent acts freely, she is, so to speak, a first or unmoved mover; no event causes her to act. Her desires, beliefs and so on may *influence* her choice, but free acts are not *caused* by those prior states.

The two conditions traditionally considered essential for libertarian freedom are the Principle of Autonomy (PA) and the Principle of Alternate Possibilities (PAP). PA says that an action is free if and only if the agent did it on her own—that is, she was the originator of her action; it was under her control. A free action is not compelled by externally caused irresistible physical or emotional forces, or by drugs and so forth. PAP says an action is free if and only if she could have done otherwise, or stated somewhat differently, if and only if she could have refrained from doing what she in fact did.

PA and especially PAP have been the subject of serious debate and refinement, and I am sure that anyone working in the field would want

---

[46]John Searle, *Freedom and Neurobiology: Reflections on Language, Free will, and Political Power* (New York: Columbia University Press, 2007), p. 43.

to refine my statements of the principles, adding definitions, qualifications and conditions. Indeed there's a thriving cottage industry inventing new counterexamples to PAP, and responding to the counterexamples by adding ever more epicycles and subscripts to PAP.[47] But for our purposes, this characterization is close enough.

Both determinists and libertarians believe that determinism is incompatible with free will (as generally understood) and also with moral responsibility; they are both *incompatibilists*.[48] But determinism and libertarianism are not the only options. *Compatibilists* hold that freedom and determinism are indeed compatible with each other, and thus even if determinism is true, that does not undermine free will. Clearly compatibilism works with a different understanding of free will from libertarianism or determinism (sometimes called "hard" determinism to distinguish it from the sort of "soft" determinism compatible with free will).

Compatibilism agrees that if determinism is true, then every human action is causally necessitated by events that obtained prior to the action, including events that occurred before the agent was born. But compatibilism claims that freedom, properly understood, is compatible with determinism. For compatibilists, freedom is willing to act on one's strongest preference. We are free to will whatever we desire, even though our desires are themselves determined. The compatibilist will either deny that PA and PAP are necessary conditions of free will, or else will significantly redefine the conditions.[49]

Evaluation. Although determinism is most consistent with naturalism (and physicalist accounts of mind), it has not drawn many open advocates, for two reasons. First, as I have already noted, it seems to fly in the face of our everyday experience: even if we believe our decisions are determined, we still find ourselves deliberating and (apparently)

---

[47]The industry got its start with the ingenious counterexamples in Harry Frankfurt's famous paper, "Alternate Possibilities and Moral Responsibility," *Journal of Philosophy* 66 (1969): 829-39.

[48]For a spirited defense of incompatibilism and libertarian free will, see Peter van Inwagen, *An Essay on Free Will* (New York: Oxford University Press, 1986).

[49]For more in-depth treatment of these positions, see John Martin Fisher, Robert Kane, Derk Pereboom and Manuel Vargas, *Four Views on Free Will*, Great Debates in Philosophy (Malden, Mass.: Blackwell, 2007).

choosing a course of action. Second, determinism seems to undermine our deepest notions of moral responsibility: if my actions are determined by something other than my own choice, then it is difficult to hold me morally praiseworthy or blameworthy for those actions.

Determinists are not without a comeback, however. For example, Derk Pereboom agrees that our best scientific theories entail determinism, and that because of this, we are not morally responsible for our actions. However, he argues that lack of moral responsibility does not undermine what is important for morality and meaning in life.[50] But in spite of such determinist protests, hard determinism has gained very little traction.

The differing compatibilist and libertarian accounts of free will become clearer as we look again at the two principles, PA and PAP, central to an adequate account of free will and consider also the role that rationality plays in the differing analyses of choice.

The autonomy condition. We can better understand the relevant notion of autonomy by asking about who (or what) is in *control* of the action. Suppose Jean extends her hand to grasp an apple. Compatibilists and libertarians agree that a necessary condition for the freedom of this act is that Jean must be in control of the act itself, but they differ radically as to what control is.

Compatibilists take cause and effect to be characterized as a series of events making up causal chains, with earlier events together with the laws of nature (either deterministic or probabilistic) causing later events. The universe is what it is at the present moment because of the state of the universe at the moment before the present together with the correct causal laws describing the universe.

Now, according to compatibilism, an act is free only if it is under the agent's own control. And it is under the agent's own control only if the causal chain of events—which extends back in time to events realized before the agent was even born—that caused the act (Jean's hand being extended) "runs through" the agent herself in the correct way. But what does it mean to say that the causal chain "runs through the agent in the

[50]Derk Pereboom, *Living Without Free Will* (Cambridge: Cambridge University Press, 2001).

correct way"? Here compatibilist accounts differ, but the basic idea is that an agent is in control of an act just in case (that is, if and only if) the act is caused in the right way by prior states of the agent herself (e.g., by the agent's own character, beliefs, desires and values). This idea is sometimes called a *causal theory of action.*

Libertarians reject the causal theory of action and the compatibilist notion of control and claim that a different sense of control is needed for the autonomy condition to be met for genuinely free will. Consider a case where a staff moves a stone but is itself moved by a hand that is moved by a man. In *Summa contra gentiles,* St. Thomas Aquinas states a principle about causal chains that is relevant to the type of control necessary for libertarian freedom:

> In an ordered series of movers and things moved [to move is to change in some way], it is necessarily the fact that, when the first mover is removed or ceases to move, no other mover will move [another] or be [itself] moved. For the first mover is the cause of motion for all the others. But, if there are movers and things moved following an order to infinity, there will be no first mover, but all would be as *intermediate movers.* . . . [Now] that which moves [another] as an instrumental cause cannot [so] move unless there be a principal moving cause [i.e., a first cause, an unmoved mover].[51]

For libertarians, it is only if agents are first causes, unmoved movers, that they have the autonomy necessary for freedom. An agent must be the absolute, originating source of his own actions to be in control. A free act is one in which the agent is the ultimate originating source of the act. If, as compatibilists picture it, the agent is just a theater through which a chain of instrumental causes passes, then there is no real control.

The alternate possibility condition. In order to have the freedom necessary for responsible agency, one must have the ability to choose one's actions. Compatibilists and libertarians agree that a free choice is one where a person "can" will to do otherwise, but they differ about what this ability is. Compatibilists see this ability as *hypothetical.* Roughly,

---

[51]Thomas Aquinas *Summa contra gentiles* 1.13.

this means that the agent would have done otherwise had some other condition obtained, for instance, had the agent desired to do so. The alternate possibility in view is counterfactual, dependent upon conditions being different than what they actually were.

Libertarians view hypothetical ability as a sleight of hand and as not sufficient for the freedom needed for free agency. For libertarians, the real issue is whether we have the *categorical* ability to will to act. This means that if Jean freely wills to grasp the apple, she could have *refrained* from willing to extend her hand to grasp it without any conditions whatsoever being different. No description of Jean's desires, beliefs, character or other things in her make-up, and no description of the universe prior to and at the moment of her choice to reach for the apple is sufficient to entail that she did reach. It was not necessary that anything be different for Jean to refrain from choosing to reach for the apple.

A third condition: Rationality. Both libertarians and compatibilists believe that rationality is a condition for free will. The rationality condition requires that an agent have a personal reason for acting before the act counts as a free, rational one. Consider again the case of Jean's extending her hand to grasp the apple. In order to understand the difference between how libertarians and compatibilists handle this case in light of the rationality condition, we need to draw a distinction between two of Aristotle's four causes, in this case, between an *efficient* and a *final cause.* An efficient cause is that *by means of which* an effect is produced. One billiard ball moving another is an example of efficient causality. By contrast, a final cause is that *for the sake of which* an effect is produced. Final causes are teleological, the purposes for which an action is done; the action is a means to the end that is the final cause.

Now a compatibilist will explain Jean's extending her hand in terms of efficient and not final causes. According to this view, Jean had a desire to eat an apple, and a belief that extending her hand to grasp the apple would satisfy this desire, and this state of affairs in her (the *belief/ desire set*) caused the state of affairs of her hand extending. On this view, a reason for acting turns out to be a certain type of state in the agent— a belief/desire state—that is the real efficient cause of her action. Persons as substances do not act; rather, states within persons cause later states to occur.

Libertarians respond by denying that reasons for acting are efficient causes. Rather, reasons are final causes only. Jean extended her hand in order to grasp the apple or, perhaps, in order to satisfy her hunger. She acted as an unmoved mover by simply exercising her powers to extend her arm. Her beliefs and desires do not cause her arm to go up; she herself does. The desire to grasp the apple serves as a final cause for the sake of which she extended her hand.

Christian worldview implications of the free will debate. Much of the argument between libertarians and compatibilists reduces to intuitions about what notion of free will is required to support moral responsibility. Compatibilists who are Christians will point to such passages as Proverbs 16:4 or Romans 9–11. The Proverbs verse reads, in the King James Version, "The LORD hath made all things for himself: yea, even the wicked for the day of evil." This sounds like it supports theological determinism. However, in a better translation, it has a different meaning: "The LORD works out everything for his own ends— even the wicked for a day of disaster" (NIV). And in the context of Paul's argument in Romans, chapters 9–11 deal with the election of Israel as the people through whom God would accomplish his salvific purposes. One cannot automatically read conclusions about individual freedom from these chapters. There are of course other texts that may be interpreted to imply a compatibilist view of free will, and of course libertarians have responses.

But there are also many texts that seem to support a libertarian view. At the risk of apparent overkill, I'll cite several. First, a cluster of verses, in which God directly appeals to people to choose, seem to presuppose libertarianism: "Be strong and very courageous. Be careful to obey all the law my servant Moses gave you; do not turn from it to the right or to the left, that you may be successful wherever you go" (Josh 1:7). "'Even now,' declares the LORD, 'return to me with all your heart, with fasting and weeping and mourning'" (Joel 2:12). "Then you will call upon me and come and pray to me, and I will listen to you. You will seek me and find me when you seek me with all your heart" (Jer 29:12-

13). "This is what the LORD says to the house of Israel: 'seek me and live'" (Amos 5:4).

Then there are the many verses in which God's spokesmen appeal for decisions. "Therefore, take care to follow the commands, decrees and laws I give you today. If you pay attention to these laws and are careful to follow them, then the LORD your God will keep his covenant of love with you, as he swore to your forefathers" (Deut 7:11-12). "Now fear the LORD and serve him with all faithfulness. . . . But if serving the LORD seems undesirable to you, then choose for yourselves this day whom you will serve, whether the gods your forefathers served beyond the River, or the gods of the Amorites, in whose land you are living. But as for me and my household, we will serve the LORD" (Josh 24:14-15). "Repent, then, and turn to God, so that your sins may be wiped out, that times of refreshing may come from the Lord" (Acts 3:19). "Timothy, guard what has been entrusted to your care. Turn away from godless chatter and the opposing ideas of what is falsely called knowledge, which some have professed and in so doing have wandered from the faith" (1 Tim 6:20-21). "For, 'Whoever would love life and see good days must keep his tongue from evil and his lips from deceitful speech. He must turn from evil and do good; he must seek peace and pursue it'" (1 Pet 3:10-11, quoting from Ps 34).

And finally that best-loved Bible verse, John 3:16: "For God so loved the world that he gave his one and only Son, that whoever believes in him shall not perish but have eternal life."

By my lights, the many verses like those just cited, which appeal directly for individuals to make decisions, are more plausibly interpreted as presupposing that the individuals addressed have both the autonomy required to make such decisions and the possibility of choosing to comply or not. Yet I must acknowledge that even though I think the preponderance of the evidence favors a libertarian position, there are significant theological, exegetical and philosophical arguments to support compatibilism.

As this is a book directed first of all at Christian philosophers, I can't refrain from noting that the issues just discussed have a direct bearing on theological debates over the freedom of the will between Augustine and Pelagius, John Calvin and Martin Luther and Jacobus Arminius, and between their many theological heirs. Over the centuries, the issues have become diffused, vocabulary has changed, and the points of many of the historical disputes are obscure to all but the historical theologians. I won't pretend to resolve the many issues involved; nevertheless, let me note three points.

First, these days the debate among Christians is often cast in terms of God's sovereignty. If God is not sovereign *of* all, it is said, he is not sovereign *at* all. As an argument: If God does not control everything, then he is not sovereign. But if humans have libertarian freedom, then God does not control everything. Therefore, if humans have libertarian freedom, God is not sovereign.

But no reasonable Christian libertarian would deny that at all times God remains in control of everything. What they deny is that he actually exercises *active* control of everything. The libertarian maintains only that some morally significant actions are free in a libertarian sense, not that all are. A Christian libertarian will maintain that God has granted limited freedom to humans, and that he can and sometimes does intervene to assure that his will is accomplished, but that this does not entail that he always intervenes. Just as God need not continually exercise all his powers to do anything in order to remain omnipotent, so too he need not actively exercise his sovereign control at all times to remain sovereign. Further, the libertarian maintains that if God actively controls every human action, then the compatibilist has a very tough job showing how it is that God himself is not the cause of sin.

Second, a libertarian can consistently maintain both that humans have (delegated) libertarian freedom and that no human can freely decide to trust Christ apart from the grace of God; libertarianism does not entail Pelagianism. That is, the inward work of the Holy Spirit, drawing the sinner to Jesus, is necessary if a person is to trust Christ for salvation; yet that person can still enjoy the sort of freedom that the libertarian believes is essential to moral accountability. On this view, a person has genuine freedom to do good or evil, but no matter how much good the person does, it will not suffice for salvation.

Third, many compatibilists are guilty of posing a false dilemma when they argue that if an action is not caused by a person's character or desires or reasons (or some such thing), then the action is random. As I noted above, libertarians believe that reasons are not efficient causes and that a free agent is a first cause herself. An agent acts, and no set of individually necessary and jointly sufficient antecedent conditions determine the action. Yet since the agent is a person, the action is not random, the product of chance quantum events in the motor regions of the brain (or some such thing).

Be all that as it may, the point stands that personal agency and free will are not to be reconciled with a physicalist account of persons, and some version of free will is a necessary condition for moral responsibility as conceived by anyone not in the grip of the dogma of determinism.[52]

Still . . . Christian (nonreductive) physicalism? Earlier I alluded to a growing position among Christians, nonreductive physicalism. I think that what I've said already suffices at least to neutralize the most common reasons for holding the view, but I owe it to those holding the position to say a bit more.

The basic idea of nonreductive physicalism (NRP) is that it can attribute more than merely epiphenomenal status to mental properties because it is top-down, not bottom-up. That is, whereas reductive physicalism offers an analysis that begins with the properties of atoms, then ascends to the level of chemical properties, and then to biological, and so explains the mental reductively in terms ultimately of microphysical properties, NRP claims that mental properties (which really are still ontologically reducible to physical properties) can exercise top-down causation. To put it a bit differently, the very complex interaction of our relationships and experiences within our environment (including humans, animals, plants and inanimate objects) affects and is affected by our mental states, so that a bottom-up analysis cannot possibly capture all of what is involved in individual consciousness.

Sometimes this is expressed by saying that the mental supervenes on the physical together with (natural and social) context. But superve-

---

[52]Further discussion of these issues can found in *Predestination and Free Will: Four Views of Divine Sovereignty and Human Freedom,* ed. David Basinger and Randall Basinger (Downers Grove, Ill.: InterVarsity Press, 1986);

nience is a very slippery term. More formally, certain properties S are supervenient on certain properties B if no two objects could differ with respect to their S-properties and not also differ with respect to their B-properties. Any change in the base properties B, then, entails a change in the supervenient properties S. However, in spite of the formality of the definition, it's not at all clear that the concept of supervenience has any real explanatory value; it seems to be the name of a problem rather than a solution.

Further, if NRP includes some reference to context, the notion is even murkier. Nancey Murphy's definition of supervenience in the context of her nonreductive physicalism is this:

> Property S is supervenient on property B if and only if something's being B constitutes its being S under circumstances c.[53]

Circumstances c would include social and other environmental contexts. But it is not at all clear that any precise meaning attaches to the claim that mental properties supervene on such things as social context: how broad is that context, what sorts of things are included, and why— these questions remain unanswered.

Finally, it is doubtful that invoking the notion of supervenience alleviates the deterministic concerns that plague physicalism. Even granting that somehow social context can affect the workings of my brain so that the antecedent physical states of my brain are insufficient to causally explain later brain states, it is still deterministic—although perhaps even more epistemically opaque to any investigator.

So I don't personally see much philosophical promise in NRP, let alone theological promise. If God, an immaterial, spiritual substance, can exert causal influence on the world, it is hard to see how Christians can balk at the idea of immaterial human souls doing the same. Moreover, if by definition, mental properties supervene on a physical base, then problems arise for the minds of angels and demons, and even God himself becomes problematic on this view.

---

[53]Nancey Murphy, "Nonreductive Physicalism: Philosophical Issues," in *Whatever Happened to the Soul?* ed. Warren S. Brown, Nancey Murphy and H. Newton Malony (Minneapolis: Fortress, 1998), p. 135.

And finally, it seems to me that issues of personal identity and the doctrine of the resurrection of the body also count against NRP. Let me explain.

THE RESURRECTION OF THE BODY

The doctrine of resurrection of the body is clearly part of a Christian worldview. Christ taught it, Peter preached it, Paul defended it, Revelation depicts it, and the creeds include it.[54] So if a physicalist view (whether reductive or nonreductive) of human persons conflicts with the doctrine of the resurrection, that's a serious problem.

To their credit, Christian physicalists for the most part have recognized the problem and have attempted to supply answers. Generally, the responses fall in to one of five camps: (1) the simulacrum view,[55] (2) the fission view,[56] (3) the constitution view,[57] (4) the nonreductive physicalist view[58] and (5) the four-dimensionalist view.[59] While I don't have space to discuss the details of the proffered answers, I believe all are inadequate and that any form of physicalism—eliminative, nonreductive, Christian, whatever—will be at best very uncomfortable with the doctrine of resurrection. As I aim to make clear, the crucial issue is that of personal identity. Whatever the account the physicalists offer of resurrection, they must show that personal identity is maintained. They must, that is, explain how a particular resurrected body is one and the same person as the person who lived and died. This is not a difficult

---

[54]For a discussion of conceptions of the resurrection in the early and medieval church, see Caroline Walker Bynam, *The Resurrection of the Body in Western Christianity, 200-1336* (New York: Columbia University Press, 1995).

[55]Peter van Inwagen, "The Possibility of Resurrection," *International Journal for Philosophy of Religion* 9 (1978): 114-21; reprinted with a postscript in *The Possibility of Resurrection and Other Essays in Christian Apologetics* (Boulder, Colo.: Westview Press, 1998), pp. 45-51.

[56]Suggested but not endorsed by Dean Zimmerman, "The Compatibility of Materialism and Survival: The 'Falling Elevator' Model," *Faith and Philosophy* 16 (April 1999): 194-212.

[57]Lynne Rudder Baker, "Material Persons and the Doctrine of Resurrection," *Faith and Philosophy* 18 (April 2001): 151-67; Kevin Corcoran, "The Constitution View of Persons," in *In Search of the Soul: Four Views of the Mind-Body Problem*, ed. Joel B. Green and Stuart L. Palmer (Downers Grove, Ill.: InterVarsity Press, 2005); Trenton Merricks, "How to Live Forever Without Saving Your Soul: Physicalism and Immortality," in *Soul, Body and Survival*, ed. Kevin Corcoran (Ithaca, N.Y.: Cornell University Press, 2001), pp. 183-200.

[58]Murphy, "Nonreductive Physicalism: Philosophical Issues," pp. 127-48.

[59]Hud Hudson, *A Materialist Metaphysics of the Human Person* (Ithaca, N.Y.: Cornell University Press, 2001).

task for dualists, who ground personal identity in the soul, not the body, and can say simply "same soul, same person." But my claim is that there are telling objections to physicalists' accounts of this identity. If I am right, then it is an interesting question as to whether Christian physicalists could express their hope in the resurrection of the dead in the same sense as did the apostle Paul before the Sanhedrin ("I stand on trial because of my hope in the resurrection of the dead," Acts 23:6; cf. Acts 24:15) or as Peter expressed in his first epistle (1 Pet 1:3).

I want to consider three arguments against any form of physicalism based on the doctrine of resurrection. I'll call the arguments respectively the Modal, the Moral and the "Where Was Jesus?" argument.

The modal argument. The modal argument is a reductio ad absurdum on the multiple realizability aspect of several versions of physicalism, most notably the nonreductive physicalist view. This view holds that at the resurrection God assembles a perfect replica of a deceased person, and that in virtue of having the same subvenient properties grounded in the elementary particles and their relations, the replica instantiates the same supervenient mental properties, thereby making the replica identical psychologically to the decedent. And since nonreductivists employ a psychological criterion of personal identity, the replica *is the* decedent.

Granting, for the sake of argument, the possibility of such supervenience, there seems to be a very serious problem here. For the replica is just that—a copy, not the original. To see this clearly, imagine that a mad scientist, not God, created a replica of me and immediately killed "me." Since multiple realizability is crucial to this view, it is logically possible that the same supervenient properties could be realized by many replicas. So the mad scientist could create one hundred exact replicas, each of which would have exactly the same psychological properties as I did moments earlier, and have equal claim to being "me." They would have, at the moment of their assembly, the same memories, beliefs, desires, fears, hopes and so forth as I had at the moment of my demise. From that point, of course, their memories would begin to diverge as they had different experiences, but if identity is grounded in psychology, all would have equal claim to be "me." And this is not a claim based on epistemic indiscernibility, but on metaphysical identity.

Further, since it is at least logically possible that the same set of psychological properties could be realized by a computer simulation, that also could claim to be "me." As could one hundred such simulations running simultaneously.

Or consider this. If the supervenience thesis is correct, God (or more likely a nefarious neuroscientist) could miraculously rearrange my brain matter so that my brain would subvene the same psychological properties as Barak Obama or Paris Hilton. But surely it does not follow that the body that my wife is married to suddenly could become president, or worse.

All such states of affairs are patently absurd. I believe that these thought experiments drive us to conclude that just as none of the computer simulations would in fact be me, so too none of the replicas would be me either. This highlights the deeply unsatisfactory nature of a psychological criterion of personal identity, especially if the psychological properties are taken to supervene on physical states as in nonreductive physicalism. But without such a criterion, the nonreductivist has no basis to claim that a resurrected body is identical to a deceased person, and so resurrection is an empty promise devoid of hope.

As a final intuitive check on this conclusion, suppose you were about to undergo serious brain surgery. The neurosurgeon assures you that even though there is a good chance you will not survive the surgery, medical technology has made it possible to create a perfect replica of you that will be pressed into service should your survival become doubtful. Would you find much hope in the knowledge that a replica of you would leave the hospital, rejoin your wife and kids, and settle into your old life?

Now, I've been directing this argument against nonreductive physicalism, but since the four-dimensionalist adopts the same psychological criterion of personal identity, the same sort of modal argument could be deployed, *mutatis mutandis,* against her.

The moral argument. The modal argument leads directly to the moral argument against physicalist resurrection. Even if we grant the supervenience thesis, the problems we have just seen with respect to a psychological criterion of personal identity makes it morally problematic that God would send a *replica* of Hitler to hell. Surely the replica didn't do the things Hitler did, even if he seems to remember that he did. Perhaps the nonreductivist will argue at this point that for this very reason, annihilationism is to be preferred over a resurrection to eternal damnation. Most evangelicals will have difficulty with this move. Be that as it may, the replica view seems equally problematic for the saved. For it is a *replica* of me that enters into the glorified state, but it was for the sins of *me* that Christ died. God in fact elected a replica for eternal life, and not me. And that robs my actions in this life of any eternal significance for *me*, and so voids the doctrine of resurrection of any real hope.

And again, since the four-dimensionalist also relies on the flawed psychological criterion of personal identity, the Moral Argument also applies *mutatis mutandis* to that position.

The "Where was Jesus?" argument. Finally, physicalists must grapple with the applicability of their view to the incarnation, and especially to the question of what happened to Christ during the time between his death and his resurrection. Whether a physicalist can give an account of the hypostatic union which agrees with Chalcedon is unclear to me. Chalcedonian Christology teaches that the Logos assumed a human nature together with a human body. But if the Divine Person assumed a human body, and physicalism is true, then a second person would supervene on the brain of that body. Why? Recall Murphy's definition of supervenience:

> Property S is supervenient on property B if and only if something's being B constitutes its being S under circumstances c.[60]

The relation between the subvenient and the supervenient properties is given in a biconditional; consequently, it is impossible that the mental properties of the Logos could be realized apart from a physical brain. But this would entail that the Logos was eternally incarnate, contrary to biblical teaching. But then the physicalist has to explain how, given her

---

[60]Murphy, "Nonreductive Physicalism: Philosophical Issues," p. 135.

definition of supervenience, the physical properties of the human brain of Jesus did not subvene a distinct person. Multiple realizability seems to lead to Nestorianism. Now, the physicalist could perhaps claim that for every other human person mind supervenes on brain, but this is not the case in the incarnation. Then how should we understand the claim that Christ was "made like his brothers in every way" (Heb 2:17)?

The problems for the physicalist seem even more acute when we ask what happened when Jesus died. Clearly the Logos did not pass into nonexistence. But what happened to the assumed human nature of Christ when the human body of Jesus died? It asks too much of orthodox Christology to allow for a "gappy" existence of the incarnate Christ. So perhaps "body-snatching" did occur. But then it was not after all Jesus who was buried, and Paul is wrong to claim so in 1 Corinthians 15. Or perhaps fissioning occurred, but then we are committed to a closest-continuer theory of human identity through time for the human part of the God-man, but something else for the divine part, all the while retaining the *unity* of the hypostasis. I could press the argument along these lines, but I believe that I've said enough to support my claim that physicalism is incompatible with the doctrine of the resurrection.

Hope reclaimed. I have argued that any form of physicalism faces serious difficulties when it comes to the issue of personal identity and the doctrine of the resurrection. So it doesn't seem to me that Christian physicalists can hope in the resurrection in the same robust sense that hope is held forth in the New Testament.

But there remains a hope, and it is what the church has believed all along. One need not be a radical Gnostic-Neoplatonic-Cartesian dualist to believe in an immaterial soul that is the bearer of personal identity. I am essentially a soul that began my life embodied as a corruptible organism, and will spend the vast majority of my life embodied in an incorruptible, glorified body. I believe in the resurrection of the dead; I believe, with the Old Testament Job, that in my flesh I shall see him—I, and not another (Job 19:26-27).

CONCLUSION

Again, as with all these issues, there is much more to say, but I must leave matters here. One thing should be clear at the end of this chapter: it is of paramount importance that we know what we are as human persons. If we don't, the effects may well be catastrophic for our relationships with other persons and other things in creation, as well as our relationship with God himself.

We have good reasons to believe what a Christian worldview implies about us as human persons:

- We are men and women made in the image of God, which implies at least capacities necessary for ruling as God's vice regents.

- We are embodied souls that function holistically, as a unified whole; our bodies (and especially our brains) affect our thinking, and vice versa.

- We are capable of disembodied existence and will exist temporarily in a disembodied state following death.

- We are endowed with free will, capable of much good but also much evil. In the words of the *Book of Common Prayer,* "we have done that which we ought not to have done, and left undone that which we ought to have done." We have freely sinned, and fallen short of the glory of God (Rom 3:23). At the same time, we are capable of freely responding to God's grace as the Holy Spirit draws us to Jesus Christ, disposing our rebellious wills to repent and receive him as Savior and Lord.

- Our hope as Christians is the resurrection of the body and life everlasting. According to God's promise and sustaining power, we are destined for endless life of blessedness in God's presence, or despair apart from him.

Finally, let me conclude with a by-now familiar disclaimer of sorts. I'm not saying that my view is the only possible Christian view on these topics, or that those Christian philosophers who hold different views—nonreductive physicalists, for example—are somehow inferior as Christian philosophers. The conclusions I've argued for in this (and other) chapters are ones I believe are correct, but I could be wrong. At the very least I hope to have demonstrated one way that a Christian can do philosophical anthropology, a way that I believe reflects the commitments inherent in a Christian worldview.

9

Understanding Nature

Philosophy of Science

We live in a society exquisitely dependent on science and technology, in which hardly anyone knows anything about science and technology.

Carl Sagan

Science is what you know.
Philosophy is what you don't know.

Bertrand Russell

Philosophy of science is about as useful to scientists as ornithology is to birds.

Richard Feynman

Fifty years ago (as I write this), C. P. Snow published his famous book, *The Two Cultures*,[1] pointing to what he saw as the dangerous, growing and seemingly unbridgeable distance between the scientific and the literary cultures. Whatever the merits (or demerits) of Snow's argument and of his political conclusions, the phrase itself is just as apt today as it was then. Public understanding of science is lamentably low, even as

---

[1] C. P. Snow, *The Two Cultures* (Cambridge: Cambridge University Press, 1959, expanded ed. 1998).

the scientific community is held up as the purveyor of unassailable truth. Television news programs looking for authoritative voices don't turn to philosophers or clergy; the scientist in a white lab coat, surrounded by fantastic and mysterious apparatus, represents the new priesthood of knowledge.

Several unfortunate consequences follow. First, since science represents the "gold standard" for knowledge, any discipline that wants its conclusions to be seriously considered in the public square *must* claim to be "scientific." And conversely, any discipline the conclusions of which are deemed somehow unacceptable in the public square *must* be written off as nonscience. This consequence makes it imperative to be able to tell what is science and what is not. But defining science—the so-called demarcation problem—is much more difficult than one might suppose.

Second, since empiricism is the "official epistemology" of science,[2] empirical evidence is tacitly accepted as by far the best, or perhaps the only, sort of evidence that can justify a knowledge claim. Claims not arrived at via "*the* scientific method" are either suspect or rejected out of hand. For example, concerns about the morality of embryonic stem cell research or human cloning, are dismissed as religious or ideological interference in the morally neutral pursuit of scientific knowledge. Ethics is relegated to the realm of personal opinion. Similarly, the claim is often heard from the bevy of "new atheists" that there is "no evidence whatsoever" for the existence of God. This is because the reasons for moral or religious beliefs are not the sort of evidence that can be subjected to the empirical investigation typical of the natural sciences.

The third consequence is that metaphysical commitments are constrained by science. Terms that figure in the best available scientific theory or explanation are widely regarded as carrying ontological commitment, whereas terms that are not part of scientific theories or explanations are widely relegated to the realm of fiction or myth. So such things as neurophysiological descriptions of brain functions are real, while immaterial minds or souls are fictions. Quantum indeterminacy,

[2]Alex Rosenberg, *Philosophy of Science: A Contemporary Introduction*, 2nd ed. (New York: Routledge, 2005), pp. 88-89.

Darwinian evolution or the extra dimensions of string theory are "fact," while the resurrection of Jesus, divine intervention in the history of life or the existence of angels or demons are myths. We are supposed to be realists about entities in scientific theories, but it is unreasonable to be realists about "metaphysical" (used pejoratively) entities such as essential human nature, or properties, relations and propositions.

The sorts of issues these consequences illustrate—definitional, epistemological, metaphysical—all belong to the philosophy of science. The attitude toward the philosophy of science illustrated by Richard Feynman (in the epigraph to this chapter) is as distressing as it is common. We desperately need to think about the philosophy of science if only because science has such a commanding presence in contemporary culture.

ISSUES AND OPTIONS

The salient issues in philosophy of science that I wish to consider in this chapter revolve around five questions: (1) Can we define science, and can we tell science from pseudo-science? (2) What is "the scientific method," and how does it relate to the epistemic status of scientific claims? (3) What is the ontological status of theoretical terms in science? (4) Should scientific research and technological applications be constrained by moral or religious considerations, and if so, how? (5) When the conclusions of science apparently conflict with conclusions of other disciplines—and I'm thinking here primarily of theology—how does one adjudicate the conflicting claims?

There are, of course, many other fascinating issues in philosophy of science, but these five seem to be where a Christian worldview has the most significant impact.

The demarcation problem. Just about all laypersons, and just about all scientists, assume that they know definitively what science is. That a layperson would think so isn't surprising: the generally poor science education in many schools, and the incessant references to "Science" (one can almost hear the capital letter) in the media surely convey the idea that there is a well-defined something called "science." That scientists think so is also understandable: they are the professionals, the practitioners, the ones mentoring the next generation of scientists, so surely they know what it is they are doing. But do they?

As I noted in an earlier chapter, the basic question in "the philosophy of X" is, "What is X?" This is a philosophical question. Accepting provisionally the characterization that science uses empirical, repeatable methods, what possible empirical methods could be used to reach and test a definition of science?

Nor can science be defined by "what scientists do." Read Kepler's journals: clearly he believed that the astrological and geometrical methods he used to derive his famous three laws of planetary motion were scientific, but today Kepler's explanations of his derivations are somewhat embarrassing to astrophysicists. Or read of Newton's almost fanatical experiments in alchemy: surely he thought that was science, but today alchemy is nowhere regarded as science. Such examples could be multiplied, but the moral is clear. The problem of defining science is a philosophical not a scientific problem.

One way to define a thing is by stating its essence. So gold is essentially that element with atomic number 79; water is that compound that is essentially H_2O, and so on. But it's obvious that science can't be defined that way—human enterprises as complex as those activities we want to call "science" don't have essences that can be displayed.

Or we could try to define science by listing a set of individually necessary and jointly sufficient conditions; any activity that met the conditions would, by definition, be science. The assumption that necessary and sufficient conditions can be identified seems to lie behind two rather famous court cases: *McLean* and *Kitzmiller*. I'll return to these putative definitions below.

A third approach would be to say science was a "cluster concept" defined by "family resemblance." Accordingly, there would be no set of jointly sufficient conditions (although there might be a necessary condition or two), but there would be a set of conditions enough of which would be sufficient to qualify a particular activity as science. These "family resemblance features" could be drawn from paradigmatic activities or episodes or theories in the history of science. The idea is that, as in epistemology, we should be particularists rather than methodists. There are clear cases in history that everyone (or almost everyone) would call science, and clear cases that are not science. Even if there is a shadowy region of questionable cases (in which category I'd put both phlogiston chemistry and sociobiology, among other examples), there is enough clarity to enable us to do a pretty good job of characterizing science.

The "scientific method." Any introductory textbook on any branch of science will, early on, have a diagram in a neat box labeled "The scientific method." While such diagrams differ in detail and execution, they all basically show something along the lines of figure 9.1. The diagrams raise several questions. First, is this methodology unique to science?

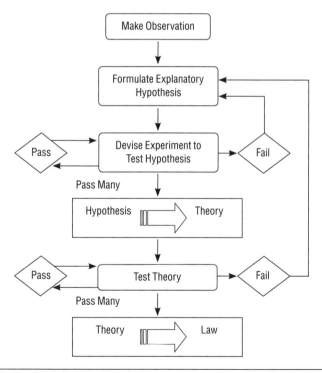

Figure 9.1. The "scientific method"

Second, does science really operate according to this methodology, or is this an after-the-fact, "rational reconstruction" of how science works?

Third, what is the relationship between this "method" and the epistemology of scientific theories? Fourth, who defines the box?

Realism versus antirealism. Scientific theories are replete with theoretical terms that seem to refer to unseen, unobservable entities. In the
past, theoretical terms referred to gravity (Newton's "occult [meaning
hidden] force"), phlogiston, the luminiferous aether and genes. Today
gravity is understood not as a hidden force but as a curvature of spacetime; phlogiston is recognized to be nonexistent since Lavoisier, the
father of modern chemistry, identified burning as a process of oxida-
tion; the aether also has been abandoned, although from time to time
certain interpretations of general relativity or quantum cosmology make
reference to something called the aether, but with quite a different conceptual content than the luminiferous aether of the late nineteenth century; and genes today are rather well understood in terms of nucleotide
sequences in the DNA molecule.

Terms playing a role in historical theories, then, have been variously
redefined with different theoretical content, replaced with new terms
with different empirical content, abandoned altogether, or retained and
cashed out with firm empirical content. With this history before us,
what should we make of terms that figure in today's cutting-edge theories: strings, quarks, dark energy, quantum wave collapse and so on?
Should we be realists—that is, accept that any theoretical term in a successful theory actually refers to an objectively existing entity? Or should
we be antirealists—refusing to commit to a realist ontology of theoretical terms, opting instead to take theoretical terms in an operationalist or pragmatic sense? Or is there a third way, an eclectic approach, and
if so, is there a principled way to decide where to be realists and where
to be antirealists?

Science and ethical constraints. It might be nice if someday scientists
discovered femto-scale[3] inscriptions of the Ten Commandments on
every proton, but that is highly dubious. In fact, science's empirical
investigation of the natural world proves radically inappropriate for
determining moral truth.[4] Yet it is clear that ethics is as important in

---

[3]A proton is approximately a femtometer in diameter—that is, 10^{-15} meter).
[4]I'm aware, of course, of the attempts to derive moral precepts from evolutionary psychology. In

science as in any other endeavor, even if science itself cannot derive ethical truth.

Ethical constraints figure in science in two broad ways. First, science must be practiced ethically. Plagiarism, data falsification, intellectual theft, the influence of funding sources on published conclusions—recent news reports have highlighted a number of ethical failures of these sorts by scientists. Like any other cooperative human activity, ethical standards must apply to how science is practiced. Scientists, scientific organizations and scientific journals recognize this, and are continually vigilant to detect and expose unethical practices. Call such restrictions "procedural ethical constraints."

But there is a second area where many people believe that ethics constrains—or should constrain—science. It seems clear enough that some lines of potential scientific research should be precluded on ethical grounds. Perhaps the paradigmatic case of immoral scientific research was the Nazi medical experiments on concentration camp victims, which virtually all ethicists regard as immoral even though some of the experiments resulted in useful information. For example, data collected in hypothermia experiments led to better exposure suits for sailors and airmen operating in the frigid North Atlantic. But in spite of useful results, such research is uniformly rejected as unethical.

While less objectionable than the Nazi experiments, research aimed at producing an undetectable performance-enhancing drug for world-class athletes still seems highly unethical. Development of an undetectable "date rape" drug seems so unethical that it should be prohibited. Call attempts to restrict certain lines of research based on ethical considerations "programmatic ethical constraints."

In many cases of possible programmatic constraints, intuitions differ. When hearing about genetic experiments involving creating human-animal hybrids, most people react strongly negatively. This no doubt reflects a certain "yuck factor," but there are, I think, widespread and

---

my opinion these attempts are woeful examples of special pleading, "just-so" stories, and suffer from a clear lack of the sort of empirical evidence that is supposed to characterize science. And even if evolutionary psychology were able to account for some moral behavior, it could not begin to explain the *oughtness* of morality (see chapter 7). Adaptive behavior conducive to survival carries no sense of *moral* obligation.

strong moral intuitions about such research.[5] And yet such research continues. The controlling principle seems to be the "technological imperative": if we can do it, we should.

The public debate over the ban on federal funding for most embryonic stem cell research, ordered by President George W. Bush in August 2001, and overturned by President Barack Obama in March 2009, illustrates the difficulties faced in trying to apply programmatic ethical constraints on a research program. Those supporting the ban argued about the morality of creating human embryos that would not be allowed to grow to maturity, solely for the purpose of research, and worried about the ethical implications for human life in general. Those opposing the ban made utilitarian arguments about the potential medical advances in treating serious conditions, which such research might lead to, and generally dismissed opposing arguments as "religion" or "someone's personal morality" trying to restrict "legitimate science."

Clearly, as the above examples show, programmatic ethical constraints should lead to prohibition of certain lines of research. But as the embryonic stem cell debate shows, there are those who would object to almost all such constraints. So who decides? Who draws the line?

Adjudicating interdisciplinary conflicts. A common perception is that theology (or the institutional church, or popular religion, or some such thing) has always been the enemy of scientific progress. The iconic image of the heroic Galileo, hounded by ecclesiastical authorities, finally being forced on pain of death to recant his heliocentric view of the solar system, is ubiquitous in our culture. That view has been reinforced in these days by the "New Atheists" whose polemical writings invariably cast religion as the enemy of enlightened, open-minded, freethinking, scientific truth seekers. But this perception is false, relying on historical distortion and omission.

---

[5]In 2003, scientists at the Shanghai Second Medical University created human-rabbit chimeras, reportedly the first human-animal hybrids. Since then, various labs have created human hybrids with cows, pigs, mice and other animals. Bioethics panels in the United States and Europe have produced widely varying recommendations to regulate such experiments (see, for example, the report of the President's Council on Bioethics, available at <http://bioethics.georgetown.edu/pcbe/reports/reproductionandresponsibility/>, but no clear legal lines have been drawn in the sand.

But it is clear that certain claims of science do apparently conflict with certain claims of Christian theology. Different positions on issues such as the age of the universe and the age of the earth, the theory of evolution, the existence of the soul, free will, life after death and so on fuel many hot debates.

In such cases, does science always win? Or theology? Or are there principles to apply on a case-by-case basis?

CHRISTIAN WORLDVIEW IMPLICATIONS

It is obvious that the Bible does not address science as a discipline. In fact, not a lot in Scripture has any clear scientific import. Yet the places that do have direct scientific implications are some of the more important (and treasured) passages. A developed Christian systematic theology will have even more areas of impact, as a systematization of biblical teaching may lead us to recognize inferences that we would not otherwise have read directly off the text itself. And if it is comprehensive, a Christian worldview will have even more implications for how science should be done and how its conclusion should be interpreted. But it is also true that science and its deliverances influence Christian theology and a Christian worldview. Christians in the sciences, as well as Christian theologians and philosophers, need to think carefully about such things. Reflective integration of all areas of life and learning within a Christian worldview remains the difficult but necessary goal.

What follows from this view of science, I think, is a qualified disciplinary integrity. Just as chemistry is not ecology or astronomy, so science is not theology or philosophy. At the same time, though, the disciplinary integrity is qualified: it is integrity, not isolation or autonomy. So any definition of science that establishes impregnable boundaries between science and other disciplines is dubious, as is any definition that elevates science's methods or deliverances to epistemological sovereignty.

A second implication that follows from this view of science is that it is an activity of men and women; it is a developing process, an ongoing enterprise. As such it probably is not possible to list a set of necessary and sufficient conditions that mark out all and only those activities that are science from all that are not. Human enterprises are much more organic, complex and fluid.

Still, as I noted above, at least two legal decisions have stipulated necessary and sufficient conditions for science. A brief look at these two will show their inadequacy. They are *McLean v. Arkansas Board of Education* (1982) and *Kitzmiller v. Dover Area School District* (2005). Both cases were successful culminations of lawsuits aimed at prohibiting certain religious interpretations of science from being taught in public schools. In *McLean*, Judge William Overton ruled against an Arkansas law mandating "equal treatment" for teaching "creation science," and in *Kitzmiller*, Judge John E. Jones ruled that even mentioning "intelligent design" in science classes as an alternative explanation of the origin of life was unconstitutional.[6]

The McLean decision ruled that there were five essential characteristics of science:

1. It is guided by natural law.

2. It has to be explanatory by reference to natural law.

3. It is testable against the empirical world.

4. Its conclusions are tentative, i.e., are not necessarily the final word.

5. It is falsifiable.

Judge Jones endorsed the *McLean* criteria and added two others relevant to the question of whether intelligent design was science:

6. The ground rules of science prohibit invoking or permitting supernatural causation.

7. Legitimate science cannot be a direct descendant of a religious theory.[7]

A little reflection reveals that these criteria are neither necessary nor sufficient for defining science. We can point to instances, both historical and contemporary, that everyone would call 'science' but that fail to

---

[6]For the *McLean* ruling, see <www.talkorigins.org/faqs/mclean-v-arkansas.html>; and for *Kitzmiller*, go to <www.pamd.uscourts.gov/kitzmiller/kitzmiller_342.pdf>.

[7]Judge Jones was ruling specifically on the issue of intelligent design (ID), and in support of his opinion that teaching ID constituted unconstitutional teaching of religion, he wrote that "ID is nothing less than the progeny of creationism."

exemplify one or another of the criteria; hence they cannot be necessary. And there are cases that are *not* clearly science that do exemplify one or another of the criteria; hence they cannot be sufficient either.[8]

With most philosophers of science, I believe that 'science' cannot be rigidly defined, but it can be adequately characterized by pointing to the most salient characteristics of paradigmatic cases of science, both historical and contemporary. The resulting characterization will be sufficient to include most of what we regard as science and exclude out most of what we would not regard as science. And while there will surely be a shadowy region where we are unsure about a particular activity, we must recognize that such is the nature of the case. At any given time, some research programs or projects may be "in" that once were "out," and vice versa. And there will probably be several moving through the shadow region, either toward acceptance as science or toward rejection.

As a characterization of science, then, I propose the following:

> Science is a structured, theoretical, cooperative, human enterprise, the goal of which is to offer progressively more accurate explanations of the natural world, which employs primarily empirical methods, and which is generally characterized by publicly accessible and replicable results.

The controversial part of this characterization is the "goal" clause. Some will argue that description, not explanation, is all that science aims at. Others will argue that the history of science does not support a notion of progress ("progressively more accurate"). And still others will claim that this clause contains an unwarranted commitment to realism. Fair enough. I'd respond, first, that while there are times and areas of research where all science can do is describe, its *goal* is to explain. Prediction, so vital to testing and confirmation of hypotheses, if

---

[8]For criticism of the *McLean* criteria, see J. P. Moreland, *Christianity and the Nature of Science* (Grand Rapids: Baker, 1989), pp. 23-42. The inadequacy of the additional *Kitzmiller* criteria is even more egregious: (6) refers to the "ground rules" of science, but there are in fact no such ground rules, only loudly stated personal prejudices. As Thomas Nagel, who has no theistic axe to grind, has argued, it is perfectly legitimate for science to conclude that the facts point to *nonnatural causes:* "Public Education and Intelligent Design," *Philosophy & Public Affairs* 36 (2008): 187-205. As for (7), if taken seriously, this criterion would rule out almost all branches of science, since most had origins in some religious context such as astrology or sorcery.

successful, must either rely on pure statistical projection or on genuine understanding of the phenomena, and the latter clearly is preferable if real-world technological applications are sought. Second, I'll acknowledge that the notion of scientific progress is a difficult one to cash out in these post-Kuhnian days.[9] Still, by my lights, we can make sense of the notion of progress by evaluating certain features of successive theories, such as empirical adequacy, predictive success, explanatory power, fruitfulness in generating new research, elegance and simplicity of explanation, and unification of earlier theories.[10]

Third, my characterization does include a modest commitment to realism, but not to the idea that every theoretical term must refer to objective, mind-independent entities. There's room for antirealism in some cases, as I'll discuss below.

I believe this characterization of science adequately preserves the disciplinary integrity of science while leaving science open to meaningful interaction with other disciplines.[11]

The scientific method. Again, as with the demarcation problem, no direct biblical teaching speaks to the scientific method. But again, as with demarcation, there are implications of a Christian worldview. Specifically I want to note two: first, the "box" around the diagram of "The scientific method," or the method-in-the-box (MIB), as I'll call the scheme diagramed in figure 9.1; and second, the epistemological status of the "outputs" of that method.

The MIB begins with observation. But of course scientific practice *does not* begin with observation *simpliciter*. Generally, scientists begin with a problem that needs to be solved, sometimes with an anomalous

---

[9]Kuhn's seminal and highly influential work has been the subject of much debate in a wide variety of fields far beyond science. Thomas S. Kuhn, *The Structure of Scientific Revolutions*, 3rd ed. (Chicago: University of Chicago Press, 1996). See also the collection of critical essays, *World Changes: Thomas Kuhn and the Nature of Science*, ed. Paul Horwich (Cambridge, Mass.: MIT Press, 1993; reissue edition, University of Pittsburgh Press, 2009).

[10]See John Losee, *Theories of Scientific Progress: An Introduction* (New York: Routledge, 2003).

[11]In the same vein, I'd characterize theology as "a structured, theoretical enterprise, the goal of which is progressively more accurate explanations of God's nature and God's relations to his creation, which employs primarily exegetical methods and utilizes any and all sources of information, and which generates publicly accessible results." And I'd suggest we make sense of theological progress in terms of exegetical adequacy, explanatory power, fruitfulness in generating new research, depth and beauty in worship, and holiness in life.

data set that needs to be investigated, occasionally with a bit of mathematical theory that suggests physical entities or interactions,[12] and now and then with an accidental, unexpected observation, for example, the sighting by an amateur astronomer of a "black spot" on Jupiter on July 19, 2009.[13] In general, though, it's only with some project in mind that any scientist knows *what* to observe and *how* to observe it. What counts as an observation is crucial, but is not patently obvious; surely what an observation is, is not itself a question answerable by MIB.

And indeed, the *what* and the *how* of observation are constrained by theory; not all observations are relevant. Observations of the extent of the polar ice cap or the geographical distribution of swine flu cases in the summer of 2009 have absolutely no bearing on the question of what caused the "black spot" on Jupiter. Nor will a more accurate value for Hubble's constant (taken from observations of red shift) be at all relevant to determining the cause of the Permian extinction event. What is observed must be deemed relevant to the question at hand, but that means that there are certain constraints on what counts as an observation that are in place *before* the task of collecting observational data begins.

A further problem with the notion of observation is that most often, at the cutting edge of science, instruments are used to make the observations. Mass spectrometers, particle accelerators, even optical telescopes depend upon a body of theory that must be accepted as accurate before observations using such equipment can be taken as veridical. Hence the slogan, "All observation is theory-laden," is about as reliable as any slogan ever is.

Next, MIB points to the formulation of an explanatory hypothesis. But here too much is omitted. What needs explaining and what counts as an acceptable hypothesis are again matters that the MIB can't determine. During the 1970s astronomers were desperately seeking the origin and explanation of observed gamma ray bursts. One hypothesis was that the bursts were caused by thermonuclear blasts in wars between

---

[12]On this last, see Mark Steiner, *The Applicability of Mathematics as a Philosophical Problem* (Cambridge, Mass.: Harvard University Press, 1998).
[13]Image at <www.jpl.nasa.gov/news/news.cfm?release=2009-112>.

space aliens. Now, that certainly could have explained the observations, but no scientist involved in gamma ray burst research took it seriously.[14] Why not? Well, the astronomers had a good intuitive sense of what counted as an acceptable hypothesis and what did not, and that sense comes from an "apprenticeship" (grad school, post-doc work, etc.) and actual practical work experience in the discipline, not from anything in the MIB.

The next stage of MIB has a bit more going for it, for once a hypothesis has been formulated, experiments can be devised to test it. However, failure of a test does not constitute falsification of the hypothesis, since any hypothesis is embedded in a mesh of other theoretical assumptions. What is disconfirmed by a failed test is a conjunction of these assumptions together with the hypothesis in question, and it isn't always clear which conjunct is the defective one. If, however, the hypothesis does survive a number of tests, then it is regarded as confirmed.[15]

When it comes to testing laws and theories, another problem arises that MIB ignores. Laws and theories are highly abstract, generalized statements that are in most cases not directly testable. Consequences are deduced from the abstract statements, and tests are devised to confirm or disconfirm these deductions (this has been called the Hypothetico-Deductive or H-D model). But disconfirmation of a deduction does not constitute falsification of the abstract statement of the law or theory, as a scientist always can—and generally will—introduce some ad-hoc hypothesis to explain why *this* test failed, but the abstract statement still holds ("The grad student forgot to clean and calibrate the equipment"; "The pressures and temperatures involved in this test opened it to unexpected quantum influences").

---

[14]The Nova program titled (rather sensationally) "Death Star," first broadcast on January 8, 2002, and available on DVD from PBS, is a very interesting study of the investigation. But it is instructive in many other ways as well, as it shows how military concerns, rivalries between scientists and labs, nationalistic pride, funding for research, and often just plain "luck," play much more of a role in scientific research than is ever acknowledged in simple diagrams of the scientific method. See more at <www.pbs.org/wgbh/nova/gamma/>.

[15]It's a bit more complicated than that, of course. A large and growing body of literature attempts to analyze the nature of confirmation: is it a statistical (probabilistic) notion, and if so, does Bayesianism correctly capture the notion? However that question is answered, virtually all philosophers of science agree that *some* notion of confirmation figures inescapably in the practice of science.

The MIB diagram confuses the nature of laws and theories when it suggests that a confirmed hypothesis "graduates" to become a theory. The relationship is more complex. A law is an abstract statement of a regularity expressed as a universal generalization.[16] A law statement may be expressed in words ("All metals expand when heated") or in a mathematical formula ("F = ma"). But neither form is self-explanatory; both leave us wanting to understand *why* the entities in question are related in this law-like way. A theory is what offers that explanation, although one theory itself may be embedded in a yet more general theory (for example, Newtonian mechanics, on many accounts, is a special case of the special theory of relativity, which itself is a special case of the general theory of relativity). So MIB errs in implying that hypotheses become theories, and theories become laws, as their degree of confirmation grows.

Rather than MIB, a more accurate (but more complex) picture emerges from historical study of how science—and indeed any theoretical discipline—really works. My understanding is based on the work of Imre Lakatos and critical interactions with his ideas.[17] The picture looks roughly like this. A "research program" has at its center a "hard core" of abstract theory, for example, Einstein's field equations for general relativity, Schrödinger's wave equation for quantum mechanics, or general statements about replication, variation and selection for evolutionary theory. This hard core "is tenaciously protected from refutation by a vast 'protective belt' of auxiliary hypotheses" together with a "heuristic," a problem-solving technique.[18] Any anomalous data resulting from testing an auxiliary hypothesis will conveniently be accommodated by questioning one or another of the auxiliary hypotheses rather than the hard core itself, or inventing a new auxiliary hypothesis, which itself then becomes something to be tested. The hard core remains untouched, let alone falsified, by the anomaly. This model describes any

---

[16]This too is an idealization. Many sciences such as biology, ecology or neuroscience do not have law statements that conform to the formal universal generalization pattern. And many laws are statistical, not deterministic.

[17]Imre Lakatos, *The Methodology of Scientific Research Programmes: Philosophical Papers Volume 1*, ed. John Worrall and Gregory Currie (New York: Cambridge University Press, 1978).

[18]Ibid., p. 4.

theoretical discipline; even theology falls into the same broad model, with a hard core, numerous auxiliary hypotheses and a problem-solving heuristic.[19]

Here are a couple examples to illustrate this process. Newtonian mechanics has as its hard core the three laws of motion together with the law of gravitation. When the motion of Uranus did not conform to the predictions of the Newtonian system, scientists did not consider Newtonian mechanics falsified. They could have reexamined hypotheses concerning extraneous causal factors (e.g., distorted propagation of light in a magnetic storm). In fact, though, the astronomers posited another planet that would account for Uranus's perturbed orbit—and found Neptune.

A second astronomical example: Planets orbit the sun in elliptical orbits; the closest point to the sun is called the perihelion. Due to the gravitational attraction of other planets, the perihelion of any planet does not remain fixed in space, but slowly rotates around the sun—it precesses. As early as 1859, astronomers knew that the observed precession of the perihelion of Mercury disagreed with Newtonian predictions. All sorts of ad hoc hypotheses were considered to solve the problem, ranging from positing another planet (called "Vulcan"), to excessive dust in Mercury's orbit, to doubting the precision of the inverse square law of gravitational attraction. None of the hypotheses worked. But the hard core of Newton's system wasn't abandoned, and the anomaly was tolerated. It wasn't until Einstein's general theory of relativity was published in 1915 that the discrepancy between observation and theory was resolved—this time, by substituting Einstein's curved space-time for Newton's Euclidean space. The Newtonian hard core was in effect subsumed as a first approximation to the general relativity model.

To show how this process works in other disciplines, take an example from biblical studies. We can legitimately think of a "conservative evangelical New Testament research program" ranging over the cultural, religious and philosophical backgrounds of the New Testament texts, textual criticism, linguistics, exegesis and so on, with commitments to

---

[19]For discussion and application of a Lakatosian model to theology, see Nancey Murphy, *Theology in the Age of Scientific Reasoning* (Ithaca, N.Y.: Cornell University Press, 1993).

the inspiration and inerrancy of the Bible as part of the hard core. So when Luke says in his Gospel that the census ordered by Caesar Augustus was "the first census that took place while Quirinius was governor of Syria" (Lk 2:1-2), that statement is taken as historically true. Luke also states (as does Matthew) that Jesus was born while Herod the Great, who died in the spring of 4 B.C., was king. But historical investigation shows that Quirinius was appointed governor in A.D. 6 and ordered a census in A.D. 6 or 7—some ten or eleven years too late to fit Luke's account. Now, conservative scholars could abandon belief in inerrancy, but that is a hard core theoretical commitment of conservative evangelicals. Various attempts (perhaps we could call them ad hoc hypotheses) to resolve the problem have been proposed, ranging from positing an earlier governorship for Quirinius, to translating the Greek of Luke to allow for a different interpretation. At this point, it seems that many conservative scholars are willing to live with the "anomaly," as astronomers did with the anomalous precession of Mercury's perihelion, and await resolution in the future.

Additional examples could easily be drawn from the history of economics, psychology, archaeology, history and other disciplines. The Lakatosian model does seem to capture the structure of any theoretical enterprise, with differences coming at the point of what sort of tests can be devised and carried out, what methods are used, and what resources (equipment, ancient texts, statistical records, etc.) are employed. The results in these other disciplines are publicly accessible and subject to peer review, as is the case with science.

So what does "the scientific method" come to? In my view, it is simply an instance of a more general theoretical methodology. Science focuses particularly on phenomena in the natural world, and employs primarily empirical methods of investigation utilizing various kinds of specialized equipment depending on the phenomena being studied. What the "box" depicts is not a unique method; in fact, *there is no unique, rigorous "scientific method"* that sets science off from other theoretical disciplines. So attempts to solve the demarcation problem by pointing to some special "scientific method" are misguided.

That leaves us to ask about the epistemic status of science. If there is no single "scientific method" that yields "assured results," then how is it that the wide population in general, and most scientists in particular, take the conclusions of science to be the clearest cases of knowledge, with other disciplines only hoping to approach the degree of certainty attached to science? I think that there are two reasons for this. First, the empiricism of science seems to be a rigorous "acid text" that only true propositions could survive; empirical results surely trump beliefs based only on "armchair philosophizing," or the "soft sciences," or "blind faith." Second is a widespread conviction that no publicly accessible reasons or evidence justify belief in nonempirical entities (such as moral facts, and the existence of supernatural beings—God and angels, for example), and therefore such beliefs must be held privately (if at all). Both reasons are grave mistakes, I think. (There is a third reason as well, related to the "terror" of religious explanations or the "cosmic authority problem" discussed in chapter three, but that reason doesn't figure into the thinking of the vast majority of Americans who, as polls repeatedly show, are at least minimal theists.)

But empiricism cannot be a complete epistemology. Here's why. In its practice of epistemic justification, in determining "starting points" for theory-building and in determining just what counts as evidence, empiricism must rely on nonempirical—that is, rational—evidence, including, importantly, a priori rational intuitions.[20] So if the claim is that only empirical evidence can be accepted as justificatory, then the claim is clearly self-defeating. But if the claim is weaker, that once the basic epistemology is in place, then only empirically justified claims are allowed, then there is no reason to think that the claim is a normative epistemological claim. As a result, the best epistemology will be a moderate rationalism according to which rational intuition, philosophical (and theological) reasoning and empirical observation all are considered prima facie justificatory evidence.

And this conclusion is just what we would expect within a Christian worldview. As I discussed in chapter three and again in chapter six, faith is not opposed to reason, but the kinds of reasons (or evidence)

---

[20]George Bealer and P. F. Strawson, "The Incoherence of Empiricism," *The Aristotelian Society, Supplementary Volume* 66 (1992): 99-138.

that justify different kinds of claims will differ. When Luke began to compose his Gospel, a largely historical (although not necessarily non-theological) account of the life of Jesus, he employed historical research (Lk 1:1-4). But clearly Luke evaluated his sources and employed some principle of selection in composing his narrative, using intuitions about justification and theological conclusions in doing so. Further, if we have good reasons to believe that a God of a particular kind exists, we may also be justified in believing that God has revealed certain truths about himself and his creation to humankind. Within a Christian worldview, then, divine revelation should enjoy the highest epistemic status possible.

The upshot is that conclusions secured on the basis of empirical investigation are not necessarily more dependable or more certain than conclusions justified on other bases. So the claim that the conclusions of science enjoy a privileged epistemic status cannot be sustained. And indeed, this is what we would expect, given the history of science, in which we see hypotheses coming and going, theories replacing others, and claims once well-justified and widely accepted being rejected or modified as new theoretical models or observational procedures come on line.

So since the theoretical methodology of science is not unique to science, and since scientific empiricism does not yield greater certainty than all other epistemological methods, there is no reason to hold the deliverances of science in such an exalted position. Science is a powerful tool to give us descriptions and understanding of the natural world, but it is only one tool to understand all of reality.

Realism versus antirealism. In the context of philosophy of science, 'realism' generally refers to the thesis that scientific theories are true (or verisimilitudinous) and not merely pragmatically useful. This realism rests on two underlying commitments: (1) Ontological realism—scientific theories are about an objectively existing world that is independent of human thought, linguistic practices, conceptual schemes or social conventions. (2) Epistemic realism—it is possible to be justified in believing that one theory is better (more verisimilitudinous) than its rivals. So when a geologist speaks of continental drift, there really are such things as tectonic plates in the earth's lithosphere. When a theoretical physicist speaks of quarks, there really are entities, described by such properties as charge, color, spin and mass, that are the constituents of hadrons. Antirealism of course would be the denial of one or both of the theses of realism.

Without doubt, the vast majority of people are realists, the pretheoretical, commonsense position. And the vast majority of scientists are at least "critical realists." They would believe in tectonic plates and quarks and so on. Where they might demure would be on such highly theoretical entities as strings; many might say, well, there's something like that, perhaps, but we're not sure just what it's like because we don't yet have the technology to observe anything that small.

So what could be the attraction of antirealism? First, questions abound about the commitment to ontological realism. Various philosophers have worried that empirical judgments cannot justify belief in the external world and have developed varieties of idealism (Berkeley, Kant, J. M. E. McTaggart or F. C. Bradley) or phenomenalism (Ernst Mach, Rudolf Carnap). Still others have questioned the validity of the correspondence theory of truth in the context of scientific theorizing and have proposed theories of pragmatism (C. S. Peirce, Nicholas Rescher, Larry Laudan), operationalism (P. W. Bridgeman) or constructivism (Robert Boyle, Bas van Fraassen) rather than realism.

Second, for a number of philosophers and historians of science, study of the history of science reveals that many (if not most) theories that were accepted in the past have been proved wrong—or worse, abjectly wrong. So what reasons do we have to believe that our current theories will not also be shown to be wrong? Today's "best" theories might well wind up on the same ash heap as indivisible atoms, geocentric cosmology, fixed continents and phlogiston chemistry.

Still, all of the antirealists mentioned above would accept some form of epistemic realism; they would agree that one can judge one theory better than its rivals (where 'better' is cashed out differently depending on one's philosophical position of idealism, pragmatism, etc.). So we can call these positions, collectively, rational antirealism, because on this view, although scientific theories are not about the external world (or, at least, cannot be known to be), we still have rational grounds for accepting (if not believing) one theory over its rivals.

But there are others who reject both ontological and epistemic realism; call them nonrational antirealists. Among these diverse philosophers are postmodern theorists like Richard Rorty (although he preferred to call himself a pragmatist), who deny that the language we use to communicate scientific theories is more than social convention, and has no purchase in "objective" reality. Willard Van Orman Quine was an epistemic coherentist who held that no beliefs—including the laws of logic—were unrevisable, depending on what happened to one's web of beliefs. Paul Feyerabend argued for "pluralism" or a "dose of theoretical anarchism" in science, and unapologetically declared, "Science is just another ideology, along with magic and astrology, against which society must be defended."[21] But more than anyone else, it was Thomas Kuhn and his theory of paradigm shifts that shaped the nonrational antirealism that survives today.[22] Kuhn's contribution was the notion that different paradigms are incommensurable. A Kuhnian paradigm is a shared way of talking about problems, methods of attacking problems and agreement on broad theoretical structures, which are relatively unanimous among professionals at a given time. But when anomalies accumulate, the old paradigm begins to look shaky, and young rebels are likely to challenge it. However—and here's the incommensurability—there is no rational way to compare rival paradigms to decide which is true (or more verisimilitudinous). As a result, paradigm shifts occur in revolutionary fashion, not as a result of careful rational argument. To shift paradigms, one must undergo something akin to a religious conversion.

How does a Christian worldview impact one's thinking about these issues? Again, indirectly. To begin with, it seems to me that the most straightforward reading of Scripture leads us to believe that there is an objectively existing, mind-independent world out there that existed

---

[21]Paul Feyerabend, "How to Defend Society Against Science," 1975; reprinted in *Introductory Readings in the Philosophy of Science*, ed. E. D. Klemke et al., 3rd ed. (Amherst, N.Y.: Prometheus, 1998), pp. 54-65.

[22]See works cited in n. 9.

before humans were created. While there have been dissenters (for example, Bishop Berkeley's idealism, Jonathan Edwards's *creatio continua*), the majority of Christian thinkers have been ontological realists in this broad sense. Further, given the venerable tradition within Christianity that humankind has been given a "cultural mandate" as stewards of the earth, rational (critical) realism in science would seem to follow. For God could not hold humans accountable for their stewardship if there were no real world, or if it were not open to rational investigation, scientific theorizing and manipulation through engineering and technology.

Second, it seems to many that the success of science is only explainable on the assumption of realism. Hilary Putnam famously offered the "miracle argument" for realism by observing, "The positive argument for realism is that it is the only philosophy that doesn't make the success of science a miracle."[23] By my lights, there is great significance in the claim that scientific progress is grounded in critical realism, coupled with the fact that critical realism fits comfortably in a Christian worldview. It's no accident of history, I submit, that modern science arose in a culture permeated with that worldview. Edward Grant observes, "It is indisputable that modern science emerged in the seventeenth century in Western Europe and nowhere else."[24] Rodney Stark "connects the dots" to explain why this is so: "The crucial question is: Why? My answer to this is as brief as it is unoriginal: Christianity depicted God as a rational, responsive, dependable, and omnipotent being and the universe as his personal creation, thus having a rational, lawful stable structure, awaiting human comprehension."[25] The dependence of modern science upon a Christian worldview was noted by no less than Alfred North Whitehead:

> When we compare this tone of thought in Europe with the attitude of other civilisations when left to themselves, there seems but one source

---

[23]Hilary Putnam, *Mathematics, Matter and Method*, vol. 1 of *Philosophical Papers*, 2nd ed. (New York: Cambridge University Press, 1979), p. 73.
[24]Edward Grant, *The Foundations of Science in the Middle Ages* (New York: Cambridge University Press, 1996), p. 168.
[25]Rodney Stark, *For the Glory of God* (Princeton, N.J.: Princeton University Press, 2003), p. 147.

of its origin. It must come from the medieval insistence on the rationality of God, conceived as with the personal energy of Jehovah and with the rationality of a Greek philosopher. . . . What I mean is the impress on the European mind arising from the unquestioned faith of centuries. By this I mean the instinctive tone of thought and not a mere creed of words.[26]

So critical realism seems to fit best with a Christian worldview, and to explain best the rise and progress of modern science.

But that is not the end of the matter. The arguments of certain antirealists such as van Fraassen cannot be lightly dismissed, and a case can be made that now-discarded concepts such as phlogiston or the luminiferous aether make sense if taken in an antirealist operationalist sense. And there are theoretical terms in several contemporary theories that are so poorly understood, stemming in many cases from the pure mathematical formalisms used to define the theory, that it's very unclear whether they should be taken as genuinely referring terms. I'm thinking here of such terms as the quantum wave packet, the collapse of the wave function, strings and superstrings, branes, multiverses, dark matter and dark energy. I see nothing amiss with withholding commitment to a realist interpretation of such terms while at the same time accepting general scientific realism.

However, if such an eclectic approach is to be viable, some principles ought to be on offer to help decide when to adopt an antirealist approach. I believe several reasonable principles can be articulated.[27] I'll illustrate my point by highlighting just two such principles. One, if the phenomena described by the theory lie outside the proper domain of natural science, or if the scientific theory reduces nonnatural to natural phenomena, then the theoretical terms in the theory may best be construed in an antirealist manner. So, for example, evolutionary psychology seems to me to be offering a natural scientific account of morality, which I would argue lies outside the proper domain of natu-

---

[26]Alfred North Whitehead, *Science and the Modern World: Lowell Lectures, 1925* (Cambridge: Cambridge University Press, 1930), pp. 12.

[27]For one well-considered approach, see Moreland, *Christianity and the Nature of Science*, pp. 202-11.

ral science (see chapter 7). Similarly, I believe a solid case can be made for substance dualism as a theory of mind (see chapter 8); hence, theories that reduce all mental phenomena to brain functions and states need not be taken as realist accounts of mind, but rather as operationalist. For example, when a subject reports seeing a green patch, or experiencing a pain, a neuroscientist may conclude that there should be a correlated brain state, but cannot correctly identify the brain state with the mental state.

Two, when a realist interpretation leads to conflict with justified conclusions in another domain, but an antirealist interpretation does not, the antirealist interpretation should be preferred. As an example, the implications of many multiverse or parallel universe theories is that there is an identical copy of me (and of you and your cat—and of Jesus?) at a distance of $10^{10^{29}}$ meters away.[28] But such theories, although mathematically consistent, are clearly at odds with concepts of personal identity, moral responsibility and salvation that are deeply embedded in a Christian worldview and are philosophically defensible. So an antirealist interpretation of the mathematics would be preferable to a realist one in this case.

So while a general commitment to scientific realism is consistent with a Christian worldview, it does not follow that all theoretical terms in all theories must be taken realistically.

Ethical constraints on science? For some, surely, there can be no question that there must be ethical constraints on science, while for others, just as surely, the thought that science is subject to anything but internal constraints is anathema. How can diametrically opposed viewpoints seem so obvious?

I think that worldviews go a long way to explaining this disparity. In a naturalist worldview, it's difficult to ground morality in any objective way (see the discussion in chapter 7; I won't consider a postmodern worldview in this context, since one would be hard-pressed to find genuine philosophical postmodernism among practicing scientists). Nev-

---

[28]Max Tegmark, "Parallel Universes," in *Science and Ultimate Reality: From Quantum to Cosmos,* ed. John D. Barrow, Paul C. W. Davies and Charles L. Harper Jr. (New York: Cambridge University Press, 2003), pp. 459-91.

ertheless, most people, including naturalists, believe that their own internal "moral compass" is both accurate and adequate for making tough moral decisions. Just as children at times rebel against parents' imposition of behavioral codes, and parishioners at times resent the church's or the pastor's pronouncement of moral values, so too scientists at times bristle at the suggestion that they need moral guidance from outside—be it from moral philosophers or religious communities.

In a Christian worldview, though, it is (or should be) easier to accept moral guidance from outside, as Christians recognize that the results of the Fall affect one's "moral compass" as well as other aspects of our nature (see Rom 2:2-15). So, at least in principle, a Christian business-man should accept input from theologians and Christian ethicists as to moral principles that apply to his business, and a Christian biologist should find it easier than her atheist colleagues to accept input as to moral principles that would constrain her research.

As the debate over using embryonic stem cells and human cloning for research purposes shows, programmatic constraints are in general harder to find consensus on than procedural constraints. Consider the widespread outrage over the fraudulent claims of the Korean biotech-nologist Hwang Woo-suk. When it was shown that he had falsified data, claiming in two articles published in the prestigious journal *Science* to have successfully produced human stem cells by cloning (somatic cell nuclear transfer),[29] there was near-unanimous condemnation from both within and outside the scientific community. But the condemna-tion was over the falsification of data, not over the idea that Hwang would attempt human cloning. The ethical offense was procedural, not programmatic; apparently, the consensus was that data falsification was wrong, cloning wasn't.

Here's the problem that this highlights. The position of those who

---

[29]Hwang W. S. et al., "Evidence of a Pluripotent Human Embryonic Stem Cell Line Derived from a Cloned Blastocyst," *Science* 303 (2004): 1669-74, and Hwang W. S. et al., "Patient-Specific Embryonic Stem Cells Derived from Human SCNT Blastocysts," *Science* 308 (2005): 1777-83. *Science* later unconditionally withdrew Hwang's papers: Donald Kennedy, "Editorial retraction," *Science* 311 (2006): 335. Hwang has since been convicted of falsifying papers and embezzlement and fired from his university position: "Disgraced Cloning Expert Convicted in South Korea," *New York Times*, October 26, 2009.

would condemn procedural ethical lapses but reject any programmatic constraints is faced with two real dilemmas. First, programmatic restrictions are generally rejected on utilitarian grounds: the research program in question has the potential to benefit many, while the harm is minor in comparison. But consistency demands that such utilitarian analysis should then be applied to procedural restrictions as well. In an age when most scientific research involves incredibly expensive equipment and procedures, if a scientist believes that his research program promises real benefit to many, but the only way to continue to receive the large grants necessary to continue the research was to publish a couple of papers with fabricated data, how can that be faulted on utilitarian grounds? Here's the real difficulty: determining the questions to which one should give a utilitarian answer. In the film *Extreme Measures*, the neurosurgeon Dr. Lawrence Myrick (the character played by Gene Hackman) asks, "If you could cure cancer by killing one person, wouldn't you? Wouldn't that be brave? One person and cancer's gone tomorrow?" What about killing (destroying) one embryo? Fabricating one paper?

The second dilemma involves the source or grounds of the moral judgment that data falsification is wrong, but no such judgment can be made about a research program. Presumably, the answer given by a scientist would be that the first transgresses the "rules" of science. But who sets those rules? Maybe the response would be that false data consumes time, effort and resources on dead-ends. But so does many a false lead, an anomalous data set, a novel but ultimately incorrect theory. If science is self-correcting in the long run, if science itself can catch the dishonest (as happened in the case of Dr. Hwang), what's the big deal? Clearly science itself, as a descriptive and explanatory discipline, lacks the resources to make normative judgments. So if the scientific community is going to regard data falsification as morally blameworthy, that judgment must come from outside science. But if so, then why can't outside judgments be brought to bear on research programs and not merely research procedures?

Ah, the reply comes, if such restrictions *are* to be proposed, they must reflect a widely held consensus reached in the public square, where religious considerations won't play a role. But why not? We can't get into this issue here, but surely, I claim, there is a place for religious thought in public debate.[30]

So it seems that the view one holds on the legitimacy of ethical constraints on science will depend profoundly on one's worldview. If a Christian worldview has major implications in this area, the need for more Christians to be thoughtfully informed on matters of both science and ethics is clear, and the importance of these matters for philosophy of science that is truly Christian is greater than is often thought.

The relation of science and theology. The last two decades have seen a flood of ink spilled and a forest of trees sacrificed to publish books dealing with science and religion, and the pace shows no sign of abating. My view is that a comparison of *science* and *religion* uses the wrong categories. Rather, it is the *beliefs or theories* of science and the *beliefs or doctrines* of theology that should be compared. Much of the study of science and of religion involves the sociology of the two institutions, their respective practices, social conventions, rituals, and so forth, but the real controversy focuses on the deliverances of the two considered as bodies of theory.

It's no secret that claims of science sometimes (some would say often) conflict with claims of theology. Adjudicating competing claims depends on accurately understanding the relationship between science and theology. A number of models are on offer that attempt to elucidate the relationship; they reduce to four broad ways of relating science and theology (or religion), with various authors proposing nuanced distinctions within the four. I'll begin the discussion using Ian Barbour's labels for the four models: Conflict, Independence, Dialogue and Integration.[31]

Conflict is probably the view of the science-theology relationship most widely held. But it's also probably the most misleading. The Conflict model sees science and theology as always in competition; either

---

[30]See Francis Beckwith, *Politics for Christians: Statecraft as Soulcraft* (Downers Grove, Ill.: InterVarsity Press, 2010).
[31]Ian G. Barbour, *Religion and Science: Historical and Contemporary Issues* (San Francisco: HarperSanFrancisco, 1997), pp. 77-105.

the freedom of scientific research and its offspring of technological innovation, making life better for all, is always under threat of suppression or outright persecution by religious zealots, or else the divine truth of Scripture is under constant assault from atheistic, anti-religious scientists. (I'm overstating the polarized positions, but not by much.) The trial of Galileo in 1633, where the Roman Catholic Church condemned Galileo and forced him to recant his heliocentric theory of the solar system, has become a potent and iconic symbol of the ignorant church persecuting an enlightened scientist.

Certainly there have been conflicts between church and laboratory, and there will certainly continue to be. But as a model of the relationship, Conflict is seriously flawed, both historically and theologically. As is generally recognized by those familiar with the history of science, conflict has not been the consistent pattern of relating. Even the Galileo affair, as popularly understood, is incorrect, as even Stephen Jay Gould, who certainly has no evangelical axe to grind, has argued.[32] In fact, Gould (and others) traces Conflict to two nineteenth-century American writers, John William Draper and Andrew Dickson White. In 1874, Draper (a physician and amateur historian) published *History of the Conflict Between Religion and Science*, and in 1896, White (the first president of Cornell University) published the two-volume *A History of the Warfare of Science with Theology in Christendom*. These two works had powerful influence on the thinking of many academics at the turn of the twentieth century, and Conflict became the "orthodox" view in most universities.[33] But the Conflict thesis is simply bad history.

Conflict is flawed theologically as well. Many theologians believe that a proper understanding of the early chapters of Genesis, both before and after the fall of Adam and Eve, supports what is often called the "cultural mandate": God's assignment to humankind was "to create cultures and build civilizations."[34] Fulfilling this mandate would be

---

[32]Stephen Jay Gould, *Rocks of Ages* (New York: Ballantine, 1999), pp. 71-75. On this and other "myths" of the Conflict model, see *Galileo Goes to Jail and Other Myths About Science and Religion*, ed. Ronald L. Numbers (Cambridge, Mass.: Harvard University Press, 2009).

[33]See Gould's brief description in *Rocks of Ages*, pp. 99-103.

[34]Nancy Pearcy, *Total Truth* (Wheaton, Ill.: Crossway, 2004), p. 47; see also the Fourth Stone Lecture (on Calvinism and Science), delivered by the Dutch theologian and politician Abra-

impossible without proper use of science, so there can be no conflict between science per se and theology. To the degree that we have good reason to think that science gives us an increasingly accurate explanation of the world, it cannot conflict with theology, no matter the worldview of the scientist who articulates it.

Barbour calls his next model *Independence,* but it is often called Complementarity as well (with a nod toward Neils Bohr's principle of complementarity in quantum mechanics). The idea is that while we need both science and theology to give us a complete picture of reality, the two describe such different domains of reality that propositions in one domain are incommensurable with (independent of) propositions in the other. Perhaps the best-known version of Independence is Gould's NOMA principle, which claims that science and religion are non-overlapping magesteria (domains of teaching authority).[35]

Essentially this is the view espoused by the medieval Islamic polymath Averroës. Writing commentaries on most of Aristotle's surviving works, Averroës became a staunch defender of Aristotelian philosophy, but found that certain claims of Aristotelian natural philosophy were not consistent with teachings of the Qur'an. Roughly, his solution was to claim that Aristotle taught truths of reason, while the Qur'an taught truths of faith, and the two domains of truth were in logic-tight compartments. This view of truth was attacked by St. Thomas Aquinas, who defended the unity of truth: he didn't, but could have used the slogan, "All truth is God's truth," as the slogan nicely captures Aquinas's understanding of truth.[36] I believe Aquinas is correct here.

We can think of it this way. The Independence claim may be understood to say that no proposition contradicting any proposition in the domain of science can be derived from any proposition in the domain of theology, and vice versa. Now, if it could be shown that the two do-

---

ham Kuyper, in 1898, available at <www.kuyper.org/main/publish/books_essays/article_17.shtml>.

[35]Gould, *Rocks of Ages.* Former Calvin College physics professor Howard Van Till champions a similar view in a number of places; see Howard Van Till, "Partnership: Science and Christianity as Partners in Theorizing," in *Science and Christianity: Four Views,* ed. Richard F. Carlson (Downers Grove, Ill.: InterVarsity Press, 2000), pp. 195-234.

[36]See, for example, the first eight chapters of Book I of *Summa contra gentiles.*

mains were as disparate as, say, history and fiction, then the claim would be plausible. For example, the proposition *Hamlet was prince of Denmark* cannot be contradicted by the proposition that *Hamlet fails to appear in the genealogy of Queen Margrethe II of Denmark*. The domain of Shakespearean fiction is incommensurable with the domain of Danish history. But the same sort of disparity between science and theology needs to be argued for, not merely asserted; it surely seems that both theology and science (at least when taken realistically) are making claims about the one reality that exists. And surely, too, certain terms have the same meanings (or referents) in theology and in science. As an example: a claim of science (at least, of evolutionary biology) is that all life on earth had a common ancestor, while a claim of theology (at least, on a certain reading of Gen 1) is that God intervened in natural history to make "kinds" in a unique way. These two claims are contradictory, so one of them must be an incorrect interpretation of the data. Thus, while many, if not most, propositions in science or theology do not entail propositions in the other domain, some do, and so Independence is not a viable model.

(I should point out here that while Conflict and Independence are often described or defended by pitting scientific realism against a naive biblical literalism, more nuanced views are preferable. A critical or eclectic realism in science and a biblical hermeneutic that recognizes diverse literary genres and seeks to discern the authorial intent of the passage are much more robust positions. And on these positions, Conflict and Independence have even less to commend them.)

Dialogue is Barbour's third model (or, rather, a family of models) according to which science and theology can learn from each other. Areas of interaction range from "limit questions"—where does science end and theology begin?—to methodological parallels to comparison of models.

Taking these in order, it seems to me that "limit questions" depend on an answer to the demarcation problem, which is not forthcoming, and to agreement on whether or not terms in the two domains are co-referring terms. Methodological parallels are often instructive (see footnote 20 above), but really only skirt the issue of apparently competing claims between the two domains. And comparison and borrowing of models often leads to incoherence, as when a theologian applies Bohr's complementarity model to the incarnation of Christ. The incoherence here is that Bohr would never have claimed that light, for example, is fully and literally particle and wave at the same time, but orthodox Chalcedonian Christology *does* claim that Jesus was fully and literally God and man at the same time.

Having been involved in a number of conferences where the Dialogue model is dominant,[37] I can say that I've learned interesting things about how different scientists view their respective fields, and how different religions look at science. But I have not seen much progress at all come out of such dialogue toward resolving apparent conflicts between science and theology.

Barbour's final model is *Integration.* Barbour sees Integration as encompassing natural theology (the attempt to infer the existence of God from natural sources and human reason alone), a theology of nature (in which science informs the theology of creation and of human nature), and finally a systematic synthesis in which both science and religion contribute toward an inclusive metaphysics (Barbour's example is process philosophy/theology).

I'm reluctant to use the term "Integration," since I believe that science and theology should retain their disciplinary integrity. Any attempt to fully integrate or systematically synthesize the two into a single discipline risks deforming one or the other or both. Rather, I prefer to use the term *Convergence.* By this I mean that science and theology *converge* on a truthful description of the world. Science and theology will sometimes tell us different kinds of things, and sometimes the same kinds of things, about the same thing (the real world). When done ideally, they will not conflict but will converge on a unified description of reality. (Of course, a complete unified description of reality will also include history, economics, psychology, sociology and so on. The Convergence model could easily be expanded to include other dis-

---

[37]It seems to me that this is the dominant model at various seminars and conferences organized by the Templeton Foundation, whose financial resources have had a very positive impact on science/religion dialogue in the past several decades.

ciplines.) However, at any point in history, conflict is possible due to the incomplete or inaccurate theories/doctrines and descriptions in one or the other (or both) disciplines. When conflict occurs, theology may correct science, or science may correct theology, or judgment may be withheld, with decisions made on a case-by-case basis.

I maintain that Convergence fits best with a Christian worldview. We live in an objectively existing world, so science investigates and makes claims about a portion of reality. But the world also includes nonnatural and supernatural entities (properties, propositions, moral facts, angels and demons, God), so both philosophy and theology likewise investigate and make claims about a portion of reality. And sometimes those claims overlap because the portions of reality under investigation overlap.

Both science and theology (and also philosophy, although I'll not include it in the discussion that follows) are theoretical disciplines that draw inferences, construct theories and make claims based on certain kinds of data. Roughly, the data of science are natural facts while the data of theology are revealed facts. In both cases, the data are given; if incompletely, or incorrectly, or inaccurately observed, our representations of the data will be in error. Then the theorizing and interpretation begins, and even if the data are completely and accurately represented, any scientist or theologian, being human, may be in error in the interpretations given. Convergence recognizes the possibility of error on both sides, so conflict is possible, but conflict then is a matter of interpretation, not some fundamental feature of the two disciplines.

Still, we are not now at the point of an ideal science or theology; human limitations mean conflicts still arise between ideas of science and theology. So if the Convergence model advises handling apparent conflicts on a case by case basis, how do we go about adjudicating any particular conflict?

Let S be a statement of science, and T be a statement of theology. (S and T are both interpretations, and as such are *in principle* revisable.) I suggest we ask the following sorts of questions:

1. Are S and T actually contradictory, or are they contrary or complementary?

2. Does S violate any theological control beliefs? Does T violate any scientific control beliefs? (A control belief, in this sense, is a belief that functions axiomatically in the discipline. For example, the belief that the laws of nature are uniform throughout most of cosmic history and across the observable universe is axiomatic for doing almost all science.)

3. How deeply ingressed in science and theology are S and T respectively? (The degree of ingression may be measured by asking how dramatically would the discipline be changed if the belief were discarded. For example, the belief that Jesus was God incarnate is very deeply ingressed in Christianity; without this belief, arguably the result would not be Christian in any historically meaningful sense.)

4. What is the relative degree of independent support for S and T? (If only one set of observations, or exegesis of only one or two passages of Scripture, supports a particular interpretation, then it has a lower degree of independent support than an interpretation supported by a number of different sorts of observations or texts.)

5. Is either S or T subject to significant internal problems? (An internal problem is one arising from recalcitrant data within the discipline. At present, the inadequacy of models of an inflationary big bang to account for dark energy weakens—but does not completely defeat—belief that we have the correct or complete physical theory of cosmogenesis.)

6. Is an antirealist interpretation of S or T preferable to a realist interpretation? Is an antirealist interpretation possible? (For example, the inability of theorists to integrate quantum mechanics and general relativity into a theory of quantum gravity raises questions as to whether either should be taken as a literal or realist—or even a complete—theory.)

7. Is it possible to suspend judgment, or is a decision forced? (For example, it may not be at all necessary or important to decide whether the "Nephilim" of Genesis 6:4 were surviving Neanderthals or simply another tribe of *Homo sapiens*.)

As I see it, a Christian worldview authorizes a division of labor; some are called to be theologians, others to be scientists (and still others to be philosophers or plumbers). But in God's plan, all are involved in furthering our understanding of our world and in bettering, where possible, the conditions for God's creatures. While theology has more to say about our highest aspirations and our ultimate destiny, we cannot adopt a gnostic denial of the importance of our physical embodiment here and now, and science is crucial in that regard. There is, in the end, no disciplinary hegemony—and certainly not a hegemony of empiricism—within a Christian worldview.

WHAT ABOUT INTELLIGENT DESIGN?

Finally, this chapter would not be complete without a brief consideration of intelligent design (ID). But these remarks will necessarily be very brief and programmatic—not because I don't have views on the matter, but because space considerations prevent a reasonably thorough discussion.

Anyone with even cursory exposure to the media in the past several years has heard ID defended and demonized, and I can't hope here to do much to end the debate! After characterizing ID, I'll argue that ID, just as surely as neo-Darwinism, has philosophical, theological and scientific aspects as part of the package, and each aspect must be evaluated on its own terms.[38]

Philosophical aspects. Philosophically, ID can be seen as exploring the epistemological question of whether design can be detected, and so intelligence inferred, from a given pattern of data. This question can be applied to such diverse fields as detecting data falsification or intellectual property theft, debunking claims of parapsychology, identifying archaeological artifacts, searching for extraterrestrial intelligence in the SETI project, or detecting putative design in nature. The philosophical work here involves interpretation of different approaches to probability theory (viz., Bayesian versus Fisherian interpretations of the probability calculus), and defending the claim that intelligent design can be in-

---

[38]Loren Haarsma, "Is Intelligent Design 'Scientific'?" *Perspectives on Science and the Christian Faith* 59 (2007): 55-62.

ferred from a pattern exhibiting small probability with specification.[39]

Theological aspects. Theologically, ID can be seen as the attempt to construct another version of the design or teleological argument, inferring the existence of an Intelligent Designer from the evidence of apparent design in the universe. Although initially proponents of ID were largely evangelical Christians (with followers of other religions and an atheist or two mixed in), they seemed to be very coy about the identification of the Designer. Some (for example, the National Center for Science Education) charged ID proponents with duplicity, since (wasn't it obvious?) they clearly intended their ID arguments to be understood as arguments for the existence of God, smuggled into school biology classes. I'll come to the scientific aspects of ID shortly, but let me first tackle the question of whether ID offers a design argument for the existence of God.

I think the ID theorists were properly noncommittal about the identity of the Designer. That's because no inductive argument, whether cosmological, teleological, moral or any other, can yield the conclusion that the God of the Bible exists. Additional premises are needed to bridge from the conclusion of natural theology to the God of Christian theology. The cosmological argument concludes to a very powerful agent as Creator; the teleological argument points to an intelligent agent as designer (and here's where an argument from ID seems to fit very well); the moral argument to a supreme lawgiver; and so on—but while the Christian God is all of these things, none of these things alone is the Christian God. Now, I believe that a cumulative case argument can be constructed from natural ("general revelation") evidence that concludes that the most probable explanation of a number of features of the universe is that a God of a certain kind exists and created the universe with those features. But to move from that conclusion to identifying that being with the God and Father of our Lord Jesus Christ takes additional moves and evidence, such as the historical argument

---

[39]See the work of William A. Dembski, notably, *The Design Inference: Eliminating Chance Through Small Probabilities* (New York: Cambridge University Press, 1998), and *No Free Lunch: Why Specified Complexity Cannot Be Purchased Without Intelligence* (Lanham, Md.: Rowman & Littlefield, 2007), and the vast literature interacting with Dembski's thesis.

for the resurrection of Jesus. So while an ID theorist may take ID as grounding one theistic argument in natural theology, it's simply wrong to think that a single natural theological argument is proof of the existence of the Christian God.[40] And it is perhaps worth noting—although I disagree—that there are theologians and Christian philosophers who deny, much like Karl Barth did, that *any* natural theological argument has much religious worth at all.

Scientific aspects. No doubt the scientific aspects of ID have attracted the greatest attention—and heat. Denounced as nothing more than "creationism in a cheap tuxedo" and worse, and declared in court not to be science (by Judge Jones; see above), ID has also been hailed as the last nail in the coffin of the theory of evolution. Of course, it is none of these things, even in its scientific aspect. The question of whether ID is science usually focuses on the philosophical or theological aspects (again, as Judge Jones did) and not in the actual scientific claims made; and further, as I argued above, absent any formal solution to the demarcation problem, it's rather hasty simply to declare ID not to be science.[41]

The scientific arguments largely focus on whether certain features in the natural world cannot be the product of a random evolutionary process. Whether irreducibly complex organelles or other biological features,[42] or the probabilistic limits of random mutations and natural selection,[43] or the information-rich structure of DNA,[44] ID claims that there are significant gaps in nature that random Darwinian evolution cannot account for. It seems that this is a clear scientific claim, and the evidence adduced by ID theorists has been accepted by many in the scientific community as constituting a scientific

---

[40]For one example, see William A. Dembski, *Intelligent Design: The Bridge Between Science and Theology* (Downers Grove, Ill.: InterVarsity Press, 1999).

[41]Even some atheists defend ID as making an interesting claim that is in some aspects scientific: Nagel, "Public Education and Intelligent Design"; Bradley Monton, *Seeking God in Science: An Atheist Defends Intelligent Design* (Buffalo, N.Y.: Broadview Press, 2009).

[42]Michael Behe, *Darwin's Black Box: The Biochemical Challenge to Evolution* (New York: Free Press, 1996).

[43]Michael Behe, *The Edge of Evolution: The Search for the Limits of Darwinism* (New York: Free Press, 2007).

[44]Stephen C. Meyer, *Signature in the Cell: DNA and the Evidence for Intelligent Design* (New York: HarperOne, 2009).

claim, one that many professional biologists have thought it necessary to refute *scientifically*.[45]

Is ID science? In the absence of any definitive solution to the demarcation problem, the answer, I think, is: in part, yes. There are clear philosophical issues involved, but so too are there philosophical issues involved in such scientific research programs as neo-Darwinian evolution (viz., what is a function, what is adaptation, what is a species, etc.) and theoretical cosmology (viz., is the concept of a temporally or spatially infinite multiverse coherent, does block four-dimensional spacetime entail Laplacian determinism, etc.). And the fact that scientific theories can be used to underwrite arguments against the existence of God without thereby becoming nonscientific,[46] so too the scientific aspects of ID can be used to underwrite theistic arguments without thereby becoming nonscientific. Whether progress will be made in generating hypotheses subject to experimental confirmation or disconfirmation from the theoretical core of intelligent design is an interesting question, but a positive answer cannot be ruled out by any a priori definition or even by the consent of any number of practicing scientists.

BRIEF EXCURSUS: THEISTIC EVOLUTION

There has been significant movement among Christians in recent years concerning the theory of evolution. The Catholic Church has been open to evolution at least since 1950,[47] and it seems that even among conservative Protestants, acceptance of some form of evolution has been growing. A recent poll by the Pew Research Center for People and the

---

[45]An informative collection of essays by both philosophers of science and practicing scientists on both sides of the ID debate is *Debating Design: From Darwin to DNA*, ed. William A. Dembski and Michael Ruse (New York: Cambridge University Press, 2004).

[46]For example, much of Richard Dawkins's work, e.g., *The Blind Watchmaker: Why the Evidence of Evolution Reveals a Universe Without Design* (New York: W. W. Norton, 1986); see also the skeptical or atheistic conclusions drawn from theoretical possibilities of a multiverse landscape of string theory, Leonard Susskind, *The Cosmic Landscape: String Theory and the Illusion of Intelligent Design* (New York: Little, Brown, 2006); or of an endlessly cyclic universe, Paul J. Steinhardt and Neil Turoc, *Endless Universe: Beyond the Big Bang* (New York: Doubleday, 2007).

[47]Pope Pius XII, *Humani Generis*, 1950; Pope John Paul II, in an address to the Pontifical Academy of Science, October 22, 1996; Pope Benedict XVI, in *Creation and Evolution: A Conference with Pope Benedict XVI in Castel Gandolfo*, trans. Michael J. Miller (San Francisco: Ignatius Press, 2008) (the conference took place in September 2006).

Press reported a significant divergence of opinion between "the public" and "scientists" on the subject of evolution.[48] While 97% of scientists agree that "humans and other living things have evolved over time," only 61% of the public agree. About a third—32%—of the public say that evolution was the result of natural processes (compared to 87% of scientists), 22% say it was directed by a supreme being (8% of scientists), and 31% believe humans and other living things have existed in their present form since the beginning of time (2% of scientists). Among white evangelical Protestants, only 9% agreed with evolution as a natural process; 20% agreed evolution was directed by a supreme being, and 57% rejected evolution altogether. (Black Protestants were not classified as evangelical or mainline, making their inclusion in the comparisons difficult.) The survey also noted a pronounced increase in the percentage of the public who accept evolution as the age drops: only 23% of those over 65 accepted evolution as a natural process, compared with 40% of those under 30. A similar increase of those who accepted evolution correlated with increasing levels of education.

Most interesting to me is the gap between scientists and "white evangelical Christians." Reading between the lines, I think it's safe to guess that "white evangelical Christians" believe that evolution is a theory contrary to Scripture. But younger and more highly educated respondents were much more willing to accept evolution, whether as a result of natural processes or guided by a supreme being. Again, reading between the lines, I would guess that this is due to two factors. First, in recent years increasing numbers of public schools have taught evolution, while alternatives (such as ID) have not been taught in public schools. Second, as the level of education rises, so too does the scientific sophistication with which evolution is presented.

Now, a thorough treatment of this topic would begin with disambiguating at least six uses of the term "evolution," offering as well thorough accounts of different versions of theistic evolution (TE), and describing different creationist positions. I'll simply offer four characterizations:

---

[48]"Public Praises Science; Scientists Fault Public, Media," July 9, 2009 <http://people-press.org/report/?pageid=1550>.

- 'Evolution' refers to the change in heritable traits (alleles) in a population (gene pool) from one generation to another.

- 'Neo-Darwinian evolution' refers to the process by which all biological diversity on earth arose by common descent with genetic modification together with some mechanism of favoring certain modifications over others (generally natural selection). In what follows, I'll use the term "evolution" in this sense—the "neo-Darwinian synthesis."

- 'Theistic evolution' refers to the process by which God providentially arranged the contingencies of the history of life on earth so that it would result in a species of creature with whom he could have a relationship.[49]

- 'Progressive creationism' refers to the view that although the universe is very old (the accepted age is 13.7 ± 0.2 billion years), as is the earth (some 4.56 billion years), God directly intervened at various points in the history of life; some evolutionary change may have occurred (in the general sense of 'evolution' above), but the theory of common ancestry for all living things is false.

As the evidence inferred from the fossil record accumulates, and as new avenues of investigation such as genetics, genomics and evolutionary-developmental biology ("evo-devo") have exploded in recent years, it seems to me that the case for evolution is strong. Yet there are still evidentiary and conceptual gaps in the theory, and in my view, were it not for the fact that for naturalists, evolution is the only game in town to explain biological diversity, it would not be defended as vociferously as it is, and alternative views would not be denounced as strongly as they are. Still, I think it is wrong for any Christian to deny the strength of the evidence and refuse to engage seriously with the complexities of modern evolutionary biology.

Here, though, I can't seriously engage contemporary naturalistic

---

[49]For thoughtfully developed presentations and defenses of TE, see Denis R. Alexander, *Creation or Evolution: Do We Have to Choose?* (Grand Rapids: Monarch, 2008); Karl W. Giberson, *Saving Darwin: How to Be a Christian and Believe in Evolution* (New York: HarperOne, 2008); Denis O. Lamoureux, *Evolutionary Creation: A Christian Approach to Evolution* (Eugene, Ore.: Wipf and Stock, 2008).

evolution, but theistic evolution does demand attention. Perhaps I should attempt to distinguish various classes of theistic evolutionary theories, varying depending on the time and the degree of divine involvement in the process of common descent. But I must resist. Instead, let me speak personally, using TE as an issue to illustrate at least one way to work through a case of apparent conflict between science and theology. Let me first acknowledge that I am no biologist, but having taught philosophy of science courses for some fifteen years, I do have more than passing acquaintance with much relevant technical, semitechnical and popular literature. Nevertheless, here I hope to be brief yet not simplistic, omitting technical discussion but not ignorant of it.

Theistic evolution, in its various forms, is an attempt to harmonize the scientific and the scriptural, retaining a role for God as creator and sustainer, providentially arranging for the process of evolution to produce what he desires (although not generally thought of as specifically *Homo sapiens,* but more generally, as sentient creatures with whom he could have a relationship). At a minimum, TE holds that God oversaw or guided (in some to-be-specified way) the contingencies of the evolutionary process to avoid extinctions, blind alleys and so forth.[50] Right away it's clear that TE differs from standard naturalistic approaches, not merely in its acceptance of the existence of God and the supernatural realm, but more particularly in seeing the evolutionary process as teleological, as opposed to the common understanding of naturalistic evolution as dysteleological.

I take it that there is indeed at least an apparent conflict between a theory of common descent (whether theistic or naturalistic) and traditional interpretations of Scripture. Genesis 1 portrays God as creating "kinds" of living things, which "bring forth according to their kinds." I won't hazard a guess as to the precise taxonomic order that corresponds to the "kinds"; I think it likely that it is somewhat higher than species or even genus, somewhat lower than domain or kingdom, but it does

[50]See Stephen Jay Gould, *Wonderful Life* (New York: W. W. Norton, 1989), or Richard Dawkins, *Climbing Mount Improbable* (New York: W. W. Norton, 1996), for discussions of the probabilities and contingencies involved, "non-random survival of random variants," in Dawkins's phrase.

seem that "according to their kinds" implies some sort of divine intervention and contradicts naturalistic common descent.

The account of the creation of humans presents stronger objections. Specifically, Genesis 2 depicts God as intervening in the world, specially creating Adam and Eve and making for them a place and purpose. Genesis 3 describes the rebellion of the pair, what has come to be known as "the Fall," the event by which sin entered into the human race. This event is rather deeply embedded in orthodox theology, and it is hard to see how common descent could incorporate a realist view of the Fall.

But I think it gets worse. In at least two places, the apostle Paul makes a significant theological point grounded in the analogy of Adam as the first man and Christ as the Second Adam (Rom 5:12-21; 1 Cor 15:20-22). It seems that the theological point is vitiated if Adam were not a literal individual. Defenders of TE have responded to such concerns of course, some even willing to grant that there was indeed a literal couple, Adam and Eve, "a pair of Neolithic farmers in the Near East, . . . to whom [God] chose to reveal himself in a special way, calling them into fellowship with himself—so that they might know him as a personal God," thus preserving the strength of Paul's analogy.[51]

In general, I agree that both defenders and opponents of TE try seriously to engage the biblical text and the theological commitments of canonical Christianity. And I firmly believe (contrary to some very conservative opponents of all forms of evolution) that one can be a "good" Christian and also an evolutionist.

The question, in my mind, is how a biblical worldview affects our evaluation of the merits of TE. Since the conflict between scientific and theological claims is real, I'll apply the criteria I gave above to illustrate how I would approach resolving the conflict. So let S be a statement of theistic evolution, say, a statement of common ancestry, and let T be a theological statement, that Adam and Eve were historical indi-

---

[51]Alexander, *Creation or Evolution*, p. 236. But even here Alexander backpedals. The words I omitted in the ellipsis are "or maybe a community of farmers." Alexander agrees that "The identification of Adam as a historical figure, just as Jesus is a historical figure (e.g., verses 14 and 17) is intrinsic to Romans 5." But is the "identification of Adam as a historical figure" upheld if "Adam" is a designation for a community?

viduals, the products of a special divine act of creation—that is, the denial of common ancestry.

1. Are S and T contradictory, contrary or complementary? As I have framed them, clearly they are contradictories. Of course, much of the literature defending TE attempts to show that either T is not a required interpretation of the biblical text, or that S and T are complementary, but for the sake of argument, as I have stated them, I'll take them as contradictory.

2. Do either S or T violate control beliefs in the other's domain? Well, T would only violate a control belief of science if methodological or metaphysical naturalism is presupposed. As I argued above, though, neither should be seen as a sine qua non of science. S, a statement of *theistic* evolution, does not prima facie violate any theological control beliefs.

3. No question, S is deeply ingressed in contemporary biological science. However, I don't think the degree of ingression is warranted. First, the gradualism assumed by almost all versions of the neo-Darwinian synthesis is not supported by the fossil record; while the punctuated equilibrium posited by Stephen Jay Gould and Niles Eldredge[52] has not been widely accepted, it does seem to me to better explain the fossil record, and it is congruent with a form of progressive creationism according to which God intervened at certain points in the long history of life to produce novel body plans—what Genesis 1 calls "kinds"—perhaps by creating new genetic information not derivable from mutational recombinations of the DNA of extant organisms. And given other evidential and conceptual difficulties with the neo-Darwinian synthesis, the degree of ingression of the notion of common descent may be unwarranted.

---

[52]Stephen Jay Gould, *The Structure of Evolution*, 6th ed. (Cambridge, Mass.: Harvard University Press, 2002). Chapter 9 of this massive work has been published as Stephen Jay Gould, *Punctuated Equilibrium* (Cambridge, Mass.: Belknap, 2007).

The central thesis of punctuated equilibrium is this:

"The history of most fossil species includes two features particularly inconsistent with gradualism:

"1. Stasis. Most species exhibit no directional change during their tenure on earth. They appear in the fossil record looking pretty much the same as when they disappear; morphological change is usually limited and directionless.

"2. Sudden appearance: In any local area, a species does not arise gradually by the steady transformation of its ancestors; it appears all at once and 'fully formed.'"

S. J. Gould, "Evolution's Erratic Pace," *Natural History* 86.5 (1977): 14.

On the other hand, I think the degree of ingression of T—that Adam and Eve were historical individuals—is strong. First, this would be the very natural way to read references to Adam and Eve throughout Scripture, although there is not a plethora of such references. But more significantly, the role that an individual Adam plays in the development of Paul's theology is significant (as even Alexander recognizes). Consider first the following summary of Paul's analogy in Romans 5:12-21, noting the repeated comparisons between Adam and Christ:

Table 9.1. Paul's Analogy in Romans 12

Adam	Christ
One man—Adam	One man—Christ
Sin entered through one man	Grace entered through one man
One act of sin	One act of righteousness
Judgment on all because of one sin	Justification to many because of one gift
Death reigned through one man	Life reigned through one man
Many died by trespass of one man	Grace overflowed by gift of one man
Disobedience of one man	Obedience of one man

It is very difficult to reconcile common descent and the gradual emergence of *Homo sapiens* with the theology Paul is developing here. Adam's Fall, the imputation of Adam's sin to humanity and the origin of the human sin nature, in contrast to the work of the Second Adam through whom comes grace, justification and the imputation of Christ's righteousness—the rich theology here has been deeply ingressed in canonical Christianity. Now, I'm aware that a number of different theological interpretations have been given to this analogy, and I can't insist that all alternative theological interpretations are heretical or even heterodox; my claim simply is that a mainstream theological position requires a literal Adam.[53] The point of the analogy is to demonstrate how

---

[53]For example, John Calvin, *Institutes of the Christian Religion* 2.2; Martin Luther, *Preface to the Letter of St. Paul to the Romans;* Thomas Aquinas *Summa contra gentiles* 3.50-52. Such examples could be multiplied.

the act of a single individual can have effects that extend to many other people.[54] So my conclusion here is that a literal Adam is more deeply ingressed in Christian theology, because of the theological weight a literal Fall event carries, than is common descent in biological science. But this conclusion is somewhat tentative, and so while I believe those who deny that T is integral to Christian theology are in error, I'm not about to call for heresy trials!

4. The degree of independent support for T and S is difficult to adjudicate. Clearly common descent plays a large role in much actual work in biological sciences, but it's not clear that such work could not proceed without that assumption. Nor is it clear (in my view) that the lines of evidence offered for common descent are not compatible with progressive creationism. Similarly, the role of a literal Adam coheres with a wide swath of biblical anthropology and Christian theology, but again it's not impossible that proponents of TE could account for the same theological claims (although very few have actually dealt with such passages as Rom 5 and 1 Cor 15 and the theological category of the Fall).

5. As for significant internal problems, both S and T have their share. S, for example, faces evidential problems, such as the origins of the first living cell (abiogenesis), the origins of the new genetic information required to produce a new body plan,[55] as well as conceptual problems, such as the definition of 'species,' whether natural selection is the only or even the primary mechanism driving evolutionary change, determining the units of selection, the meaning and power of adaptation, and so on. T faces its own internal problems, such as questions about the literary genre of Genesis 1–3, and moral difficulties involved in the doctrine of imputing the guilt of Adam's sin to all subsequent humans.

6. Is an antirealist interpretation of either S or T possible? Perhaps surprisingly, I would say yes. I once was involved in a debate with an evolutionary biologist broadcast on public radio in Boulder, Colorado. I knew I could not go toe-to-toe with him on details of biology, so I

---

[54]C. E. B. Cranfield, *Romans: A Shorter Commentary* (Grand Rapids: Eerdmans, 1985), pp. 110-25; Douglas J. Moo, *The Epistle to the Romans* (Grand Rapids: Eerdmans, 1996), pp. 290-328.

[55]See the arguments in Michael J. Behe, *The Edge of Evolution: The Search for the Limits of Darwinism* (New York: Free Press, 2007); Meyer, *Signature in the Cell.*

opened with the philosophical claim that given the evidential and conceptual gaps in the neo-Darwinian synthesis, we would be well advised to treat the theory in an antirealist fashion. To my great surprise, he agreed, saying that he never told his students that evolution was true, but only that it explained (in an instrumental sense) certain observable phylogenetic similarities in species. (Later, after the debate was over, though, he insisted to me that he *did* know it was true.) And although with greater skepticism, I'll also allow that T might be understood in an antirealist sense, taking the names 'Adam' and 'Eve' as symbolic of early hominids (presumably *H. sapiens*) who grew into God-consciousness. In my own view, as I said above, arguments stemming from both exegesis and theology count against an antirealist reading of T, and certainly the prevailing sense of the biological sciences community counts against an antirealist reading of S, so although antirealism about both is possible, I don't think antirealism is preferable in either domain.

7. Is it possible to suspend judgment? Possibly so. But in our day, when evolution is such a polarizing issue, to do so would be to appear either cowardly or uninformed. And frankly, I don't think suspending judgment here is the correct option to take.

So where does this leave me (since I'm being very personal here)? Although as I said, I regard the scientific evidence (which includes the coherence and explanatory power of the theory) for evolution as strong, and so TE as a live option, at the end of the day I am swayed more by the exegetical and theological arguments. T has been deeply ingressed in Christianity for two thousand years, while S has been ingressed in science only for 150 years. I'd say that on this issue, I've reached a place of "reflective equilibrium," and am most comfortable defending an old-earth, progressive-creationist account of Genesis 1–2.[56]

---

[56]Although I have said nothing about the age of the earth, it seems to me that many independent lines of scientific evidence point to an old earth, and several lines of interpretation of the early chapters of Genesis allow for an old universe and an old earth. See, for example, Davis A. Young and Ralph F. Stearley, *The Bible, Rocks and Time: Geological Evidence for the Age of the Earth* (Downers Grove, Ill.: InterVarsity Press, 2008); Henri Blocher, *In the Beginning: The Opening Chapters of Genesis* (Downers Grove, Ill.: InterVarsity Press, 1984); John Sailhammer, *Genesis Unbound: A Provocative New Look at the Creation Account* (Portland, Ore.: Multnomah, 1996); or John H. Walton, *The Lost World of Genesis One: Ancient Cosmology and*

Here ends the "brief" excursus into theistic evolution. No matter where you find yourself in this debate, we can all agree on two things: One, that much more study, exposition, argument and honest engagement with the natural sciences is needed; and two, that in the debate, we must all strive to practice Christian charity—a virtue much more deeply embedded in a Christian worldview than any position on evolution.

---

the *Origins Debate* (Downers Grove, Ill.: InterVarsity Press, 2009). My own view is closest to Blocher's, but the point is that there are several hermeneutical approaches to the early chapters of Genesis that may be preferable to reading it literally as a historical, young-earth-24-hour-days narrative.

PART FOUR

THE END OF THE MATTER

*If Christian belief is to have an integrating role in the world of ideas,
then we must learn to see things as the interrelated whole they are,
rather than compartmentalizing them. If Jesus Christ is indeed creator,
redeemer, and lord of all, then we must cultivate a philosophy
that recognizes this and beware of what is simply
"according to tradition" (Col. 2:8).*

ARTHUR F. HOLMES

*Wisdom is supreme; therefore get wisdom.
Though it cost all you have, get understanding.*

PROVERBS 4:7

The end: was it worth it? Only if it affects how we live our lives.
Which is precisely the end—the goal, the aim—of wisdom.

If you've come this far with me, thinking and arguing along the way,
then surely you know the exhilaration of philosophy, the pure intellectual joy of seeking wisdom. But in the end, if we're honest, we realize
that philosophy in itself cannot fully limn the end. To paraphrase the

sage of Ecclesiastes, there is nothing *in* life big enough to give meaning *to* life.

And yet we have learned much along the way. The Christian philosopher values both the effort and the conclusions, however incomplete and tentative. Philosophy is intrinsically worthwhile, a worthy calling for rational, imaginative creatures, such as ourselves. At the same time, it is instrumentally valuable, offering guidance in skillful living.

The Christian philosopher also knows that the overarching vocation of his or her life—indeed, the calling of all Christians in any station of life—is daily to become more like the Lord Jesus Christ. This is the end of the matter. And philosophy can help us toward that end.

10

TRANSFORMING THE SOUL

PHILOSOPHY AND SPIRITUAL FORMATION

The greatest need you and I have—the greatest need of
collective humanity—is renovation of our heart. That spiritual place
within us from which outlook, choices, and actions come has been formed
by a world away from God. Now it needs to be transformed.

DALLAS WILLARD

And we, who with unveiled faces all reflect the Lord's glory,
are being transformed into his likeness with ever-increasing glory,
which comes from the Lord, who is the Spirit.

PAUL THE APOSTLE (2 COR 3:18)

To many minds, philosophy and spiritual formation are like aardvarks and carburetors—the words hardly belong in the same sentence. But as I conclude, I want to suggest that not only are spiritual formation and philosophical work compatible, but in fact they are rather closely related—as means and end.

To make this argument I'll need to characterize spiritual formation as the goal of the Christian life this side of the eternal city, and then show how the study and the doing of philosophy contribute to the pursuit of that goal.

THE CHRISTIAN STORY

Every culture and every person has a conscious story, a narrative they tell themselves by which they make sense of their past and on which they base their plans and projects for the future. In essence these stories are what we call a worldview. This is not to say that the postmodern notion of incommensurable micronarratives in the absence of a metanarrative is correct, but it is to recognize that we tell ourselves stories that constitute the matrix of meanings within which we live. Some conform more closely to reality than others, and those that are more correct provide better frameworks for living wisely and lead to greater human flourishing.

The Christian story—the sweeping panorama, historical, existential and eschatological—can be told in four movements: creation, fall, redemption and glorification. Naming the movements, of course, is a bit like naming the movements of a Mahler symphony, or identifying the tonic of a Bach fugue: it is only a coarse-grained description. The details, the intricately interwoven melodies, harmonies, counterpoints and rhythms with all their texture and beauty, perhaps can only be sung by the concerted voices of all the redeemed gathered around the throne of God. But this much all Christians agree on (with only small and spasmodic dissent in the history of the church): We are redeemed by the grace of God, appropriated by faith in Christ, but are not yet glorified. We are destined for heaven, but are not yet fit for heaven. In this in-between time, we live in the tension of the already and the not yet. In a striking comment on the sacrificial death of Jesus, the author of the Epistle to the Hebrews says that "by one sacrifice he has made perfect forever those who are being made holy" (Heb 10:14). Note the inherent tension: "he has made perfect" is in the perfect tense in the original Greek, while "being made holy" is a present passive participle. The perfect tense indicates an action completed in the past with results continuing in the present, and the present participle indicates ongoing action in the present.

Theologians speak of "positional" and "progressive" states. *Positionally* we have been made prefect; in union with Christ, we have been credited with his righteousness (see St. Paul's extended argument in

Rom 3–6). But we know, as surely as we know anything, that we are not yet perfect, not yet wholly righteous. We know what we should be, but we know well that we willingly rebel (see Paul's anguished confession in Rom 7:7-25), and so *progressively* we must change, or, more correctly, be changed, to conform to the image of Christ (Rom 8:29). This process of progressive change is what the New Testament calls our sanctification.

Through the centuries the church has employed a number of different concepts to describe this process. The early fathers, especially in the Eastern church, spoke of *theosis* or divinization—not implying that humans would become gods, but that God's communicable attributes would be exemplified by believers to a greater and greater degree. *Catechesis* generally referred to the oral teaching of doctrine prior to baptism or confirmation. *Christian education* was somewhat broader, including both Bible and church history in addition to doctrinal summary. *Discipleship* was employed by and variously understood by many parachurch organizations, but generally focused on practices such as prayer, Bible study, evangelism and Christian fellowship, and then was defined with various understandings of the knowledge and behaviors required to become a disciple. Practice of the *spiritual disciplines,* including prayer, fasting, silence, solitude, worship, service, and so on, characterized many different movements within the church, and sometimes resulted in a strict legalism. In contrast, a "let go and let God" strand of thought emphasized that spiritual transformation must be the work of the Holy Spirit; sometimes this strand spoke of a "second work of grace" or "full surrender" or "lordship." And there are many other movements, strands and concepts of sanctification, too many to recount. Common to all, though, is the recognition that sanctification does not come naturally or easily to redeemed sinners. Hence, the pervasive New Testament use of the category—not merely a metaphor—of spiritual warfare.[1]

These days the term very much in vogue is *spiritual formation.* The term finds biblical warrant in Galatians 4:19, where Paul speaks of

---

[1]As a representative sample, see 2 Cor 10:4; Eph 6:10-18; 1 Tim 6:12; 2 Tim 2:3-4; 4:7. Further, Paul refers to companions as "fellow soldiers" in Phil 2:25 and Philem 2.

Christ being formed in his readers in the church in Galatia. "Formation" highlights a process; in all but Wesleyan/Holiness traditions, the process of being transformed into the image of Christ is understood to be lifelong and will not be completed as long as we see though a glass darkly: glorification awaits that moment when we enter the bright day of God's presence.

The problem: Disordered desires, false beliefs. As I said, we Christians find ourselves in the third movement, between redemption and glorification, but the reason for the tension—the battle—is the second movement, the Fall. As used by theologians, the term refers to Adam and Eve's fall from innocence—not from absolute perfection—in the Garden of Eden.

As told in Genesis 2 and 3, it is the story of the first two humans, Adam and Eve. Being made in the image of God, they were endowed with rationality and rich creativity (Adam, remember, named all the animals, a considerable intellectual feat). And they were gifted by God with the dignity of a free will. Further, they were probably more genetically perfect than any humans since (because created directly by God), living in a more perfect environment that any since (because planted directly by God), and enjoying a more direct communication with God than any human since (with the exception of Jesus Christ). Yet they were not robots, programmed to obey God mindlessly. They voluntarily rebelled against God's command and "fell." Adam and Eve could not blame genetics, or the environment, or even the hiddenness of God for their rebellious act.

As punishment, first and foremost, death rather than life became their state and destiny (Gen 2:9; 3:17, 22). Death in the Bible connotes separation—of the soul from the body in physical death, and of the person from God in spiritual death. At the moment of eating the forbidden fruit, at the moment of rebellion, Adam and Eve were separated from God; they died spiritually. And the long slow process of physical death followed. Secondarily, Adam and Eve came under a curse (Gen 3:16-19) that profoundly affected their relationship and their work. Finally, they were punished by expulsion from Eden (Gen 3:23-24). The perfect environment and the perfect occupation were lost to them forever, the way back barred by an angel with a flaming sword. The history of humankind since has been one of trying to sneak back into paradise through religious acts or to recreate paradise by autonomous effort. Neither path can be successful for us, children of rebellion.

According to the apostle Paul (Rom 5:12-21), and as developed in the theological understanding of the church through the ages, that rebellious streak runs through each of us, not merely potentially but actually, as our "sin nature." That judgment is well confirmed in the experience of every self-reflectively honest person since. But there's more.[2] As the theologians make clear, the Fall has stained every aspect of who we are. We are not tainted intensively but extensively—that is, we are not as bad as we could have been, but each part of us is affected. Our rationality is incomplete, our emotions are at times inappropriate to their objects, our beliefs may be false, and our desires misdirected.[3]

This is the problem for which spiritual formation is proposed as the solution. And it is here that I believe philosophy can become an indispensable ally of spiritual formation. When we act rationally and voluntarily (on a personal agency theory of action; see chapter 9), we are exercising our capacity to deliberate on the possible courses of action open to us, and to decide to act to (attempt to) bring about the best of the possible courses that we have considered. What is involved in this process? Six things at least: desires, beliefs, emotions, rational deliberation, intentions and actions. It's the business of philosophy to help to clarify each of these so we can better understand ourselves and our actions. Much philosophical work has recently gone into analyzing these components of personal agency and action theory, often making insightful use of empirical results from psychology. At first, the analysis may seem to greatly over-complicate the simple matter of deciding to act, but I submit that the extra work required to disentangle these concepts will in the end help us understand much better both the nature of the ten-

---

[2]For my purposes, I don't need to try to untangle the concepts of original sin, sin nature, our participation in Adam's sin though "federal headship," or other thorny and much-debated theological knots. All that's necessary for the thread I'm following here is the recognition that, as St. Paul said, "All have sinned and fall short of the glory of God" (Rom 3:23).

[3]Even nature has been affected by the Fall (see, for example, Gen 3:17-19; Rom 8:18-23), so "natural evil" occurs without God's primary causal involvement.

sion facing us and the role of spiritual formation in the solution.

Desires. Adam and Eve had desires, just as surely as we do. A desire, let us say, is an attraction toward some object, real or imagined, material or immaterial, that we deem to be good for us. An object may be desired intrinsically as a good in itself; or instrumentally, as means toward the realization of some other good; or both intrinsically or instrumentally. (I take it that this broad definition is compatible with many animals having desires.)

It's been traditional to speak of natural and unnatural desires, with much debate going into the classification of desires into the two categories. However, I think that a more nuanced approach is correct.[4] Surely the desire for food or drink or sex arises "naturally" in a properly functioning human (and in most higher animals also). But such natural desires easily give way to gluttony, drunkenness and promiscuity, and there is no high wall, no bright line, separating the one from the other. Similarly, the desire to express oneself in speech can issue equally in words that heal or wound, and the legitimate use of force to work the ground for food, or to protect oneself and one's family, can turn to violence and bloodshed all too easily.

One clear difference between humans and other animals is that animals' desires are narrowly confined, while human desires, it seems, can range over almost anything in creation, and given a fertile imagination, over things beyond creation. And invariably some desires conflict with others. The problem isn't merely to decide which desires are natural and which are unnatural, but to properly order or configure our desires.

What happened in Eden, when the serpent approached Eve and enticed her to eat the forbidden fruit, was a disordering or a reconfiguring of her proper desires, shaped by communion with God and recognition that in God's will lay genuine flourishing. Perhaps we can call the configuration of desires in Eden before the Fall, ordered by submission to the will of God, "natural" desires, and perhaps the same can be said of

---

[4]A suggestive—and, by my lights, largely accurate—exploration of the nature of desire is Paul J. Griffiths, "The Nature of Desire," *First Things* 198, December 2009, 27-30. For a related but distinct understanding, see Martha Nussbaum, *The Therapy of Desire: Theory and Practice in Hellenistic Ethics* (Princeton, N.J.: Princeton University Press, 1994).

the desires of all the redeemed after our resurrection. But between these two points, after the Fall and before glorification, we all suffer from disordered desires.

Traditionally, St. Paul has been understood to lament the disordering of desires he finds within himself: "I do not understand what I do. For what I want to do I do not do, but what I hate I do. . . . For I have the desire to do what is good, but I cannot carry it out. For what I do is not the good I want to do; no, the evil I do not want to do—this I keep on doing" (Rom 7:15, 18-19).

So one way to look at the problem that spiritual formation aims at addressing is this: post-Fall, "east of Eden," we find in ourselves a jumbled, disordered confusion of desires, and progress toward holiness is a reordering of those desires so that, more and more consistently, we exemplify the image of Christ. But desires alone are not the end of the story.

Beliefs. As with desires, we all find ourselves believing very many things, and disbelieving many others. A good proportion of our beliefs range over our desires and their objects. We believe, say, that it is good to desire to tell the truth, even when it may put us at a disadvantage. We believe that it is wrong to desire (or as the commandment says, covet) to seduce a neighbor's wife or steal his property. Further, we have beliefs about the means available to us to fulfill our desires. A desire for adequate food is proper, but fulfilling that desire by stealing from the grocery is not. A desire to demonstrate compassion in practical ways is proper, but getting extra money to give to the poor by falsifying an expense account is not.

We also have second-order desires, as when we don't really desire to exercise to lose weight, but we have a desire to desire to exercise, or when an addict has no desire to break her addiction, but does have a second-order desire not to be an addict.[5]

At least for meaningful decisions we make, the mix of beliefs and desires will generally be very complicated. I think this is what we grasp when we acknowledge that we often have mixed motives. But one thing

---

[5]Harry Frankfurt explored this notion in an original and influential essay, "Freedom of the Will and the Concept of a Person," *Journal of Philosophy* 68 (1971): 5-20.

is clear: The more true beliefs we have, and the fewer false ones, the better our ultimate decisions will be.

Think again of Eve in Eden (Gen 3:1-7). Surely among her beliefs was the belief that God had commanded that she and Adam not eat of the Tree of the Knowledge of Good and Evil. And surely she also had the belief that what God commanded was not only morally right, but also conducive to her ultimate happiness. Then she encountered the serpent (doubtless an embodiment of Satan). He begins by undermining her belief about God's command, not seeking to get her to believe the contradictory, but simply weakening it: "Did God really say . . . ?" Next he flatly contradicts Eve's belief about what God had commanded, but offers an explanation for the command. "You will not surely die. . . . For God knows that when you eat of it your eyes will be opened, and you will be like God, knowing good and evil."

Once Eve's belief set had been shaken, she was able to consider her desires in a new light. "When the woman saw that the fruit of the tree was good for food and pleasing to the eye, and also desirable for gaining wisdom, she took some." These desires in themselves are not improper—food is a necessity, aesthetic beauty is a value, and wisdom is worth pursuing. But when the general proper desire finds its satisfaction in a specific improper object, when the desires become disordered, trouble awaits. When beliefs about God's commands and about human flourishing are weakened or replaced by false beliefs, desires are knocked out of their proper order; they become deranged.

In what is very likely a meditation on Eve's temptation, the apostle John shows that the love of the Father is incompatible with "the lust of the flesh [Eve's disordered desire for food] and the lust of the eyes [Eve's disordered desire for aesthetic beauty] and the boastful pride of life [Eve's disordered desire for wisdom]" (1 Jn 2:16 NASB).

There's one further aspect to consider. Beliefs are degreed; they come in various strengths (sometimes analyzed in terms of epistemic probabilities, or what betting odds one would accept based on a belief). In general, for a rational thinker, the strength of a belief is dependent on the strength of the evidence for the belief (where 'evidence' need not be empirical—see the discussion in chapter 6). The better the evidence, the stronger the belief. As beliefs become stronger, they become convictions and lead to the sort of intention we call resolution or commitment (see below). So it follows that by considering the evidence for our beliefs, it is possible that an earlier weak belief can be strengthened and play a more powerful or decisive role in deliberation.

Emotions. Many thinkers distinguish *emotions* from *affects* or "raw feelings."[6] A raw feeling has no particular object, while an emotion does. The child who wakes up at night terrified but doesn't know what he's afraid of, the worker who has a nagging, free-floating anxiety but can't identify the cause, the student who wakes up happy but isn't sure why she feels that way—these people are experiencing "raw feelings." But an emotion is an intentional state; it is a feeling about or directed toward an object. So one might feel fear of driving at night or of an upcoming midterm exam; feel disgust at the thought of pornography or of eating asparagus; feel delight when anticipating a reunion with a loved one or deep gratitude while watching a spectacular sunset over the mountains. In these cases, the feeling has an object, and it is this sort of mental state that is properly called an emotion, in distinction from the affect.

Now, emotions may be proper or improper. That is, a particular emotion may be appropriate or inappropriate to its object. Excitement at the thought of an extramarital affair is improper, while anger directed at a politician convicted of having taken large bribes is appropriate. But as soon as this is pointed out, we see with clarity that emotions can easily be manipulated. Our beliefs and desires already color our emotions, and such things as friendships and films can maneuver us into inappropriately linking an emotion with an object. A friend confides in us how unhappy she has been in her marriage, and we can find ourselves feeling positive about her desire for a divorce. We watch a film where a young woman, seemingly without any other options, seeks out an abortion doctor, and we feel more than compassion—we feel approving of her decision. For sake of argument, let's say that in these two examples, the divorce and the abortion would not be the righteous

---

[6]See, for example, Robert Solomon, *Not Passion's Slave: Emotions and Choice* (Oxford: Oxford University Press, 2003).

choice. It's easy to see how an emotion can be inappropriate to its object, given the whole context of life. Since emotions can seemingly strengthen or weaken desires, and can serve as evidence for beliefs, a picture of rational agency must take them into account.

I believe that emotions *do* serve as evidence for judgments, albeit often incorrectly or illicitly, and at best can only serve as weak evidence.[7] So along with beliefs and desires, the process of rational deliberation takes into account emotions as well. But it is absolutely essential that emotions be evaluated rationally, as they are so easily open to influence and manipulation.

Rational deliberation. Some people act almost wholly and unreflectively on the basis of desires (Harry Frankfurt calls them "wantons"). But 2,500 years of philosophical tradition, as well as our thoughtful self-reflection, commend acting only after rationally deliberating. We think carefully (or should) about the desires, we examine the appropriate beliefs about those desires and about the means of satisfying them, we interrogate our emotions to insure that as much as possible they are appropriate to their object, and we consider our own personal plans and projects—what kind of people we want to be.

Rational deliberation will take into account all these "internal" factors, as well as such considerations as our past experiences, our duties, others' expectations and needs, and on and on. But the result of such deliberation is a choice—the act of forming an intention to do (or refrain from doing) some action.

As for Adam and Eve, we don't know how long Eve deliberated, nor much at all about Adam's deliberation. But it's clear enough that deliberation with disordered desires and weak or false beliefs will not conclude in a right intention.

Intentions. Intentions are a special sort of mental state, not reducible

---

[7]See Martha C. Nussbaum, *Upheavals of Thought: The Intelligence of Emotions* (New York: Cambridge University Press, 2001). I'm in partial agreement with Nussbaum's "neo-stoic" theory of emotions, but cannot delve deeply into the issues here. However, it seems to me that the early medieval-scholastic doctrine of God's impassibility tended to bend Christian folk psychology in the direction of full-on Stoicism, where emotions were denied or suppressed. This is both psychologically unhealthy and, in my view, a denial of an important aspect of who we are as creatures made in the image of God—a God who has emotions.

to desires and beliefs. While an intention may be quite specific ("I intend to leave for the airport at 2:30 this afternoon"), quite often they are more general, ranging over types and not merely tokens of actions. As such, our intentions enable us to act in many cases when we don't have sufficient time or even information to deliberate thoroughly.

Intentions are not themselves actions, of course; they are more like dispositions—being "spring-loaded" to act in a certain way in the right circumstances. Forming an intention to act generally will involve at least a vague representation of the circumstances that would trigger the action. Such circumstances may be simply the physical possibility of the action, as when I form the intention to pick up a loaf of bread on the way home, and the triggering circumstances include stopping at the grocery and its not being out of bread. But the circumstances may be represented much more richly, including the possibility of encountering contrary evidence challenging a relevant belief, or of realizing the presence of some other competing and mutually exclusive intention. In such cases, perhaps a person will have a considered strategy for revising intentions, perhaps not, but in many cases we understand, at least tacitly, that intentions are subject to revision.

But what about those cases where we want our intentions to be firm, (nearly) unrevisable? We may identify a special sort of intention—a resolution—that is designed to remain resolute, unchanging in the face of temptation or contrary information. Especially in cases where we may anticipate having contrary inclinations or encountering new evidence, a resolution is, we may say, accompanied by a second-order intention not to revise or abandon the resolution.[8] This is how we can understand the strong intentions that constitute New Year's resolutions: I resolve to not to cheat on the final, even though a higher grade will help my grad school application; I resolve not to gossip, no matter how juicy the tidbit I just heard; I resolve to be more faithful in giving to my church, no matter how tempting another ski trip may be. But it applies equally in much more serious cases: a resolution not to be unfaithful to

---

[8]See Richard Holton, *Willing, Wanting, Waiting* (New York: Oxford University Press, 2009) for an illuminating discussion of beliefs, desires, intentions and resolutions, temptation, weakness of will, and so forth.

one's spouse even when the opportunity and the inclination are present and the chances of being caught are negligible, or the martyr's resolution not to deny Christ even when faced with intense pain and imminent death.

Actions. Finally, we act. The circumstances are right, and we exercise active power; we *do* something. It seems to me that very often, courses in ethics stop at beliefs: we want students to learn what Aristotle and Hobbes and Kant had to say, but (sometimes for legitimate reasons) we don't press students to consider the intricate web linking their own ethical beliefs, their desires, their deliberations and formation of intentions and resolutions. And then we evaluate actions somewhat in isolation from the rest.

To their credit, a number of institutions and even businesses have developed character development programs that seek to bridge the gap between beliefs and actions. To cite one example, the United States Air Force Academy (full disclosure: my undergrad alma mater) has created a Center for Character Development with the following mission:

> The center's objective is to graduate officers who have the forthright integrity and voluntarily decide the right thing to do; who are selfless in service to the United States, the Air Force and their subordinates; who are committed to excellence in the performance of their professional and personal responsibilities; who respect the dignity of all human beings; who are decisive, even when facing high risk; who take full responsibility for their decisions; who bear the self-discipline, stamina and courage to do their duty well; and who appreciate the significance of personal values and beliefs to their own character development and that of the community.[9]

A statement like this clearly reflects a richly textured understanding of the complex psychology of character formation. Spiritual formation must be similarly articulated.

Yielding to temptation. Temptation, on this analysis of agency, arises from diverse sources. The source of temptation may lie within a person; certainly desires play a key role, as the apostle James taught: "Each one

---

[9]See <www.usafa.af.mil/Commandant/cwc/?catname=cwc>.

is tempted when, by his own evil desire, he is dragged away and enticed" (Jas 1:14). Temptation can also come from watching others (Gal 6:1) or from Satan and, I presume, his minions (Gen 3:1-4; Mt 4:1; 1 Cor 7:5). But whatever the source, temptation involves either an appeal to desire or a challenge to belief—both often accompanied and reinforced by inappropriate emotions.

Yielding to temptation, whatever its source, is often attributed to weakness of the will. Traditionally, weakness of the will has been understood along the lines Aristotle developed in considering *akrasia* (literally, "lack of command [of oneself]").[10] On this view, one simply fails to act according to one's judgment as to what action is best. Introspectively and anecdotally, this seems right; how many times have we heard someone say, "I acted against my better judgment"? But this view has been subject to much criticism from those who take a more Platonic line, according to which one always does what one believes to be the best.[11] A third view is that weakness of the will involves failure to stick with one's intentions, revising them too easily in the face of new or unexpected aspects of the circumstances.[12]

I don't think it's necessary here to pursue the ins and outs of this debate. What is clear is that actions flow from intentions, and intentions (at least those involved in rational decision-making, as opposed to decisions made under the influence of drugs, alcohol, significant brain chemistry imbalance, etc.) are formed by a deliberative process in which beliefs and desires figure prominently. So it's clear as well that the more true beliefs a person has, the stronger those beliefs are, the more well-ordered her desires and the more appropriate her emotions to their objects, the easier it will be for her to form intentions and resolutions that will enable her successfully to resist temptation.

It seems to me that much that goes on in the church skips from beliefs to actions without much thought of what must go on in between. Sermons, Sunday school and Bible studies do a pretty good job of teaching the right biblical and theological beliefs (although often these

---

[10]Aristotle *Nichomachean Ethics* 7.1-10.
[11]Developed especially in the *Protagoras*.
[12]See Holton, *Willing, Wanting, Waiting*, chaps. 4-5.

beliefs are taught simply as dogma with little concern given to presenting the supporting evidence for the beliefs). And often the sermons and
so on offer clear application—suggested actions or attitudes that are
entailed by the beliefs.

But an inadequate understanding of the rich texture of decision
making leaves many in the church puzzled about why the church resembles secular society so closely: why "love" would not be the first
word generally associated with Christians, why meaningful and practical care for the poor and powerless is rare, why "good girls" in the youth
group get pregnant, why alcohol abuse increases even in the church in
times of economic stress, why domestic violence occurs at all in Christian families, why so many Christian marriages fail, or why the associ-
ate pastor ran off with the organist. It won't do to babble platitudes that
"Satan is alive and well," and "They have free will," and "There but for
the grace of God go I."

Clearly something hasn't been going right in much of the church;
progress toward holiness and righteousness—progressive sanctification—is often hard to spot. If philosophical thought can help illuminate the mental processes involved in forming intentions and resolutions and acting on them, then perhaps it can also contribute to
understanding and strengthening the process of spiritual formation.

Inadequate responses. If we could take a bird's-eye view of the church
throughout history, we would see at least three seriously inadequate
conceptions of spiritual formation.

Legalism. As already noted, emphasis on what kind of behavior is
expected by a church community can often lead to legalism. In essence, this is a "lowest common denominator" form of spirituality: it's
enough that one follows (most of) a code of behavior accepted by the
community, with no encouragement or expectation to real transformation. But history and experience teach that effort devoted to meeting
certain behavioral standards is insufficient for being formed in the image of Christ.

Let go and let God. At the opposite end of the spectrum from legalism
lies a passive conception of spiritual formation in which we do nothing
and God does it all. Recognizing that nothing done "in the flesh"—by

human effort alone—can please God, the reaction is to wait for God to do it all. Bill comes to believe that he should stop smoking, but waits for God to remove the desire; Sue is convicted about her lack of spending time praying, but waits for God to wake her up early every morning. And so seldom is there any progress in sanctification.

Grace covers all. Then there is the approach that resembles aspects of Neoplatonism and its spawn, early Gnosticism. Emphasizing the infinite grace of God that covers all our sin, this approach simply denies that there are any significant consequences to anything we do in this life, sinful or not. It misconstrues Martin Luther's maxim to "Love God and do as you please," not grasping the richness of Luther's understanding of what loving God entails.

Of course, those who promulgate lists of behaviors to avoid do not often see the dangers of legalism, and those who teach the concept of complete surrender to the Holy Spirit do not often see the dangers of spiritual stagnation. Nor do those who emphasize the infinite richness of grace and the extent of the atonement intend to sanction unbridled licentiousness. I don't want to judge motives too harshly; it's the results that I question, and I believe I have biblical warrant for doing so.

As for the temptation to overemphasize grace, the apostle Paul recognized the error. Laying the stress on grace, he wrote, "But where sin increased, grace increased all the more, so that, just as sin reigned in death, so also grace might reign through righteousness to bring eternal life through Jesus Christ our Lord" (Rom 5:20-21). But he immediately addressed the error that might follow: "What shall we say, then? Shall we go on sinning so that grace may increase? By no means! We died to sin; how can we live in it any longer?" (Rom 6:1-2).

And as for the polar errors of legalism and passivism, the New Testament throughout teaches both-and: Each believer must *do* certain things, but also must *yield* to the Holy Spirit and depend on his power to do them. Here are just two such passages: "if by the Spirit you put to death the misdeeds of the body, you will live" (Rom 8:13). Note that *you* put to death the misdeeds of the body, but you do it *by the Spirit.* Both/ and. "I have been crucified with Christ and I no longer live, but Christ lives in me. The life I live in the body, I live by faith in the Son of God, who loved me and gave himself for me" (Gal 2:20). Paul says, *I have been crucified, I no longer live,* but immediately says, *the life I live, I live by faith.* Both-and.

Whatever we say, then, about the process of spiritual formation, it must take account of the synergism we find in the New Testament—not a synergism with respect to salvation—that is God's work through and through, to which I contribute no effort at all, but a synergism of sanctification, in which I "work out [my] salvation with fear and trembling" (Phil 2:12), and in which I am transformed (passive voice) into the image of Christ.[13]

Toward a solution: Spiritual (trans)formation. In the *locus classicus* on these matters, the apostle Paul tells us that only by the transformation of our minds will we be able experientially to experience true flourishing in the will of God:

> Therefore, I urge you, brothers, in view of God's mercy, to offer your bodies as living sacrifices, holy and pleasing to God—which is your spiritual worship. Do not conform any longer to the pattern of this world, but be transformed by the renewing of your mind. Then you will be able to test and approve what God's will is—his good, pleasing and perfect will. (Rom 12:1-2)

This passage rewards the exegetical labor of unpacking it.

Paul couches his words as a plea—he urges or beseeches or appeals to us—and not a command. He is not averse to commanding, and does from time to time in his epistles. But what he will urge—the self-sacrifice that leads to transformation—cannot be commanded. Grudging compliance, reluctant obedience, is not the path to a renewed mind. In the language we've explored, self-sacrifice must be a resolution, not a revisable intention, and that frame of mind cannot be commanded from without.

The opening word of the passage, "Therefore," indicates that the

---

[13]For various reasons I have not touched on the legitimate role that psychology may play in spiritual formation. First, the focus of this chapter is on philosophy and spiritual formation; second, to discuss the contributions and limits of psychology would make this chapter inexcusably long. See, however, John H. Coe and Todd W. Hall, *Psychology in the Spirit: Contours of a Transformational Psychology* (Downers Grove, Ill.: InterVarsity Press, 2009).

appeal is a logical inference from what has gone before. So what is the basis for the appeal? It might be the immediately preceding verses, the doxology that closes chapter 11. However, most exegetes see the doxology itself as the conclusion of Paul's extended theological argument in the first eleven chapters. Paul begins with an indictment of every person as unrighteous sinners, falling short of God's glory (Rom 3:23), and meriting the wages of sin—death (Rom 6:23). He then demonstrates God's faithfulness, justifying freely (counting as righteous) those who by faith receive the redemption that comes through Jesus Christ (Rom 3:21-31). This is God's nature, as seen even in the Old Testament example of Abraham (Rom 4:1-22). But how can it be, a reader might ask, that justification, life, peace with God (Rom 5:1), come through the death of one man, Jesus? Paul draws an analogy (Rom 5:12-21) between Adam, through whom sin came to all since all sin, and Christ, through whose death grace comes to all who receive it.

Consequently, those who are spiritually united with Christ are no longer slaves to sin (Rom 6:1-13). Though no longer slaves to sin, we are not free from the enticements of sin (Rom 7:7-15); however, those who live by the power of the Holy Spirit are free to live the God-pleasing life that culminates in glorification (Rom 8:1-17). And since this all is God's plan, from foreknowledge through predestination to sanctification (being conformed to the likeness of Jesus) and glorification (Rom 8:28-30), nothing "in all creation will be able to separate us from the love of God in that is in Christ Jesus our Lord" (Rom 8:39).

Paul then considers, in a parenthetical discussion in chapters 9–11, a potential defeater. If God chose the people of Israel, but now has chosen Gentiles in Israel's place, doesn't that show that God is unjust, going back on his promise? The answer is surely no—Israel collectively rejected God's grace, which resulted in the gospel being offered directly to Gentiles, but in the end "all Israel will be saved," "for God's gifts and his call are irrevocable" (Rom 11:26, 29). And then follows the great concluding doxology:

> Oh, the depth of the riches of the wisdom and knowledge of God!
>   How unsearchable his judgments,
>   and his paths beyond tracing out!

"Who has known the mind of the Lord?
    Or who has been his counselor?"
"Who has ever given to God,
    that God should repay him?"
For from him and through him and to him are all things.
    To him be the glory forever! Amen. (Rom 11:33-36)

Paul's extended argument shows that salvation, justification, redemption—Paul knows that one single word cannot capture the momentous transaction—comes when one receives God's grace by faith in Jesus Christ. Further, this transaction unites us inseparably with the love of God and frees us from sin to live righteous lives. Paul's "therefore," the ground of his plea, draws the inescapable inference: because of what God has done for us, because of his mercy, here's what we should do now.

And what is it that we should do? Sacrifice ourselves! For it is only by renouncing our autonomy—our plans and projects formulated while we were slaves to sin, enemies of God—that we will be able to live truly flourishing lives that prove out in experience that the will of God is good, pleasing and perfect. Paul has already shown the possibility of this life—no longer slaves to sin, predestined to be conformed to the likeness of Jesus. But with chapter 12 he moves into the practical portion of his letter to the Romans: just *how* do we live this way?

"Offer your bodies as living sacrifices," Paul says. Why does he mention our bodies? I think this is to ward off an error associated with the Neoplatonism and perhaps an incipient Gnosticism of Paul's day. One implication of these schools of thought was that matter is evil, or at best, irrelevant, to the true self, the immaterial soul. What one did bodily would not affect one's soul. It's easy to see how such teaching gave license to just about anything, bracketing off the soul from any fulfillment of physical desires. However, the will of God is not something that is done only inwardly, only in one's soul (or mind); it must involve the whole person. Humans are, in this life, functional unities of the material and immaterial: body and soul. Say that I am disturbed at the weight I've gained over the holidays. I can "offer my mind" to a program of diet and exercise, visualize my thin self, and go my merry way, not ever "offering my body" to the treadmill. So Paul says that doing the will of God must involve our bodies; he'll come to the mind shortly.

But I think there's more here. Paul isn't just thinking about how we "use" our bodies—whether we use our hands to harm or steal, whether we yield to sexual urges and so on. Clearly how we conceive ourselves, our life projects and our plans for tomorrow involve our bodies: how could they not? And often those plans and projects, and our self-concept, is focused on sensual pleasure, or on acquiring material possessions or power or prestige. Those too must be placed on the altar as an offering. Very likely Paul here is recalling Jesus' teaching, "If anyone would come after me, he must deny himself and take up his cross and follow me. For whoever wants to save his life will lose it, but whoever loses his life for me will find it. What good will it be for a man if he gains the whole world, yet forfeits his soul? Or what can a man give in exchange for his soul?" (Mt 16:24-26).

To emphasize this point, Paul says that our bodies must be offered as "holy and pleasing to God." What pleases God is not partial sacrifices, imperfect leftovers, grudgingly and sporadically given (see Mal 1:6-14); rather, complete, whole-hearted, pure and grateful offerings are required.

Such offering, Paul says, is our "spiritual" worship (NIV). I'd suggest that this translation is a bit misleading. The Greek here is a form of *logikos,* one of Plato's favorite words. It indicates what is in conformity with *logos,* the rational principle, and is usually translated "rational." And I think that's how Paul intends it here. As we consciously examine our beliefs and rightly order our desires, the intention that should be formed by rational deliberation is to offer ourselves. Any other response to God's mercy would be less than rational. And the sort of worship that honors and pleases God is not a mindless self-flagellation, a rote mouthing of words or an automatic performance of rituals; it's the product of conscious, rational thought.

Two alternatives then face us: conform or be transformed. "Do not conform any longer to the pattern of this world," Paul says, using a Greek verbal form, the middle voice, which indicates "do not conform yourselves." As J. B. Phillips translates it, "Don't let the world around you squeeze you into its own mould." Conforming is easy: going along with the crowd doesn't take much thought, and it's often safer too, avoiding ridicule, rejection, even persecution. Conformity is natural, Paul would say—it's what we unconsciously do, it's our autopilot mode.

The alternative is to "be transformed," to be changed into something quite different, something, in fact, that we were made to be, for this is the word used of the transfiguration of Jesus, when he was transformed into what he would be as resurrected and glorified (Mt 17:1-8). The word is in the passive voice—transformation is something that does not come naturally to us, this side of the Fall. Now, as we have seen, even in this very epistle of Romans, Paul teaches a both-and, a symbiosis of sanctification. There are things we must do to become holy, but, almost paradoxically, they are things we cannot do on our own. His use of the passive voice here, I think, underscores the fact that we must rely on the power of the Holy Spirit. It is as we offer ourselves (active) that we are transformed (passive).

Transformation comes "by the renewing of your mind." Just here the discussion earlier about personal agency becomes relevant, for I take it that Paul's use of "mind" refers to our entire intellectual apparatus, including (at least) beliefs, desires, rationality, deliberative capacity, and intentions and resolutions resulting in voluntary actions. The renewal of that whole package results in transformation. As evidence for beliefs is examined, false beliefs are discarded, justified beliefs are properly weighted; as desires are reordered and emotions adjusted, as reflection and deliberation continue, the result is the formation of intentions and resolutions that result in living one's life in such a way as to experientially test and approve the goodness, pleasantness and perfection of God's will. As Dallas Willard emphasizes, those "living the life" will, among other things, *"Discover remarkable changes in their beliefs, fundamental attitudes, and emotional conditions."*[14] The result: a life that is truly flourishing, the "life to the full" of which Jesus spoke (Jn 10:10).

What could be more philosophical than this? Philosophy—thinking

---

[14]Dallas Willard, *Knowing Christ Today: Why We Can Trust Spiritual Knowledge* (New York: HarperCollins, 2009), p. 161; emphasis in the original.

critically about the most important questions—surely applies to thinking critically in the process of being transformed by the renewing of the mind. Here's how it seems to me that it works: I pray, consciously submitting myself to the Lordship of Christ and the work of the Holy Spirit. I read Scripture, and the Spirit makes salient to my mind specific applications of certain texts—that is, specific places where the teaching of the Bible impacts my life. I reflect on my beliefs, desires, emotions, attitudes and actions, and I form intentions to change where necessary or resolutions to remain firm, where appropriate. As I am saturated with Scripture and guided in my thinking by the Holy Spirit, as my mind is renewed, then to an ever greater degree I will be able to say that I "have the mind of Christ" (1 Cor 2:16).

There are habits of thought that go with being a good philosopher, dispositions toward the employment of the intellectual virtues, and these virtues are indispensable in the process of "renewing the mind." So I say that in an obvious way, a philosophical orientation contributes significantly to spiritual transformation—if its starting point is the self-sacrifice with which Paul begins.

This is not to say that a person with no philosophical training cannot be spiritually transformed; however, I believe that a spiritually formed, mature, believer will have developed the intellectual virtues and a critical, self-evaluating objectivity regardless of her formal training. Nor is this to say that any philosopher who is a Christian will be automatically further down the pathway to holiness, for we retain the freedom to pursue disordered desires or to accept falsehoods, and so to form wrongful intentions.

If the process unfolds as it should, I will develop "habits of holiness," dispositions to think, desire and intend that are in ever-greater conformity to the will of God. Yet there will never cease to be a tension; for just as soon as I have reordered certain desires and formed renewed habits of intending and acting, God through Scripture and the Holy Spirit will bring to my attention some new area where attitudes need changing, where emotions are inappropriate to their object, where action is called for. And so the "pilgrim's progress" continues.

What of the spiritual disciplines? God's people throughout the ages have learned that certain practices can assist the process of spiritual transformation. Chief among them is the discipline of obedience—obedience to God first of all, to his commands as recorded in Scripture, but also obedience to legitimately constituted spiritual authorities. For God's people, both national Israel and the multinational church, have been organized to some degree or another in a hierarchical structure. The life pleasing to God is not—and cannot be—lived in isolation or in anarchy. Obedience to legitimate authority is always a challenge to one's self-sufficiency and pride, and can be especially onerous for the young. So St. Peter writes, "Young men, . . . be submissive to those who are older [in context, the *presbyteroi*, a general title for church leaders]. . . . Humble yourselves, therefore, under God's mighty hand, that he may lift you up in due time" (1 Pet 5:5-6). It seems that we learn obedience to God by practicing obedience to legitimate authority. Astonishingly, even Jesus, we are told, learned obedience (Heb 5:8), a necessary step for the one who was fully human as well as fully God.

Other disciplines that have been recognized over the centuries include prayer, meditation, fasting, simplicity, solitude, service, giving, worship and a few others.[15] All can play a most helpful role in the process of spiritual transformation. But note: not all can be practiced simultaneously, and so will be of more or less value to any individual in different seasons of life, and different individuals will find different disciplines valuable. No concrete program or algorithmic progression can be prescribed for every believer in every age and every culture.

And note also: the disciplines are *means*, not ends. Focus on the disciplines themselves, and they will lead to a dry legalism. Ignore them, and spiritual progress will be more meander than march. In the end, a spiritual discipline is simply a method, a technique, for facilitating the process of reflectively reordering desires, reexamining beliefs, readjusting emotions and reforming intentions. The point isn't to practice a discipline but to be transformed by renewing the mind.

---

[15]There is no canonical list of the spiritual disciplines. See the now-classic studies by Richard Foster, *Celebration of Discipline: The Path to Spiritual Growth* (New York: HarperCollins, 1978), and Dallas Willard, *The Spirit of the Disciplines: Understanding How God Changes Lives* (New York: HarperCollins, 1988).

Through the years it has seemed to me that some advocates of spiritual formation forget that point. There's always a tendency to draw principles out of one's own experience and to advocate for everyone else what one has found helpful for one's own self. Such tendencies should be avoided. In Romans 14, Paul notes that among believers in Rome, a variety of different practices are observed. But he forbids those who observe one practice from condemning those who don't, "for God has accepted him" (Rom 14:3). "Therefore let us stop passing judgment on one another. . . . For the kingdom of God is not a matter of eating and drinking, but of righteousness, peace and joy in the Holy Spirit" (Rom 14:13, 17). Charity must rule in such matters.

THE END OF THE MATTER

The end: Has the journey to this point been worth it? Only if it affects how we live our lives. Which is precisely the end—the goal, the aim—of *philosophia,* the love of wisdom. For a Christian reflecting on doing philosophy *as a Christian,* the doing must be more than a fascinating intellectual expedition through ideas that form cultures and shape empires, and it must be more than a vocation that allows us to have an effect, sometimes profound, on eager young minds.

In chapter three, I stated my thesis of what it means to do philosophy as a Christian:

> Doing philosophy as a Christian means doing philosophy under the authority of the Lord Jesus and the Bible, the Word of God. It means reasoning within the bounds of religion. It means, in the end, doing philosophy in a way that aims intentionally at the ultimate goal of personal transformation into the image of Christ, and of extending a meaningful invitation to others to enter into that transformation—that is, of extending the kingdom of God on earth.

It follows, I think, that the more closely one approaches to the likeness of Christ, the more fully one will do philosophy "under the authority of the Lord Jesus."

Spiritual formation, as I've come to understand it, and as I outlined above, intimately involves the Holy Spirit. After eating the Last Supper with his disciples, Jesus gives them final instruction in what is called the Upper Room Discourse (Jn 14–16). Several times Jesus promises the coming and ongoing ministry of the Holy Spirit. He will "teach you all things and will remind you of everything I have said to you" (Jn 14:26). He is the "Spirit of truth" who will testify about Jesus, though the disciples also must testify (Jn 15:26-27). The Spirit of truth "will guide you into all truth" (Jn 16:13). And significantly, "He will bring glory to me" (Jn 16:14). So the work of the Holy Spirit in the life of the believer leads to bringing glory to Jesus. Is anything less to be expected of the role of the Holy Spirit in the life of a Christian philosopher?

Saint Paul exhorted believers, "whether you eat or drink or whatever you do, do it all for the glory of God" (1 Cor 10:31). The end of the matter must be this: the glory of God the Father, and of our Lord Jesus Christ. May the end—the goal and the result—of our doing philosophy as Christians, realize the prayer of Jude 25:

> To the only God our Savior be glory, majesty, power and authority, through Jesus Christ our Lord, before all ages, now and forevermore! Amen.

SELECT BIBLIOGRAPHY

Abraham, William J., Jason E. Vickers and Natalie B. Van Kirk, eds. *Canonical Theism*. Grand Rapids: Eerdmans, 2008.

Adler, Mortimer. *Truth in Religion: The Plurality of Religions and the Unity of Truth*. New York: Macmillan, 1990.

Anderson, Ray S. "On Being Human: The Spiritual Saga of a Creaturely Soul." In *Whatever Happened to the Soul?* Edited by Warren S. Brown, Nancey Murphy and H. Newton Malony. Minneapolis: Fortress, 1998.

Anderson, Walter Truett. *Reality Isn't What It Used to Be: Theatrical Politics, Ready-to-Wear Religion, Global Myths, Primitive Chic, and Other Wonders of the Postmodern World*. New York: HarperCollins, 1990.

Annas, Julia. *The Morality of Happiness*. Oxford: Oxford University Press, 1993.

Anselm. *Proslogion*. Translated by S. N. Deane. 2nd ed. Chicago: Open Court, 1962.

Aquinas, Thomas. *Summa contra gentiles*. Translated by Anton C. Pegis. Notre Dame, Ill.: University of Notre Dame Press, 1975.

———. *Summa theologica*. Translated by the Fathers of the English Dominican Province. 5 vols. New York: Benzinger Brothers, 1948.

Augustine. *City of God*. In *Political Writings*. Edited by Michael W. Tkacz and Douglas Kries. Indianapolis: Hackett, 1994.

———. *Contra academicos*. In *Against the Academicians and The Teacher*. Translated by Peter King. Indianapolis: Hackett, 1995.

———. *Tractates on the Gospel of John*. Translated by John W. Rettig. Washington, D.C.: Catholic University of America Press, 1988.

Ayer, A. J. *Language, Truth and Logic*. 2nd ed. London: Victor Gollantz, 1946.

Baker, Lynne Rudder. "Material Persons and the Doctrine of Resurrection." *Faith and Philosophy* 18 (2001): 151-67.

Barbour, Ian G. *Religion and Science: Historical and Contemporary Issues*. San Francisco: HarperSanFrancisco, 1997.

Barnes, Jonathan. *The Presocratic Philosophers*. Rev. ed. New York: Routledge, 1982.

Basinger, David, and Randall Basinger, eds. *Predestination and Free Will: Four Views of Divine Sovereignty and Human Freedom.* Downers Grove, Ill.: InterVarsity Press, 1986.

Bealer, George. "'A Priori' Knowledge and the Scope of Philosophy." *Philosophical Studies* 81 (1996): 122-42.

———. "Materialism and the Logical Structure of Intentionality." In *Objections to Physicalism.* Edited by Howard Robinson. Oxford: Oxford University Press, 1993.

———. "Mental Causation." *Philosophical Perspectives* 21 (2007): 23-54.

———. "Mental Properties." *Journal of Philosophy* 91 (1994): 185-208.

Bealer, George, and P. F. Strawson. "The Incoherence of Empiricism." *The Aristotelian Society, Supplementary Volume* 66 (1992).

Beckwith, Francis. *Politics for Christians: Statecraft as Soulcraft.* Downers Grove, Ill.: InterVarsity Press, 2010.

Behe, Michael. *Darwin's Black Box: The Biochemical Challenge to Evolution.* New York: Free Press, 1996.

———. *The Edge of Evolution: The Search for the Limits of Darwinism.* New York: Free Press, 2007.

Bird, Alexander. *Nature's Metaphysics: Laws and Properties.* Oxford: Oxford University Press, 2007.

Block, Ned. "Troubles with Functionalism." In *Readings in Philosophy of Psychology.* Edited by Ned Block. Cambridge, Mass.: Harvard University Press, 1980.

Blomberg, Craig. *The Historical Reliability of the Gospels.* Downers Grove, Ill.: InterVarsity Press, 1987.

Bloom, Paul. "First Person Plural." *The Atlantic,* November 2008 <www.theatlantic.com/doc/200811/multiple-personalities>.

Bock, Darrell L. *The Missing Gospels: Unearthing the Truth Behind Alternative Christianities.* Nashville: Thomas Nelson, 2006.

Bonjour, Laurence. *Epistemology: Classic Problems and Contemporary Responses.* Lanham, Md.: Rowman & Littlefield, 2002.

Borchert, Donald M., ed. *The Encyclopedia of Philosophy.* 2nd ed. Farmington Hills, Mich.: Macmillan, 2006.

Bynam, Caroline Walker. *The Resurrection of the Body in Western Christianity, 200-1336.* New York: Columbia University Press, 1995.

Calvin, John. *Institutes of the Christian Religion.* Translated by Henry Beveridge. Grand Rapids: Eerdmans, 1962.

Chafer, Lewis Sperry. *Systematic Theology.* Vol. 1. Dallas: Dallas Seminary Press, 1947.

Chalmers, David J. *The Conscious Mind: In Search of a Fundamental Theory.* New York: Oxford University Press, 1996.

Chisholm, Roderick. *The Problem of the Criterion.* Milwaukee: Marquette University Press, 1973.

Churchland, Paul. *Matter and Consciousness.* Cambridge, Mass.: MIT Press, 1984.

Coe, John H., and Todd W. Hall. *Psychology in the Spirit: Contours of a Transforma-*

tional Psychology. Downers Grove, Ill.: InterVarsity Press, 2009.

Cooper, John W. *Body, Soul, and Life Everlasting: Biblical Anthropology and the Monism-Dualism Debate.* Grand Rapids: Eerdmans, 1989.

Copan, Paul, and William Lane Craig. *Creation Out of Nothing: A Biblical, Philosophical, and Scientific Exploration.* Grand Rapids: Baker, 2004.

Corcoran, Kevin. "The Constitution View of Persons." In *In Search of the Soul: Four Views of the Mind-Body Problem.* Edited by Joel B. Green and Stuart L. Palmer. Downers Grove, Ill.: InterVarsity Press, 2005.

———. *Rethinking Human Nature: A Christian Materialist Alternative to the Soul.* Grand Rapids: Baker, 2006.

Craig, William Lane. "Classical Apologetics." In *Five Views on Apologetics.* Edited by Steven B. Cowan. Grand Rapids: Zondervan, 2000.

———. *The Cosmological Argument from Plato to Leibniz.* New York: Harper & Row, 1980. Reprint, Eugene, Ore.: Wipf and Stock, 2001.

———. *Time and the Metaphysics of Relativity.* Philosophical Studies Series 84. Dordrecht: Kluwer Academic, 2001.

Craig, William Lane, and J. P. Moreland, eds. *Naturalism: A Critical Analysis.* New York: Routledge, 2000.

Craig, William Lane, and Quentin Smith, *Theism, Atheism and Big Bang Cosmology.* New York: Oxford University Press, 1995.

Cross, Richard. *The Metaphysics of the Incarnation.* Oxford: Oxford University Press, 2002.

Davies, Stephen. *The Philosophy of Art.* Malden, Mass.: Blackwell, 2006.

Davis, Stephen T., Daniel Kendall and Gerald O'Collins, eds. *The Incarnation: An Interdisciplinary Symposium on the Incarnation of the Son of God.* New York: Oxford University Press, 2004.

Dawkins, Richard. *The Blind Watchmaker: Why the Evidence of Evolution Reveals a Universe Without Design.* New York: W. W. Norton, 1986.

———. *The God Delusion.* New York: Houghton Mifflin, 2006.

Dembski, William A. *The Design Inference: Eliminating Chance Through Small Probabilities.* New York: Cambridge University Press, 1998.

———. *Intelligent Design: The Bridge Between Science and Theology.* Downers Grove, Ill.: InterVarsity Press, 1999.

———. *No Free Lunch: Why Specified Complexity Cannot Be Purchased Without Intelligence.* New York: Roman & Littlefield, 2007.

Dembski, William A., and Michael Ruse, eds. *Debating Design: From Darwin to DNA.* New York: Cambridge University Press, 2004.

DePaul, Michael R. Preface to *Resurrecting Old-Fashioned Foundationalism.* Edited by Michael R. DePaul. Lanham, Md.: Rowman & Littlefield, 2001.

DeWeese, Garrett J. *God and the Nature of Time.* Aldershot, U.K.: Ashgate, 2004.

———. "One Person, Two Natures: Two Metaphysical Models of the Incarnation." In *Jesus in Trinitarian Perspective.* Edited by Fred Sanders and Klaus Issler. Nashville: B&H Publishing, 2007.

———. "Toward a Robust Natural Theology: Reply to Paul Moser." *Philosophia Christi* 3 (2001): 113-18.

DeWeese, Garrett J., and J. P. Moreland. *Philosophy Made Slightly Less Difficult.* Downers Grove, Ill.: InterVarsity Press, 2005.

DeWeese, Garrett J., and Joshua Rasmussen. "Hume and the *Kalām* Cosmological Argument." In *In Defense of Natural Theology: A Post-Humean Reassessment.* Edited by Douglas Groothuis and James Sennett. Downers Grove, Ill.: InterVarsity Press, 2005.

DeWitt, Calvin B., ed. *Caring for Creation: Responsible Stewardship of God's Handiwork.* Grand Rapids: Baker, 1998.

Dyrness, William. *Themes in Old Testament Theology.* Downers Grove, Ill.: InterVarsity Press, 1979.

Eagleton, Terry. "Awakening from Modernity." *Times Literary Supplement,* February 20, 1987.

Erickson, Millard F. *God in Three Persons: A Contemporary Interpretation of the Trinity.* Grand Rapids: Baker, 1995.

Evans, Craig A. "Jesus: Sources and Self-Understanding." In *Jesus and Philosophy: New Essays.* Edited by Paul K. Moser. New York: Cambridge University Press, 2009.

Farley, Benjamin W. *In Praise of Virtue: An Exploration of the Biblical Virtues in a Christian Context.* Grand Rapids: Eerdmans, 1995.

Feldman, Richard. *Epistemology.* Upper Saddle River, N.J.: Prentice-Hall, 2003.

Feyerabend, Paul. "How to Defend Society Against Science." Reprinted in *Introductory Readings in the Philosophy of Science.* Edited by E. D. Klemke et al. 3rd ed. Amherst, N.Y.: Prometheus, 1998.

Fisher, John Martin, Robert Kane, Derk Pereboom and Manuel Vargas. *Four Views on Free Will.* Great Debates in Philosophy. Malden, Mass.: Blackwell, 2007.

Foster, Richard. *Celebration of Discipline: The Path to Spiritual Growth.* New York: HarperCollins, 1978.

Frankfurt, Harry. "Alternate Possibilities and Moral Responsibility." *Journal of Philosophy* 66 (1969): 829-39.

———. "Freedom of the Will and the Concept of a Person." *Journal of Philosophy* 68 (1971): 5-20.

Freddoso, Alfred J. "Human Nature, Potency, and the Incarnation." *Faith and Philosophy* 3 (1986): 27-53.

Gale, Richard M., and Alexander R. Pruss. "A New Cosmological Argument." *Religious Studies* 35 (1999): 461-76.

Ganssle, Gregory E. "Necessary Moral Truths and the Need for Explanation." *Philosophia Christi* 2 (2000): 105-12.

Geivett, R. Douglas, and Gary R. Habermas, eds. *In Defense of Miracles: A Comprehensive Case for God's Actions in History.* Downers Grove, Ill.: InterVarsity Press, 1997.

Gergen, Kenneth. *The Saturated Self: Dilemmas of Identity in Contemporary Life.* New York: Basic Books, 2000.

Gettier, Edmund. "Is Justified True Belief Knowledge?" *Analysis* 23 (1963): 121-23.

Goetz, Stewart. "Modal Dualism: A Critique." In *Soul, Body, and Survival: Essays on the Metaphysics of Human Persons.* Edited by Kevin Corcoran. Ithaca, N.Y.: Cornell University Press, 2001.

Goetz, Stewart, and Charles Taliaferro. *Naturalism.* Grand Rapids: Eerdmans, 2008.

Gould, Stephen Jay. *Rocks of Ages.* New York: Ballantine, 1999.

Grant, Edward. *The Foundations of Science in the Middle Ages.* New York: Cambridge University Press, 1996.

Greco, John. *Putting Skeptics in Their Place: The Nature of Skeptical Arguments and Their Role in Philosophical Inquiry.* New York: Cambridge University Press, 2000.

Green, Joel B. "'Bodies—That Is, Human Lives': A Re-Examination of Human Nature in the Bible." In *Whatever Happened to the Soul?* Edited by Warren S. Brown, Nancey Murphy and H. Newton Malony. Minneapolis: Fortress, 1998.

———. *Body, Soul, and Human Life: The Nature of Humanity in the Bible.* Grand Rapids: Baker, 2008.

Gregory of Nazianzus. "Fourth Theological Oration." In *Christology of the Later Fathers.* Edited by Edward R. Hardy. Philadelphia: Westminster Press, 1954.

Griffiths, Paul J. "The Nature of Desire." *First Things* 198, December 2009, 27-30.

Groothuis, Douglas. *On Jesus.* Wadsworth Philosophers Series. Florence, Ky.: Wadsworth, 2003.

———. "Truth Defined and Defended." In *Reclaiming the Center.* Edited by Millard J. Erickson, Paul Kjoss Helseth and Justin Taylor. Wheaton, Ill.: Crossway, 2004.

Grossmann, Reinhardt. *The Existence of the World: An Introduction to Ontology.* New York: Routledge, 1992.

Habermas, Gary R. *The Historical Jesus: Ancient Evidence for the Life of Christ.* Joplin, Mo.: College Press, 1997.

Habermas, Gary R., and Michael R. Licona. *The Case for the Resurrection of Jesus.* Grand Rapids: Kregel, 2004.

Harris, Sam. *The End of Faith.* New York: W. W. Norton, 2003.

Hart, David Bently. *The Beauty of the Infinite: The Aesthetics of Christian Truth.* Grand Rapids: Eerdmans, 2004.

Hauser, Marc. "Origin of the Mind." *Scientific American* 301, September 2009, 44-51.

Hirsch, Eli. *Dividing Reality.* New York: Oxford University Press, 1993.

Hitchens, Christopher. *God Is Not Great.* New York: Hatchette, 2007.

Hoffman, Joshua, and Gary S. Rosenkrantz. *Substance: Its Nature and Existence.* London: Routledge, 1997.

Holton, Richard. *Willing, Wanting, Waiting.* New York: Oxford University Press, 2009.

Horwich, Paul, ed. *World Changes: Thomas Kuhn and the Nature of Science.* Cambridge, Mass.: MIT Press, 1993.

Howard-Snyder, Daniel, and Paul K. Moser, eds. *Divine Hiddenness.* New York: Cambridge University Press, 2002.

Hudson, Hud. *A Materialist Metaphysics of the Human Person.* Ithaca, N.Y.: Cornell University Press, 2001.

Issler, Klaus. "Jesus' Example: Prototype of the Dependent, Spirit-Filled Life." In *Jesus in Trinitarian Perspective.* Edited by Fred Sanders and Klaus Issler. Nashville: B&H Publishing, 2007.

Jackson, Frank. "Epiphenomenal Qualia." *Philosophical Quarterly* 32 (1982): 127-36.

———. "What Mary Didn't Know." *Journal of Philosophy* 83 (1986): 291-95.

James, William. "The Present Dilemma in Philosophy." In *Pragmatism.* New York: Longmans, Green, 1907.

Kant, Immanuel. *Critique of Judgment.* Translated by Werner S. Pluhar. Indianapolis: Hackett, 1987.

———. *Foundations of the Metaphysics of Morals.* Translated by Lewis Beck White. 2nd ed. New York: Macmillan, 1990.

———. *Religion Within the Limits of Reason Alone.* Translated by Theodore M. Greene and Hoyt H. Hudson. La Salle, Ill.: Open Court, 1934.

Kenneson, Philip D. "There's No Such Thing as Objective Truth, and It's a Good Thing, Too." In *Christian Apologetics in the Postmodern World.* Edited by Timothy R. Phillips and Dennis L. Okholm. Downers Grove, Ill.: InterVarsity Press, 1995.

Kim, Jaegwon. *Mind in a Physical World.* Cambridge, Mass.: MIT Press, 1998.

———. *Philosophy of Mind.* Boulder, Colo.: Westview Press, 1998.

Kripke, Saul. *Naming and Necessity.* Malden, Mass.: Blackwell, 1972.

Kuhn, Thomas S. *The Structure of Scientific Revolutions.* 3rd ed. Chicago: University of Chicago Press, 1996.

Kvanvig, Jonathan L. *The Value of Knowledge and the Pursuit of Understanding.* New York: Cambridge University Press, 2003.

Lakatos, Imre. *The Methodology of Scientific Research Programmes: Philosophical Papers Volume 1.* Edited by John Worrall and Gregory Currie. New York: Cambridge University Press, 1978.

Lamont, John. "A Conception of Faith in the Greek Fathers." In *Analytic Theology.* Edited by Oliver D. Crisp and Michael C. Rea. New York: Oxford University Press 2009.

Lewis, C. S. *Mere Christianity.* New York: Macmillan, 1960.

Lindsey, F. Duane. "Essays Toward a Theology of Beauty." *Bibliotheca Sacra* 131 (1974): 120-36, 209-18, 311-19.

Losee, John. *Theories of Scientific Progress: An Introduction.* New York: Routledge, 2003.

Lowe, E. J. *An Introduction to the Philosophy of Mind.* Cambridge: Cambridge University Press, 2000.

———. *The Possibility of Metaphysics: Substance, Identity, and Time.* New York: Oxford University Press, 1989.

———. *A Survey of Metaphysics.* New York: Oxford University Press, 2002.

Mann, Robert B. "The Puzzle of Existence." *Perspectives on Science and the Christian Faith* 61 (2009): 139-50.

Martin, Michael. *The Case Against Christianity.* Philadelphia: Temple University Press 1991.

Mavrodes, George I. "Religion and the Queerness of Morality." In *Moral Philosophy: A Reader.* Edited by Louis P. Pojman. Indianapolis: Hackett, 1993.

Mawson, T. J. "Omnipotence and Necessary Moral Perfection Are Compatible: A Reply to Morriston." *Religious Studies* 38 (2002): 215-23.

McGinn, Colin. *The Mysterious Flame.* New York: Basic Books, 1999.

Merricks, Trenton. "How to Live Forever Without Saving Your Soul: Physicalism and Immortality." In *Soul, Body and Survival.* Edited by Kevin Corcoran. Ithaca, N.Y.: Cornell University Press, 2001.

―――. "Split Brains and the Godhead." In *Knowledge and Reality: Essays in Honor of Alvin Plantinga on His Seventieth Birthday.* Edited by Thomas Crisp, Matthew Davidson and David Vander Laan. Dordrecht: Kluwer Academic, 2006.

Meyer, Stephen C. *Signature in the Cell: DNA and the Evidence for Intelligent Design.* New York: HarperOne, 2009.

Mitchell, Basil. "War and Friendship." In *Philosophers Who Believe.* Edited by Kelly James Clark. Downers Grove, Ill.: InterVarsity Press, 1993.

Monton, Bradley. *Seeking God in Science: An Atheist Defends Intelligent Design.* Buffalo, N.Y.: Broadview Press, 2009.

Moore, G. E. "A Defence of Common Sense," and "Proof of an External World." In *Philosophical Papers.* London: George, Allen & Unwin, 1959.

Moreland, J. P. *Christianity and the Nature of Science.* Grand Rapids: Baker, 1989.

―――. "If You Can't Reduce, You Must Eliminate: Why Kim's Version of Physicalism Isn't Close Enough." *Philosophia Christi* 7 (2005): 463-73.

―――. *The Recalcitrant* Imago Dei: *Human Persons and the Failure of Naturalism.* London: SCM Press, 2009.

―――. "A Response to a Platonistic and a Set-Theoretic Objection to the *Kalām* Cosmological Argument." *Religious Studies* 39 (2003): 373-90.

―――. *Scaling the Secular City: A Defense of Christianity.* Grand Rapids: Baker, 1987.

―――. *Universals.* Central Problems in Philosophy. Chesham, U.K.: Acumen, 2001.

Moreland, J. P., and William Lane Craig. *Philosophical Foundations for a Christian Worldview.* Downers Grove, Ill.: InterVarsity Press, 2003.

Moreland, J. P., and Garrett DeWeese. "The Premature Report of Foundationalism's Demise." In *Reclaiming the Center.* Edited by Millard J. Erickson, Paul Kjoss Helseth and Justin Taylor. Wheaton, Ill.: Crossway, 2004.

Moreland, J. P., and Scott B. Rae. *Body and Soul.* Downers Grove, Ill.: InterVarsity Press, 2000.

Morris, Thomas V. *The Logic of God Incarnate.* Ithaca, N.Y.: Cornell University Press, 1986.

Morriston, Wes. "Omnipotence and Necessary Moral Perfection: Are They Compatible?" *Religious Studies* 37 (2001): 143-60.

Moser, Paul K. *The Elusive God: Reorienting Religious Epistemology.* New York: Cambridge University Press, 2008.

Murphy, Nancey. *Bodies and Souls, or Spirited Bodies?* New York: Cambridge University Press, 2006.

———. "Nonreductive Physicalism." In *In Search of the Soul: Four Views of the Mind-Body Problem.* Edited by Joel B. Green and Stuart L. Palmer. Downers Grove, Ill.: InterVarsity Press, 2005.

———. "Nonreductive Physicalism: Philosophical Issues." In *Whatever Happened to the Soul?* Edited by Warren S. Brown, Nancey Murphy and H. Newton Malony. Minneapolis: Fortress, 1998.

———. *Theology in the Age of Scientific Reasoning.* Ithaca, N.Y.: Cornell University Press, 1993.

Nagel, Thomas. "What Is It Like to Be a Bat?" *Philosophical Review* 83 (1974): 435-50.

———. *The Last Word.* New York: Oxford University Press, 1997.

———. "Public Education and Intelligent Design." *Philosophy & Public Affairs* 36 (2008): 187-205.

Numbers, Ronald L., ed. *Galileo Goes to Jail and Other Myths About Science and Religion.* Cambridge, Mass.: Harvard University Press, 2009.

Nussbaum, Martha C. *The Therapy of Desire: Theory and Practice in Hellenistic Ethics.* Princeton, N.J.: Princeton University Press, 1994.

———. *Upheavals of Thought: The Intelligence of Emotions.* New York: Cambridge University Press, 2001.

O'Connor, Timothy. *Theism and Ultimate Explanation: The Necessary Shape of Contingency.* Malden, Mass.: Blackwell, 2008.

Packer, J. I. *Knowing God.* Downers Grove, Ill.: InterVarsity Press, 1973.

Page, Don N. "Our Place in the Vast Universe," and "Does God So Love the Multiverse?" In *Science and Religion in Dialogue.* Vol. 1. Edited by Melville Y. Stewart. Malden, Mass.: Blackwell, 2010.

Papineau, David. *Philosophical Naturalism.* Oxford: Blackwell, 1993.

Pearcy, Nancy. *Total Truth.* Wheaton, Ill.: Crossway, 2004.

Penrose, Roger. *The Emperor's New Mind: Concerning Computers, Minds, and the Laws of Physics.* New York: Oxford University Press, 1989.

Pereboom, Derk. *Living Without Free Will.* Cambridge: Cambridge University Press, 2001.

Plantinga, Alvin. "Advice to Christian Philosophers." *Faith and Philosophy* 1 (1984): 253-71 <http://faithandphilosophy.com/article_advice.php>.

———. "A Christian Life Partly Lived." In *Philosophers Who Believe.* Edited by Kelly James Clark. Downers Grove, Ill.: InterVarsity Press, 1993.

———. *Does God Have a Nature?* Milwaukee: Marquette University Press, 1980.

———. "Materialism and Christian Belief." In *Persons: Human and Divine.* Edited by

Peter van Inwagen and Dean Zimmerman. New York: Oxford University Press, 2007.

———. *Warrant and Proper Function.* New York: Oxford University Press, 1993.

———. *Warranted Christian Belief.* New York: Oxford University Press, 2000.

Popkin, Richard H. *The History of Scepticism from Savonarola to Bayle.* Oxford: Oxford University Press, 2003.

Pruss, Alexander R. "The Leibnizian Cosmological Argument." In *Blackwell Companion to Natural Theology.* Edited by William Lane Craig and J. P. Moreland. Malden, Mass.: Blackwell, 2009.

Putnam, Hilary. "The Meaning of 'Meaning'." In *Mind, Language and Reality.* Volume 2 of *Philosophical Papers.* New York: Cambridge University Press, 1975.

Quine, W. V. "On What There Is." *Review of Metaphysics* 2 (1948): 21-38. Reprinted in *From a Logical Point of View.* Cambridge, Mass.: Harvard University Press, 1953.

Rad, Gerhard von. *Old Testament Theology.* New York: Harper & Row, 1962.

———. *Wisdom in Israel.* Nashville: Abingdon, 1972.

Rosenberg, Alex. *Philosophy of Science: A Contemporary Introduction.* 2nd ed. New York: Routledge, 2005.

Russell, Robert John. "T=0: Is It Theologically Significant?" In *Religion and Science: History, Method, Dialogue.* Edited by W. Mark Richardson and Wesley J. Wildman. New York: Routledge, 1996.

Saucy, Robert. "Theology of Human Nature." In *Christian Perspectives on Being Human.* Edited by J. P. Moreland and David M. Ciocchi. Grand Rapids: Baker, 1993.

Schultz, Walter. "Dispositions, Capacities and Powers." *Philosophia Christi* 11 (2009): 321-38.

Schwartz, Jeffrey M., and Sharon Begley. *The Mind and the Brain: Neuroplasticity and the Power of Mental Force.* New York: HarperCollins, 2002.

Searle, John R. *Freedom and Neurobiology: Reflections on Language, Free Will, and Political Power.* New York: Columbia University Press, 2007.

———. "Minds, Brains and Programs." *Behavioral and Brain Sciences* 3 (1980): 417-57.

———. *Rediscovering the Mind.* Cambridge, Mass.: MIT Press, 1992.

Sire, James W. *Habits of the Mind: Intellectual Life as a Christian Calling.* Downers Grove, Ill.: InterVarsity Press, 2000.

———. *Naming the Elephant: Worldview as a Concept.* Downers Grove, Ill.: InterVarsity Press, 2004.

Smith, Quentin. "The Metaphilosophy of Naturalism." *Philo* 4 (2001): 195-215.

Smith, R. Scott. "Language, Theological Knowledge, and the Postmodern Paradigm." In *Reclaiming the Center.* Edited by Millard J. Erickson, Paul Kjoss Helseth and Justin Taylor. Wheaton, Ill.: Crossway, 2004.

Smolin, Lee. *The Life of the Cosmos.* New York: Oxford University Press, 1997.

———. *The Trouble with Physics: The Rise of String Theory, the Fall of Science, and What Comes Next.* New York: Houghton Mifflin, 2006.

Snow, C. P. *The Two Cultures*. Cambridge: Cambridge University Press, 1959. Expanded reprint edition, 1998.

Solomon, Robert C. *Not Passion's Slave: Emotions and Choice*. Oxford: Oxford University Press, 2003.

Stark, Rodney. *For the Glory of God: How Monotheism Led to Reformations, Science, Witch Hunts, and the End of Slavery*. Princeton, N.J.: Princeton University Press, 2003.

Steiner, Mark. *The Applicability of Mathematics as a Philosophical Problem*. Cambridge: Harvard University Press, 1998.

Steinhardt, Paul, and Neil Turok. "Cosmic Evolution in a Cyclical Universe." *Physical Review* D 65 (2002): 126003/1-126003/20.

———. "A Cyclic Model of the Universe," *Science* 296 (2002): 1436-39.

———. *Endless Universe: Beyond the Big Bang—Rewriting Cosmic History*. New York: Doubleday, 2007.

Stoner, James R., Jr. "The 'Naked' University: What If Theology Is Knowledge, Not Belief?" *Theology Today* 62 (2006): 515-27.

Stott, John. *Christ the Controversialist*. Downers Grove, Ill.: InterVarsity Press, 1970.

Strevens, Michael. *Depth*. Cambridge, Mass.: Harvard University Press, 2008.

Stroud, Barry. *The Quest for Reality: Subjectivism & the Metaphysics of Colour*. Oxford: Oxford University Press, 1994.

———. *The Significance of Philosophical Scepticism*. Oxford: Oxford University Press, 1984.

Studtmann, Paul. "Aristotle's Categories." *Stanford Encyclopedia of Philosophy*. Fall 2008 Edition. Edited by Edward N. Zalta. <http://plato.stanford.edu/archives/fall2008/entries/aristotle-categories/>.

Susskind, Leonard. *The Cosmic Landscape: String Theory and the Illusion of Intelligent Design*. New York: Little, Brown, 2006.

Swinburne, Richard. *The Evolution of the Soul*. Rev. ed. New York: Oxford University Press, 1997.

Taylor, Richard. *Metaphysics*. 4th ed. Englewood Cliffs, N.J.: Prentice-Hall, 1991.

Taliaferro, Charles. *Consciousness and the Mind of God*. Cambridge: Cambridge University Press, 1994.

Tegmark, Max. "Parallel Universes." In *Science and Ultimate Reality: From Quantum to Cosmos*. Edited by John D. Barrow, Paul C. W. Davies and Charles L. Harper Jr. New York: Cambridge University Press, 2003.

Tertullian. *De Carne Christi*. In *Tertullian's Treatise on the Incarnation*. Edited and translated by Ernest Evans. S.P.C.K., 1956. Reproduced by permission of SPCK and available at <www.tertullian.org/articles/evans_carn/evans_carn_04eng.htm>.

———. *Prescription Against Heretics*. In *Ante-Nicene Fathers*. Vol. 3. Edited by Alexander Roberts and James Donaldson. Peabody, Mass.: Hendrickson, 1994.

Van Inwagen, Peter. *An Essay on Free Will*. New York: Oxford University Press, 1986.

———. "The Possibility of Resurrection." *International Journal for Philosophy of Religion* 9 (1978): 114-21. Reprinted with a postscript in *The Possibility of Resurrection and Other Essays in Christian Apologetics*. Boulder, Colo.: Westview Press, 1998.

Van Till, Howard. "Partnership: Science and Christianity as Partners in Theorizing." In *Science and Christianity: Four Views*. Edited by Richard F. Carlson. Downers Grove, Ill.: InterVarsity Press, 2000.

Vilenkin, Alex. *Many Worlds in One: The Search for Other Universes*. New York: Hill and Wang, 2006.

Waltke, Bruce K. "The Book of Proverbs and Ancient Wisdom Literature." *Bibliotheca Sacra* 136 (1979): 221-38.

Walton, John H. *The Lost World of Genesis One*. Downers Grove, Ill.: InterVarsity Press, 2009.

Wenham, John W. "Christ's View of Scripture." In *Inerrancy*. Edited by Norman L. Geisler. Grand Rapids: Zondervan, 1980.

Wennberg, Robert. *Terminal Choices: Euthanasia, Suicide, and the Right to Die*. Grand Rapids: Eerdmans, 1989.

Wesley, John. "An Address to the Clergy." In *The Works of John Wesley*. London: Wesleyan Methodist Book Room, 1872. Reprint, Grand Rapids: Baker, 1979.

Whitehead, Alfred North. *Science and the Modern World: Lowell Lectures, 1925*. Cambridge: Cambridge University Press, 1930.

Wilkins, Michael. *In His Image: Reflecting Christ in Everyday Life*. Colorado Springs: NavPress, 1997.

Willard, Dallas. *The Divine Conspiracy*. San Francisco: HarperSanFrancisco, 1998.

———. "Jesus the Logician." *Christian Scholar's Review* 27 (1999): 605-14.

———. *Knowing Christ Today: Why We Can Trust Spiritual Knowledge*. New York: HarperCollins, 2009.

———. "Knowledge and Naturalism." In *Naturalism: A Critical Analysis*. Edited by William Lane Craig and J. P. Moreland. New York: Routledge, 2000.

———. *Renovation of the Heart*. Colorado Springs: NavPress, 2002.

———. *The Spirit of the Disciplines: Understanding How God Changes Lives*. New York: HarperCollins, 1988.

Williams, Bernard. "A Critique of Utilitarianism." In *Ethics: Discovering Right and Wrong*. Edited by Louis Pojman. 2nd ed. Belmont, Calif.: Wadsworth, 1995.

Woit, Peter. *Not Even Wrong: The Failure of String Theory and the Search for Unity in Physical Law*. New York: Basic Books, 2006.

Wolterstorff, Nicholas. *Art in Action: Toward a Christian Aesthetic*. Grand Rapids: Eerdmans, 1998.

———. *Reason Within the Bounds of Religion*. 2nd ed. Grand Rapids: Eerdmans, 1984.

Wright, Crispin. "The Conceivability of Naturalism." In *Conceivability and Possibility*. Edited by Tamar Szabo Gendler and John Hawthorne. New York: Oxford University Press, 2002.

Wright, N. T. *The Challenge of Jesus: Rediscovering Who Jesus Was and Is*. Downers Grove, Ill.: InterVarsity Press, 1999.

———. *The Resurrection of the Son of God*. Minneapolis: Augsburg Fortress, 2003.

Zagzebski, Linda Trinkaus. *Virtues of the Mind*. New York: Cambridge University Press, 1996.

Zimmerman, Dean. "The Compatibility of Materialism and Survival: The 'Falling Elevator' Model." *Faith and Philosophy* 16 (1999): 194-212.

Author and Subject Index

Scripture Index